SPREADING DEMOCRACY AND THE RULE OF LAW?

Spreading Democracy and the Rule of Law?

The Impact of EU Enlargement on the Rule of Law, Democracy and Constitutionalism in Post-Communist Legal Orders

Edited by

WOJCIECH SADURSKI
European University Institute, Florence, Italy

ADAM CZARNOTA
University of NSW, Sydney, Australia

and

MARTIN KRYGIER
University of NSW, Sydney, Australia

Springer

A C.I.P. Catalogue record for this book is available from the Library of Congress.

ISBN-10 1-4020-3841-0 (HB)
ISBN-13 978-1-4020-3841-6 (HB)
ISBN-10 1-4020-3842-9 (e-book)
ISBN-13 978-1-4020-3842-6 (e-book)

Published by Springer,
P.O. Box 17, 3300 AA Dordrecht, The Netherlands.

www.springer.com

Printed on acid-free paper

Printed in the Netherlands.

Contents

PART II: CONSTITUTIONALISM

PART III: THE RULE OF LAW

Preface

The accession of eight post-communist countries of Central and Eastern Europe (and also of Malta and Cyprus) to the European Union in 2004 has been heralded—rightly—as perhaps the most important development in the history of European integration so far. European enlargement and the resultant "coming together" of the two parts of Europe raise a number of crucial questions about the operation of constitutionalism, democracy and the rule of law at both the European and the national level. While the impact of the enlargement on the constitutional structures and practices of the EU has already generated a voluminous and rich scholarly literature, the influence of the accession on constitutionalism, democracy, human rights and the rule of law among the new member states has been largely ignored. And yet it is a matter of fundamental importance not just for those new member states but for the European Union as a whole.

This book attempts to fill this gap, and to address the question of the consequences of the "external force" of European enlargement upon the understanding and practice of constitutionalism, the rule of law and human rights among both the main legal–political actors and the general public in the new member states. We have invited a number of legal scholars, sociologists and political scientists, both from Central and Eastern Europe and from outside, to address these issues in a systematic and critical way. Work on this volume has been greatly facilitated by a workshop held at the European University Institute (EUI) in Florence in November 2003 at which the authors had an opportunity to present and discuss their drafts. The editors are grateful to the EUI and its Research Council, to the Representation of the EU Commission in Rome, to the European Law Centre of the University of New South Wales, and to the Australian Research Council which generously funded the workshop. We also wish to thank Mehreen Afzal, Claire O'Brien and Cormac MacAmhlaigh, researchers at the Law Department of the EUI, for their assistance with the manuscript and to Marlies Becker for her excellent assistance with the workshop and with the volume.

W.S., A.C. and M.K.

List of Contributors

Miriam Aziz was, at the time of writing her chapter for this book, a Marie Curie Fellow at the Robert Schuman Centre for Advanced Studies (RSCAS) at the European University Institute in Florence, Italy

Sergio Bartole is Professor of Constitutional Law in the University of Trieste, Italy

Christian Boulanger is a Ph.D. candidate in the Department of Political Science at the Free University Berlin, Germany

Adam Czarnota is Associate Professor at the University of New South Wales in Sydney, Australia, and co-director of the European Law Centre at that University

Claire Gordon is Temporary Lecturer, Department of Government and European Institute, London School of Economics and Political Science

James Hughes is Reader in Comparative Politics, Department of Government, London School of Economics and Political Science

Martin Krygier is Professor in the Faculty of Law, University of New South Wales in Sydney, Australia, and co-director of the European Law Centre at that University

Vittorio Olgiati is Associate Professor of Sociology at the University of Urbino, Italy

Daniela Piana was, at the time of writing her chapter for this book, a Jean Monnet Fellow at the Robert Schuman Centre for Advanced Studies (RSCAS) at the European University Institute in Florence

Istvan Pogany is Professor of Law at the University of Warwick, UK

Jiri Priban is Professor in Legal Philosophy and Sociology, Charles University, Prague, and Senior Lecturer at Cardiff Law School, University of Wales

Enrica Rigo was, at the time of writing her chapter for this book, a Jean Monnet Fellow at the Robert Schuman Centre for Advanced Studies (RSCAS) at the European University Institute in Florence

David Robertson is Professor of Politics at the University of Oxford and a Fellow of St Hugh's College

Wojciech Sadurski is Professor of Law at the European University Institute in Florence, Italy and the University of Sydney, Australia

András Sajó is Professor of Legal Studies at the Central European University in Budapest, Hungary, and Professor in the Global Faculty, New York University School of Law

Gwendolyn Sasse is Lecturer in East European Politics, in the European Institute and Department of Government, London School of Economics and Political Science

Daniel Smilov is Programme Director in the Centre for Liberal Strategies, Sofia, and Recurrent Visiting Professor in the Legal Studies Department, Central European University, Budapest

Dionysia Tamvaki is a Researcher in the Department of Social and Political Sciences at the European University Institute in Florence, Italy

Lauso Zagato is Professor of International Law at the University of Venice, Italy

Marek Zirk-Sadowski is Professor of Legal Theory at the University of Lodz and Judge of the Supreme Administrative Court, Poland

Introduction

Introduction

Martin Krygier

The essays in this collection range widely. All, of course, are concerned with implications of European enlargement in the post-communist accession states. However, they approach these from a large variety of viewpoints and disciplinary approaches, and with a variety of particular questions in mind. This is apt because so many domains are affected and intertwined in the process of enlargement. The story of enlargement is indeed in a profound sense a story of multiple interactions: between nations, states, economies, regions, social structures, political systems, and all of the above with all of the above. And just as borders are becoming blurred on the ground of Europe, so too, any appreciation of what is happening and likely to happen will tend to overrun the boundaries of established disciplines.

The chapters speak for themselves. Rather than attempt the invidious and somewhat pointless task of summarising in brief scope what each of them has to say, it seems more useful, by way of introduction, to suggest a few underlying and interwoven themes or questions to which all the chapters, in their own different ways, respond. I would suggest four. In practice answers to them will overlap, but analytically at least they can be distinguished. First, what are the goals and underlying values of enlargement? Second, what are the major challenges it has faced and continues to face? Third, what is the character of the process, in particular what characterises the means employed to achieve it? Fourth, what are the likely prospects? In relation to any and all of these questions, of course, neither the chapters nor this introduction makes any pretence to definitiveness, a pretence that, even if we had been tempted to it, is absurd in relation to this subject. No one knows what Europe will be in even ten years, still less over a longer term. All we can offer at this stage is our best-informed guesswork.

1. Goals

A story is told of a London cab driver who, on recognising his passenger to be T.S. Eliot, mentioned that he had had the honour to drive other eminent thinkers in his cab from time to time. One of them was Bertrand Russell. He explained that he had seized this opportunity for edification by asking his passenger, "Lord Russell. What's it all about? And you know what? He could not tell me." Perhaps Eliot, fortified by faith, did a better job, but for the rest of us it's a question hard to answer, in general and even in relation to something as relatively specific as the European Union (EU). What *is* the EU all about, what are the overarching themes of the Union and its enlargement? Many answers, little agreement.

Wojciech Sadurski et al. (ed.), Spreading Democracy and the Rule of Law?, 3–24.

One reason the question is so difficult is that there are so many interested parties with different values, understandings and ambitions. Of course, at its largest that includes all citizens of the Union, and constitutionally all Member States and the overall constitutional structure of the Union itself. But even if we seek to simplify by concentrating on the major categories of political orders involved, the European Union at the moment of enlargement represented at least three very distinct sorts. Sergio Bartole speaks of the duplex character of the Union, always accommodating two different points of view – that of the European legal order as a whole, and those of the internal systems of law of the interested states – but of course that second category, at the time of accession and for the immediate future at least, is itself duplex. It includes the enlargers of the West, and the enlargees of the East, whose positions and aims are far from the same. Add to that the newly augmented club itself which the former created and will continue to dominate, and the complexities and divergences can be readily appreciated. What serves the West may, but it may not, serve the East, and vice versa. What serves the Union as a whole may not always be the goal or option of choice of its constituent parts. Not to mention that goals have changed over time, and are not always consistent with each other.

The focus of this book is on enlargees, and specifically those of post-communist Central and Eastern Europe. Even within this relatively circumscribed domain, however, all three entities are in play, though it is not always clear that they are playing the same game by the same rules. And of course, one of the players is also the selector, coach and umpire. Where differences emerge, will/should the goals of the hosts prevail or will/should they be subverted by local actors with other agendas? Answers to this question depend in important part on an estimation of the goals and values that underlie the enterprise of enlargement.

Are the political values which Europe professes universal goods, only for contingent historical reasons better instantiated in the West than in the East? Are they what E.P. Thompson took the rule of law to be: "a cultural achievement of universal significance?".[1] If so, the attempt to spread and secure them through enlargement looks like an admirable idea from which all stand to benefit. *Unless* the professed values are not the real ones, *or* the ways in which they are being spread are counterproductive, *or* they are embodied in practices, institutions and traditions so tied into local cultures and histories that they do not transplant well, *or* because the specific practices, institutions and traditions of the accession states are peculiarly ill suited to the grafts on offer. And what if they are not universal after all? All the options mentioned are explored in this volume.

Wojciech Sadurski is an EU universalist. He believes the spread of democracy, constitutionalism and the rule of law are central among the real and legitimate goals of enlargement. Transplanting them to countries, some of which had never known them, is to do good, even if not all the beneficiaries appreciate this. So, for

1 *Whigs and Hunters. The Origin of the Black Act* (Harmondsworth: Penguin 1977), p. 265.

him the asymmetry of power, prosperity and appeal between West and East, which has allowed the former to call most of the shots, is not an embarrassment but a useful resource. It does not result in the imposition by force of "western values", especially since it has been most successful when it "resonated with domestic preferences and political aims." Rather, it enables the spread of values good for all. Not only has the accession process required necessary modifications in the accession states" institutions, but accession itself is, overall, likely to continue to strengthen the hands of the good guys of post-communism, who might have more difficulty resisting "threats from authoritarian, populist, nationalistic forces" without it. If there are benighted easterners who do not hold all these truths to be self-evident, then it is a good thing the West has had the carrots of prosperity and democracy, and the sticks of conditionality, with their double standards that other authors decrie, to bring them in line.

Much of this looks like a particularly eloquent portrayal of what might be called the missionary position, except that Sadurski stresses – as he indeed personally embodies – the commonality of liberal democratic values, whether their bearers come from West or East. The likely and welcome result, he believes, is that

> the EU increasingly becomes a community of values, not merely a community of interests, and the values that these days predominate within the Union resemble closely the values of civic liberal-democrats in the post-communist area of Europe.

Values cross boundaries, as do threats to them. Enlargement is, he believes, a potent source of strength to the former, and opposition to the latter, whether they occur in Italy, Austria or Slovakia.

Even more than Sadurski, David Robertson stresses autochthonous sources of support for "European values" from the East. Not all wisdom moves from West to East. He argues that the specific predicaments that transitional states face appear to generate deeper consideration of common commitments than is available among many of the old guard. Focusing on the jurisprudence of post-communist constitutional courts, particularly the contrasting approaches to lustration – more broadly, dealing with the past – of the Hungarian and Czech courts, he is full of praise for them both. The novelty of the issues with which Central East European (CEE) courts have had to deal requires them to delve at greater depth into issues which the more established jurisprudence of Western European states might glide over. Thus:

> [T]o a large extent a western court analyses a troubling statute against a relatively well-established definition of a constitutional right to see if it passes scrutiny. There is, as it were, only one puzzle. Here there is a double puzzle – the statute needs to be analysed, but the right has to be as well – they are interdefined. There is thus a self-reflexivity in the process of constitutional jurisprudence over

> this period and in these countries which is highly unusual and crucial . . . the great advantage is that there is far more, more thoughtful, and less formulaic discussion of absolutely core questions than one finds anywhere except in similar transition states. This cannot be stressed enough.

Democratic values, rule of law, constitutionalism: Robertson finds them all in remarkably good shape, at least at the level of the discourse of elite judicial institutions in the transitional/accessional/enlargee states. And all of it is helped by the systematic determination of these institutions to look over their shoulders at how things are done in the more established, though not necessarily more committed or reflective, western states.

In contrast, several other contributors are doubtful whether professed goals are always the real ones, and even if real, whether the grafts being attempted will take. Vittorio Olgiati believes that what is really going on is the repeat of an old story, self-defence by expansion:

> In short it has always been a question of defending-by-modernizing the legacies of the Enlightenment's features and the constitutional architecture and lifestyle (universalistic values and particularistic interests) deriving from Euro-centric liberal ideology.

What press releases (and Sadurski) might describe as the magnanimous (and expensive) spread of goods such as democracy, constitutionalism and the rule of law, he views as "a process of socio-economic colonisation" favouring "foreign investors above all", together with a "veritable policy of colonisation", of "legal implantation of western-styled legal standards", virtually forced in a top–down process that brooks no opposition, often not even discussion. Olgiati seems to suggest that what are euphemistically called negotiations amounted, in effect, to offers that could not be refused, on conditions not subject to alteration, to weak if willing supplicants, with nowhere else to go. In all this, "bottom–up social trends played the role of mere secondary adjustment patterns." Local elites were simply co-opted or willingly volunteered, to "domesticate and localise the incoming foreign models and goods."

Daniel Smilov's critique, while milder, is if anything even more radical. While focusing on a specific question – judicial independence – he highlights flaws that he believes go much deeper. With regard to that value he argues there is no underlying coherent theory or account of what the EU demands. But Smilov says a lot more. First, that notwithstanding the absence of a coherent account of judicial independence, and notwithstanding frequent inconsistent decisions and evaluations of the conditions for judicial independence in different countries, the EU propagates the myth that it has such an understanding. Second, that this is no accident, since the myth serves a number of useful functions for the EU elites. It saves bureaucrats' time; "creates a certain picture of the EU as a polity based on common principles and standards", and strengthens the Commission's bargaining position. But third, it is not a benign myth, like, say, children's belief in Santa Claus, because while it promises presents if the children behave, it does not always deliver. Even worse, what it does deliver is not necessarily what its beneficiaries want or need. In particular it "conceals the growing political power of judges and courts", rather than encourage ways of dealing with it, "reinforces a grander myth of the EU as a community based on common normative principles and values", and expels the central *political* character of this process from sustained and serious discussion. Finally, do not just think this mischievous myth making is restricted to judicial independence. It infects EU policies on enlargement all the way up and down. Judicial independence is, he suggests, just the tip of the iceberg that is "the accession process in general."

Adam Czarnota's skepticism moves in the other direction. He doubts that the reasons why the "Old Europe" has invited the new are the same as, or even always consistent with, the reasons the latter have accepted the invitation. Nor does he believe it obvious that either old or new will get what they want. One goal popular among many of the former is to override the dysfunctional consequences of national sovereignty. This is less likely to have appeal, as Czarnota notes, among those just beginning to learn what sovereignty is like. All the more so when these newly sovereign states recognise their even newer status as subordinate members of a union of some sort, dominated by its older members. He argues on the one hand, that the Europe the countries of CEE wanted to join is not the one they are about to join. They wanted money and they wanted status, and they might get both, but did they want to pool sovereignty? Does *Solidarność* extend to the French? To Germans? They wanted a normal economy, and they are getting into a quite abnormal, indeed unique polity, and one in which – just after they regained sovereignty, or even gained it for the first time – they are being asked to pool it in a conglomerate where they are unlikely to be major players. Not only Poles but most of the enlargees, Czarnota suggests, "will find it difficult to surrender their own sovereignty to the EU, when they are only beginning to enjoy it themselves." This is enough to raise suspicions of enlargement, particularly among enlargees who have for some time felt themselves the objects of suspicion, otherwise known as conditionality, by those they have been so keen to join. Rich in collective memories, they will find that memories in the West, of the same events, are different. Not rich in traditions of legality or democracy, they are asked to exhibit both. Czarnota does not deny that many benefits might flow from joining Europe, but there will be inevitable costs too, and he even worries that "the entire project of European integration could be derailed because of eastern enlargement."

2. CHALLENGES

Accession occurred some fifteen years after the collapse of communism. Eight of the ten enlargees are beneficiaries of that collapse. Like all the post-communist states, those eight have been spoken of as enjoying or enduring a "transition" to democracy, constitutionalism and the rule of law ever since. Thus, unlike other enlargees, before and now, the countries of Central and Eastern Europe, as Gwendolyn Sasse *et al.* stress, are navigating a double transition: from communism and to Europe. Inevitably peculiarities of the first will affect the second, just as the unprecedented nature of the latter has already become intertwined with the former.

Long before "joining Europe" had become a practical matter of swallowing 80,000 pages of regulations, joining Europe in a larger sense was a dream of many, particularly elite central and east Europeans. Often it was spoken of as a "return". Not everyone thinks that language is realistic, nor the ambition realizable. Partly this has to do with alleged historical legacies, some of them very old. At the dawn of the "transition", even before talk of joining the EU, the Polish historian, Jerzy Jedlicki pointed out that this is not the first time that many East Europeans have sought to "return to Europe." He seems to suggest that, notwithstanding dreams of such "return" from at least the eighteenth century, they were never really there in the first place. And he argues that many of the reasons for their backwardness and marginality continue to weigh on the countries of the region. While the chances are not closed, that more recent attempts to "return" might succeed, he does not seem to regard them as highly promising:

> [I]f all those peoples who live in the narrow space between the old Russian, German, Austrian, and Turkish empires share any basic experience and any common wisdom, it boils down to this: that no victory is ever final, no peace settlement is ever final, no frontiers are secure, and each generation must begin its work anew. There is no linear development in East European history, but rather a Sisyphus-like labour of ups and downs, of building and wrecking, where little depends on one's own ingenuity and perseverance.[2]

More melodramatically, John Gray insisted that:

> [I]n throwing off the universalist institutions that supposedly nurtured Homo Sovieticus, the post-Soviet peoples have not thereby adopted the Western liberal self-image of universal rights-bearers, or buyers and sellers in a global market. Instead, they have returned to their pre-Soviet particularisms, ethnic and religious – to specific cultural traditions that, except in Bohemia, are hardly those of Western liberal democracy . . . not, manifestly, an ending of history, but rather its resumption on decidedly traditionalist lines – of ethnic and religious conflicts, irredentist claims, strategic calculations, and secret diplomacies. This return to the historical realities of European political life will remain incomprehensible, so long as those realities are viewed through the spectacles of ephemeral Enlightenment ideologies. We will not, for example, understand current developments in Poland if our model for them is the transitory nightmare of Marxian Communism;

[2] Jerzy Jedlicki, "The Revolution of 1989: The Unbearable Burden of History," *Problems of Communism* (July–August 1990), pp. 39–45 at 40.

we will gain insight into them if we grasp them as further variations on historical themes . . . that are millennial.[3]

The authors in this book are not given to any such millennial determinism, but they are not unaware of the history that prompts it, or the legacies that may still haunt present efforts. Jiří Pribáň stresses that ethnic nationalism occurs in many western European states, but he concedes that it was much stronger in the younger states of central and eastern Europe. And, as Adam Czarnota emphasises, some of these states, if not the nations that have just come to power within them, are very young indeed.

Moreover, András Sajó observes that

> [O]ne of the striking features of East European nationalism is that it results in a value system that is indifferent (at best) to modernity and finds its values in past (ascribed and mystical) national glory. This mental attitude does not generate much popular interest in the ethics of modernity that is instrumentalized in the rule of law.

Elsewhere he points out, even more pithily, that:

> [U]nlucky Hungarian history, unfortunate Romanian history, and for that matter, any other history in East and East Central Europe are responsible for all sorts of constitutional ideas. History nestled all sorts of political ideas into people's minds, except that of classical constitutionalism.[4]

Overlaying whatever ages-old legacies are attributed to them, the post-communist states are, of course, just that: post-*communist.* And there is a vast literature on what that legacy entails. Communism established a unique array of institutional attributes, aptly compressed in Gellner's phrase, "Caesaro-Papist-Mammonism,"[5] and generated a distinctive set of social behaviours, caricatured but not without foundation in the phrase "homo sovieticus". It left a unique combination of transformations to accomplish, exacerbated by the facts that they were all supposed to be dealt with at once (the "simultaneity" problem), and that several generations of subjects had known nothing else. Though this is not the first enlargement of the EU, it is, consequently, unique in the range of problems it presents.[6]

---

3 John Gray, "From Post-Communism to Civil Society: The Reemergence of the Western Model", 2 *Social Philosophy and Policy*, (1993), pp. 10–27.

4 A. Sajó, *Limiting Government. An Introduction to Constitutionalism* (Budapest: CEU Press 1999), p. 1.

5 Ernest Gellner "Civil society in historical context," International Social Science Journal, 129 (1991), p. 495; *Conditions. of Liberty. Civil Society and its Rivals* (London: Hamish Hamilton 1994), pp. 4–196.

6 On the distinctiveness of the post-communist combination of challenges, see Jon Elster, Claus Offe, and Ulrich Preuss, *Institutional Design in Post-communist Societies: Rebuilding the Ship at Sea* (Cambridge: Cambridge University Press 1998).

There is no shortage of institutional advice, forthcoming from the EU and elsewhere, about how to deal with such matters. But though most emphasised in the accession process, formal institutions are only part of the picture. As Miriam Aziz points out, we need to distinguish "between the formal process of implementation (adoption of the *acquis*) and the legal norms and legal culture which will inform the implementation of the *acquis* in the day-to-day process." For it is these norms and culture which will be decisive in whether new or even old institutions count as normative components in social behaviour and imagination, resources and constraints in everyday life. That is a general truth, and it is all the more salient in societies where for a long time they have not and where not all contemporary trends are calculated to make them do so. On this score, our contributors *from* the region are less optimistic than our westerners who write about it.

Perhaps the most sustained examination of these issues comes from Marek Zirk-Sadowski, who combines his insider's knowledge as professor of law and judge, and his experience as a collaborator in the annual report on Poland's readiness to join the EU,[7] to offer a disturbing account of the way not-altogether-European law functions in now-European Poland. Zirk-Sadowski's argument is complex and nuanced, but essentially it is that in Poland at least there is no conception, either among citizens or among lawyers, of law as an argumentative tradition, a discourse, mastery of which might enable some disciplined, convergent but yet often novel legal responses to new situations. Rather, law is seen socially as a source of at one stage oppressive rules, at another of potential bonuses to be grabbed, but in either case "still regarded as 'received' and not resulting from negotiations or discussions", in neither case recognised as a hermeneutic practice in which beneficiaries and victims of law themselves are legitimately involved. It is viewed purely instrumentally, and as an elite imposition or gift, sometimes for elite purposes, sometimes foisted on the country by the arbiters of Europeanness.

Apart from this profound discursive incompetence, Zirk-Sadowski implies, nothing much else is good in Polish law either. Underfunded, overworked judges watch delays mount, and can do nothing about them. Society had naive hopes that post-communism would bring them justice; instead, as the former East German dissident, Bärbel Bohley, complained, "we demanded justice; we got the rule of law." But the Poles did not even get an effective version of that. And like every other arm of state, the judicial arm withers, while people watch with scorn and without sympathy, and with increasing anomie. The result of these layers of pathology is a paradoxical sort of

> disintegration in legal consciousness . . . there exists a sense of the presence of law, of its validity but it is accompanied by the sense of destruction of normativity. Law is a collection of texts, a source of certain goods but it is not a duty. . . . There exists law, legal institutions but there is no legal order.

---

7 See the EU monitoring reports on Poland, Vols. I–VII.

And Polish lawyers, simplistic positivists all, are themselves bereft of the argumentative equipment to *interpret* law. They simply know how to apply rules, apparently with machine-like repetitiveness and lack of imagination: "they did not presume that a new role in the social discourse was required of them, and especially of judges." This makes them particularly inept receivers of European law, quite unable to deal with "soft law" and more generally the kind of argumentative participation in legal discourse that it demands. Instead of a language, all they have is a book of rules. And another paradox of "integration" is that a form of law that *depends* upon all these discursive and semantic capacities that Poles lack is being introduced in a way that leads

> . . . to the strengthening of the tendency to instrumentalise law. The disintegration of legal order is a result of the narrow understanding of the harmonisation of law as the implementation of new texts. They were introduced to Polish legal order without a reference to the achievements of the European legal discourse. The consequences of this primitive implementation of law have led today to alarming phenomena.

Complementary accounts appear in the articles by Czarnota and Sajó. Czarnota also adds to these "software" considerations, ones of hard and evident realities. The new countries are poor, both in money and in infrastructure, indeed at times worse than poor: what they have is not what anyone would want, products of mis- and not merely under-development. And not all forms of transition from that state are helpful. Sajó notes what he calls some perverse effects of the ways in which accession is being managed, and their interactions with inherent perversities of already-existing "transition." Together, he suggests, these tend to reinforce harmful behavioural and attitudinal legacies of communism. We will return to these suggestions in the final section below.

Now if these pessimistic tones are warranted, they represent a serious source of concern, since no one suggests that Poland and Hungary are the *worst* prepared of the new members of the EU. On the other hand, we should heed Aziz's warning against the common tendency to speak in an undifferentiated way of the "legacies of communism" and "transition" as though all post-communist states share the same legacies and must travel the same path. Instead she insists, the legacies varied, and so too the paths from communism. We have already mentioned Robertson's enthusiasm for post-communist constitutional jurisprudence. And one reason why one occasionally finds more committed democrats in post-communist states than in more established ones, is that not all legacies were necessarily bad, and some aspects of communism that *were* bad spawned good legacies. Thus Daniela Piana suggests that

> since history is constituted by change and tradition, by novelties and memories, it is also reasonable to assume that people have learnt something useful, and helpful in the reconstruction of their political life, even from their experiences

under the communist regimes – in the negative or in the positive sense of the word.

One aspect of this sort of learning from experience is that "people who lived within communism have collective preferences about what they do not want in a new political system. This idea was often stronger than a clear idea about what they want." This accords with the observation that a number of people have made over the years, that people who experience the *absence* of something valuable, more especially its active denial, often show more insight into its worth than people who have never known life without it.[8] But such insights, though precious, are often lopsided, better at telling us what to avoid than what to have and how to get it How enduring even those negative insights are, and how easily sustained in the absence of the conditions that generated them, are among questions to which we might learn answers from the experience of post-communist entrants to the European Union.

3. PROCESS

Not only are the specific challenges faced by this latest and largest EU expansion in many ways unprecedented; so too is the way it was brought about. While our contributors evaluate this process differently, they describe it in pretty comparable terms. First of all, this was manifestly *not* a discussion among equals, but bargaining in a very lopsided sellers' market. No room here for Groucho Marx's disdain for a club which would have him for a member. Here the club had laid down stringent ground rules which had, in its estimation, to be satisfied before it would consider admitting eager applicants. And so the famous 80,000 pages.

Not only was this asymmetry of condition and enthusiasm underlined by the conditionality process itself, with its double standards requiring of new applicants what had not been and still was not required of existing ones. But it was also conceived as a *didactic* process, as a result of which applicants would only be admitted once they had been taught, and persuaded existing members that they had learnt, what insiders purportedly already knew, and had institutionalised what insiders, again purportedly, already had. As Dionysia Tamvaki points out, "[n]ever before has the EU taken such an active stance in teaching proper state conduct to aspiring entrants." The ambition, as she puts it, "assumes the characteristics of a socialisation process, through which Western Europe diffuses its shared beliefs and institutional practices to the 'untrained' East."

---

8 Adam Podgórecki makes a similar point about the insights to be gained from the experience of "crippled rights" in "Human Rights Revolution," in *A Sociological Theory of Law* (Milan: A. Giuffre 1991), pp. 102–103. I have followed him on this point in a number of places, e.g., "Virtuous Circles. Antipodean Reflections on Power, Institutions and Civil Society", *East European Politics and Societies* (11.1) (Winter 1997), p. 80.

This combination of conditionality and pedagogy assumed an asymmetry of attractiveness, competence, and knowledge-worth-having which had its own reflections in the process of implementation. As many of our authors note, it was elite driven, instrumentalist, technocratic, undemocratic, and formalistic. Hardly an exercise in progressive, participatory, dialogical education. This was both because the assumption was strong that the west knew what the east had to learn, and also that in regard to democracy, the rule of law etc., little value was placed on the *process* of achieving the benchmarks set. What mattered were the results. This top–down and instrumental orientation, perhaps inevitably, led to a process with a number of salient characteristics the desirability of which is a matter of argument.

Not only was this a process driven by elites, but it was doubly so. Criteria were devised by Eurocratic elites who "knew" what they should be, and had to be learnt and satisfied by enlargee national elites who needed to show that they too could come to know and apply them. Since the prize was so attractive to the latter, they were reluctant to endanger it by opening it up to the vagaries of domestic politics any more than was unavoidable. That had a certain logic. Fulfilling the criteria was treated primarily as a technocratic, apolitical matter, where expertise rather than values ruled. So Eurocrats met in committees primarily with national bureaucrats and executives more generally. This "comitology" had, in general terms, an anti-political character, and more specifically an anti-democratic one, involving as it did a certain sidelining of parliaments and wider democratic involvement in the accession process within accession states. As Přibáň notes,

> [t]he committee based form of European governance is neither constitutional, nor unconstitutional. It is beyond the reach of the constitutional discourse because it exceeds its concepts of different branches of government, checks and balances, principles of delegation and separation of power etc. The expansion of government by committees contradicts the proclaimed ascendancy of a common European citizenry and its ethos of public control and political accountability. It is much closer to the decisionist concept of law and state elaborated by Carl Schmitt in his critique of the liberal democratic rule of law.

Since bureaucrats had the expertise, even if parliaments had some claim to represent values, the pressures of accession tended to move power from parliamentary to executive elites, and more generally from political to bureaucratic elites, not only in Brussels but in national capitals as well. On the one hand, as Sadurski emphasises, conditionality in any case loads up the position of bureaucrats *vis-à-vis* parliaments. All the more when negotiations were conducted in secret, and more still when "a good deal depended upon informal contacts among negotiators on both sides, not easily subjected to formal control." And when matters got to parliament, there were disincentives to make them subjects of larger domestic public debate. As Přibáň points out:

> the harmonization of the EU law and national legal systems of the accession countries seriously affected the quality of democratic deliberation in those countries because national parliaments favoured a smooth integrative process and mechanically, without an adequate political debate enacted most of the proposals harmonising national laws with the EU legal framework.

And the focus on national elites meant that sub-national elites were also sidelined. As Sasse, Hughes and Gordon show with regard to regionalisation, this has left those sub-national elites ill-informed on matters where ultimately their participation will be crucial, but which hitherto have seemed to them a game played above their heads for stakes that were unlikely to fall into their hands.

According to Tamvaki, Olgiati, and several other observers, and again not surprisingly in such a "benchmarking" venture, "it is mainly the formal adaptation that matters at the elite level", leaving grounds for concern about the extent of penetration of reforms that have satisfied benchmarkers but have yet to play their role in social life. Indeed one might speculate, and Zirk-Sadowski implies, that formal conformity might be bought directly at a price in terms of social embeddedness. Thus he observes of Poland what is unlikely to be too different elsewhere:

> There is the domination of the process of developing legal institutions in the normative dimension over the cultural process of assimilating values and legal principles. The implementation of the Community law was not a process of historical evolution but a purely formal operation of introducing certain legal texts into the system of law. Thus legal institutions have been left suspended in a specific culture vacuum and therefore the actors of the legal institutions assume a purely instrumental attitude towards them; they are not able to fill the legal institutions with rational discourse. This purely external attitude to law, the absence of a social hermeneutics of law, results in the fact that legal institutions do not generate common, socially accepted symbols and meanings. . . . The lack of the rooting of law in culture brings about the attitudes of legal nihilism and legal instrumentalism. No connections are discerned between the normativity of law and moral conventional normativity.

As we have seen, Olgiati views this whole way of doing business as misconceived. Lauso Zagato, too, is sharply critical of the way in which a lot of the implementation was carried out. Thus he claims that "exporting the *acquis* has often consisted in a blind, bureaucratic operation, carried out in some countries without any criterion," and, as the examples he adduces suggest, with little attention to facts on the ground. So much has this elision of "guiding function" and "takeover" tended to ignore local developments, he claims, that

> [p]aradoxically, however, this has ended up weighing especially heavily on the legal systems of the more advanced CEEC, the first States which managed to enact legislation on competition (Poland, the Czech Republic, Hungary). In these countries the provisions were modelled *roughly* on Community law, but had

their basis in the local system; this is particularly true of the Polish legislation on concentrations. Local experiences of this sort (involving the creation of expertise on the part of administrative and judicial organs, and of the operators themselves) have been wrecked by the activity conducted by the Association Councils of Issuing Implementing Rules (IR). The latter have naturally imposed immediate implementation, pure and simple, of primary and secondary EU law, in the manner of pre-accession strategy.

Sadurski, on the other hand, takes precisely the rigidity and inflexibility of the enlargers to work to the benefit of enlargees. As he writes, provocatively since much that he praises is precisely what many others condemn:

> The combination of the relative inflexibility and rigor of principle of conditionality, on the one hand, with the relative malleability, open-endedness and speed of the political transformations in post-communist states, on the other, contributed to the high degree of effectiveness of the attempt to transplant the rule of the "club" to the "applicants". The EC/EU could dictate the terms because the candidates had more interest in joining than the Union did in enlarging. The democratic forces in the CEE states could bravely design new institutions because the forces of the *ancien regime* were demoralised, traumatised and easily embarrassed.

Christian Boulanger mounts an argument that in part supports Sadurski's. He focuses on the Hungarian constitutional court, and emphasises the extent to which "the prospect of joining Western institutions also has an informal, culturally based impact on constitutional politics." Local elites were speaking to more than local audiences, and they knew it, partly because they could feel the breath of Eurocrats on their necks, but partly too because they *wanted* to be participants in a European discourse. They consequently were concerned to appear proto-Europeans not merely in the local context but at large, partly because they wanted to think of themselves and their country as European already. Now Boulanger emphasises that this cultural identification and aspiration is not uniformly spread around the region. It is important to ask how realistic it is, and to the extent that it is not, how quickly and successfully it might become so? And then it is important to know who, apart from the highest elites, shares it.

4. PROSPECTS

The Copenhagen criterion most relevant to the concerns of this book is the one which requires "the stability of institutions guaranteeing democracy, the rule of law, human rights and the respect for and protection of minorities." Taken literally, there are three aspects of the passage worth noting. One is the success language. To qualify for accession, you need to ensure your institutions are *stable*, and they must *guarantee*. It is hard to know how you ensure stability of such things in a short time (1997–2003), let alone how you can know you have done so. But more striking, a guarantee is an extraordinarily ambitious requirement for things as complex as democracy, the rule of law, human rights and "the respect for and protection of minorities." Particularly since the assumption must be, for otherwise the criterion would be otiose, that they had not been in less than perfect shape hitherto. If candour had been thought appropriate about what institutional design can accomplish, starting in several cases from scratch (or behind scratch), in hard circumstances, in a very brief period, it might have been more honest, if rhetorically somewhat flatter, to require something like

> institutions that appear to have some prospect of lasting, and which there is some hope might, *ceteris paribus*, contribute positively to the achievement of some degree of democracy, the rule of law, [etc.] or in any event not render such degree of achievement impossible.

But that sort of candour is unlikely in an official benchmarking document.

A second notable feature is that it is *institutions* that are to do all this good work. That is not an innocent assumption, though it is a common one. Marc Galanter once observed[9] that, just as health is not found primarily in hospitals so legal institutions are not necessarily the first place you should look to find law. That is a remark with a rather long central and eastern European pedigree, of course, stretching from the Bukovina (Eugen Ehrlich) through Cracow (Bronislaw Malinowski) to St Petersburg and later Warsaw (Leon Petrażycki). Whatever you think about it as applied to *law* writ large,the remark has particular pertinence to the rule of law, human rights, minority protection, and so on. I also think it is true of democracy,[10] though that is more controversial. Whoever wants these things wants a social and political *outcome*, not just laws and legal institutions. They want certain ways of behaving to be established and generalised and above all to become *normative*. They want the norms on which these thing depend to *count*, in people's heads and in their acts, as reliable restraints on, and resources and channels for, the ways in which social and political power are routinely exercised and contested.

What makes such things count in such places and ways is only partly dependent upon the formal institutions one has. Sometimes, if you inherit a strong legal or liberal culture you can have a good deal of legality and liberality even when your institutions are lousy, as happened in the convict origins of my own country. Other times, your institutions might in fact be way better than the legality in the surrounding culture and ways of behaving, but no one much notices. That is one way of interpreting Kathryn Hendley's remarks that post-communist Russia has

9 "Justice in Many Rooms: Courts, Private Ordering, and Indigenous Law," *Journal of Legal Pluralism*, 19 (1987), pp. 1–47.

10 See Krygier, "The Quality of Civility: Post-Anti-Communist Thoughts on Civil Society and the Rule of Law," in András Sajó (ed.), *Out of and Into Authoritarian Law*, (Amsterdam: Kluwer 2002), pp. 221–56 at 231–236.

not such a bad *supply* of appropriate laws and legal institutions in some areas, but often still less than optimal demand.[11] So, if Olgiati is right to allege that "the transition towards a Western-style constitutional democracy and market system of former Socialist countries was considered accomplished with the 'adoption' of a cluster of imposed and heteronomous, formal-official parameters", that conclusion is at the very least premature.

A third point is that what Daniel Smilov shows of judicial independence is true of the key political and legal requirements mentioned in this criterion: their meanings are highly contested and the EU has not rendered perspicuous the specific meanings favoured.[12] So the enlargees were asked to ensure *stable* institutions that *guarantee* something the meaning of which is uncertain, even apparently to those who ask for it. That is a challenge. As Smilov shows, it is already hard enough in the much more specific context of judicial independence, and since no one says that independence is all that you need for democracy, the rule of law, human rights or minority protection, it is exponentially harder in the larger context.

I would not belabour these linguistic quibbles so, if I did not think that they reflected some rather common beliefs. One is that a stable and effective rule of law, not to mention other good things like democracy, is something specifiable, tangible, and constructible, and that the tools for construction are laws and legal institutions. Another is that we know which ones will work (as distinct from which ones have worked, which is not the same thing).

Anti-communist dissidents knew democracy, the rule of law, human rights, were great things (and some thought about minority protection too), since they knew something about life without them. But for all their fineness, wisdom, and at times heroism, they also typically shared (with the rest of us), over-simple ideas of what these good things might require. Thus, it was common in 1989 to insist that what distinguished these revolutions from any of their forebears was that the former intended "no more experiments." Successful models existed in normal countries, and the job was to adopt them, not even to adapt them. Timothy Garton Ash faithfully captures what this was taken, at least by many prominent activists, to mean at the time:

> In politics they are all saying: There is no "socialist democracy", there is only democracy. And by democracy they mean multi-party, parliamentary democracy as practiced in contemporary Western, Northern, and Southern Europe. They are all saying: There is no "socialist legality", there is only legality. And by that they mean the rule of law, guaranteed by the constitutionally anchored independence of the judiciary.[13]

---

11 See Kathryn Hendley, Stephen Holmes, Anders Åslund, András Sajó, "Debate: Demand for Law," 4 *East European Constitutional Review*, 8 (1999), pp. 88–108.

12 See, for a similar argument re the rule of law, Dale Mineshima, "The Rule of Law and EU expansion", *Liverpool Law Review*, 24 (2002), pp. 73–87.

13 "Eastern Europe: The Year of Truth", *New York Review of Books*, February 15, 1990, p. 21.

This taste for democracy and legality "without adjectives", as dissidents used to put it, can be readily appreciated. They had more than enough experience of distasteful adjectives being forced upon fine nouns to glorify ghastly parodies. They were rightly allergic to such substance-cancelling qualifiers. But, to the extent that saying "there is only legality" might suggest that there exists one obvious incarnation of legality which merely needs to be copied by eager imitators, then the taste for legality unqualified is misleading. *Mutatis mutandis*, democracy, human rights, minority protection.

For we have no recipes to produce such results, even less single general recipes. We know what democracy and the rule of law are about (more controversially human rights), but we can more easily recognise them where they are well established, than we can specify the particular institutions that will promote them, with any combination of generality, detail and ability to travel. What might go to accomplishing (or thwarting) them will vary with time, place, history and tradition. That makes it a complicated matter to decide what might foster them or even affect them. These complications are evident in the variety and controversy among the authors in this book.

Sadurski focuses on institutions. He is concerned about the bypassing of parliaments, though he thinks it can be exaggerated and that there are counter-trends. He also worries about the increasingly powerful position in which accession will place constitutional courts in the accession states. This novel implant has thrived unexpectedly in its new soil, and Sadurski worries that the issues to be resolved at the intersection of the EU and national constitutional orders in an enlarged Europe will augment the role of these courts as "significant political and legislative players" still further. As a democrat he favours neither over-powerful executives nor over-active courts.

Still, notwithstanding these particular sources of concern, Sadurski is confident that the larger consequences of accession will be positive for the acceding states, and for Europe as a whole. On one hand,

> by providing the democratic forces within the post-communist states with additional support, encouragement and discursive assets against the threats from authoritarian, populist, nationalistic forces, the democratic transition itself has been strengthened. In this sense, the position of democratic elites in new member states will not be all that different from the position of liberal and democratic forces in, say, Italy or Austria, where those with authoritarian tendencies invariably find themselves in the "anti-European" corner, because the institutional and ideological structure of the European Union tends to support liberal and democratic arguments.

And as this last sentence already begins to suggest, Sadurski believes that the positive effects of enlargement will not all travel one way. Indeed, it is the *Europeanisation* of issues to do with democracy, etc., the discovery, or reaffirmation, that so many of the key issues are ones that do not start or stop in particular nations, that he sees as *the* great significance of enlargement. He believes national identity will become less and less salient, to the extent that

> [t]he understanding of who is part of the *demos* will inevitably be transformed: traditional loyalties and the ethnic and cultural sense of belonging will need to give way to something more akin to "constitutional patriotism", under which the polity is bounded by common civic rights and duties rather than by tradition and ethnic identity.

Pessimists might agree that the need is there, but not on how likely it is to be satisfied.

These are examples of what might be called Sadurski's maximalism. His minimalist position is that "[a]ccession to the EU may not be a panacea for all of the problems of political democracy but it may well be a reasonably good protection against possible future disasters." In this hope and prediction he is strongly supported by Přibáň, who sees "[t]aming ethnos in European nation states ... [as] the primary purpose of both economic and political integration." Already during the lead-up to accession, the EU has played a crucial role "as a neutralizing force of ethno-national divisions, tensions and conflicts." That central role is not due to diminish. How is this to occur, given that there is no European demos? The answer, it appears, is not to attempt to build such a demos on infertile soil, but rather, not to presume that it is necessary:

> [u]nlike the utopian image of one European people, the European identity is most likely to be constructed as a hybrid mixture of common civil ethos and persisting different national loyalties. It will be the dilemmatic identity which will be impossible to consolidate at the symbolic level. European identity and legitimacy will thus remain an open-ended process of the symbolisation of the common social, cultural and political space. ... The European constitution-making is therefore accompanied by multi-dimensional identity which is disentangled from the traditional concepts of solidarity, community, and face to face relations. Cultural rigidity is replaced by flexibility of social networks and multiplied personal choices. ... The European identity can emerge only as a symbolic space of heterogeneity, permanent contestation of existing practices, compromise-oriented negotiations and the conversational model of politics.

Can this possibly work? Yes, says Miriam Aziz, so long as Europe works. That is,

> [w]hether sovereignty resides at the level of the nation state or elsewhere is largely irrelevant. What is important is that sovereignty *exists*. It will, by nature, command affiliation and trust. The level at which sovereignty resides is irrelevant to the affiliation of the trust of the citizen because sovereignty is intrinsic to whether citizens feel confident that states perform certain duties and the citizens feel comfortable with the obligations. Drawing on performance theories, the

following expectation can be voiced: If the EU performs, it will attract both support and affiliation.

Aziz emphasises that in the new Europe, performance operates in a multiplicity of domains and at a multiplicity of levels. Foci of trust and allegiance will proliferate, and so "[m]atters of trust and loyalty also have to be reconfigured in the face of the plurality of public spheres."

But what does it mean to perform? Sasse *et al.* emphasise that now that accession has been won by the new member states (though not by all who have sought membership), there will necessarily be a shift in focus, from satisfaction of formal criteria to

> the implementation and sustainability of the institutions, rules and norms adopted over the last decade. Thus, the post-enlargement context will add a new impetus to the discussion about the successful transition and consolidation of states, democracy and market economies in CEE.

Formal implementation has been, above all, the concern of national elites, but sustainability will need to delve more deeply, as it spreads more broadly. In their study of regionalisation, Sasse and her colleagues stress the different interests, stakes, and commitment of national and sub-national elites, a difference of increasing significance given that

> [d]espite the weak attitudinal "Europeanization" of sub-national elites, their position and functional importance guarantees their involvement in key policy areas, thereby raising doubts about effective implementation of EU policy, at least in the short-to-medium term.

And, though elites are key, they are not the only people who need to be persuaded to support the European enterprise, and not everyone will find persuasive what persuades elites. Tamvaki points out that while the focus has hitherto been on formal adaptation of institutions, and while the bulk of the scholarly literature focuses on "the international aspect of social learning", formal adaptation matters most at elite level and "the internalisation of EU norms by the public is taken for granted or is even ignored." She does not suggest that is wise. On the contrary, what will be crucial over a longer term, and what we do not know much about, is transformation of what she, following March and Olsen, calls "the logic of consequentiality" to "the logic of appropriateness." The latter involves habituation, and that is crucial, Tamvaki argues, since:

> Habituation as opposed to institutionalization is expected to go beyond individual decision-makers and reach the public. If that is not accomplished then the long-term effectiveness of socialization cannot be guaranteed, because it is not just the State that constitutes the people. The people, in turn, form the State, and their readiness to abide by the new norms determines state actors' future behaviour in the international arena.

Piana, similarly, stresses that

> [f]or the CEECs, the development of a democratic culture depends not only on the presence of democratic institutions and the rise of civil society, but also on the willingness of the citizens to view the emerging democratic framework as historically legitimate.

This, she insists, is not something that can just be imposed from outside, but must mesh with internally generated attitudes, histories, and developments. These, in turn, differ significantly among the new members of the EU and have to be taken into account.

And so, beyond the caution that top–down requirements, however refined, can only be *part* of a successful accomplishment, these arguments serve as a reminder that different recipients will respond differently, and a crucial element in successful transition is the state of the recipients themselves. Our contributors from the region, as we saw in section 2 above, speak with some apprehension of that. Like Zirk-Sadowski, Czarnota does not find much aptitude for the rule of law in Poland or other CEECs, and particularly not aptitude for *European* law. At the level of elites, again, it is the national centre that has controlled. Czarnota believes that most lawyers in the region, and particularly lower court judges, have little understanding of European law and are poorly trained to understand it, let alone interpret and implement it. Like Zirk-Sadowski, he believes that "[y]ears of training in a positivist perception of law and with 'judicial dependence' in thinking has left Central and Eastern European courts ill prepared to become part of the European legal space."

More broadly, there is one thing that post-communists – citizens as well as elites – are well trained in, and that is what the sociologist Adam Podgórecki, called "fellowships of dirty togetherness", or what Czarnota calls "informal operations due to the distrust of authorities." That might, he darkly suggests, be a real source of comity between the accesses "with their own networks and façade type rule of law" and the European network-based "infranationalism" that Joseph Weiler describes as a central feature of the EU. Czarnota concludes, with sardonic gloom, that "[i]n this sense post-communist rule of law will join a post-democratic European Union. But then such a marriage will be at the expense of the average citizen on both sides of the Elbe River."

As we have seen, Sajó, too, is less than enthusiastic about the propensity of his fellow citizens for "democracy, rule of law, human rights and respect for and protection of minorities." Moreover, he suspects that the way accession has been implemented might operate, at least in the short term, to reinforce already-entrenched proclivities inconsistent with these goals. Thus he argues that "the accession process as well as the drafting of the European Constitution has reinforced the irrelevance of constitutional democracy in the eyes of the public who continue to see it as a matter of majoritarianism" and more broadly that

> [s]o long as "European solutions" are felt as being imposed and detrimental to local self-interests, "modernity" (i.e. efficiency considerations and pragmatism in decision-making, irrespective of traditional values and communitarian sentiments) will be detested.

And Sajó suggests that it is not only "primordial" attachments that challenge Europeanisation while, at least short term, being accentuated by aspects of its implementation. There are also characteristics engendered by communism that the top–down process of accession and the "prevailing solidarity culture" of the more prosperous welfare states of the Union might reinforce, particularly "socialist welfare dependence". This has "dramatic" fiscal consequences that enlargee states can ill afford, and will perpetuate the phenomenon of "complaint-subjects", that is, "citizens who behave like subjects of a paternalist state, who refuse to take responsibility for their fate through democratic participation, and whose 'voice' ... remains limited to complaints."

Still, in what passes for optimism in CEE, Sajó concedes that the upshot of these pathologies and high-handed dealings might not be all bad:

> [T]he long-term perspectives are not hopeless for constitutionalism in the new member states. After all, the emerging supranational separation of powers adds to what remains of separation of powers at the national level. With regard to restricting the chances of elected dictatorship the changes are favourable to constitutionalism. It will take time to learn to live with, use and perhaps appreciate the new constitutional arrangement where the traditional branches of power operate within (and complement) networks of interest representations which have limited democratic legitimation and partial representativity. It is possible that these alternative interest representations will operate as new checks and balances: it certainly does not satisfy traditional expectations of democracy and popular representation but may perhaps provide counterbalances and at the same time contribute to a more efficient steering of the European administrative state.

Whatever their enthusiasm for the Euro-project, none of our authors denies that the benefits of Euro-membership will fall unequally: on states, on citizens, and on inhabitants who are not citizens. In discussion at the European University Institute in Florence over the early drafts of chapters included in this volume, Jan Zielonka pointed out that a major challenge to be faced will have to do with the *quality* of membership and democracy. State members are not and will not be equal, members will be more and more differentiated, and this will generate difficult political issues. And, of course, the differentiations will not merely be between states.

In his close study of the post-communist conditions of the Roma of CEE, Istvan Pogany argues that, notwithstanding Euro-monitoring and financial incentives to acceding states,

> for the bulk of an estimated six million Roma, or Gypsies, constituting by far the largest ethnic minority in the region, the post-Communist era has brought

neither improved living standards nor the genuine enjoyment of democracy or basic freedoms. On the contrary, Roma poverty has worsened dramatically during the transition from Communism.

Moreover, he fears that in some accession states, with the hurdle of membership now jumped, the situation of the Roma might worsen. Indeed, Pogany observes, "it may seem as if the *territorial division* of the continent has been replaced by the erection of new 'borders' that are essentially social, cultural and economic in character, rather than geographical." This claim is echoed by a number of authors who have other subjects than the Roma in mind.

Rigo, Olgiati and Zagato each stress that "joining Europe" is not simply a matter of warm inclusion. Zagato argues that

> it is the Commission itself that seems willing to take upon itself a policy of dramatic closure towards the planetary migrations of desperate hordes, in pressing for the creation of a European immigration agency, requiring new Member States meanwhile to incorporate in their laws the full weaponry with which the historical Member States are endowed: readmission agreements, etc. There is a strong impression that the 'archangel' approach within the Union and at its immediate borders counterbalances an extreme carelessness verging on cynicism on the part of the Unionist institutions in handling relations of a global character. Nor would this be for the first time.

Rigo agrees and argues further that the exclusory distinctions now insisted upon do not merely (if that is the appropriate word) stay at the border. Rather, the "transformation of European borders creates a system of 'differentiated' memberships which questions the normative assumption that post national communities are potentially inclusive". New distinctions are drawn between individuals who are members, "semi-members" and never-to-be members of the new Europe. These distinctions are no longer confronted just at borders, though they are rigorously enforced there too, but

> borders are dragged into the core of Europe because they follow the biographies of the individuals whose mobility is limited ... The enlargement process challenges the theory and practice of defining European membership exactly because it brings into light how the deterritorialisation and relocalisation of the EU polity's borders leads to a fragmentation of the legal subjectivity of the *citizen*. In other words, any eastern border of Europe is a border drawn within Europe itself.

***

The European project is a monumental one. It promises to affect every aspect of the life of its members. This book attempts to examine some of the early effects and their likely consequences. As we have seen, controversies are plentiful, and criticisms too. Notwithstanding the reservations and criticisms expressed by a number of authors in this book, however, many of them are Euro-enthusiasts and even the more hesitant are not thoroughgoing Euro-skeptics. Most of the criticisms come from Euro-supporters, expressing sorrow rather than anger, disappointment rather than hostility, anxiety rather than rejection. And not everyone is critical. Perhaps Czarnota is right, and eastern Europeans have already abandoned Eros for Euro, but however satisfying the consummation the affair promises to be long-standing. Moreover there is one thing on which all contributors to this volume agree with the sage Yogi Berra, and which should nurture hope as much as it does fear: it's tough to make predictions, especially about the future.

Part I: Democratic Institutions and Practices

1. EU Enlargement and Democracy in New Member States

Wojciech Sadurski *

1. Introduction

Public opinion polls in the accession states of Central and Eastern Europe (CEE) have consistently shown that, among the pro-accession motives, the hope of the European Union (EU) modernizing and stabilizing the political system figures very highly. For example, a Polish public-opinion expert reported:

> Respondents [to public-opinion surveys] expect that our membership in the Union will lead to improvement of the functioning of the political system, strengthen the rule of law, improve the level of knowledge and education of Poles, and improve the protection of the environment.[1]

This hope was echoed in the public discourse and in the literature. At a minimum, accession was viewed as providing CEE states with a guarantee against things going really bad and thus with extra protection against potentially sliding into chaos, authoritarianism, and uncontrolled corruption. Even if it will not add any positive features to the democratic institutions of these countries, the accession (it was thought) will at least help cushion democratic institutions against the worst threats should a crisis situation occur. In a word: it will render democratization irreversible.

This hope was accompanied—and supported—by a general sense of frustration with the state of democracy in the new member states. Citizens of CEE do not trust and do not particularly like their own states: 15 years after the advent of democracy, the belief in their own democratic institutions is very low. This is undoubtedly a legacy of the immediate past; as George Schöpflin notes, "[T]he state, having been seen as an alien, impenetrable, inauthentic and hostile entity, continues to be regarded with suspicion, and reliance on personal connections is widely preferred, as real."[2] In all CEE countries there is a clear contrast between a very small number

---

* My thanks to Ms Ania Slinn for excellent research assistance. An earlier, and largely different, version of this chapter appeared in *European Law Journal* 10 (2004), pp. 371–401.

1 Ewa Bojenko-Izdebska, "Postawy i oczekiwania wobec integracji Polski z Unią Europejską," [Attitudes and expectations regarding the integration of Poland within the European Union], in Marian Grzybowski and Marta Berdel-Dudzińska (eds.), *Prawo i ustrój Rzeczypospolitej polskiej w perspektywie integracji z Unią Europejską* (Rzeszów: Wydawnictwo Wyższej Szkoły Informatyki i Zarządzania 2002), p. 87.

2 George Schöpflin, "Post-Communism and the Perceptions of Europe," in Stefano Bianchini, George Schöpflin and Paul Schoup (eds.), *Post-Communism as a European Problem* (Longo Editore: Ravenna 2002), p. 100.

Wojciech Sadurski et al. (ed.), Spreading Democracy and the Rule of Law?, 27–49.

of people that declare their trust in the fundamental democratic institutions of their own country, on one hand, and those that harbour a rather high level of support for the institutions of the EU on the other.[3] This trust has a somewhat mythical quality (because the level of knowledge about how the EU institutions work is quite low), but it nevertheless constitutes an asset that responsible national political elites may use for the benefit of reforming the state.

This mix of distrust in one's own state and a quasi-mythical trust in "Brussels" (largely derived from the old, Communist-era conviction that anything coming from the West is good) offers a socio-psychological background against which the possible contribution of the accession process to the state of democracy in new member states can be evaluated. It can also be considered against the background of the contribution *already* made to the consolidation of democratic rules and institutions by the process of Europeanization in general, as well as the more specific prospect of accession to the EU. It is this contribution that may, at least in part, account for the high level of support overall that the accession process enjoyed among the citizens of candidate states, despite the uncertain calculus of material costs and benefits. CEE candidate states in the period leading up to accession attempted to emulate, with varying degrees of success, the models of liberal-democratic principles in their own institutional design and practice; no doubt a major incentive for such emulation was provided by the prospect of joining the EU, and it acquired the form of political conditionality. Its effectiveness will be discussed in the first part of this chapter; more specifically, I will discuss the extent to which the effectiveness of political conditionality is likely to survive after the accession takes place. In the three remaining parts of this chapter, I will consider in more detail those areas of democratic institutions and practices that may be affected by the entry of CEE states into the EU (and that have already been effected, to some degree, by the process leading up to accession): the relationship between the legislature and the executive, the position of constitutional courts, and the decentralization through regionalization.

2. Political Conditionality Before and After Accession

In the years immediately after the fall of Communism, EC conditionality was focused mainly on human rights and on general democratic stability; it was the period in which the CEE states set up their basic institutional frameworks. Conditionality operated through co-operation and association agreements with CEE states and by the major assistance programme, PHARE. The turning point, however, was the

[3] A Eurobarometer poll of Autumn 2003, published in December 2003, showed that the average level of trust in the acceding and candidate states for the country's parliament was 20% and for the country's government, 23%, while for the European Union: 44%. (Note that this is an average for the 10 acceding countries and three candidate countries). See http://europa.eu.int/comm/enlargement/opinion/, visited 4 March 2004.

Copenhagen summit of 1993, which established, as the political conditions for the new entrants, the "stability of institutions guaranteeing democracy, the rule of law, human rights and respect for and protection of minorities." Nevertheless, in the period of 1993–1997 the principal focus of conditionality was on the internal market *acquis*, with the main pre-accession strategy in this domain determined at the Essen European Council in 1994. Political conditionality acquired real bite after 1997, when the Commission began evaluating the progress of all candidates in the annual reports, which included sections on "Democracy and the rule of law" (with sub-sections on the parliament, the executive, the judicial system, and anti-corruption measures) and "Human rights and the protection of minorities" (with sub-sections on civil and political rights, economic, social and cultural rights, and minority rights and the protection of minorities).

To what extent was the consolidation of democracy in CEE the result of EU conditionality? Lately, there has been a lively scholarly debate mainly among political scientists concerning the nature and relative importance of the transmission of democratic and liberal norms to the candidate states: whether it was largely voluntary or involuntary, driven mainly by external or internal forces; whether the most efficient measures were those that operated through the mechanisms of conditionality (with the coercive element inherent therein), or rather "lesson drawing" and "social learning" by the candidate states, which voluntarily adapted to the models they saw as dominant among EU member states.[4] There is no room here to enter this debate but a few observations may be helpful for the purpose of reflecting upon how membership in the EU will affect the consolidation of democracy, human rights and the rule of law in the future.

To begin with, one must acknowledge that some of the most important institutional innovations, especially in the first period of democratic change, were taken predominantly under *domestic* public pressure. There have been some obvious demands made from the outset: for free elections to the parliament, independence of the judiciary, free press, etc. They coincided with what was perceived as the "normal" democratic system, and the elites of the CEE states more often than not found it perfectly natural to model their own systems on Western European institutions that they saw to be functioning successfully. This emulation had often been pre-configured by dissident elites before the fall of Communism. In addition, some (although admittedly not many) institutional innovations *preceded* the transition and had been installed, albeit in a carefully limited way, by the old regimes, as was the case of the Constitutional Tribunal in Poland. Also, in terms of the self-perception of the motives for reform by the elites in CEE, there has been a strong *noblesse oblige* type of view under which it was improper to accord too high importance to EU conditionality. Many institutional changes that occurred at a later stage

---

4 See the papers presented at the workshop convened by Professor Frank Schimmelfennig *The Europeanization of Eastern Europe: Evaluating the Conditionality Model* (The Robert Schuman Centre for Advanced Studies at the European University Institute, 4–5 July 2003).

of the 1990s were driven by the locally felt need to introduce corrections to the system as a response to the experiences with lapses in democracy; for instance, the reforms initiated by the Dzurinda government in Slovakia after 1998 were based on the lessons drawn from the authoritarianism of the Mečiar era; decentralization and regionalization may serve as examples of this type of action.

This is not to say that conditionality was unimportant but rather that it was most efficient when it resonated with domestic preferences and political aims, where there existed significant domestic factors in the "importing" states that favoured the importation, adoption and the maintenance of these mechanisms. These domestic factors came in different shapes and sizes. One major factor has been the extent to which an imported rule or institution has resonated with public opinion and those widely shared values within a given community: the relative ineffectiveness of measures aimed at protecting the Roma minority throughout the region may be largely traced to a broad social hostility towards and prejudice against this group in CEE and thus to the absence of resonance between the externally required anti-discrimination measures and the local consensus. Another factor was the "density" of the previously established rules, practices and institutions in any given area in each candidate state: the more entrenched these practices were, the higher the resistance to the rules imported from the EU. Yet another factor, obviously related to the former two, was the magnitude of social costs incurred by the domestic political elites in adopting a rule advocated (or imposed, in the form of "conditionality") from the outside.

It also needs to be remembered that conditionality was a broader phenomenon that just the highly structured, formalized EU policy towards its applicants. Right from the outset, there were a number of outside sources, other than the EU, that provided their advice, inspiration and pressure upon post-communist transitional states: Council of Europe and its related bodies and agencies (including the Parliamentary Assembly and the very active and influential Venice Commission), the Organization for Security and Cooperation in Europe (OSCE), NATO (which had made accession subject to the same conditions as the EU), and various NGOs, in particular Open Society Institute, the Helsinki Committee, etc. It is clear that the impact of these sources was the strongest whenever there was a high degree of consistency among those various influences. One good example is the case of Latvia's law and practice regarding its Russian speaking minority. Here the EU had followed the policy of the OSCE and its High Commissioner on National Minorities (HCNM). As early as December 1993 the EC made it clear that Latvia would have to change its citizenship law if it wanted to be admitted, and in the 1997 Opinion on the applicant countries, the European Commission reiterated the concerns of the HCNM regarding then position of the Russian-speaking minority in Latvia. As a result of these combined pressures, Latvia kept gradually changing its naturalization and state language laws, initially in a way judged unsatisfactory by the West, but eventually in conformity with EU demands, thus opening the way to accession negotiations.

More often than not, however, the influence of conditionality was not in the form of suggesting very specific institutional solutions and devices—perhaps for the simple reason that there is no single model of democracy and rights-protection in the EU—but rather through general templates or thresholds. Those thresholds had the form of certain minimal conditions to be fulfilled rather than of specific institutional designs to be installed. The very fact, however, of the generality of these templates or the minimalistic nature of the thresholds renders it very difficult to trace the "emulation" to one specific source—or even to determine whether it was indeed emulation in the first place. To be sure, the degree of specificity of EU political conditionality varies from one domain to another, and so political conditionality might have been much more effective where there was a determinate set of rules that the candidate states were expected to observe than in cases in which the criteria laid down could at best be characterized as a vague template.[5] The credibility of the conditionality varied depending upon whether they corresponded to the seriousness and determination with which the EU has held *its own* member states to those standards. When the EU set certain political conditions that were not part of the EU legal system and *in addition* were not actually shared by the current members states themselves (such as minority rights), the credibility and hence effectiveness of this area of conditionality must have been suspect. Apart from the legitimacy and "double standards" problems, candidate states could not know what exactly was expected from them.

But what will happen to conditionality now that the "candidate states" have become "new member states"? The formal measures of conditionality have, of course, expired: there is no more political *acquis*, no more annual Commission Reports, no more scrutiny for membership eligibility towards new member states. A rich body of expertise and advice stored in, among other things, the annual Commission Reports will ostensibly retain only a historical value.[6] New member states will be judged—alongside the others—on their continued compliance with theexisting EU rules rather than on their suitability to join. This may mean a

[5] Compare, for example, the conclusions by Antoaneta Dimitrova who found high effectiveness of conditionality in the area of civil service reform ("Conditionality meets post communism: Europeanisation and administrative reform in Central and Eastern Europe", paper presented at the workshop "The Europeanization of Eastern Europe: Evaluating the Conditionality Model", The Robert Schuman Centre for Advanced Studies at the European University Institute, 4–5 July 2003, p. 33) with the conclusions by Martin Brusis who claims that if conditionality had been an important factor, we would not be able to explain the significant differences in the regionalization policies between the Czech Republic and Slovakia ("Instrumentalized conditionality: regionalization in the Czech Republic and Slovakia", paper presented at the same workshop, pp. 13–14).

[6] See Bruno de Witte, "The Impact of Enlargement on the Constitution of the European Union," in Marise Cremona (ed.), *The Enlargement of the European Union* (Oxford: Oxford University Press 2003), p. 240.

dramatic reduction in the strictness of the standards by which they will be judged, and so will radically transform the pattern of incentives for adopting and preserving the rules of democracy, human rights and the rule of law. The huge carrot of conditionality (with an extremely desired prize in the form of an invitation to the club) will be replaced by the not-too-threatening stick of Article 7 TEU, further enhanced by a Treaty of Nice (the "lex Austria" clause), sanctions—or rather, its equivalent in the future Constitutional Treaty of the EU, if and when it is adopted.[7] According to this provision as it now exists, a member state found to be in "serious and persistent breach" (or, after Nice, when there is "a clear risk of a serious breach") of the values of the Union (which include democracy, the rule of law and respect for human rights) will risk having its Union membership rights suspended.

But will such a decline in the EU's effect upon the institutional, non-*acquis* related structures and norms in new member states really happen? It is unlikely. For one thing, while formally stating that all member states are equal, the truth is that some are more equal than others, and the inequalities between them vary from one domain to another. New member states will be for some time suspect in the eyes of the general public of Western Europe, and the awareness that the democratic institutions and the rule of law are of a rather new pedigree will surely affect the way in which they will be perceived by more established democracies. It is very probable that the elections in, say, Slovakia or Latvia will be, whether we like it or not, more critically scrutinized than those in Austria or Italy. After all, the annual Commission Reports will not simply be erased from the institutional memory of the Union, and its critical comments will be able to be revisited at will. Moreover, the membership of the Union will be a powerful strategic and rhetorical asset in the domestic politics of new member states. Both the governing and opposition parties (as well as various "veto players", such as disgruntled trade unions, NGOs, extra-parliamentary opposition, etc.) will be able to use the argument from membership in their political actions. Some of these actions will have the form of demands for constitutional and other institutional changes. The argument: "We need to adopt the rule *X* because our membership in the Union so requires" admittedly has a different force than the argument "We need to adopt rule *X* because this is a condition of our accession." The answer: "So much the worse for the accession decision" applies to the latter but not to the former argument. One can, of course, reply: "We told you so; we should not have asked to join the EU", but this response will ring increasingly hollow with time, and will sound more like a grumbling loser's complaint—not a good rhetorical device for any political actor to adopt.

This suggests that the pattern of incentives regarding the adoption and maintenance of rules, standards and institutions of liberal democracy will be altered

7 Article I-58 of the Draft Treaty establishing a European Constitution.

compared to the pre-accession circumstances. One may speculate that these changes will have at least two forms, leading in two opposite directions. On the one hand, the burden of argument will shift even more to those seeking to *resist* the adoption of the rules or institutions presented as in compliance with EU standards: if such a characterization of a particular measure is credible, there will be a strong presumption in favour of its adoption, and resistance to this will be more difficult. On the other hand, however, those supporting the adoption of such a rule or institution will not benefit from the argument about the *other* gains of accession to the EU: the argument, "We have to adopt this rule, otherwise we will not be admitted," will no longer be valid. In the situation of lowered sanctions for non-adoption, what could have previously been represented as part of a non-negotiable package that on balance is good for the candidate state, will from the moment of accession take on a much more discretionary character for each new member state.

Naturally, the alteration of the pattern of incentives and of the calculi of costs and benefits will affect much more than the discursive assets on both sides of any future domestic controversy over rule adoption. There will be also a very substantial alteration of control in terms of knowledge of the relevant facts, of which the most important will be: to what extent a proposed rule or an institution is indeed part of the EU *acquis*, part of the "EU model", part of the "common constitutional traditions" of EU Member States, or part of any other such formula that suggests that membership in the EU *commits* a Member State to adopt a given rule or institution. Once in the EU, some elites in new Member States will be able to claim a better expertise in what the EU *really* requires than others: they will be able to gain public and political support for their knowledge-claims based on proximity to the EU centres of power, due to the much higher level of interaction between national governing elites and the "Eurocracy" than was the case during the accession negotiations. One can speculate that the governing parties, which will all have extra incentives to be "pro-European" regardless of their official positions pre-2003, will acquire this asset of inside knowledge and be able to use it more effectively against the "anti-European" oppositions, with the knowledge-claims of the latter suffering from lower credibility, and thus less potency in resisting the claims for the adoption of any given rule.

3. THE ROLE OF PARLIAMENTS

Both the very process of managing the preparations for accession by a *candidate* state, and the dynamic of participation in the EU decision-making process by a *member* state, inevitably strengthen the powers of the executive branch of government to the detriment of the legislature. The former phenomenon has already left its imprint upon the government-parliamentary relationships in CEE, and with good reason; with only minor exaggeration it has been stated that conditionality "can be seen as the functional equivalent of war: [it] give[s] the executive more power to by-pass parliament and to justify the lack of consultation with the public by the need to avoid economic crisis."[8] Even the formal institutional set-up emphasized the primacy of the respective executives in the whole strategy of adjusting each legal system to EU requirements: Europe Agreements established Association Councils (or Association Committees) composed of the representatives of the EU and of the candidate country concerned (usually, members of the government), with formidable powers to take legally binding decisions taking precedence over national law. In addition, the negotiations, due to their delicate nature, were largely conducted in secret, thus further reducing the potential of the parliament to balance the power of the executive; moreover, a good deal depended upon informal contacts among the negotiators on both sides, not easily subjected to formal control.

This focus on the executive meant that parliamentarians often lacked sufficient knowledge as to the details of the laws being passed in conformity with the *acquis*. The sheer volume of the *acquis* meant that parliaments had to adopt fast-track procedures for passing the related laws, and this inevitably lowered the importance of parliaments *vis-à-vis* the governments. Although some countries have resisted this move to speed up the legislative process (for example, the Slovenian parliament rejected a proposal to introduce a faster and less thorough legislative process for *acquis*-related law)[9] the Commission put pressure on them to co-operate in this way. Thus, the 1999 Commission Report on Slovenia (before the above-noted rejection by parliament) stated that the legislative process there was too slow. In some cases, the parliamentary route was side-stepped altogether: in Slovakia, the constitution was amended in 2001 and the new Art 120(2) allowed the government to issue decrees in execution of the Europe Agreement. In Romania, the government has adopted *acquis* into national law through the use of extraordinary governmental decrees, which require only retrospective approval by parliament. The overall system of incentives created by the EU put a premium on efficiency over democracy in the accession process.

However, the picture was not as bleak as presented thus far. Whilst there has undoubtedly been a shift in power to the executive, there have been also factors pointing in the other direction. For one, the EU has on occasion acted to control abuses by the executive in candidate states. Thus, the *démarche* against Slovakia during the Meciar regime "included a concern over the growing power of the executive in Slovak politics, attempts to undermine parliamentary control and the

---

8 Report of the Reflection Group chaired by Jean-Luc Dehaene, *The Political Dimension of EU Enlargement: Looking Towards Post-Accession* (Robert Schuman Centre for Advanced Studies at the European University Institute, Florence 2001), http://www.iue.it/RSCAS/e-texts/Dehaene_report.pdf, p. 63.

9 Darina Malovà and Tim Haughton, "Making Institutions in Central and Eastern Europe, and the Impact of Europe," in Peter Mair and Jan Zielonka (eds.), *The Enlarged European Union: Diversity and Application* (London: Frank Cass 2002), pp. 111–112.

opposition parties . . . ".[10] It managed to prevent the worst abuses of the parliamentary system, such as the expulsion from Parliament of a democratically-elected party. More generally, the sections on parliaments in the Commission's Regular Reports have, at times, pointed out negative phenomena, such as the lowering of parliament's ability to effectively scrutinize legislation as a result of the increased volume of legislation combined with tighter deadlines and limited resources;[11] the disturbing growth of legislation through ordinances, adversely affecting the importance of parliament *vis-à-vis* the executive;[12] the malfunctioning of certain parliamentary committees resulting from the unwillingness of some parliamentary parties to take seats in them;[13] the failure to fulfill a constitutional obligation to ensure the direct parliamentary representation of minorities;[14] doubts as to the adequate staffing of the parliamentary administration responsible for EU integration,[15] etc. Even when a section of the Report devoted to the parliament opened with the ritualistic phrase: "The Parliament continues to function properly . . . " and further contained no critical remarks, the very fact that the parliaments themselves were placed under the spotlight emphasized the existence of critical and careful scrutiny.

So much for the pre-accession period. Once in the EU, the political dynamic of a Member State renders the executive the most powerful body in relation to the Union. Indeed, very few Member States' parliaments can control or veto the position of their government in the Council; the power of national parliaments is therefore curtailed as the EU's growing competencies reduces the exclusive sphere of national competence.[16] There have been, on the part of current member states, some brave attempts aimed at countering this trend, and also, since the Maastricht Treaty, there has been a tendency within the EU to emphasize, through various declarations and protocols, "the role of national parliaments in the European Union". They call for an increase in the role of national parliaments in the EU in order to offset the inevitable

---

[10] Geoffrey Pridham, "The European Union's Democratic Conditionality and Domestic Politics in Slovakia: the Meciar and Dzurinda Governments Compared," *Europe-Asia Studies* 54 (2002), p. 212.

[11] 2002 Regular Report on Romania Part B.1.1, see http://europa.eu.int/comm/enlargement /report2002/ro_en.pdf, p. 21.

[12] *Id.*

[13] 2002 Regular Report on Slovakia Part B.1.1., seehttp://europa.eu.int/comm/enlargement/ report2002/sk_en.pdf, p. 21.

[14] 2002 Regular Report on Hungary, Part B.1.1., see http://europa.eu.int/comm/enlargement/ report2002/hu_en.pdf, p. 20.

[15] 2002 Regular Report on Bulgaria, Part B.1.1., see http://europa.eu.int/comm/enlargement/ report2002/bu_en.pdf, p. 20.

[16] See Eric Carpano, " 'La transformation des régimes parlementaires : des réalités dans les Etats membres aux perspectives ouvertes par la constitution pour l'Europe," in Jacques Ziller (ed.), *L'Europeanisation des droits constitutionnels à la lumière de la Constitution pour l'Europe—The Europeanisation of Constitutional Law in the Light of the Constitution of Europe* (L'Harmattan: Paris 2003), p. 164.

weakening of their role resulting from the transfer of competencies from the national to the EU level. Some remedial action has been taken at the level of member states; for example, the German, Finnish, Portuguese, Austrian. Swedish, French and Belgian Constitutions were all amended to ensure parliamentary participation in EU affairs. In Denmark, the executive is controlled by the opinion of parliament; this is, however, the only example of such a strong parliamentary role. The Austrian and German parliamentary resolutions are stronger in effect than those of France, Italy and Portugal, which do not constrain the government at all in any legal sense but which may, nevertheless, have a political effect.

What will be the likely involvement of the parliaments of new member states in EU affairs? The most probable institutional mechanism will be that of non-binding resolutions to the governments regarding their positions in the Council. Looking at the constitutional amendments adopted in this regard, it can be seen that parliaments have *not* been given a strong post-accession role. Although experts in the Czech Republic suggested that the Parliament should be able to bind the government with its resolutions regarding EU issues, when the Constitution was actually amended it only allowed for the parliament to express its opinion—this in no way being binding on the executive.[17] The Hungarian constitutional amendment provides that, in matters related to European integration, parliamentary "supervision" and harmonization (understood as consultation) between Parliament and the government is to be determined by a law adopted by two thirds majority. This seems to have weakened the level of parliamentary supervision that had been envisaged in an earlier draft, which stated that the government should act "in cognizance" of the parliament's position when participating in the decision-making procedures of the EU institutions.[18] The *draft* amendment (of February 2003) to the Lithuanian Constitution does, however, provide for a stronger role for Parliament, as it states that the executive shall "take into account" the parliament's views.[19] In other new member states, including Poland, no constitutional provisions have been introduced aimed at including the respective parliaments in the European policy-making. At present, the only formal mechanism that most MPs have at their disposal regarding their government's European policy is a routine question to a minister within the framework of parliamentary question time.

It has to be said, however, that the new Member States will join the EU at the time when awareness is growing of the need to strengthen the role of national parliaments in the EU process; the parliaments of the new Member States may benefit from this dynamic. The Convention on the Future of Europe has adopted a Draft Protocol on the Role of National Parliaments in the European Union, which

---

17 András Sajó, "Accession's Impact on Constitutionalism in the New Member States," in George Bermann and Katarina Pistor (eds.), *Law and Governance in an Enlarged Europe* (Oxford: Hart, 2004), pp. 415–435.

18 *Id.*

19 *Id.*

suggests a number of ways meant to "encourage greater involvement of national parliaments in the activities of the European Union and to enhance their ability to express their views on legislative proposals . . . ".[20] The proposal includes various means of informing the national parliaments about EU legislative proposals, such as sending to them Commission consultation documents, the annual legislative programme, policy strategy documents, legislative proposals, agendas and minutes of Council meetings, and the Court of Auditor's annual report. It then states that national parliaments would have the right to send their opinion to the relevant EU organs as to whether a particular legislative proposal contravenes the principle of subsidiarity. To facilitate this, legislative proposals would have to be sent (except in cases of urgency) to the national parliaments at least six weeks before they are to be adopted. Finally, the draft suggests that the European Parliament and the national parliaments should work out together how to more effectively implement inter-parliamentary co-operation.

If these proposals are fully implemented, it would go some way towards redressing the shift of power in favour of the executive. The core problem of the lack of information would be partly remedied (also through the simplification of procedures) and the possibility of sending opinions to EU bodies could potentially increase the number of parliamentary debates on EU issues and also galvanize public opinion thereby encouraging more of a debate, and one which is better-informed in that sphere. The parliaments of new Member States are likely to join the bandwagon—especially given that participation in European affairs is seen as a prestigious and lucrative role for MPs, and that only very few of them can count on being elected to the European Parliament. They will, therefore, have incentives to keep parliamentary involvement in European policy lively, and in this way to send the message to their electorates and party leaders about their "European" credentials and competence. This will not, of course, remedy the continuing transfer and consolidation of power to the executive after accession, and one can easily imagine the situation in which the national parliaments from CEE will happily and actively participate in the European fora while maintaining a rather meek position *vis-à-vis* the governments of their own states in terms of EU law and policy. In the end, some observers may conclude that this will be a natural correction of these parliaments' perhaps unduly inflated role in the first years following the collapse of Communism.

4. CONSTITUTIONAL COURTS

Constitutional courts in CEE have played a very important role, often becoming an independent and active player in the law- and policy-making processes; it may be expected that accession to the EU will, if anything, create the opportunity for these

---

20 Preamble to the Draft Protocol on the Role of National Parliaments in the European Union, CONV 797/1/03 REV 1, Annex 1.

courts to assume an even more powerful role. This prediction may be informed by analyses of the experience of constitutional courts in the older Member States, and also by the behaviour of these courts in the new Member States even before the accession, and, in particular, their perception of the relationship between EU law and national constitutional law. The point is to try to gauge the likelihood that the constitutional courts of the region will attempt to carve out for themselves an important and independent role as an actor that has to be reckoned with by other branches of government in the context of their European policy.

Indeed, whether they want it or not, these courts will probably face an obligation to sort out the constitutional position of new Member States *vis-à-vis* EU law, and, in particular, the position regarding "direct effect" and the supremacy of EU law over national constitutions. This task will not be made easy by the strong pro-sovereignty orientation of most of the constitutions of new Member States, combined with a pragmatic, minimalist approach to constitutional amendments as accession approaches. As is well known, there is no such thing as a "constitutional *acquis*": the EU does not prescribe whether and how the relevant countries' constitutions should be changed to make them fit for accession. Significantly, the Regular Reports from the EU Commission on progress towards accession did not mention any required constitutional changes. When one considers the experience gained from for previous accession processes, it is readily evident that the candidate states at the time did not follow the same constitutional model for entry to the EU (and this is true also of the six original member states)[21]: some opted for allowing a limitation of national sovereignty, although without mentioning the EU directly,[22] while others opted for allowing entry specifically into the EU.[23] Regarding the domestic effect of EU law, some member states did not mention this at all in their amended constitutions,[24] while others stated that EU laws are binding at a national level,[25] or that Parliament must ensure compliance with them.[26]

Judging by the experience thus far, one may expect that the constitutional courts of new Member States will be invited—or tempted—to pronounce on questions on whether EU laws should take precedence over the national constitution, who should adjudicate in cases in which it is claimed that the EU acted *ultra vires*, and what to do about specific constitutional provisions that are in conflict with the EU

21 Bruno De Witte, "Constitutional Aspects of European Union Membership in the Original Six Member States: Model Solutions for the Applicant Countries?," in Alfred E. Kellermann, Japp W de Zwann, Jenö Czuczai (eds.), *EU Enlargement: The Constitutional Impact at EU and National Level* (The Hague: T.M.C. Asser Press, 2001), pp. 65–80.

22 For example, the first six member states and Denmark, Greece, Spain and Portugal.

23 For example, Ireland, Austria, Finland and Sweden.

24 For example, the first six member states.

25 Ireland.

26 Spain and Portugal.

treaties. So far, the constitutional position of the EU *vis-à-vis* the current Member States has been shaped both by the ECJ and by the constitutional courts of Member States, with at least some national courts reacting against the ECJ's view that EU law has supremacy over national constitutions. Constitutional Courts in Germany (the Solange I,[27] Solange II[28] and Maastricht[29] cases), Italy (the Granital[30] and Frontini[31] cases) and Denmark (the Maastricht[32] case) have all stated that they can declare EU law unconstitutional if it contradicts the fundamental aspects of their own constitution, or exceeds the bounds of the authority granted to the EU. The German Maastricht decision announced that the constitutionally entrenched principles of democracy (and in particular, the constitutional right to vote which at this stage is best exercised through election to the federal Parliament) dictate the limits on the extension of the functions and powers of the EU. The French Maastricht decision[33] went further, though in narrower domains: the *Conseil constitutionnel* declared squarely the Maastricht Treaty unconstitutional in three specific areas (Union citizenship, a single European currency and the right of non-French nationals to vote in French municipal elections), and it was only after France amended its Constitution to eliminate these conflicts that the *Conseil* determined that the Treaty could be ratified.[34] The same sequence was repeated in France with respect to the 1997 Treaty of Amsterdam.

This shows that there is significant space for the activism of constitutional courts at the intersection of the EU and national constitutional legal systems, especially with regards to the identification of the outer parameters beyond which EU law must not infringe upon the national constitutional legal order (as in German Solange cases where the absolutely entrenched constitutional rights of German Basic Law were erected as insurmountable limits to the expansion of EU competence),[35] and for mandating national constitutional amendments in order to remove

27 [1974] 37 BverfGE 271.
28 [1974] 73 BverfGE 378.
29 German Constitutional Court Decision Concerning the Maastricht Treaty [October 12, 1993], (1994) 33 ILM, pp. 388–444.
30 Decision No. 170, 1984.
31 Decision No. 183, 1973.
32 Danish Supreme Court's Judgement of 06.04.1998, I 361/1997.
33 92-308 DC of 9 April 1992.
34 92-312 DC of 2 September 1992.
35 In Solange I, of 1974, the German Federal Constitutional Court found that the standard of fundamental rights under Community law did not yet show the level of legal certainty to satisfy the fundamental rights standards of the German Constitution, and this limited the transfer of sovereign rights from federal Republic to the Community. In Solange II, of 1986, the same Court expressed its satisfaction that the EC by this time ensured an effective protection of fundamental rights, and therefore the Court would no longer review secondary Community legislation by the standards of fundamental rights as contained in the German Constitution.

the inconsistencies between these orders (as in the French Maastricht decision). How does it augur for the role of constitutional courts in new Member States?

At first blush, there would exist a certain irony if those courts were to replicate, at today's stage of the development of EU law, the Solange-I doctrine of the German Constitutional Court of 1974 based upon a concern for the standards of protection in EC law of domestic constitutional rights—a doctrine now rendered obsolete by developments in EC law since that time. However, there are other grounds that can be used by constitutional courts in new Member States to mark their activism. As a foretaste of what may follow one can consider the Hungarian Constitutional Court's decision of 1998 regarding the Europe Agreement, in which it held that the *acquis* had no direct effect before accession or its explicit implementation by national statutes, and in which it, in effect, dictated the need for constitutional amendment preceding accession. The Court found unconstitutional a provision of the Implementing Rules to the Europe Agreement with Hungary (stating that the Hungarian Office of Economic Competition had to take into account Articles 81 and 82 of the EC Treaty when making their decisions).[36] The Court stated that

> The constitutional issue is whether the norms of the domestic law of another subject of international law, another independent system of public power and autonomous legal order . . . can be applied directly by the Hungarian competition authority without these foreign norms of public law having [first] become part of Hungarian law.[37]

The Court held the provision of the Rules (but not of the Europe Agreement itself) to be unconstitutional (although it delayed a decision on annulment). It did this on the basis of Article 2 of the Constitution, which declares Hungary to be a sovereign and a democratic state based on the rule of law. The Court thus suggested in this judgment that a constitutional change allowing for the transfer of sovereignty to an international organization was necessary, and indeed such change was made on 17 December 2002.

We have to be cautious about drawing any conclusions from this decision: the Hungarian Court did not suggest that it would not accept the notion of direct effect *after* accession but rather its decision related to the lack of direct effect *prior* to accession (and in the absence of a relevant constitutional amendment). And yet this may suggest that the Hungarian Court—and other constitutional courts of the region—could follow the path of the German Court's Maastricht decision. Indeed, in its earlier decision—the Preliminary Issues Judgment[38]—the Hungarian Con-

---

36 Decision 30/1998 (VI.25)AB 25 June 1998.

37 Decision 30/1998 (VI.25) 25 June 1998 III.I, quoted in Janos Volkai, "The Application of the Europe Agreement and European Law in Hungary: The Judgment of an Activist Constitutional Court on Activist Notions", Harvard Jean Monnet Working Paper 8/99, http://www.JeanMonnetProgram.org/papers/99/990801.html at 9.

38 Hungarian Constitutional Court Decision 4/1997 (I.22) AB. 22 January 1997.

stitutional Court declared that it had the competence to conduct *ex post* review of international treaties (or rather, the national law that promulgates the treaty); in doing so, it made explicit reference to the Maastricht decision of the German Constitutional Court, and stated that national constitutional courts have the power of review over the constitutionality of EU laws that have direct effect in the relevant country. At least one Hungarian legal scholar has argued that the Hungarian Constitutional Court's decisions allow one to tentatively predict how the Court will act after Hungary's accession to the EU, and he has suggested that it may well continue to imitate the German Constitutional Court, and "thereby develop a conflictual relationship with the Community legal system after accession."[39]

Be that as it may, it may be anticipated that, immediately after accession, the constitutional courts of new member states will adopt an activist stance towards the relationship between EU law and the respective national constitutions, and to the questions of the direct effect and supremacy of EU law. They have some useful constitutional instruments for this purpose. First, almost all constitutions of new member states contain provisions to the effect that the constitution is the supreme source of law in the country, or (which comes to the same thing) that any law that violates the constitution is invalid; on this basis, some top constitutional justices in these countries have already announced their hostility towards the primacy of Community law towards the domestic order, in particular, toward the constitutional rules of their states.[40] Second, all of these courts have the power of preliminary review of the constitutionality of treaties (or rather, of the instruments of ratification), and in addition, the constitutional courts of Hungary, Poland and Estonia have the power of *ex post* review of treaties. Therefore, even though national law is subject to international agreements entered into by the State, such agreements are still themselves subject to the national Constitution. Third, as the above-mentioned decision of the Hungarian Constitutional Court indicates, these courts will adamantly insist that Parliament must not change the Constitution "by the back door," for example by ratifying a Treaty containing provisions that conflict with it, but rather that any change to the Constitution can be only made by using the proper amendment procedures. By adopting the position of supervisor over whether a legislative or constitutional amendment path should be adopted, the constitutional courts may become significant players in the European policy of new member states.

The argument is not that the constitutional courts in these states will in any way be a hindrance towards adopting the principles of direct effect and the supremacy of EU law, or that they will be obstacles to the process of legal integration of the new member states within the Union. On the contrary, it seems that most of the judges in these courts are strongly "pro-European": this is what their social and educational

---

39 Volkai, *op. cit.* n. 37, p. 31.

40 See, e.g., Marek Safjan, "Konstytucja a członkostwo Polski w Unii Europejskiej," *Państwo i Prawo* n. 3, 2001, pp. 9–10. Professor Safjan is President of the Constitutional Tribunal of Poland.

background, aspirations and political views incline them to. Some of the courts have even been eager to make use of EU law and EU legal principles well before accession. The Estonian Constitutional Review Chamber was so enthusiastic that, as early as 1994, it referred to the general principles of the Council of Europe *and EU law* as sources of Estonian law, even though, according to the Estonian Constitution, the courts should administer justice in accordance with the Constitution and the laws.[41] The point here is rather that accession will provide these courts with an extra opportunity to herald their importance as significant political and legislative players.

5. REGIONALISATION

The relationship between regionalization and democratic consolidation is not self-evident. There is no necessary truth in the statement that the more decentralized and "regionalized" the state, the more democratic it is. But it is a reasonably plausible contingent truth: all else being equal, decentralized states, especially when the local or regional units have responsive and elected institutions, tend to provide more spaces for spontaneous political actions of citizens, and, by establishing multiple focal points of power, spread the capacity for political action more widely within the community. Regions and local units are also attractive political alternatives to those "insular" minorities that may be voiceless nationally (due to small numbers, or traditional prejudices) and yet numerous and powerful enough to organize themselves at a sub-national level.

The Commission has shown a preference for democratically elected regional self-governments with significant financial and legal autonomy. The aspiration for this type of multi-level governance is due to the EU's desire, firstly, for democratic stability (the promotion of cohesion with the EU and reducing economic disparities is seen to be a good way of consolidating democracy), and secondly, for the effective management of the EU Structural Funds: regional and local authorities are considered as "partners" of the central government in managing those funds. However, before 1997, the Commission did not express a preference or demand for regionalization in CEE. For example, whilst talking of administrative reform, the Commission's 1995 White Paper did not refer to regionalization. This was based on the prevailing idea that aiding regions would help particularly backward regions at the expense of the better-off ones which, in turn, would slow down economic growth in the CEE countries.[42] It was only after 1997 that the Commission did push for regionalization, as by then it had been decided that the candidate states

41 Decision II-4/A-5/94 of 30 September 1994, discussed in Julia Laffranque, "Co-Existence of the Estonian Constitution and European Law," *Juridica International* 7 (2002), pp. 12–22.

42 Martin Brusis, "Between EU Requirements, Competitive Politics, and National Traditions: Re-creating Regions in the Accession Countries of Central and Eastern Europe," *Governance* 15 (2002), p. 541, referring to Martin Hallet, *National and Regional Development in*

would have to implement all of the *acquis* before accession, and this "implied that the accession countries needed to improve their administrative capacities at the regional level in order to manage Structural Funds."[43] In addition to the Accession Partnerships—for example those of Bulgaria, the Czech Republic and Slovakia in March 1998—that explicitly stated that the countries in question should set up regional administrative structures in order to be able to take advantage of the structural funds, the Commission's pressure was also based on the direction of PHARE resources towards regional assistance, and the setting up of twinning programmes. The Commission's Regular Reports made remarks on the extent of administrative reforms in the relevant states, though there is a very clear emphasis on the administrative capacity for the management of structural and cohesion funds, and on effective monitoring, financial management and control at regional level rather than on democratic self-government and autonomy.

The *acquis* includes (in Chapter 21) the requirements of regional administrative capacity, inter-ministerial co-ordination of regional policy and means for monitoring structural programmes. The candidate states must also organize their territory to fit within the so-called NUTS (*la Nomenclature des Unités Territoriales Statistiques*) classification system used to implement the Structural Funds.[44] Regarding these, the regions need to be autonomous enough to be credible partners to the Commission in the Structural Fund partnership process: the principle behind the co-management of the Structural Funds is to create policy not just for the regions, but also by them—that is, to ensure that local governments and NGOs, etc. are involved in the administration and management of the funds, within a collaborative process. The Structural Funds implement over 90% of all EU structural funding, the most important objective of which is the promotion of development in economically backward regions with GDP per capita of less than 75% of the EU average.

When evaluating the importance of the EU accession factor in the decentralization of CEE states, it should be emphasized that a high degree of regionalization in the countries of the region could well have occurred anyway, without any such pressure from the EU. Brusis has shown that much of the impetus towards regionalization came about due to the traditions of the countries and their move away from Communism, and also due to the preferences of the political actors on the scene in the 1990s.[45] Indeed, in relation to local government, many CEE states introduced reform well before the Commission or other EU bodies became active in promoting regionalization. For example, Poland did so in 1990 and then introduced another reform in 1993, the Czech Republic did so in 1990, with Hungary

---

Central and Eastern Europe: Implications for EU Structural Assistance (Brussels: European Commission/DG for Economic and Financial Affairs, 1997), p. 25.

43 Brusis, *id.* at 542.

44 See Dan Marek and Michael Baun, "The EU as a Regional Actor: The Case of the Czech Republic," *JCMS* 40 (2002), pp. 895–919 at 897–898.

45 Brusis, *op. cit.* n. 42, pp. 546–548.

starting from 1991. It is true that, with the exception of Hungary, the reform of regional government (in which there were more vested interests and disinterest in reform) did not take place until after 1997 when the Commission began to pressure explicitly for regionalization. Could it be said that the EU directly influenced these moves? Whilst it certainly may be true that the agenda for reform came about due to EU pressure, the actual formation of the new regions did not always correspond to NUTS areas. The general picture is that regions were created in the country (the real regions) and then amalgamated to form administrative regions *only for* NUTS purposes. This occurred in Bulgaria, the Czech Republic, and in Hungarian and Romanian regions (with the larger regions being formed to comply with NUTS II). The Polish regions were created in 1999 to comply with NUTS but they are "managerial and administrative rather than political entities."[46] It is not clear how effectively the NUTS-driven units will interact with the original "real" regions. Of the examples mentioned above, all but Poland have weak institutionalization of the NUTS areas (being merely administrative concepts created for the purpose of the Structural Funds), which "indicates that they constitute artificial elements in the traditional (and re-created) territorial-administrative structure."[47] Indeed, in the Czech Republic, the artificiality of the NUTS areas created "a potentially awkward situation by grouping together, in some of the NUTS II units, regions that have not always historically co-operated, and in some cases have even been rivals."[48]

The evaluation of the EU factor is also difficult because the pressure from the EU—in the Reports and through PHARE funding—was not towards any specific, detailed model for the construction of regions: their size, form of funding, exact capabilities, and level of fiscal autonomy were largely left open. The Commission has been very cautious in dispensing its advice: it merely required "that "appropriate" systems of regional administration and governance be in place by the time of accession, without trying to define these in any concrete way."[49] Consequently, there are big differences between the regional structures in the various countries of CEE: between Bulgaria, the Czech Republic, Hungary, Poland and Slovakia, the size of the regional units varies, as does the level of integration between territorial state administration and regional self-governments.[50] The form that regionalization takes is dependent upon the geographical and political contexts, thus such differences are not surprising given that the CEE states have different population densities and sizes.

There is some evidence, however, that the Commission Reports made a difference to the trend towards regionalization. Most fundamentally, the influence of the EU

---

46 Report of the Reflection Group, *op. cit.* n. 8, p. 120.
47 Brusis, *op. cit.* n. 42, p. 553.
48 Marek and Baun, *op. cit.* n. 44, p. 903.
49 *Id.*, p. 898.
50 Brusis, *op. cit.* n. 42, pp. 538–539.

institutions was crucial in putting the very issue of regionalization on the agenda. As the authors of the "Dehaene Report" observed,

> [w]ith the exception of Poland, where regional reform was recognised early on as a[n] essential part of the transition process, regionalisation only became an issue following pressure from the Commission which directly or indirectly shaped the process in a number of CEECs.[51]

The pressure was also occasionally effective in remedying specific detailed problems. After the Czech Republic was criticized in 1997 because higher units of territorial administration were lacking, it remedied the situation by 2001. Furthermore, other aspects of regionalization that were criticized in the Reports (such as financial management) were also at least partially remedied, with the Commission noting substantial progress in its 2002 Report. As Marek and Braun observe, EU pressure and the prospect of accession "probably accelerated the process of regionalization in the Czech Republic".[52] In addition, to fulfill the requirements of decentralization contained in the PHARE cross-border co-operation programme, the Czech Republic established Euroregions—cross-border structures along the Czech borders with its neighbours—and even more decentralized regional bodies used for administering the small projects fund which invest in border areas. These were, however, seen as a big success by the Commission and recommended to other countries of CEE.

On balance, the effect of EU accession upon regionalization in the candidate states has been positive, though indirect, diffuse and not particularly strong. This is for a number of reasons. First, there is no single West European model to imitate in this respect, and consequently there is no specific *acquis* regarding the details of the organization and status of regional governments. Although Professor Alessandro Pizzorusso may be right when he notes that recognition of *a* form of regional autonomy belongs to the common constitutional traditions in Europe, nevertheless he himself acknowledges the existence of a great variety of forms of such recognition, ranging from a federal design (as in Germany, Austria and more recently in Belgium) to unitary states in which autonomy is "purely administrative" (as in France, the Netherlands or the Scandinavian states).[53] Hence, it is understandable that the pressure from the Commission was only by "indirect and underformalized methods".[54] Secondly, the societal pressure from below was relatively weak in the

---

51 Report of the Reflection Group, above n. 8 p. 121, referring to Jim Hughes, Gwendolyn Sasse and Claire Gordon, "The Regional Deficit in Eastward Enlargement of the European Union: Top Down Policies and Bottom Up Reactions," *ESRC "One Europe or Several?" Programme*, Working Paper 29/2001.

52 Marek and Baun, *op. cit.* n. 44, p. 903.

53 Alessandro Pizzorusso, *Il patrimonio costituzionale europeo* (Bologna: Il Mulino 2002), pp. 150–151.

54 Brusis, *op. cit.* n. 42, p. 535.

states of CEE, perhaps with the exception of Poland. This is due to a number of factors: the small size of many of the candidate states, the newness of these states, the relative frequency of boundary shifts in the past—all of these contributed to the relatively low intensity of the sense of regional identity, with the regions created being more "artificial creations rather than historically and culturally anchored regional units".[55] The demands for strong regional autonomy based on historical identity in those few cases in which they occurred—in Silesia in Poland, or in Moravia in the Czech Republic—were quickly marginalized and rejected by all major parties in these countries. As Brusis explains, the relative weakness of regionalism in CEE can be explained by lack of correlation between ethnic and historical regionalism: significant national minorities do not have traditions of regional units (as is the case in Estonia, Lithuania or Slovakia), while historically entrenched regions lack separate ethnic identity (as is the case of Czech Republic; Poland is an exception but the ethnic German minority in Silesia represents less than one percent of the population).[56] However, this weakness of indigenous support for regionalization at the same time indicates that, without the external pressure, there would have been no attempt to regionalize at all and that the matter would not even have made it on to the political agenda. Thirdly, the EU push towards regionalization has been largely offset by the by-and-large technocratic nature of the accession process, which has inevitably led to centralization: the EU demand for speedy implementation of the *acquis* and efficient use of resources strengthened national actors to the detriment of regional ones.

Nevertheless, accession is likely to consolidate and deepen the push towards regionalization. If we look to the lessons of history in this regard, there have been some examples in the EU of regional identities being created—or at least, greatly fostered—within regions set up initially for administrative reasons, as is the case of North-Rhine-Westphalia; a consensus seems to exist among many scholars that the EU cohesion policy has mobilized support for regions in the existing member states and strengthened their political position.[57] There is no reason to believe that a similar effect will not occur in CEE. The example of some Polish regions having established their own interest groups to lobby in Brussels on their behalf may suggest that the EU exerts some pull towards increasing regional awareness, if not in terms of cultural or political identity, then at least at the level of economic and political interests.

6. CONCLUSION

Since the fall of Communist rule, the countries of CEE have profoundly transformed themselves into constitutional, liberal democracies. Much of the transformation has

---

[55] Report of the Reflection Group, *op. cit.* n. 8, p. 123.
[56] Brusis, *supra* n. 42, pp. 550–551.
[57] See *ibid.*, p. 1, referring to the literature of the subject.

been by imitation, emulation and transplant of Western (including Western European) templates of democratic institutions. Since the early 1990s, the transformations have been also dictated by "conditionality": a set of more or less vague requirements that had to be met if a state were to qualify for membership in the EC/EU. The combination of the relative inflexibility and rigor of principle of conditionality, on one hand, with the relative malleability, open-endedness and speed of the political transformations in post-communist states, on the other, contributed to the high degree of effectiveness of the attempt to transplant the rules of the "club" to the "applicants". The EC/EU could dictate the terms because the candidates had more interest in joining than the Union did in enlarging. The democratic forces in the CEE states could bravely design new institutions because the forces of the *ancient regime* were demoralized, traumatized and easily embarrassed. The constellation of external and internal conditions was therefore favourable to rapid and thorough democratization although the specific parameters varied from country to country and from issue to issue. In general, the interaction between the "external" factors of conditionality and the domestic calculus of the costs and benefits of transforming an institution (or adopting a rule) provides the best lens through which to evaluate the impact of "conditionality" upon the speed, depth and resilience of adoption and maintenance of particular democratic rules or institutions in the candidate states.

This explanatory lens will maintain its validity also after accession, although the patterns of incentives will change somewhat, as was suggested in Part 1 of this chapter. The three specific areas in which accession is likely to make a difference for the institutional set-up in the new Member States are the relationship between the executive and legislative branches, the position of constitutional courts, and the significance of regional and local administration and self-government, discussed in Parts 2–4 of this chapter. In all of these three areas the changes will not be qualitative in character, but will instead continue the trends already set in motion by the process of accession negotiations and preparations. Their overall significance for democracy in general is difficult to assess; from my point of view, the strengthening of constitutional courts and the weakening of the legislatures both give cause for concern, while the decentralizing tendencies should be applauded. Others will attach different values to these trends. What *is* important is to realize that accession will not leave the political systems in new Member States untouched, and that a prudent strategy at this point for these countries would be to anticipate and attempt to limit the possible negative effects of accession (for instance, strengthening the legislatures by providing them with better expert infrastructure, or by introducing constitutional amendments in order to prevent constitutional courts from "dictating" legislative changes to parliaments), while at the same time taking advantage to the greatest degree possible of the positive effects.

In the end, the most fundamental positive effect will be at a macro- rather a micro-level: by providing the democratic forces within the post-communist states with additional support, encouragement and discursive assets against the threats from authoritarian, populist, nationalistic forces, the democratic transition itself has been strengthened. In this sense, the position of democratic elites in new member states will not be all that different from the position of liberal and democratic forces in, say, Italy or Austria, where those with authoritarian tendencies invariably find themselves in the "anti-European" corner, because the institutional and ideological structure of the European Union tends to support liberal and democratic arguments. Thus, the EU increasingly becomes a community of values, not merely a community of interests, and the values that these days predominate within the Union resemble closely the values of civic liberal-democrats in the post-communist area of Europe. The anxiety that the leaders of most of the EU member states displayed in response to the likelihood—and then, the reality—of a coalition government including a nationalistic, xenophobic, authoritarian party in one of its member states (I have in mind, of course, the Austrian debacle of 2000) illustrates clearly that the EU can be mobilized against such trends, and that there is a degree of transnational solidarity on the part of liberal-democratic forces that can count on the political resources of the Union. When the awareness that a possible lapse into a nationalist-authoritarian option in new Member States in the CEE is not merely an "internal domestic affair" but rather an immediate "European" problem penetrating the public opinion in these states, the political mechanisms for preventing and countering such collapses will themselves become more resilient. Accession to the EU may not be a panacea for all of the problems of political democracy but it may well be a reasonably good protection against possible future disasters.

This will be a principal democracy dividend stemming from the reconfiguration of traditional focal points of identity and sovereignty that will necessarily follow upon the accession to the EU. That reconfiguration—a process of "transnational articulation of societies"[58]—has already begun to occur, but it will be greatly accelerated after the actual accession. Many social forces in the new member states—political parties, NGOs, women and environmental organizations, etc.—will find their counterparts in the other member states to be the most obvious partners for co-operation and common action. Indeed, the process of transnational party co-operation, with CEE parties included within EU party federations and various political internationals, has already begun, and the introduction of parliamentarians from CEE into the European Parliament will be a powerful additional stimulus to such political transnationalization. Traditional patterns of loyalty will be altered: as "local" matters become, by definition, "European", the notion of "washing one's dirty linen at home" will lose its persuasive force. Just as the appeal to the Strasbourg Court has established—and legitimated—a route outside the state to make one's grievances heard, so will the EU-based institutions, procedures and organizations erode the trumping power of "state sovereignty", once capable of silencing the voices raised in defence of democratic and liberal values.

---

[58] Stafano Bianchini, "Post Communism, Post-Westfalianism, Overcoming the Nation-State," in Bianchini, Schöpflin and Schoup (eds.), *op. cit.* n. 2, p. 197.

The identity of the polities will also undergo significant changes. For example, the extension of the right to vote in elections to the European Parliament to any EU citizen regardless of where they happen to be, and also, in local elections, to resident non-citizens of member states—such changes will drive home to many people the contingency of citizenship and the weakness of ethno-national criteria in defining the membership of a polity. The understanding of who is part of the *demos* will inevitably be transformed: traditional loyalties and the ethnic and cultural sense of belonging will need to give way to something more akin to "constitutional patriotism", under which the polity is bounded by common civic rights and duties rather than by tradition and ethnic identity. The same will apply to an increasing knowledge of foreign languages and the consequent evaporation of the "monopoly over language" by the nation states,[59] as to the EU-driven removal of legal prohibitions upon the purchase of real property by non-citizens. In a longer-term perspective, the adhesion to the Euro-zone will undercut another traditional symbol of national identity: a local currency and the dominant position of a central bank. All of this will put the nationalistic forces (who also happen to be, more often than not, authoritarian and illiberal) on the defensive. Attempts to re-establish identity along the lines of national, ethnic or religious patterns will no doubt be undertaken, but, with the growing integration of the new Member States in the EU, those doing so will be facing increasingly uphill battle. Accession will reconfigure political and discursive assets and incentives in ways that help the liberal-democratic and hinder the authoritarian political forces in new Member States. This is perhaps the best thing about the democracy dividend of the EU accession process.

---

[59] See *id.*

2. The Eastern EU Enlargement and the Janus-headed Nature of the Constitutional Treaty

Vittorio Olgiati

"*Ce sont des problèmes pour lesquels Thémis n'a pas de balance*"*

1. Introduction

Leafing through the history of European unionism, cleavages and differences within and among socio-legal orders do not seem to have been taken on as a major concern when favorable conditions for the enlargement of the Community borders occurred. If and when a *status necessitatis* provided for such conditions, geo-political *arrondisages* were immediately pursued, often in spite of other, not less relevant, governance issues.[1] Following the fall of the Berlin Wall, the accession of Eastern European countries as EU Member States is just the last case in point at present.

Hence, one wonders: is there a socio-technical *archè*, i.e. an original source, or core matrix, laying behind current affairs that presides over, or works for, the type of strategy that the EU adopted so far? What structural and symbolic limits or boundaries, if any, can be ascribed, or are inherent to geo-political EU incrementalism? In sum: is it there an inner format that can explain the relationship between the logic of EU enlargement and the way in which EU institutions have been constructed?

As one can easily see, these questions are not rhetorical. It is even possible to reframe the above interrogatives into technical/doctrinal legal terms as follows: is it there a coherent mix in the *Ratio Status et Ratio Juris* of the EU enlargement process and policy? Is the ongoing mixture of the *necessitas rerum jus constituit* and *auctoritas, non veritas, facit legem* reference standards, i.e. the combination of legal realism and legal formalism, either in the form of decisionist/jusnaturalistic tenets of legal institutionalism or voluntaristic/rationalistic tenets of legal constructivism, a coherent normative framework to manage the problems raised by EU expansionism? Is the constitutionalization of the EU a plausible and socially adequate response to current and prospective EU governance systems?

---

* Carl Schmitt (Glossarium).

1 Ian Ward, "A Decade of Europe? Some reflections on an aspiration", *Journal of Law and Society* 30 2 (2003), pp. 236–257.

Wojciech Sadurski et al. (ed.), Spreading Democracy and the Rule of Law?, 51–71.

The leading hypothesis of this study is that the entry of Eastern European countries to the EU gives room to the official claim of there being actual subsistence in "common" European legal tradition, but by contrast exacerbates a variety of paradoxical outcomes of late-modern EU legal arrangements. This is the inevitable challenge for creating a wider and stronger European Union which has to deal with—as Szucs, following Braudel, put it—the irrepressible spatial existence of a historical variety of Europes (Western, Central and Eastern).

In this respect, the temporal coincidence of EU enlargement towards Eastern countries and the drafting of an EU Constitutional Treaty not only provides us with a veritable laboratory-like field to test the consistency of the above interrogations. It also provides us with a highly problematic socio-legal scenario.

2. THE "DEMOCRATIC TRANSITION" OF EASTERN EUROPEAN COUNTRIES AND THE EU ENLARGEMENT POLICY

As a starting point for our discussion, a *tour d'horizon* on the major socio-institutional changes that have occurred in the last decade in Eastern European Countries seems opportune.

As we know, both Western and Eastern European countries depicted the EU enlargement/accession strategy as a common task. In practice, however, it was not so, for it concerned quite different needs, interests and expectations. The solution given to such a mismatch has been the enactment of (i) an enormous flow of financial investments, and (ii) a large program of legal implantation of Western-styled legal standards, so as to (a) soften social-institutional problems of the transition and (b) raise a sufficient political-ideological loyalty towards the newly-created order.

The flow of financial investments has been extraordinary indeed. The EU only devolved to Eastern States over 40 billion Euro as pre-adhesion support between 1994 and 1999. Besides, EU Member-States individually provided financial support to implement specific economic projects and favor the so-called de-localization of Western private enterprises. If one then adds the amount of money poured in by USA formal and informal agencies and corporations since the fall of the Berlin Wall, on can easily imagine the overall political result: to render licit and consensual—if not legitimate and voluntary—a veritable form of aggressive economic merger. As a matter of fact, the privatization wave concerned foreign investors above all. Hence, as the pre-exiting economic system had to be dismantled, and the newly created one had to be shaped in this manner, one can reasonably decipher the final outcome as a process of socio-economic colonization.[2]

The legal implantation of Western-style legal standards has also been pursued as a veritable colonization process. Surely, this implantation has been made appealing and has been socially and institutionally accepted by virtue of the flow of financial

---

[2] Josef Langer, "Shortcomings of Enlarging the European Union Eastward", *ISIG Quarterly of International Sociology*, XII, 1–2 (2003), pp. 16–18.

investments mentioned above. Yet it is fair to say that it also gained ideological and political support on the part of those local/national groups that were concerned with the advancement of enlightened ideals and life-styles. In any case, such a legal strategy has implied top–down (a) enactment of foreign legal tools produced by foreign legal sources (e.g. EU accession criteria, EU directives, international quality standards, etc.), (b) settlement of foreign institutional/professional agencies/expertise, (c) importation of western-style legal culture, and, last but not least, (d) politicization of judicial systems (the so-called "judicial activism").

To sum up, if one considers the way in which the process of either the "democratic transition" or EU-oriented alignment have been carried out, it is apparent that the rationale of Western EU Member States' policy—leaving aside the special cases of Eastern Germany, Czechoslovakia and Yugoslavia—has been that of (a) maintaining, in as far as possible, those State borders already in existence (in accordance to the *uti possidetis* legal principle), so as to (b) ease a systematic overturn of the overall Eastern socio-institutional contexts in terms that could hardly be matched with the legal principle of national self-determination.

This does not mean to say that, by assessing an extreme variant of the neoliberal theory of the interdependence of legal-economic orders, the same did not foster socio-institutional pluralism as well as the rise of a new sort of civil society.[3] But such transformations did not change the nature of the trend since bottom-up social trends played the role of mere secondary adjustment patterns so much so that—contrary to the principles of national independence and sovereignty officially proclaimed in their new-born democratic constitutions—either political leaders attached to the previous regimes or the new ones not only did not consider a fight for self-determination as an alternative way, but simply worked to domesticate and localizing the incoming foreign models and goods.[4] Within this framework, it comes as no surprise therefore that—as Stompka put it—common people lacking personal resources and/or disoriented by ongoing changes, did not raise social protests, but rather inclined towards individual quests for functional substitutes of trust in a better future, such as EU welfare's providentialism.[5]

Given the above, it is noteworthy to mention the way in which either repeated re-adjustments of constitutional systems, or the impact of judicial activism—otherwise labeled "transitional justice"—have been analyzed and discussed in the meanwhile. In fact, studies carried out by Eastern scholars stressed the unstable country-specific space–time juncture, and noted recurrent conceptual shifts as regards the political meaning of the legal items under consideration. In particular,

---

3 Jacek Kurczewski and Joanna Kurczewska, "A Self-Governing Society Twenty Years Later: Democracy and the Third Sector", *Social Research*, 68, 4 (2001), pp. 937–976.

4 Nina Bandelj, "Particularizing the Global: Reception of Foreign Direct Investments in Slovenia", *Current Sociology*, 51, 3–4 (2003), pp. 375–392.

5 Piotr Sztompka, "Trust and Emerging Democracy. Lessons from Poland", *International Sociology*, 11, 1 (1996), pp. 37–62.

the rising politicization of the justice systems raised a number of theoretical and political "dilemmas" as regards the very notion of "transition" to Western-styled democracy: "dilemmas" that could not be easily resolved just because of concurrent social changes and constitutional variability.

By contrast, studies undertaken by Western scholars emphasized the importance of slow yet evolving "achievements", and the support provided by both the elite and the people. Therefore they stressed the rising effectiveness of the democratic transition, despite the need to further improve it with additional "aids". In brief, they provided quite a linear interpretation of the problematic issues under consideration. So much so that some analysts were even inclined to give credit to a substantial equivalence between the politicization of the law and justice systems occurring in Eastern countries as well as the politicization of the law and the justice systems that occurred in the same period in Western countries.[6]

Needless to say, official EU representatives had no difficulty in assuming this sort of scientific literature as a reference framework. Relying on it, and recognizing that in the case of self-styled or newly-created democratic society to "reckon with the past" cannot be carried out to the point of damaging the economy and the State,[7] a lenient attitude towards the so-called lustration was suggested. Then, the accomplishment of western-style parameters was declared step by step. The official admittance of ten North Eastern Countries in May 2004 is the certification that such accomplishment has been formally achieved.

3. THE RISING POLITICAL AND LEGAL DILEMMAS OF EU ENLARGEMENT

The fact that the transition towards a Western-style constitutional democracy and market system of former Socialist countries was considered accomplished with the "adoption" of a cluster of imposed, and heteronomous, formal-official parameters is not the only striking issue of the 2004 EU enlargement. In fact, it perfectly clashes with the period of gestation and the drafting of the EU Constitutional Treaty.

As epochal events of this sort do not happen by chance, and occur even less by chance in the same time-frame, one might wonder whether the formal-legal certification of the accomplishment of the democratic transition has, or has not, resolved the conceptual/political "dilemmas" mentioned above. If not, did these "dilemmas" raise further questions within the EU inner circles? In other words: is the coincidence of the two epochal events a sign that the EU project reached such a problematic geo-political contour to require the enforcement of a formal-official EU identity framework to stabilize and defend its promoters? After all, how could one ignore that typical of post World War II transitions is the attempt to promote a

---

6 Wojciech Sadurski, "Decommunisation, Lustration and Constitutional Continuity: Dilemmas of Transitional Justice in Central Europe", EUI Law Department Working Paper, 2003/15.

7 Helmut Quartisch, *Giustizia politica. Le amnistie nella storia* (Milano: Giuffré 1995).

damnatio memoriae—i.e. a mix of amnesia and amnesty—about past constitutional experiences and that this sort of *damnatio* cannot rely on mere economic "buying and selling," although this is an essential condition, but rather requires either a sort of self-identification with the new order or a symbolic Manifesto to improve the "social learning" about the overall socio-political change?[8]

To answer these questions and explain how and why the EU agenda reached the stage of setting up, at one time, a formal constitutionalization and the largest accession so far, it is useful here to recall major historical cleavages of European unionism.

As is known, European unionism was originally promoted by elite factions within historical national blocks of a number of European countries as a precautionary measure to tackle domestic and international issues and prevent undesirable socio-political upheavals within the post-war political order. In fact, given that constitutional experiences occurred in the first half of XX century, the European project has been, from the start, carried as a veritable "defensive modernization" strategy to come to terms with (1) the historical decline of the bourgeois domination of the overall functioning of the State; (2) the historical dissolution of the European rule in various non-European countries; (3) the historical emergence of new powerful political constituencies and economic corporations at world-system level. In short it has always been a question of defending-by-modernizing the legacies of the Enlightenment's features and the constitutional architecture and lifestyle (universalistic values and particularistic interests) deriving from Euro-centric liberal ideology.

From the Treaty of Rome (1957) up to the Single European Act (1986), the above was performed by levering on essentially economic imperatives. Since the 1980s, however, this practice proved to be absolutely inadequate in relation to changes triggered by global/local processes at either the international or the domestic level. In a nutshell, it became clear that existing private interest governments were imperiled at the national level and only weakly empowered at supranational level.[9] Consequently the European elite power was compelled to change its political agenda (from socio-economic communitarianism to political unionism) to better protect the European fields of strategic interests and values. And it did so up to the point of contradicting even the cautionary, reformist early imprinting of the project, as the interference of some EU Member States in civil conflicts occurring, just beyond the boundaries of the Union, in a neighboring country (i.e. former Yugoslavia) demonstrates.[10]

---

8 *Ibid.*

9 Philip Schmitter, "The Future of Euro-Polity and its Impact upon Private Interest Governance within Member-States", *Droit et Societé*, 28 (1994), pp. 659–675.

10 Vittorio Olgiati, "The EU Charter of Fundamental Rights. Text and Context to the Rise of a "Public Interest" EU-oriented European Lawyer", *International Journal of the Legal Profession*, 9, 3 (2002), pp. 235–250, and Vittorio Olgiati, "L'Unione Europea verso

Needless to say, the change mentioned above also occurred in relation to—and at the same time as—the dismantling of the communist rule in Eastern European countries. In this juncture the idea to set up a European Confederation of these countries to facilitate a smooth socio-political transition, in view of their prospective integration into the EU, suggested in 1991 by Mitterand—or at least a "Visegrad Triangle" as envisaged by Havel, Walesa and Antall—was immediately abandoned. By contrast increasing efforts were devoted to the enactment of the Maastricht and Schengen Treaties and the planning of the Euro Currency system.

This sort of EU policy gave rise to two diverging trends: an increasing interest on the part of Eastern European countries to establish closer links with the USA, and an apparent competition among Western European countries to re-set their own pre-World War sphere of influence in the area. Then the Serbia–Kosovo war—i.e. the very first war on European continent since World War II—occurred. And it made apparent the paradox: i.e. that the USA's and the EU's pretensions to "inspire" Eastern countries to enact human rights, democracy, rule-of-law, etc. coupled with the breach of basic rules of national and international law—under the guise of self-claimed humanitarian aids and war to rouge regimes—by the very same USA and EU Member-States.

Given such a geo-political context—in which (1) only a veritable financial and legal colonization of Eastern European countries made their entry into the EU possible and acceptable, and this in turn was carried out in the course of (2) a concurrent blatant violation of the letter and the spirit of the *Jus Publicum Europaeum* on the part of the same EU Western countries predicating to be guardians of the rule of law and democracy principles—it is by no means fortuitous that additional serious "dilemmas" about the (democratic) nature of the EU policy's "style" have come to the fore. If then one adds the prospective political-economic impact of the EU enlargement at world-system level,[11] one can easily see what sort of historical conditions were on the EU agenda in the space–time under consideration.

As it will be outlined in the following paragraphs, the drafting of the EU Constitutional Treaty—with the inclusion of the section of the Nice Treaty labeled "Charter of Human Rights and Fundamental Freedoms"—is the official response to the disquieting state of EU affairs that has just briefly been described.

4. THE SEARCH FOR EU GOVERNANCE LEGITIMACY

To fully understand the legal and political meaning of the drafting of the EU Constitutional Treaty and the inclusion of the EU Charter of Fundamental Rights

---

una costituzione virtuale?", Paper presented at the International Conference "Le identità mediterranee e la costituzione europea" (Salerno, 2003).

11 Neil Winn, "Europe's Role for Global Peace and Conflict Resolution", *ISIG Quarterly of International Sociology*, XII, 1–2 (2003), pp. 14–16.

as a way to handle the dilemmatic consequences of the EU policy after the fall of the Berlin Wall, it is necessary to consider the implications of the Euro firstly.

As it has been noticed, with the enforcement of the Euro currency system, the European elite set up the EU as a financial "fortress", to defend, by modernizing, a system of productive resources and a network of economic-social relations which could otherwise have been taken over or dispersed by aggressive foreign players. The political problem of the Euro, however, is that its enforcement was incapacitated by "economicism." Let us use an analogical example to make this statement clear. As with every "dowry institution"—each citizen of each EU Member State participating to the venture having given his or her share—the birth of the Euro ought to have been consequent upon the celebration of the EU basic interests/values "wedding", that is upon a procedurally correct and socially visible ceremonial act such as to permit the immediate recognition not only of the actors legitimately involved, but also of their respective legitimization to act.

This apparently extravagant analogy would not be significant were it not for a substantial reason: that is—as we learn from the unsurpassed historical model of *Austria Felix*—when a marriage of political/property interest is celebrated to avoid a conflict between neighbor States and/or defend or "round out" a sovereign territory, it is good practice for the wedded couple to appear on the balcony of the palace so that all the people know who has married who, and who among the relatives and connections has been excluded from the symbolic and material benefits of the union.

Unfortunately, in the case of the Euro this good ancient rule was completely ignored: to the extent that, even today, common European citizens know what the Euro currency looks like, but are not at all aware of who, behind the windshield of the official institutions, came together to rule the matter and whether it was done on equal terms or otherwise. To put it in another way: it is not true that the enactment of the Euro system preceded the rise of a proper EU ruling class. In fact, the contrary is true, for the dominating EU historic block—concealed behind the complexity of the EU governance system—did not include some Member States and still less some fractions internal to certain national elites. With the Euro, therefore, the original and unresolved problem of the EU "democratic deficit", far from being mitigated has actually been aggravated: for the first time in EU history, it has taken on importance and visibility which is not solely declamatory, but openly conflictive even at the very top of the European socio-political ladder.[12]

Alongside the recognition of the power of immediate or postponed self-exclusion (opting-out) or entry (opting-in)—a sign of the lack of a common co-alignment, and therefore, of a latent conflict (as in the case of Britain and Denmark)—dominant EU power elite fractions enacted a preventive and discriminatory selection to the detriment of other fractions also. It is important to state—aside from the rigidity

12 Vittorio Olgiati (2003), *op. cit.* n. 10.

of the Maastricht Treaty parameters and their subsequent violation—the spatial-temporal coincidence of events that appear otherwise quite distinct when seen from a superficial light: (1) the political attack conducted—even through judicial activism—against certain political parties and financial groups which were considered, on various heads, not to be organically oriented towards the EU "common" values and interests (the case of Belgium, Italy, France, etc.); (2) the political vindication of the right of secession of highly industrialized sub-national entities (the case of Italy); (3) the sudden establishment of transversal political alliances between and within opposite parties (the case of Italy, Germany, The Netherlands, etc.); (4) the political obstructionism about a non-negotiated restructuring of the Euro system in the event of EU enlargements (the case of Ireland); (5) the *sine die* postponement and/or re-proposition of national political referendums about the Euro and overall EU *Struckturbildung*; and, last but not least (6) the sudden decision of the USA for the inclusion of Eastern European countries into NATO before their entry into the EU.

As one can see, the number of variables that provide evidence of an open conflict of interest/values and a lack of a democratic rule-of-the-game within and among EU and EU Member States power elites is quite large. Actually, it has grown even larger in the last few years, as demonstrated by the standing of some European countries in relation to the USA pre-emptive war against Iraq—and the end of Globalization as a post Cold-war international order system[13]—as well as the subsequent failure of the EU inter-governmental conference held in Rome in October 2003 to discuss the draft of the EU Constitutional Treaty.

In this context, how can EU constitutionalization be heralded as a sign of the democratic rule-of-law oriented interests/values of the European community as a whole? How can it be officially claimed that it "seals" off the common destiny of the European society? And, how far can one think that a paper-Treaty is the best way to raise social consensus and political legitimization towards the kind of European unionism that the same Treaty is supposed to constitutionalize?

5. EX OCCIDENTE SALUS?

As if the disquieting state of the EU affairs discussed thus far were not enough, additional technical issues add up to worsen the situation of the EU strategy: the epochal crisis of Western formal-official codification and legal positivization. As a matter of fact, a paradoxical aspect of EU constitutionalization is that it is taking place at a problematic historic moment of the "law's empire." Both constitutionalism as a politico-legal discipline and constitutionalism as a concrete form of order are, at present, far from being anchored to secure theoretical and practical bases. Attempts

13 Vittorio Olgiati, "Constitutional Instability. A World-system Issue", in Alessandro Gobbicchi (ed.), *Globalization, Armed Conflics and Security*, Atti del Convegno CEMISS-Centro Militare di Studi Strategici, (Soveria: Rubettino 2004) (in print).

at a revision of existing Western-style constitutional systems are in progress in almost any country in the world. A condition of constitutional instability is also apparent in any country, due to either the so-called "explosion" of legal pluralism, the erosion of Nation-State sovereignty or the rise of new political strategies such as pre-emptive war and terrorism.[14]

In Europe the above is further complicated by the fact that there is no country in which the theory and practice of the Constitution do not, in one way or another, recall the codification model as a pivotal structure of State-centered nationalism: a historical legacy that the EU tends to go beyond. Besides this, the EU (a) is not and does not take a State-form, for it is the product of mere international treaties, and consequently (b) it does not have the possibility of setting up a proper, autonomous constitutional system, and even less a self-styled democratic constitutional system rooted, as in the case of State/Nation, in the principle of legality and on the criterion of the fiduciary mandate lacking, as it does, any exclusive sovereignty over its own people and its own territory. If one then adds the fact that the so-called "EU citizenship" is *de jure* no more than a "social label" (as, e.g., England is a (1) common law, (2) monarchical, (3) confessional, and (4) colonial State ruling a European colony within Europe, while for example Finland or Italy are not), one can easily understand why an international legal act such as the Constitutional Treaty has been drafted by a group of (not democratically elected) State representatives, gathered in an informal setting called the "convention."

To conclude it is apparent that the EU Constitutional Treaty is not, and cannot be, a way to substantiate the (self-styled democratic) rule-of-law, division-of-powers, etc. principles. However, as its structure and functions are anyhow technically and politically relevant for prospective EU scenarios, let us comment on its "mimetic" discursive content.

6. THE BINARY NATURE OF THE EU CONSTITUTIONAL TREATY

The EU Constitutional Treaty represents the quintessence of the EU law-policy, as has been performed so far: a mix of voluntaristic-rationalistic legal constructivism and jusnaturalistic-decisionist neo-institutionalism. As a constructivist regulatory model, the Treaty is for sure a sort of creative/regressive re-issue (in late-modern key) of Rousseau's "social contract." Urged by a veritable *status necessitatis*, it is the result of a contractual agreement between EU Member States acting as private agents, intentionally disposed to limit their own sovereignty so that it can be implemented (by virtue of the EU legal principles of "direct effect" and "supremacy") by EU agents (devoid of a substantial democratic legitimization) *as if* it were the expression of the general will (of European society), in the interest of the pacific cooperation of each (State) and all (citizens), and therefore in the general interest of the overall Europe as formally constituted by the Union.

---

[14] Vittorio Olgiati (2002, 2003), *op. cit.* n. 10.

As one can see, in the articulation of its essential elements, the EU Constitutional Treaty does not appear to diverge greatly—*mutatis mutandis*—from that hypothesized by Rousseau to give credit to the shift from a "state of nature" to a "civil society."[15] The only exception—intriguing and innovative—is that (1) the agents are not physical persons, but States and EU organs, and consequently (2) there is no original "state of nature" except that given by the political and legal systems of the current *pouvoir constituée*, just as (3) there is no civil and political society except through the re-enforcement of the same political and legal constituted power. The novelty of the Treaty, therefore, is that it is the result of a self-interactive process, an act of self-observation and self-recognition of mere vested interests and values, brought about and intentionally oriented to function in the absence of an explicit, visible and substantial, popular *pouvoir constituant*.

In technical legal terms the rationale of the Treaty is therefore clear: to do (or not to do) things with words, by means of the use of the constructivist "as if" (*Als Ob*) legal device as a pivotal *fictio intellectualis*[16] of a political project that, for fifty years, has been portrayed as a veritable self-fulfilling prophecy but that has actually been consolidated according to the *Ratio Status* or "Doctrine of State Interests", as suggested by the century-old, but living still, *Arcana Imperii* European legal tradition.[17]

In turn, as a neo-institutional regulatory model, the Treaty is an equally interesting case of creative/regressive re-issue (in late modern key) of a well-known constitutional trend leading to the constitutional hypostatization of the Judiciary as "supreme power" of existing institutional domains. To have an idea of this trend (and consequently of the politicization of the Justice system) it is sufficient to consider that the claim of traditionally self-styled universal values and principles typical of early Enlightenment and Classic Political Economy overlap upon a late-modern constitutional architecture that, for historical reasons, cannot but deal with a "bifurcation" of Western European constitutionalism that occurred after the failure of the Weimar Republic and the Nazi experience. As the trauma of these events had to be covered, such a "bifurcation" has been officially formalized. This is the case of post-war Italian and French constitutional systems. In short, it is about the process of "de-personification" (Italian case) and of "presidentialization" (French case) of the formal/material State sovereignty.

Now, if one reads either the Preamble or the text (so far available) of the EU Constitutional Treaty, it is apparent that the emphasis put on liberal-democratic values and principles as the EU legal foundations recalls the Italian constitutional model enforced in 1947, in which no real subject—be it either a political leader, a particular class, a king or the people—seems to hold the "supreme power", i.e. the

[15] Jean Jacques Rousseau, "Extrait du project de paix perpétuelle de monsieur l'Abbe de Saint-Pierre", in *Œuvres completes*, vol. III (Paris, 1964).

[16] Hans Vaininger, *Die Philosophie des Als Ob* (Berlin, 1911).

[17] Vittorio Olgiati (2003), *op. cit.* n. 10.

sovereignty of the State is totally de-personified. On the other hand, the emphasis put on the functioning of the EU institutions and decision-making procedures recalls, in turn, the French constitutional model enforced in the 1950's by De Gaulle, in which the State sovereignty is individualized not by means of a somewhat *legibus solutus* leader, but by an agent/agency provided with relatively discretional—presidential—powers in order to by-pass the overall formal-legal design of the political dynamic of the State machinery governance. In short, the supreme power is embodied by a sort of powerful, politically independent, "commissioner" able to act also in case of a daily (i.e. not exceptional but recurrent) state of necessity. Being so, the EU Constitutional Treaty not only combines, but up-to-dates the logic of the above mentioned constitutional models, by enlarging and refining either the range of fundamental values and principles or the prerogatives of the commissarial system.

6.1. The Pillar of EU Constitutionalism: the Court of Justice

Paradoxically, the way in which the above technical solution could actually work can hardly be found in the works of the Convention that drafted the EU Constitutional Treaty. In fact, to have more information on this issue, one has to focus on the works of another Convention that drafted another EU Treaty, now officially included in the former, i.e.—as has been said—that part of the Nice Treaty entitled "Charter of Human Rights and Fundamental Freedoms of the European Union." As a Treaty, the Charter is a political document. Yet it has been written "as if" it is a legal text suitable for action in Court. Its aim, therefore, is to provide the European Court of Justice with both wider competence and a formal cover, "as if" the same Court—embodying the Law—is and acts as a truly "impersonal" and "independent" organ.

Unfortunately, however, such a double fictionalism cannot mask the fact that the EU is not ruled by the division-of-power principle and that modern legal theory rejects the idea of judges as mere Law speakers. Hence, simply by virtue of the Charter's drafting, the EU Court has been provided with the most discretionary—supreme—decision-making power over any other European institution and the overall EU governance system.[18]

This result should not be surprising. It is a direct consequence of the inclusion of the fictional implications of the above mentioned constitutional "bifurcation" into a unique body. In fact, the more State sovereignty and supreme constitutional power appear de-personalized, or somehow detached, from the ordinary political playground, the more the legal presumption that only the Law—as a pure value—can provide undisputed democratic legitimization to the constitutional system comes to the fore. Yet, the Law cannot be performed by any other than human "carriers" in actual practice. Hence, sooner or later, the organized body of judges—either constitutional or ordinary—objectively and subjectively transpose the Law's aims thus turning into the real sovereign agents.

---

[18] Vittorio Olgiati (2002, 2003), *op. cit.* n. 10.

As current judicial activism shows, the above evolutionary legal trend has been tacitly accepted and widely enforced by almost all European countries over the past decades. This is particularly apparent at present simply because it increasingly challenges traditional prerogatives formally ascribed to other State organs. The constitutional model envisaged by the EU Constitutional Treaty, therefore, does not constitute an exception. Rather it is one of the most remarkable, refined and advanced examples.

Indeed, the whole story of the European Court of Justice is the story of a highly decisionist judicial activism, as demonstrated by the enforcement of *ex novo* self-referential EU standards even against national Constitutional Court decisions. Accordingly, therefore, it is hardly deniable that the EU Justices are indeed the subjects that, in the final instance, legally hold—and will hold even more in the future—the reins of the overall EU constitutional asset.

This being so the case, the technicalities of the EU Treaty throw an even more disquieting light on the general EU constitutional scenario discussed above, for, in actual practice, they further politicize the EU legal system in a non-democratic way—Courts being, by their very nature, autocratic—and leave open and unresolved the conflict between and within the fractions of the EU power elite—Courts being, by their very nature, based on social conflicts and legal disputes.

The implications of all the above are of extraordinary importance to Eastern countries. In fact, they add up to the fact that there is hardly any chance that the EU, through its Court, will consider the entry of Eastern European countries as a way that could undermine the already achieved *acquis communautaire*: an *aquis*—it is worth noting—that not only does not constitute a legal tradition "common" to these countries, but also does not offer, by its very nature, any chance either to them or to any Western country "to reckon with their past" in a non-conflictual way.

7. TAKING EU FUNDAMENTAL RIGHTS SERIOUSLY

The fact that the architecture of the EU Constitutional Treaty might not fit adequately to Member States that, for more than fifty years, shared neither the alleged Western "common" legal tradition nor the Community's *acquis* is not the only legal variable that deserves attention. The overall normative dimension of the EU policy also was shaped and pursued according to values and interests typical of Western European socio-legal contexts only. Being unlikely that this legacy will be re-framed on equal basis between Western and Eastern EU Member States, a focus on the doctrinal nature of basic legal issues such as EU fundamental rights and liberties cannot be left aside.

7.1. The Idealistic Nature of the EU Constitutional Treaty's Preamble

The Preamble of the Draft Constitutional Treaty solemnly recalls a (subsequently deleted) statement of an ancient Greek historician, Thucydide II, in order to stress the never-ending "civilizational mission" of Europe in the world and its still living attachment to everlasting humanistic values, such as those now formally recognized under the label of the inviolable rights of the subject and the respect for the law. No mention is made, by contrast, of the Manifesto of Ventotene written in the Ventotene prison by one of the leading promoters of the European unionism, Altiero Spinelli. In that Manifesto, the ideal of a United Europe is historically conceived as the only way-out to overcame—verbatim—the "civilizational crisis" of continental European societies: i.e. the rupture of Western *Weltanshauung*, and the turn of one of its constitutive patterns towards extreme forms of authoritarianism and totalitarianism. In other words, the EU Constitutional Treaty not only ignores what was—and still is—the core rationale of the EU project (see *supra* par. 2), but also hides the fact that the Community's founding-fathers aimed at a veritable "civilizational transition" from what might be called modern Western barbarism, i.e. nothing less than a substantial "transition from within."

Besides, no mention is made in the Treaty about other, subsequent continental European "transitions" such as those occurring to Greece, Portugal and Spain on the one hand, and in East Germany, on the other. Even less is mentioned about European countries "transitions" from colonialism, i.e. about the ways in which e.g. Belgium, England and France reacted against the claim for Western-style national independence, civil rights and self-determination made by Asian and African colonized countries.

Last, but not least, the Preamble simply "forgets" that for about forty years the European unionism grew up in a state of limited sovereignty because Western European countries had to comply with the military and financial rule of the *Pax Americana*, and that some legacies of such a foreign rule are still influential, albeit in a different fashion.

In brief, the Preamble not only is idealistically constructed, but avoids any historically determined account of the real issue at stake: "to reckon with the past" on the part of the whole—Western and Eastern, modern and contemporary—European society *vis-à-vis* either itself or the World-system.

Of course one could argue that those who drafted the text opted for legal amnesia in a technical sense. Yet, this does not excuse the lack of any reference to another unavoidable issue, i.e. the problematic evidence of what Giddens called the dark consequences of (western-style) Modernity, i.e. the collapse of major tenets of Enlightenment's and Classic Political Economy's narratives, as epitomized at present by the intelligence failure of a number of high-tech devices and the rise of the so-called *Risikogesellshaf*.

As legal ideals and economic principles of such narratives are the basic reference standards of the Preamble, the lack of any concern about what are now known as the "false promises" of (western-style) Modernity cannot be undervalued here: it signals that, besides the above mentioned political-cultural rupture, the EU constitutional project is ideologically repressing also a plausible and socially adequate representation of what current and prospective EU governance is and will be like.

7.2. The Vanishing Nomic Function of Contemporary Written Constitutions

Misrepresentations contained in the Treaty appear even more apparent if one recalls the Rousseauian-styled functional-fictional constructionist nature of the EU Constitutional Treaty (see *supra* par. 5.1) and consider it in relation the vanishing guarantee of rationality of Western formal knowledge and know-how[19] in the field of law, i.e. in relation to current theory (and practice) of democracy in the final instance.

As is well known that the constitutionalization of fundamental rights and values in self-styled democratic legal systems has been a recurrent *vexata quaestio* among legal scholars. In the late 1920s it was claimed that such constitutionalization would reduce conflicts deriving from the rising wave of social and cultural pluralism, while hiding the weakening of the organic hegemony of traditional power elites. The post-war Italian constitution formalized this option and acted as a model. In the past decades, however, multiculturalism and legal pluralism have undermined altogether the core rationale of all written constitutions—namely its judicial interpretation[20]—as it already had undermined not only legal codification but also the traditional function of official law as a generalized medium of social control.[21]

Quite paradoxically, there is no sign of such evidence in the EU constitutional Treaty. Rather, the universalistic pretence of EU fundamental rights and the claim for the *nomic* potentials of the rule-of-law are stated as a dogma, to assure European "citizens" that, if provided with them, they can forge their "common destiny" democratically. Unfortunately for EU "citizens" the "nature of things" are not as they appear to be. To have some insight, let us consider two, for brevity sake, major items: current notions of human/fundamental rights and democracy.

7.3. Cognitive and Operational Shifts about the Notion of Human Rights

Contrary to common understanding of lay people, the so-called "human" rights lost any universal and/or human character *strictu sensu* as soon as they were formally positivized and codified (for the space–time contingency of positive law makes them

---

19 Immanuel Wallerstein, "Social Science and Contemporary Society: the Vanishing Guarantees of Rationality", *International Sociology*, 11, 1 (1996), pp. 7–25.

20 Francesco Belvisi, "Un fondamento delle costituzioni democratiche contemporanee? Ovvero: una costituzione senza fondamento", in Gustavo Gozzi (a cura di), *Democrazia, Diritti, Costituzione. I fondamenti costituzionali delle democrazie contemporanee* (Bologna: Il Mulino 1997), pp. 231–267.

21 Vittorio Olgiati, "The Conceptual Shift of a Key-Concept. Norm Production in Contemporary Sociology of Law in Europe", *Journal of Legal Pluralism and Unofficial Law*, Special Issue, 41 (1988), pp. 89–109, and, Vittorio Olgiati, "Vers une refonte des communautes epistemiques en Europe", in Lorena Parini (dir.), *State et Mondialisation. Strategies et Roles* (Paris: L'Harmattan 2001), pp. 191–223.

(1) changeable and debatable at whim or by force, (2) subjected to a pluralistic legal interpretation, and (3) subdued to occasional power-game social constraints). At the time of the Weimar Constitution, the notion of "fundamental" rights was thus suggested not only to cover such a semantic and operational disempowerment, but also to assess a totally different institutional system. Actually, since then, the binary-model of human/fundamental rights no longer expresses the individual freedoms of personhood, but rather general political-institutional ordering principles of the given system that enforces them.[22] Accordingly, therefore, what for example the Nice Treaty still labels as human rights cannot be conceived as any other than protection rules of the EU institutional agents (EU Member States in particular), or as legal provisions sustaining the EU vested constituencies in the first instance, rather than as a direct guarantee of/for individual subjects.

A similar cognitive and operational shift has occurred to the notion of "democracy". If one reads any official EU legal document, the term democracy merely means official parliamentary acts and procedures performed by elected political representatives only. Also in this case, we owe, to the fear of the power elite for the risks inherent to rising pluralism, the legal positivization and codification of the concept. In turn, the traditional notion of "rule-of law" as the quintessence of a democratic system—forged in the second half of XIX Century by liberal ideologues to contrast democratic ideals[23]—was not abandoned: it simply lost is formal-abstract universal character, became an indicator of, or synonymous to, the so-called Administrative State and, lastly, took on the meaning of official law as a mere binding procedure. So, when one reads "rule-of-law" in any EU legal document, one has to aware that the term lacks any general substantive content.

7.4. Law's Empire as a Procedure

The theory and practice of positive law as a mere procedure constitutes a remarkable cognitive and operational shift in contemporary Western legal systems.

The core problem with this shift is that, notwithstanding the most refined systematizing efforts made in the last fifty years, it does not fit at all with either Classical Political Economy or Enlightenment constitutional tenets. These tenets are centered not on the added value provided by a type of decision-making implying relational/negotiable role-plays carried out within the framework of the self-referential logic of pre-defined proceedings and programs, but—as anybody knows—on individual actors' rational choices, i.e. a type of decision-making that excludes *a priori* that, e.g. common (political) values could match perfectly with personal (civil) in-

---

22 Gustavo Gozzi, *Democrazia e diritti. Germania: dallo stato di diritto alla democrazia costituzionale* (Roma: Laterza 1999).

23 Maurizio Fioravanti and Stefano Mannoni, "Il "modello costituzionale" europeo: tradizioni e prospettive", in Gabriella Bonacchi (a cura di), *Una Costituzione senza Stato* (Bologna: Il Mulino 2001), pp. 23–70.

terests. Given this apparent contradiction, therefore, the enforcement of the law as a mere procedural system has been enhanced for decades informally, just to by-pass the limits of the traditional model without questioning its updated rationale. So much so that, in the meanwhile, the spread of two special structures, organically related to the new arrangement, completely change the constitutional scenario of any national and international western-style legal order: (a) the so-called "collegial formations," i.e. a sort of professionalized guilds, acting as semi-autonomous legal agents and embodying the procedural know-how required by the given legal field, and (b) sets of "qualitative procedural requisites", i.e. a sort of uniform body of legal standards, so as to establish a procedural threshold of interpretation of different variables.[24]

Needless to say, typical prototypes and the most notorious examples of these two structures today are just the EU Commissions, on the one hand, and the list of (so far 14) "fundamental" rights/liberties set up by the EU Court of Justice's praetorial jurisprudence,[25] on the other. As these structures are officially acknowledged as a constitutive part of the EU governance, it follows that the legal system already in force in the EU totally differs from the one that the liberal ideology contained in the Preamble suggests.

This conclusion would not be shocking if only the above issues were a mere matter of ideology. But it is not the case. Once treated procedurally—as Luhmann would put it—citizenship rights lose any political meaning because de-politicization is the structural–functional prerequisite of any legal procedure. They thus indicate mere social-cultural variables, i.e. social difference, not a proper political identity! Furthermore, once performed procedurally, citizens' participation to electoral competition is not an exercise of a fundamental right of democracy but a token of the degree of self-legitimation of the given political system. Once conceived procedurally, the division-of-powers principle—upon which the democratic value of the rule-of-law traditionally stands—does not guarantee any right or claim for it merely signals the cyclical turn-over of those in charge of given power structures. Once defined procedurally, even the expressions of sovereignty do not signal the full right of a supreme power, but a certain type of functionally differentiated status-role.[26]

In other words, in as far as the procedural logic of the so-called "societal constitutionalism"[27] has de-constructed traditional constitutional theory and practice, centered on the State-society divide, the substantive *ratio juris* of positive-codified

---

24 David Sciulli, "Towards Societal Constitutionalism: Principles from Communicative Action and Procedural Legality", *British Journal of Sociology*, 39 (1988), pp. 377–407.

25 Petri Helander, "Supremacy and Scope of Community Law—Room for Principles?", *Turku Law Journal*, 3, 1 (2001), pp. 43–58.

26 Niklas Luhmann, *Legitimation durch Verfahern* (Frankfurt-am-Main: Suhrkamp Verlag 1983).

27 David Sciulli (1988), *op. cit.* n. 24.

law has eroded and the legal representation of social dynamics have turned into a veritable artifice. Surely this evidence was not the kind of legal experience that many citizens in Eastern European countries expected when complying with the EU entry conditions.

8. EX ORIENTE LUMEN?

Upon initial inspection, the list of problematic socio-legal issues that the EU Constitutional Treaty embodies is so large that it has been argued that the Treaty could only work—as Sigfrid Kracauer would put it—as a mere *ornament der masse*. Yet, this conclusion is both superficial and misleading. A sketchy look at the power games currently going on at social level provide us with a rather different view-point and make apparent a much more intriguing framework.

In the course of the discussion, the hybrid nature of the EU Constitution Treaty has been outlined as it mixes in a paradoxically synchronic way XIX Century-old individualistic legal principles and Late-Modern processual/transpersonal socio-legal interactions. Within, but also beyond, this structure, however, another "bifurcation" exists—also typical of XX century European constitutionalism—and plays an extremely relevant role: that between "substantive" and "formal" constitutions (the former being the expression of the vital force of politically active social groups able to establish a relatively stable and visible normative order in a given space–time, and the latter being the expression of the formal institutionalization of such a legal construction in proper technical legal terms.)[28]

As it is known, this sort of "bifurcation", running internally within any socio-normative realm, becomes scientifically apparent in the Thirties, as soon as the decline of the bourgeois' legal project matched with the rise of new social, political and cultural "capitals". Since then, it signals the existence of a cleavage between official and unofficial constitutional variables, or, if one prefers, a dialectical relationship between the manifest and latent socio-legal positions that social forces take on in the course of the ups and downs of their conflictive interactions, especially in relation to what is occurring at the institutional level. Moreover, it also signals the fact that collisions and collusions between normative facts and legal rules—between living laws and official laws—are as much irrepressible as the conflictive compositions of values and interests involved. Hence, their overall dynamics are particularly relevant for the social reproduction of social groups and the way in which their own particular interests and values fit or not into the established forms of a given constitutional system.

Needless to say, also in this respect, the process of EU constitutionalization does not make an exception. So much so that it is impossible to fully understand the above mentioned paradoxical synchronic wave without considering the

[28] Costantino Mortati, *La costituzione in senso materiale* (Milano: Giuffré 1940).

contradictory scenarios in which the EU ruling elites seem to place themselves vis-à-vis prospective EU constitutional patterns.

As the ideal of European societies' integration is not in the EU agenda, and due to the fact that current EU policy emphasizing diversity cannot but produce such a type of hybrid and spurious constitutional syncretism mentioned *supra*, it follows that the EU power elites are also moving towards a Janus-headed socio-political system: a model that in theoretical terms revitalizes—as has been said—the Rousseauian model, but that in technical legal terms resembles a veritable (albeit democratically self-styled) "Double-State", i.e. a political-institutional form of governance in which the superimposition of a special normative layer over pre-existing ones rules them in a relatively discretionary way.[29] Two diverging—but nevertheless complementary also—hypotheses, therefore, could be envisaged.

8.1. Towards a "Felix Austria" EU Model?

The original aim of European unionism was to end the devastations of the wars of the XX Century by means of a defensive modernization policy against any potential "Enemy". Yet, the fall of the Berlin Wall and the peaceful *acquis* of Eastern countries makes the EU single space larger than that conquered and subdued by—or anyhow politically prone to—Napoleon's or Hitler's army. Hence, one might wonder: what about the interior/exterior "enemy" now? Is that original aim still valuable?

In a recent study devoted to prospective world-system geo-political scenarios, an American scholar argued that the EU turned into a selfish "fortress". More precisely, the EU defends its domestic welfare rather than defending common Western strategic interests and values at global level, the burden of which is nicely delegated to the USA. Given this new sort of "splendid insulation", the EU gains twice: it avoids certain responsibilities in case of "dirty work", and enjoys the benefits of a "good" internal and international standing.[30] Unfortunately it is impossible to deal with this international issue here. For brevity sake, let us simply stress its extraordinary relevance for prospective interior *vs.* exterior EU constitutional governance trends.

However, the argument offers us the chance to deal with the other side of the coin, i.e. to discuss constitutional "visions" about future Europe from the inside. For the purpose of this study, this means to focus in a prospectivist way on the way in which the EU constitutional process is constructing a proper intra-European geo-political hegemony, or—if one prefers—is assessing the symbolic (and material) power asset of the EU power elite in both social and legal terms. In short: what sort of "fortress" are we talking about?

---

29 Ernst Fraenkel, *Il doppio-stato. Contributo alla teoria della dittatura*, (Torino: Einaudi 1983).

30 Robert Kagan, *Of Paradise and Power* (New York: Knopf 2002).

With regard to this topic, it is quite apparent that the "visions" of the future Europe were already formulated in the past.[31] Even though ideologically raised, the claim about the "common destiny", the "civilizing mission", the "common cultural tradition" of Europe made in the Preamble of the EU Constitutional Treaty, recalls a governance model that Montesquieu, following Machiavelli, envisaged, i.e. that of the search for an equilibrium between the different European constituencies. In turn the regulatory standards for a more centralized, reinforced EU governance system recalls not only the problem raised by either Voltaire or Burke, i.e. that due to the diversity of European countries any equilibrium is unstable and conflicts inevitably occur, but also the solutions provided respectively by Leibniz and Rousseau, i.e. that either a balanced dualism between top–down and bottom-up constituencies, or directorial guarantees stemming from a superior confederate asset is needed.

If so, how can one miss that the French-German cooperation within the EU revitalizes the myth/reality of the leading "civilizing mission", "common destiny" and "common tradition" of Mitteleurope: i.e. the myth/reality of a never-ending historical trend spanning from the Holy Roman Empire—as a legacy of ancient Rome—up to the "Universal" Habsburg Empire? And how can one exclude that the claim for a formal "reinforced" cooperation could be a stepping-stone for a renewed Holy Alliance to impede that not only a sort of Auschwitz, but also a sort of Termidore could occur again, and eventually on a European scale?

In any case, whatever way in which one looks at the matter, there is no doubt that the Habsburg *Austria Felix* governance model, especially when shaped as a "Double Monarchy" legal system, seems to offer an appealing historical reference to promote a long-lasting EU rule. On the one hand, it could reinforce the structure and the image of the new (democratic-style) EU "Double-State" system, as somewhat created by the EU Constitutional Treaty, without repressing the interior diversity of the each EU country. On the other hand—as Bagehot would put it—it could raise a sentiment of reverence for the venerable symbolism evoked by a traditional form of power and authority. In other words—and, of course, *mutatis mutandis*—one could even venture as far to say that a sort of up-to-date Mitteleuropean governmentality model might not have been so far, or be now, unrealistically imagined as a possible way out of the kind of challenges—i.e. multicultural fragmentation and political instability—that the EU power elite inevitably has to face, and will have to face even more in the near future.

As a number of indicators suggests—from the letter of Otto von Habsburg, published by an Austrian newspaper in 1987, to praise the enforcement of the Maastricht Treaty, up to the election of Simeon of Saxony–Coburg–Gotha at the Bulgarian parliament—there is no apparent contradiction between the EU policy and a prospective monarchic constitutional revival in Europe. Actually, if one

31 Bo Petersson and Anders Hellstrom, "The Return of the Kings. Temporality in the Construction of the EU Identity", *European Societies*, 5, 3 (2003), pp. 235–252.

excludes the struggle for the organizational dominance[32] that Nation-States and new powerful corporate socio-legal orders are carrying out at patrimonial and symbolic level at present—a matter that unfortunately cannot be dealt with in detail here—one hardly notices any contrast within European aristocracy—whether by old-blood or by new-money—as regards the advantages offered by the EU constitutional process to strengthen typically selective and exclusive clan ties.

8.2. Towards a "Legal Bukowine" EU Model?

Having said the above, however, it would be naïve to undervalue the limits that are inherent of the Mitteleuropean model, and, more particularly, socio-political risks stemming from any form of clan ties. It is well known that the historical weakness of both the Holy Roman and the Habsburg empires' model is that the dynamic of interior cultural, political and legal diversity, matched with the recurrent instability and mobility—by enlargements and contractions—of their formal-official borders. In this respect one can hardly speak of a "common" destiny, tradition, or civilizing mission even within the Mitteleurope. The good, old, highly refined, structures of the so-called *Rechtspublizistik*, and its related "Empire Patriotism" were not able to counteract the recurrent claim for what Ratzel called *Lebensraum*, either in the form of the enforcement of the *cuius lex, ejus rex* or *cuius regio, ejus religio* rules, or in the form of the struggle for a *Sonderweg* to national irredentism, independence and self-determination. It is, therefore, not by chance that we owe to Gumplowicz one of the most radical studies of the human history as a never-ending form of "tribal war", and to Ehrlich the first conscious approach to legal pluralism as a general theory of law. The reference model for Gumplowicz's theory was his personal experience of the historical turn of order and disorder stemming from occasional, temporary and arbitrary territorial partitions and aggregations in the Baltic, Northern Slavonic and Southern Slavonic regions, areas in which the oppressed cyclically turned into oppressors and vice versa. The reference model for Ehrlich's theory was his personal experience of the force of multicultural living conditions *vis-à-vis* formal-official law in the Bucowine region, the most central region within the central geo-political realm of the whole European continent.

As one can see, there are serious historical records in Europe that cannot be hidden or ignored. Even less so when a constitutional process of continental dimensions such as that that has been described so far is currently in progress.

9. CONCLUSION

As it has been stressed, the historical coincidence of the process of EU constitutionalization and the EU Eastern enlargement has exacerbated a variety of theoretical

---

32 Mancur Olson, *The Logic of Collective Action* (Cambridge, MA: Harvard University Press 1966).

and practical "dilemmas" concerned with the a-systematic functioning and the "democratic deficit" of the overall EU *Struckturbildung*. Such a coincidence also acted as a political catalyst to reinvigorate the still-living ideology of Europe as an expansionist, self-fulfilling "civilization" model *vis-à-vis* both neighboring countries and the world-system. In this respect, a last—but by no means least—issue cannot be left aside at the conclusion of this study: no mention at all can be found in the Treaty of a boundary or a dead-line about the EU territorial incrementalism, especially beyond commonly acknowledged, traditional *limes* of what is meant by "Europe". As there is any notion in the EU Constitutional Treaty of Europe as a *Finis Terrae* of the Eurasian continental platform, the option for a new sort of new European imperial policy at transcontinental level cannot, therefore, be reasonably excluded.

Significantly, in no way is this lacuna a sign of a lack of attention or an occasional mistake. The fact is that there is a growing internal cleavage—but also a common networking role-play—within the EU power elite between those fractions that are still culturally and politically attached to the State-nation territorially constituted interests and values, and those fractions that, by contrast, are more and more culturally and politically attached to transnational corporate socio-legal orders pursuing, at economic and institutional level, interests and values *sans Patrie*. Unfortunately—as has been previously said—the struggle for the organizational dominance that is currently going on between nation-State oriented and trans-national corporation oriented groups[33] is a theme that cannot be dealt with here. But it is clear that, being open and unresolved the issue of the *limina* of the EU single space, this is a major problem that all EU "citizens" will have to face in the future.

---

33 Vittorio Olgiati (2001), *op. cit.* n. 21.

3. A Problem of their Own, Solutions of their Own: CEE Jurisdictions and the Problems of Lustration and Retroactivity

David Robertson

1. Introduction

The idea of the rule of law is very rich and deep, allowing much legitimate variation in its implication. When a difference between local constitutional interpretations takes one system out of the category of "a state governed by the rule of law" but leaves another within it is essentially a judgment call. I am concerned with the pragmatic question of what precise rules or constitutional court decisions are necessarily implied by the avowed preference "*non sub homine, sed lege e dei.*" No analysis of the problem I address could be intellectually honest were it to insist on a simple and uniform definition being applied everywhere in the CEE area. In the end if will be for the reader to decide whether, for example, the differences between the Czech and the Hungarian approach to the rule of law falls within the necessary area of what the ECHR has called a "margin of appreciation", or whether we must rule one or other state to have failed the test. What is very important indeed is how the Constitutional Courts have gone about assessing the legitimacy of the policies covered here. What the rest of Europe will gain, or suffer from, is very much a matter of high doctrine. Such doctrine constitutes further building blocks in the constructive writing of democratic political theory by courts as they move towards an international constitutional common law.[1] What the Hungarian, Czech, Polish, Slovenian, Lithuanian and Estonian High Courts have thought when asked about the constitutional validity of some methods of dealing with the problems of the past could be of enormous value in this long term endeavour. At the very least their difficulties draw our attention to how little worked out are many of our legal assumptions and icons in this area.

---

1 I have discussed the idea that the CEE courts are working towards a common constitutional law in David Robertson, *Democratic Transitions and a Common Constitutional Law for Europe.* (Oxford: Europaeum 2001). It is clear that at least some of the leading CEE jurists themselves have an idea very close to this, and an ambition to share in developing such an international approach. See, especially, László Sólyom, "Opening Address, 10th Conference of European Constitutional Courts", in *Bulletin on Constitutional Case Law* (Budapest: Council of Europe 1996).

Wojciech Sadurski et al. (ed.), Spreading Democracy and the Rule of Law?, 73–96.

2. THE NATURE OF THE CASE LAW

The way in which concepts like "the rule of law", "a state under the rule of law" and so on are worked out and used in CEE court decisions needs to be understood in terms of the very nature and context of the case law, which is very different from that of established Western courts. To start with the material I deal with comes from the very early years of the development of curial authority in CEE jurisdictions. The consequence of this is that these courts did not assess the constitutionality of, for example, lustration statutes against a background either of well-established constitutional rights doctrine, or even of well-established structural constitutional doctrine. Rather the lustration cases were, *inter alia,* precisely part of the material used by the courts to develop their doctrines on vires and rights. It was not, in other words, quite a matter of asking whether s.5 of Act No 198/1993 of the Czech Parliament, (on retrospective punishment) breaches guarantees of legal certainty which are of vital constitutional importance, as it might be in a longer established court. It is much more a matter of using reflection on s.5 to work out what legal certainty means and how important such legal certainty is to a democratic constitution and the rule of law. The difference is that to a large extent a western court analyzes a troubling statute against a relatively well-established definition of a constitutional right to see if it passes scrutiny. There is, as it were, only one puzzle. Here there is a double puzzle—the statute needs to be analyzed, but the right has to be as well—they are interdefined. There is thus a self-reflexivity in the process of constitutional jurisprudence over this period and in these countries which is highly unusual and crucial. These (and of course many other types of decisions) are what have made the constitutional doctrines the rest of Europe will have to cope with and which it may benefit from. From our point of view the great advantage is that there is far more, more thoughtful, and less formulaic discussion of absolutely core questions than one finds anywhere except in similar transition states.[2] This cannot be stressed enough. This idea of reflection on complex problems is crucial, though its relative frequency between countries is also one of the keys to the differences in constitutional understanding one finds on the rule of law. Decisions of the Czech

---

2 Transitions need not be dramatic to be useful to us in this way—not only does the South African Court give us similar original reflection, but so does the Canadian Court on receiving its Charter. On the latter see Claire L'Heureux-Dubé, "Realising equality in the twentieth century: The role of the Supreme Court of Canada in comparative perspective", *International Journal of Constitutional Law* Vol. 1 No. 1, January 2003; for a South African case exhibiting the degree of open and flexible thought typical in some CEE cases, consider *Republic of South Africa vs. Grootboom,* 2001 (1) SsA. 46. The rival constitutional theories behind the South African Bill of Rights are well depicted in Martin Chanock, "A Post-Calvinist Catechism or Post-Communist Manifesto? Intersecting Narratives in the South African Bill of Rights Debate" in Philip Alston (ed.), *Promoting Human Rights Through Bills of Rights: Comparative Perspectives* (Oxford: OUP 1999).

court are perhaps the best examples: frequently there is a depth of reflection on democracy and on the relationship between law and core socio-political values that one could never find in an established western court—indeed which no western court *has ever* undertaken. One good example in the case on the constitutionality of the statute *Regarding The Lawlessness of the Communist Regime and Resistance to it*[3] which I discuss later.[4] A case less commonly analyzed is the Court's (retrospective) validation of the 1945 Benes decree, from October 1945, "On the Confiscation of Enemy Property and the Funds of National Renewal."[5] The case arose because of a challenge to the legality of the confiscation of property belonging to German citizens and Czech sympathizers the end of the Second World War. It could have been handled by a short and technical demonstration of the constitutional status of the interim government in 1945, and indeed the court did give such an answer. But far more of the judgment is dedicated to answering the plaintiffs claim, hopeless in terms of positive law, that the Benes decrees "violated the legal canons of civilized European societies and that, therefore, they must be considered not as acts of law but of force." In answering this, the court made a series of assertions which characterize the way it looks at the past, and at the foundations of a democratic legal order. In particular, the sense of the primacy of the political base for the legitimacy even of procedural law comes across clearly.

The constitutional requirement laid down in the 1920 Constitutional Charter that the Czechoslovak state have a democratic character, is rather a concept of a political science character (and which is juristically definable only with difficulty) which, however, does not mean that it is a meta-legal concept, hence not legally binding. On the contrary, the constitutional principle mandating the democratic legitimacy of the governmental system was a basic characteristic feature of the constitutional system which as a result meant that, in the 1920 Constitutional Charter of the Czechoslovak Republic, this principle *was ranked above and prior to requirements of formal, legal legitimacy.*[6]

It is, of course, possible to make the argument that any court which does indeed think that any principle can rank above "formal, legal legitimacy" does not understand the rule of law, and it is arguable the Hungarian Court, for one, would take that position. I believe, with the Czech court, that the rule of law, or the idea of a "state under law", especially in a transition period, actually requires this politically informed depth of analysis. Much is made in this ruling of the nature of human

---

3 Act No 198/1993 Sb.

4 This has been very ably analyzed elsewhere by another contributor to this book, Jiri Priban, to whom I owe a great debt in my understanding of this entire topic, and whose work I admire without, necessarily, actually agreeing with it. See Jiri Priban, "Moral and Political Legislation in Constitutional Justice: A Case Study of the Czech Constitutional Court," *The Journal of East European Law*, 8:1 (2001), pp. 15–34.

5 Pl. US. 14/94—Benes Decree No. 108.

6 *Ibid.*

political responsibility, in a way which is vital for the other decisions where the rule of law has to be interpreted in relation to dealing with the past.

This decree has a more general scope and can be considered as one of the documents reflecting the age-old conflict between democracy and totalitarianism. The dividing line was drawn according to which side of the conflict a person chose to support.[7]

Similarly the very nature of human political society can be seen to be based on a human political and moral obligation:

> It is mankind's fate that human beings are placed into power relations, and this situation gives rise to their responsibility to champion the forces which will make human rights a reality. The grounds for social, political, moral, and in some cases even legal, responsibility is thus precisely the person's neglect to make a contribution in the structuring of power relations, his failure, during the struggle for power, to act in the service of right.[8]

A court which thinks in this way is unlikely to produce the sort of formalistic application of the idea of the rule of law which might please some—it is equally a court which cannot easily be accused of indifference to the deepest moral and political questions of legal legitimacy.

It must be said as a general comment that it would be odd if the jurisprudence of the CEE courts was deficient in respect for the rule of law, because of a special feature of their work. These courts all show very considerable commitment to a comparative methodology. It is important to each of them that the solutions used elsewhere to the special problems of transition states are taken into account. But equally constitutional law from a wide range of countries is cited in aid of developing the local rule—not only other CEE states and Germany, though the latter looms very large, but other western countries, for example France, and when possible common law constitutional jurisprudence from North America.[9] The exact way in which they use external jurisprudence is more controversial. Some commentators seem to think there was more of an automaticity about the process than do the leading jurists themselves. On the one hand, for example, we have the powerful and detailed analysis of the Hungarian court's debt to Germany given by Catherine Dupré which only partially coincides with the account the court's chief legal

---

7 *Ibid.*

8 *Ibid.*

9 The mere fact that Germany allowed a potentially retroactive prosecution in its "Border Guards" case might lead one to wonder why the CEE countries were peculiarly thought to lack respect for the rule of law. For a good discussion of this in the context of transition law, see Manfred J. Gabriel, "Coming to Terms with the East German Border Guards Cases", *Columbia Journal of Transnational Law*, 38 (1999), pp. 375–417. A more theoretical treatment is Peter E. Quint, "The Border Guard Trials and the East German Past-Seven Arguments", *American Journal of Comparative Law* 48 (2000), pp. 541–571.

architect, Lászlo Sólyom himself gives. Sólyom is more prone to stress the differences in actual results, Dupré the reliance on German reasoning.[10] Sólyom is however also our best source for how influential foreign law in general and German law in particular has been for other CEE national constitutional courts.[11] If constitutional law, so heavily influenced by Western Europe, is deficient in respect for the rule of law, something very strange must have happened in the process of legal borrowing. From their beginnings all of these courts show every sign of working towards something that can be seen as a comparatively constructed common understanding of democratic constitutionalism.

A final important characteristic may only be noteworthy to those used to looking through common law eyes, and with an Anglo-American perspective on constitutional rights. This is the extent to which at least some of the courts take are to spin a coherent web of rights jurisprudence, rather than treating each case and each issue as largely free standing. There is a surprising degree of reference to a court's own decisions wherever analogies can be made even though at such an early stage in curial history there are seldom other cases so directly relevant that they must be brought to bear. Even where precedent like references are not made, we need to be clear that much of what shapes an interpretation of what "the rule of law" requires in one case is the use a court hopes or needs to put the concept to in some likely future application to a different question. One way to interpret the Hungarian Courts very narrow and positivistic interpretation of "legal certainty" on the retrospective punishment issue is-to note the very far from narrow and positivistic use they made of the concept in striking down social security reductions, as discussed later. In the same way the entire Czech "methodology of constitutional interpretation" in the Benes degree case is clearly connected to the approach in the earlier lustration case before the Czechoslovakian court and the later decision on retroactivity of the Czech court. Again the Hungarian court, in the eyes of its interpreters,[12] was very conscious of shaping tools of general utility in its constitutional interpretations.

I proceed by examining three sets of cases, covering different aspects of the problems of dealing with the past. Especially in the first section I pay close attention to the arguments made by the justices—these are the building blocks, both for the CEE and for the rest of Europe, of twenty-first century constitutional law, rather than the decisions themselves.

---

10 Catherine Dupré, *Importing the Law in Post-Communist Transitions: The Hungarian Constitutional Court and the Right to Human Dignity* (Oxford: Hart Publishing 2003). Contrast the account given by Lászlo Sólyom himself, in "The Role of Constitutional Courts in the Transition to Democracy", *International Sociology*, 18:1 (2003), pp. 133–161.

11 See also, *Bulletin on Constitutional Case Law* 1996, *op. cit.* n. 1.

12 This is a major theme in Dupré, *op. cit.* n. 10.

3. RETROACTIVITY, LEGAL CERTAINTY AND SUBSTANTIVE JUSTICE

I have used, and largely continue to use, the word lustration in a rather broad sense, mainly to avoid the cumbersome but more appropriate "problems arising from dealing with the past." What is not often fully appreciated is that these cases, whether they be technically lustration, or retroactive punishment or property compensation or whatever, are about the past in two rather different ways. They are, as is obvious, about the constitutionality of attempts to deal with injustices past and present arising from the previous ruling political ideology and system. But they involve questions of the *legal* impact of the past, and indeed generally of the passing of time in a more abstract sense.[13] This is because courts have chosen, or been unable to avoid, dealing with these issues partly in terms of the doctrine of legal certainty. It is a question of some interest whether this was an avoidable route. Certainly the insistence of all the courts, but especially the Hungarians, that legal certainty is at the very core of the idea of "a state governed by law" involves a stance which in many eyes marks their doctrine out as a very "legalistic" approach. To many, "legal certainty" is the lawyer's value par excellence, and too often used by conservative judges to restrict innovations by their brethren. It is also the hallmark of a constitutional jurisprudence favoring procedural over substantive values, favoring a traditional continental European formalism. Yet to the extent that a major problem of the past regimes in central and Eastern Europe was not the imposition of cruel law but the failure to obey existing law, a common theme in the judicial arguments in these cases, it may not be possible to take a more relaxed attitude to legal certainty. Compounding this problem is the difficulty arising from the story the new regime tells about its birth. New CEE regimes vary a good deal about how much they wish to see their origins in a revolution. It is no accident that the court which most stresses legal certainty as the corner stone of a democratic constitution is the one which has most tried most ardently to tell a story about the essentially unrevolutionary and *legal* nature of the transition—Hungary. Lászlo Sólyom makes a strong defense of the Hungarian decision about retroactive punishment, which rested on making "legal certainty" a prime constitutional virtue under the aegis of rule of law. His claim is that Hungary before the revolution had been a very mild regime in which much freedom was allowed to the citizens. To mark the difference under the new regime, where "permissions" were replaced by "rights", required a firm commitment to procedural values in order to establish that the constitution now really was the sole source of legal authority.[14] If this was really the motivation the presumed contrast with the Czech Republic must be that Czechs, because they had had a rougher experience of the last days of communism could be trusted to value their new constitution highly enough to allow it to

---

13 The best analyses I know of the entire nature of the problem of the past is Jiri Priban, *Dissidents of Law*, (Aldershot: Ashgate-Dartmouth 2002), especially Chap. 4.

14 Sólyom 2003, *op. cit.* n. 10.

be interpreted in a more substantively just manner. Oddly one country with good institutional grounds for such an account, the only one whose constitutional court pre-dates transition, Poland, is much less likely to tell itself that story and to cite legal certainty as core.

The issue above all in which legal certainty has mattered most is that of retroactive punishment. One of the problems of comparative constitutional law is finding cases from two or more jurisdictions sufficiently similar to make comparison effective. We are thus very lucky that this issue has arisen in so similar a way in two countries, the Czech Republic and Hungary to be, in old lawyer language, "on all fours" with each other. We are even luckier that the two constitutional courts gave completely opposed decisions, and luckiest of all that they discussed almost exactly the same issues in coming to these radically opposed understandings of how to deal with the past under democratic constitutions. The cases both involved an attempt by the respective legislatures to make open to prosecution people who had committed crimes under the communist regime but had not been prosecuted precisely because their criminal behavior was carried out on behalf of the regime. Many such offenders were, by the early nineties, immune from prosecution because the statute of limitation written into the law at the time of the commission of their crimes, had run its course. In both cases, the statutes attempted to treat such offenders as though the clock had stopped for the whole or part of the period of the previous regime, thus giving the new regime time to deal with the cases. But also in both countries it was decided not to make all alleged criminals from that period who had not been tried, face renewed legal vulnerability. Instead only those whose prosecutions had not taken place for "political reasons" were to be vulnerable to a re-started clock.

The Hungarian President declined to promulgate the act *On the Prosecution of Serious Criminal Offences not previously prosecuted for Political Reasons*[15] and addressed a series of questions to the Constitutional court. Essentially these alleged that a recommencement of the statute of limitations "conflicted with the rule of law, an essential component of which was legal certainty", and secondly, that it was based on "overly general provisions and vague concepts", which also offended against legal certainty, and finally that distinguishing "between perpetrators of the same offence on the basis of the State's reason for prosecuting such offences" was in violation of a constitutional prohibition on arbitrariness and of the equal protection clause of Article 70/A(1) of the constitution.[16]

The Hungarian court did find the act unconstitutional on all of these grounds; in doing it developed further a doctrine it had enunciated since its beginning, that the change of system in Hungary in 1989 had been fully legal by the predecessor

15 Act (IV/1991).

16 László Sólyom and Georg Brunner, *Constitutional Judiciary in a New Democracy: The Hungarian Constitutional Court* (Ann Arbor: University of Michigan Press 2000), pp. 214–216.

system's own law, and that this very fact imposes an even stronger obligation to obey the new constitution than might otherwise have been the case.[17]

The change of system has been carried out on the basis of legality. The principle of legality imposes on the state under the rule of law the requirement that legal regulations regarding the legal system itself should be abided by unconditionally. The politically revolutionary changes adopted by the Constitution and all the new fundamental laws were enacted, in full compliance with the old legal system's procedural laws on legislation, thereby gaining their binding force. The old law retained its validity. With respect to its validity there is no distinction between "pre-Constitution" and "post-constitution" law.[18]

This sense of legal continuity is somehow or other found compatible with a clear sense of how the new system differ from the past—"The Republic of Hungary is an independent democratic state under the rule of law"—is taken to have "conferred on the State its law and the political system a new quality, fundamentally different from that of the previous regime." But this difference is seen as potentially fragile, requiring great purity of legal purpose to preserve it:

> That Hungary is a state under the rule of law is both a statement of fact and a statement of policy. A state under the rule of law becomes a reality when the Constitution is truly and unconditionally given effect. For the legal system the change of system means, and the change of the legal system is possible only in that sense, that the whole body of law must be brought into harmony—and new legislation kept in harmony—with the new Constitution. Not only must the legal provisions and the operation of state organs comply strictly with the constitution but the constitution's values and its conceptual culture must permeate the whole of society. This is the rule of law, and this is how the Constitution becomes a reality. The realization of the rule of law is a continuous process.[19]

This is, in effect, a highly legal equivalent to the oft heard cry from those inside CEE countries who are opposed to lustration that "We are not like them!" The need to be perfectly consistent in following the rule of law arises simultaneously from the fact that the old system was not law abiding, and that the new system has its origin in abiding by the old procedural laws. It does not follow from any of this, of course, that legal certainty is quite so crucial an element of the rule of law, but this second move is stated more than justified. Having defined legal certainty as requiring, *inter alia*, the protection of vested rights, and non-interference with legal relations already executed, the primacy of legal certainty is made almost tautologous—and a very powerful tautology at that:

---

17 Though Priban makes the point that the continuity of the pre and post transition Hungarian system is largely a legal fiction, *op. cit.* n. 4.

18 Sólyom, *op. cit.* n. 16, p. 200.

19 *Ibid*, p. 219

> ... individual legal relations and legal facts become independent of the statutory sources from which they emerge and do not automatically share their fate. Were this otherwise, a change in the law would necessitate in every instance a review of the whole body of legal relations. Thus, from the principle of legal certainty, it follows that already executed or concluded legal relations cannot be altered constitutionally by enactment of a law or by invalidation of a law by either the legislature or the Constitutional Court.[20]

Whether the Court really believes the last sentence, there is no doubt left about the role of legal certainty in constitutional definitions of the rule of law. Citing an earlier case,[21] the court insists "the consequences of the unconstitutionality of a law must be evaluated primarily with reference to their impact on legal certainty."[22]

I cannot stop at this point if I am fully to draw out the nature of this decision, because the Court was fully aware of the pragmatic arguments from the epical nature of the pre-transition crimes, and develops here an almost chillingly formalistic view of the constitution which occurs elsewhere as well, especially in the economic compensation cases. Shortly after these statements, they say quite bluntly that "the unjust result of legal relations does not constitute an argument against the principle of legal certainty"; this develops into "the requirement of the rule of law as to substantive justice may be attained within the institutions and guarantees ensuring legal certainty. The Constitution does not and cannot confer right for substantive justice", and finally:

> The basic guarantees of the rule of law cannot be set aside by reference to historical situations and to justice as a requirement of the state under the rule of law. A state under the rule of law cannot be created by undermining the rule of law. Legal certainty based on formal and objective principles is more important than necessarily partial and subjective justice.[23]

The arguments go on like this—further quotation though hard to resist would add very little to the point. Throughout, an intensely fierce commitment to procedural principle is shown, often in language making the demands of this principle greater than the justices themselves can really have believed. We are told that legal guarantees can *never* be denied by a state under the rule of law, that criminal law

---

20 *Ibid*, p. 220.

21 The earlier case was Decision of 10/1992.

22 This case occurred after the first two "compensation" cases [Sólyom, *op. cit.* n. 16, pp. 108, 151] in which past legal relationships had been protected and before the Social Security case [Sólyom, *op. cit.* n. 16, p. 322] where legal certainty was used to strike down benefit reductions. As such one can see the way in which a concept can take on an unavoidable constitutional importance in some contexts, beyond the point, perhaps, the court might wish because of its importance as a tool in other contexts.

23 Sólyom, *op. cit.* n. 16, p. 221.

constitutional provisions cannot even be restricted or suspended in "a state of national crisis, a state of emergency or a state of danger." There is real fear of the risk of law being misused permeating the judgment—while admitting that the criminal law is not merely an instrument but "protects and embodies values", it turns out that the values it protects are "the principles and guarantees of constitutional criminal law." More importantly, "though criminal law protects values, as a guarantee of freedom it cannot become an instrument for moral purges in the process of protecting values." Quite simply, under the law in place at the time, ruthless criminals killing people to serve the political masters of the state were entitled to become free of risk of prosecution a set number of years after their crime, and the constitution of the new republic would be put at risk denying them their entitlement. It must be stressed that this supremacy of legal certainty has been extensively used by the Hungarian court, often in quite brave ways—it was the basis, for example, on which they struck down important budgetary policies which trimmed too far, in their eyes, legitimate expectations of welfare payments. It may be for this reason that the court refused to look at all at the logic of limitation rules, and consider whether the values they sought to protect were in fact the sort that legal certainty is actually intended to promote. Statutes of limitations are rather low on the scale of basic human rights—they vary enormously from jurisdiction to jurisdiction, and have their main justification from the fact that a very long delayed criminal trial may produce evidentiary problems. It would have been an easy task to support the challenged legislation on the grounds that the normal reasons for such limitations did not apply, and that evidentiary questions could always be handled by trial judges. But to open up the question of why and when legal certainty needed to be seen as a high constitutional value would have weakened the court's ability to use it in other contexts.

It might not be worth spending as much time as I have in showing the nature of the thought processes in this judgment, which is, in its own way, a flawless development of a purely procedural orientation to constitutional law, but for one fact. The fact is that another court in another country with a similar history looked at the same issue and came out totally the other direction. But before discussing the Czech case, a further chapter in the Hungarian story is worth mentioning, because it under scores the formalism of the court. A year later the parliament, still determined to wield some substantive justice in this area took another and highly creative tack. It attempted to pass an act *On the Procedure of Certain Criminal Offences committed during the 1956 October Revolution and Freedom Struggle* which got round the statute of limitations problem by applying international laws against war crimes and crimes against humanity, which by a 1968 agreement to which Hungary was signatory, had no statute of limitations. This act was also found to be unconstitutional, largely because of bad draftsmanship. But the court was so eager to show that Hungary now *had* found a way to proceed against some of the worse offenders of the past regime in a way which was procedurally proper that it not only set out how the act could be remedied, but went even further and essentially announced that the relevant international law had direct effect in Hungary and did not need statutory support! What this does to legal certainty in a substantive sense is anyone's guess.[24] Nonetheless the decision, based on a very strong interpretation of the constitution's recognition of the supremacy and automatic incorporation of international law, demonstrates the typical openness of the new democracies' constitutional judiciary to foreign and international jurisprudence. It would certainly have been possible to avoid granting direct effect which, given the failure of the parliament to draft adequately, would have continued the immunity of communist era criminals.[25]

4. HARD LUSTRATION

The contrast between the Czech and Hungarian approaches—as in general with lustration issues—is enormous. To start with, the context within which the Czech case arises is vastly different. The issue of extending the date at which prosecutions become time barred was buried in a very strange statute, probably unique amongst CEE nations. The statute itself, *Regarding The Lawlessness of the Communist Regime and Resistance to it*,[26] was primarily concerned with making a statement about collective moral and political guilt for the past, and condemning the Communist Party and its members. By the terms of the act itself most of the language, even when cast in pseudo legal terms of criminal law, was not intended to create any criminal liability, though it was attacked as doing just this, as well as for many other things. However, the Court used its answer to objections about the general unconstitutionality of such a statement to set a context within which it became much easier to uphold the really controversial aspect, which was the prolongation of the prosecution period for politically protected crime. So completely different is the Czech view on legal continuity that one wonders whether it was in part written with an eye to the Hungarian case which had been decided a year earlier—though there is no reference at all to it in the Court's opinion.[27]

This section of the opinion requires explication because it is at least as important in helping us draw conclusions about our topic as the more legally concrete later section. The group of 41 Czech deputies who brought the action claimed that the statement in s.2 of the act whereby the previous regime was declared illegitimate

---

24 Described, with his own commentary, in Sólyom, *ibid.*, pp. 281–283.

25 One interpretation of why the court decided the second version of the limitations issue this way is that throughout the 1990s it was involved in a negotiation process with the Hungarian parliament so that it usually gave them part of what they wanted in return for the parliament accepting their authority by demanding less a second time around. See Kim Lane Scheppele, "Constitutional Negotiations: Political Contexts of Judicial Activism in Post-Soviet Europe," *International Sociology* 18:1(2003), pp. 219–238.

26 Act No 198/1993 Sb.

27 Pl US. 19/93, taken from the Court's Website: http://www.concourt.cz

must be unconstitutional because the new republic was a successor state in which inherited statutes, rules and other legal obligations remain in force. As the court put the claimant's case "this 'substantive continuity of domestic and international rights' is . . . an indication of the legitimacy of the governmental and political regime during the period 1948–1989." In fact the claimants argument in part could have been taken directly from the Hungarian judgment:

> If the statutory statement concerning the illegitimacy of the government and political system during the period . . . were correct and remained in effect, then the legal acts adopted during the stated period would no longer have been valid as of 1st August 1993; naturally this did not occur, for legal certainty is one of the basic characteristics of a law-based state, and that certainty depends on the constancy of legally expressed principles in particular areas of the law, on the constancy of legal relations.[28]

The Czech court clearly had a problem in answering this, but it was a problem they seem to have relished, and the answer, which depends on a trenchant rejection of some forms of legal formalism, has real implications for constitutional law throughout Europe. The Court asserts that the positivistic legal tradition that pre-dated the early development of post 1918 democracies in Central Europe, though it had strengthened legal certainty and the stability of laws had, in its later development "many times exposed its weaknesses. Constitutions enacted on this basis are neutral with regard to values." They argue such positivism lead directly to Hitler's ability to claim legality for his destruction of Weimar. They cast early post 1945 Czechoslovak history as the victim of such legal positivism in a resounding paragraph:

> After the war this legalistic conception of political legitimacy made it possible for Klement Gottwald to "fill up old casks with new wine." Then in 1948 he was able, by the formal observance of constitutional procedures to "legitimate" the February Putsch. In the face of injustice, the principle that "law is law" revealed itself to be powerless. Consciousness of the fact that injustice is still injustice, even though it is wrapped in the cloak of law, was reflected in the post-war German Constitution and, at the present time, in the Constitution of the Czech republic.[29]

---

[28] *Ibid.*

[29] *Ibid.* The fact that Germany has allowed a similar prolongation of the statue of limitations for East German alleged politically protected criminals is important later in their argument. But it is noteworthy that the Hungarian court, usually close to German thinking does not cite it at all, whereas the Czech court gives this distinctly non-positivistic reading to the German constitution. An extremely interesting account of the German situation, which also suggests some ways of squaring the circle between the Hungarian and Czech positions is James McAdams, *Judging the Past in Unified Germany*, (Cambridge: CUP 2001).

But note the way, as we saw earlier, this historically informed style of argument was used to legitimize the Benes decrees, which occurred in the brief period between Nazi and Communist regimes. It is certainly a fine line one walks if one is to pick and choose between substantive and procedural constitutional legitimacy. The court goes on to spell out the way that the Czech constitution is not value neutral, is not "merely a demarcation of institutions and processes", but is suffused with the core values of democracy which must be used in legal interpretation. It becomes an important interpretative point—one initially developed earlier in the first lustration case as I shall go on to discuss. Here the point is made in words that require full quotation:

> The Czech Constitution accepts and respects the principle of legality as a part of the overall basic conception of a law based state; positive law does not, however, bind it merely to formal legality, rather the interpretation and application of legal norms are subordinated to their substantive purpose, law is qualified by respect for the basic enacted values of a democratic society and also measures the application of legal norms by these values. *This means that even while there is continuity of "old laws" there is discontinuity in values from the "old regime."*[30]

In other words, the old laws must be interpreted via the new values, and not as a value free procedural system. What this ends up as is the idea that in order actually to be faithful to the values of a modern democratic state something akin, in the terminology of commercial law, to a "piercing of the corporate veil" is required. Ironically it is the specifically Hungarian stress, borrowed from the Italians, on looking at the "living law", though here the living law of the past, that is needed and used. This has to be the case because, as both the complainant deputies here and the Hungarian court point out, mere anarchy would follow from a generalized removal of legal certainty. This becomes clearer when the Czech court turns to the issue of stopping the clock on the statute of limitations for the whole duration of the previous regime. Doing so in general is justified by the now statutory illegitimacy of the past, but somehow it is necessary to show that no real violence is done to legal certainty, but rather, a very ambitious aim, legal certainty actually *requires* such a move. The argument they use is essentially one of empirical common sense. No one really believes that the state had any intention of prosecuting its own agents for illegal behavior—"Political power founded on violence should, in principle, take care not to rid itself of those who carrying out its violence." They then define the actual legal condition for a statute of limitations—it depends on the state actually wishing and trying to prosecute. Without this the concept of limitation is empty and the very purpose of the legal institution is beyond fulfillment. A statute of limitations can only exist:

---

[30] Pl US. 19/93.

> ...if there has been a long term interaction of two elements: the intention and the efforts of the state to punish an offender and the on going danger to the offender that he may be punished, both giving a real meaning to the institution of the limitation of actions.[31]

Courts must always have the last word, so it is hardly surprising that the Czech court makes the ultimate move—legal certainty requires this analysis: the orthodox application of the idea, treating the situation as the running of a limitation period that was not permitted to run would produce "a quite paradoxical interpretation of a law based state", the validation of a different legal certainty, the certainty the perpetrators originally had that they were safe. More fully: "This 'legal certainty' of offenders is, however, a source of legal uncertainty to citizens (and vice versa). In a contest of these two types of certainty, the Constitutional court gives priority to the certainty of civil society ...".[32]

Indeed, the Court argues, any other answer would legitimate a dictatorship *as law based*, giving a sign that "crime may become non-criminal". In competition to the Hungarian idea that strict application of traditional legal certainty is vital for the health of the new democracy, the Czechs argue instead that such an approach would mean "the loss of credibility of the present law-based state." In fact it would infringe Article 9 (3) of the constitution, "... legal norms may not be interpreted so as to authorize anyone to do away with or jeopardize the democratic foundations of the state."

Further, to demonstrate this technique of showing that formal legal values may better be protected by doing the opposite of what they seem to require, it is well to point out how very briefly the court dealt with the discrimination argument. In both Hungary and the Czech Republic it had been argued that removing time-barring only for one sort of offender, the politically protected, but not others who happened to have escaped prosecution involved unequal treatment. The Hungarian court had agreed that this was unjust discrimination. The Czech answer is short and characteristic. Not at all: actually "this is the way to rectify their inequality with those who had already faced the possibility of being put on trial because, not only were they not under special political protection, but it was the state's wish and in its political interest to prosecute them."

As the interpretative methodology of the Czech approach is so different from the Hungarian, and potentially so important to our assessment of the CEE in this area, it is worth, rather more quickly, looking at what is probably its origin, in the first Lustration case.[33] Here I am now using "lustration" in the more technical sense of investigating the past records of people in the public life of the new democracies. It is, of course, well known that Czechoslovakia was the first CEE country to take

---

31 *Ibid.*
32 *Ibid.*
33 Pl US 1/92.

such a policy with any rigor.[34] Considering that the Czech policy, though rather milder and affecting far fewer people than often thought, is one of the strongest, it may alarm some how easily the statute got through the Constitutional Court of the Republic of Czechoslovakia. The opinion, which, again, contains a good deal of instant history of the past regime to act as an empirical justification, starts with a very clear statement of the Court's overall attitude to constitutional adjudication. They describe the setting up of the new constitution in ambitious words, "thus an entirely new element of the renaissance of natural human rights was introduced into our legal order." They also stressed that the new constitution was not to be value free, in language already familiar from the limitations case, dismissing the merely procedurally legitimate "the concept of the law-based state does not have to do merely with the observance of any sort of values and any sort of rights, even if they were adopted in the procedurally proper manner." But it is when they come to talk directly of legal certainty that the determination to produce a novel form of constitutional adjudication become clear, all the more strongly because legal certainty as an argument hardly appears in the judgment once they turn to the issues rather than to introductory noises. Indeed it is not very clear, in the bulk of the argument, why they need discuss legal certainty at all. Nonetheless: "... not even the principle of legal certainty can be conceived in isolation, formally and abstractly, but must be gauged by those values of the constitutional and law-based state which have a systematically constitutive nature for the future."[35]

This is spelled out with an early version of the concern for the public legitimacy of the new state found in the statute of limitations case, and needs to be quoted in full:

> As one of the basic concepts and requirements of a law-based state, legal certainty must, therefore, consist in certainty with regard to its substantive values. Thus the contemporary construction of a law-based state which has for its starting point a discontinuity with the totalitarian regime as concerns values may not adopt a criteria of formal-legal and material-legal continuity which is based on a different value system, not even under the circumstances that the formal normative continuity of the legal order makes possible. Respect for continuity with the old value system would not be a guarantee of legal certainty but, on the contrary, by calling into question the values of the new system, legal certainty would be threatened in society and eventually the citizens' faith in the creditably of the democratic system would be shaken.[36]

---

34 Although the decision of the unified Czechoslovakian court remained good law in post divorce Slovakia for some years, the policy was never implemented, and the statute was ultimately repealed. See Herman Schwartz, *The Struggle for Constutional Justice in Post-Communist Europe*, (Chicago: University of Chicago Press 2000), Ch. 7.

35 Pl US 1/92.

36 *Ibid.*

The purpose of the statement in the context of the arguments that follows on the legitimacy of the Czechoslovakian lustration policy is logically unclear, but symbolically vital, because the main proposition they embrace is that the new state is entitled to be sure that those in leadership positions fully share the new values. When it comes to discussing the technical constitutionality of the statute the court actually takes refuge in highly definitional moves. The Czech lustration system required citizens to present a certificate proving that they had no unacceptable connections to the old security regime before they could hold a position above a certain level in a variety of institutions. For the Court there was no question of retroactivity, no question of discrimination, no breach of any international obligations under employment law. All that was happening according to them was that the state was setting an extra qualification for holding a post. This was future oriented, hence no retroactivity, it was equally applicable to all, so no discrimination, and was equivalent to similar practices elsewhere, even where it involved taking membership of a group as determinative of unsuitability without individuation of judgment.[37] And the state's entitlement to set such a qualification was the paramount need to ensure the elite of the new republic fully held to its new democratic values. The dismissal of merely "formal" rights from the past is acknowledged and dismissed:

> If compared with the preceding legal order, these conditions might appear to be, from a formal perspective, a restriction on civil rights; however, in the current legal order the basic criteria which will serve as the guide for our actions in the future are those found in the charter . . .[38]

Just as the realities of actual safety from prosecution of those working for the state had been cited to show that the statute of limitations had never been running, here the partisan employment practices of the old regime are cited as justification. But the connection is, of course, a very different one, and the Court's argument weak on this point despite the impressive rhetoric of the new meaning of legal certainty. The lustration policy was re-visited much later because parliament removed the time restriction—the original act had been intended to lapse in 1996—and the court of the Czech Republic decided an appeal, again by parliamentarians opposed to the act, in 2001. A large part of the judgment was involved in working out the status of the previous decision—did it mean the issue was *res judicata*, and if not, to what extent could the court of the *Czech* republic still follow the ruling of the court of the CSFR? It was an issue that had to be dealt with precisely because of the earlier court's stress on the irrelevance of formal continuity, but one easily enough handled because of the same stress on value continuity. The doctrine enunciated was a form of common law *stare decisis*—to the extent that the world had changed, so could the

---

[37] Again they cite Germany, though the only example they could find was a prohibition on some people who been involved with the Stasi working in advanced armaments firms.

[38] Pl US 1/93.

ruling. But, and this was crucial, the world was judged not to have changed enough, and the second court was careful to limit the extent that the first court had relied, as it had, on the short term nature of the original lustration restrictions. They derived a form of "political question" doctrine to insist that it was for the legislature not the court to solve the sociological question of when a state was secure enough to do without lustration. Instead they emphasized the right of a democracy to defend itself, usefully relying on ECHR rulings on the notion of "a democracy capable of defending itself."[39] The new court did clearly regard the external legal environment as, if not decisive, certainly vitally important. They note that no international court has decided the question of the legitimacy of lustration laws and that they are thus forced to use other "indicators", leaving no doubt that any future case arising after such an international decision might be handled very differently. As it is they recite the usual list of similar measures elsewhere, taking especial care to note the 1996 Resolution of the Council of Europe legitimizing lustration as long as it is not punishment but protection of democracy.[40] The temper of the second decision is much more even, with greater acknowledgement of the problem of passing time from the old days, and, as noted, with very careful reference to the external legal world. However no single doctrinal aspect of the first decision is doubted, and we are left unsure quite what Czech law does think about the role of legal certainty in a state ruled by law.

There are two forms of lustration. One, the Czech model, restricts access to positions of power directly. The other, the Hungarian and Polish models, operate essentially by a "name and shame" policy—all that is formally at risk is that, if an individual does not resign, his past will be made public (Hungary) or if a citizen is found to have lied in his account of his past, he will be debarred from office for ten years (Poland). Other states of course have used the Czech model, and nowhere has a Constitutional Court banned it. Lithuania, for example, banned anyone who had worked for the KGB from a wide list of offices and employment sectors, taking much the same line as the Czechs—no discrimination is involved, because it is simply a matter of a legitimate technical qualification for a post applied prospectively.[41] Nor was the challenge, also found elsewhere, under the right to freely choose an occupation seen as relevant. Lithuania did object to the machinery of adjudication as not providing an adequate appeal mechanism, but in fact the original Czech decision had done the same. Some more far reaching cases about the past which are not lustration but fit in no obvious category have been dealt with by a different attitude to the continuity of the past, one more in keeping,

---

39 In particular they cited *Glasenapp* v *Germany* (1986) and *Vogt vs. Germany* (1995).

40 Resolution No. 1096 (1996).

41 "On the Assessment of the USSR Committee of State (NKVD, NKGB, MGB, KGB) and Present Activities of the Regular Employees of This Organisation", Decision of the Constitutional Court of the Republic of Lithuania, Vilnius, 4 March 1999. The Court's Website is at: http://www.lrkt.lt.

perhaps with the formalism of the Hungarians. Thus the Ukraine's Constitutional court overturned legislation banning the Communist Party of the Ukraine by finding that the current party was legitimately registered in 1991 and had no institutional continuity with its predecessor. Given this, the ban on it breached the freedom of association clause of the constitution. But, neatly, as there was no institutional continuity, the party had no claims over its predecessors property either, thus giving the government much of what it wanted.[42] It is fairly clear that this case had as much to do with asserting the Court's authority within the separation of powers as solving the substantive rights claim—something which, as I have noted earlier, characterizes much of the litigation. A powerful example of this was the Polish case on retroactivity in punishing judges who had, in their words, "transgressed against the duty of issuing independent and impartial decisions in political trials conducted before 1989."[43] The Tribunal struck down the legislation because of procedural improprieties. However they clearly saw the procedural lapse in question, failing to consult the National Judiciary Council as required by legislation, as extremely important. In fact they developed a complex and far reaching doctrine covering such consultation rights, based on a scale of constitutional importance of the issues in question, which his\itself of major constitutional importance. There is no reason, therefore, to disregard what they did say about the substantive issue, in which they made it clear that the crucial necessity of an impendent judiciary did justify such retroactivity in this case. They should, therefore, be seen as on the Czech side of a robust preparedness to deal with some past injustices regardless of legal formalism. It might be thought this is even more remarkable given that judiciaries tend to be protective of their brethren. In making my point about the fact that the cases were dealt with are seldom only about the issue we look at, it might be thought particularly powerful that it was procedural propriety that stopped the court overruling a concern for procedural propriety. This is not some undisciplined court bowing to political pressure and likely to be indifferent to human rights—it is a court delicately balancing conflicting rights demands, albeit an unusual version of such a clash.

There are other examples of cases on what one might call the Czech end of the lustration spectrum, often dealing specifically with the judiciary,[44] but while nowhere has the basic principle been found unconstitutional, nor has such a developed argument about the nature of legal continuity and its relation to on value

42 The case is reported in Alexei Trochev, "Ukraine: Constitutional Court invalidates ban on Communist Party", *International Journal of Constitutional Law* 1:3 (July 2003).

43 Judgment K. 3/98, delivered 24th June 1998: Website of the Constitutional Tribunal is at: http://www.trybunal.gov.pl.

44 For example, the Slovenian case in which assessment of whether or not a judge had been guilty of favouritism to the old authorities was made a condition for his promotion or confirmation in office. *Constitutional Court of the Republic of Slovenia* U-I-83/94, 1994.

discontinuity been developed as in the Czech cases. I shall return to consider the implications of this at the end.

5. SOFT LUSTRATION

The first decision on what I have called "soft lustration", systems involving simply publicizing some individuals' past record was rendered in Poland on the early ill fated and politically transparent attempt in May 1992 which ultimately caused the fall of the Prime Minister. The case is almost infamous, and could not have got through even the laxest of constitutional reviews.[45] It is important to us because it is perhaps the best example, even more than the Polish case on retroactivity for punishing judges, to show the interaction between structural constitutional decisions and more obviously human rights issues. It is part of my thesis here that the alertness of the CEE courts to structural power issues in their constitutional jurisprudence is as much of value in their contribution to a united Europe as would be a simple "good" and "liberal" approach to individualized rights issues—but also that the two aspects have been inextricably interlinked. In this case, the Sejm gave a very ill defined instruction to the Minister of Internal Affairs to provide

> complete information regarding government officials from the level of voivode upwards, deputies, senators, prosecutors, barristers, township councilors and members of township management boards who collaborated with the UB Security Bureau and SB Security Services . . .

This instruction was issued as a mere resolution of the parliament, rather than a statute or any more normal form of regulatory instrument. Whether the format had been chosen to try to avoid judicial review or for other reasons is unclear, but it incensed the Constitutional Tribunal when the parliament tried to argue the Tribunal had no right of review over such motions. The Tribunal produced an immediate and wide interpretation of their over-view powers in what they themselves described as an "all encompassing interpretation of the provisions of the Constitution and the Constitutional Tribunal Act" which effectively said that if anything is done purporting to be a legally enforceable norm, then they get to review it. In fact, the Tribunal produced what was almost a tautology, and one that certainly empowers them:

> in a democratic state under the rule of law—a state founded on the separation of powers—legal norms cannot be established whose conformity with the constitution is not evaluated in a manner facilitating the removal of any inconsistencies.[46]

They describe this as literally "unthinkable".

[45] Case U. 6/92, 19th June 1992.

[46] Case U. 6/92, 19th June 1992.

In a word, anything the Sejm wanted to do important enough to worry the Tribunal was by definition, a fit subject for the Tribunal. Casting the instruction as a resolution was fatal to the Sejm, because the Tribunal went on to take the position that any such intrusion into private life was a huge breach of constitutional rights, given that protection "of one's honor" was crucial to human dignity. This form of "personal interest" is "inseparably coupled with the essence of a human being." It follows from the fact that this is such a major intrusion on human rights that it most certainly could not be carried out by anything less than a full statute, and, of course, the statute itself would have to pass constitutional review. It was also cause to fail the resolution, in the Tribunal's eyes, that there had been procedural irregularities even in the process of passing it as a resolution, irregularities that prevented its proper debate in the Sejm. This accords with the style of objection in the judicial discipline case cited above—the Tribunal is very concerned about the actual working of the institutions it supervises. It is notable that Poland uses the form "a democratic state under the rule of law", not merely "a state under." As to the substance, it is unconstitutional because of vagueness—collaboration was not even defined, and, most important, because the vagueness prevented the natural assessment of whether the intrusion authorized was proportional to the good it might do—hinting at a very strong rational connection test that would have been applied.

This recognition of the human dignity aspect is stronger than anything found even in Hungry, and fully in keeping with the best standards of any Western European state. It is noteworthy that the Tribunal cites legal textbooks, in French, Italian and German on the "inalienability of human rights" as well as international human rights documents. It is also at least in part a pragmatic understanding of the cost to anyone listed in the sort of search the Sejm was calling for, building that into the understanding of the right itself by stressing that "not only the subjective feelings of the person . . . should be taken into account, but also the objective reaction of public opinion." In rendering this opinion the Tribunal was keen to buttress it with earlier opinions of its own, mainly on the structural aspect. It was typical of the decision on the Hungarian form of lustration that it should demonstrate very well this one of my initial points—the new courts' concern to weave a coherent rights jurisprudence by self-reference wherever possible. It is also a valuable further sign of how varied the concerns identified by CEE courts can be that the Hungarian Court worried a good deal less about the affront to the dignity of those exposed than about an aspect of these old secret police records which no other court appears to have noticed.[47] The records are, they say, unconstitutional in themselves, and always have been. Thus part of the problem for the constitutionality of the statute is that it failed to accept that those records not made public had to be dealt with in some other way—they could not simply be kept under lock and key. In doing this the court was relying

47 Decision 60/1994, of 24th December 1994.

heavily on its own, already by then extensive, jurisprudence on what is called, in the Hungarian Constitution "informational self determination."[48] The act as a whole was declared unconstitutional for a variety of reasons, though none went to the basic question of disclosing the past of those in public life—the court relies on an American style concept of those in public life necessarily having a restricted "scope of private life". This is made all the more pressing by the fact of the transition and the need for transparency in public life. The court indeed regards the general thrust of the act as exhibiting "a confluence of the moral obligation that remained in the wake of the transition: the unveiling of deceit, publicity rather than punishment, and the value system normal to a state under the rule of law." They do however have very considerable concern about the way the act makes the government arbiter of what may be made public, not because they fear unfair publicity, but because of this problem of the rights of everyone to control data about them. Unusually for the court they come close to recognizing an American style "political question" doctrine in admitting that there is much room for policy latitude in working this balance in the details of this act, but they note in an apt phrase that "this political decision could not be based on the Constitution but rather on the constitutional certainty that the records can neither be kept secret not brought entirely to light." The Hungarian Court has the probably unique power of ruling that the legislature has allowed or created a state of "Constitutional Omission" and ruled that failure to provide for citizens to see and destroy those secret service records which were *not* going to be disclosed as part of the lustration process was such an omission which had to be dealt with by statute. For the court:

> The fundamental right to the protection of personal data and to access to information of public interest shall be interpreted in light of each other. This is natural for informational self-determination and the freedom of information are two complementary preconditions for individual autonomy . . . when freedom of information conflicts with the protection of personal records it cannot simply be said that the latter must always be strictly interpreted and must take precedence. In the light of the subject of the Act at issue, the Constitutional Court has established a hierarchy of these two basic rights.[49]

The other problem the Court found with the act related to the charge that unconstitutional discrimination was involved in the categorization of who would be vulnerable to these background checks. The approach here does not fit the idea that it is happy to allow much in the way of a margin of appreciation to legislatures. In keeping with much of their work during the nineties, the judgment might actually be seen in many ways as an illegitimate intrusion into policy making at the micro level,

48 The key early decision which laid down very strong personal rights to control data collected on one by the government was Decision 15/91 of 13th April 1991, on the use of personal data and PIN numbers.

49 Decision 60/1994, of 24th December 1994.

à la Stone Sweet.[50] The discrimination argument was upheld on the grounds that the categories used in the act were variously too broadly or too narrowly defined to "establish consistent constitutional criteria to distinguish between public and private data." Just what these criteria would look like the court did not say, but they were quite certain that records of university and college officials and top business executives of state enterprises "were not information of public interest since such people neither exercised public authority nor took part in (public) political affairs." This can only be regarded as a bizarre judgment: and even if the claim that that circulation figures were no basis to decide when a newspaper editor might have political influence was not bizarre, it was equally clearly no business of a court to so judge. Indeed excluding academics as opinion formers went ill with the other objection, that restricting such checks to the press corps but not to other opinion formers such as church leaders, trade union leaders and political parties produced too narrow a group. We need not, perhaps, be concerned by this tendency of the court. Human Rights can probably only be strengthened, if other aspects of policy are weakened, by over active courts who verge on legislation—and it is certainly something which is commonly found in Western Europe. A large number of judgments of unconstitutionality rendered by the French *Conseil Constitutionnel*, for example, are based on detailed objections to categories used in legislation, thus arguably producing discriminatory problems.[51]

6. CONCLUDING REMARKS

One thing above all stands out—at least at the level of rhetoric, and surely much more—the idea of the state governed by law, or the democratic state governed by law is central to the way the CEE courts have dealt with their legislatures' attempts to deal with the past. The concept is the starting point of all these judicial discussions, and it is usually analyzed with considerable care, if not always to the same conclusion. Whatever may be allowed or forbidden, it is done through this intellectual sieve. Only if one is prepared to be an extreme judicial realist and discount the language of decisions completely could one doubt that the conceptual framework used is fully fitting potential members of an enlarged democratic and liberal Europe. It is equally important to see that assessments via this check relate as much to how a proposed accounting with the past is made as with its substance. Had the CEE courts simply ruled out particular proposals that western liberals might dislike without being over concerned by procedure we would have nothing but the happenstance that, in certain specified cases, policies were measured against

50 See his general criticisms of European Constitutional Courts usurping the legislative function, particularly in Alec Stone Sweet, *Governing with Judges: Constitutional Politics in Europe* (Oxford: OUP 2000).

51 See Dominique Rousseau, *Droit du Contentieux Constitutionnel* (6th edn.), (Paris: Montchrestien 2001), especially pp. 409–427.

relatively inchoate values. It is precisely the great care taken over other constitutional matters that reassures us for the future. A state ruled by law is, at least in the eyes of Central and Eastern European Constitutional Justices, a state abiding strictly by the separation of powers and careful to ensure legislative procedure is abided by.

Nor does it make much sense to worry about the fit of these decisions to western legal practices when one notes the concern to cite and test against legal opinion both within the CEE itself and within the rest of Europe. One consequence of this comparative citation is that it would be hard to fault these countries without also raising serious concern about Germany, given the centrality of their experience after unification to the case law of CEE states. (One might also suggest that the ease with which many CEE justices feel at referencing the ECHR requires any doubter either to accuse them of improbable duplicity or seriously to question the standards of the ECHR itself).

There is one serious question to resolve, however. It arises primarily in the Hungary versus Czech Republic contrast. What are we to make of the radically different approach to assessing the requirement that a policy satisfies the standards of a state ruled by law? One knows, of course, that the political background to transition sharply affects the context within which a court as well as a legislature have to come to terms with the past. Were it simply a matter of accounting for why the Czechs did, and the Hungarians did not, allow an extension of the statute of limitations, it might be enough to point to their respective histories in the decades before transition.[52] I have already pointed out that much of the difference comes about by the story the two countries choose to tell about themselves. What is problematic is the fact that both courts claimed to be doing the same thing—abiding by the requirements of a state ruled by law *where legal certainty is a major part of the definition of such a state*. Because it simply cannot be the case that legal certainty is compatible both with allowing and forbidding the extension of time during which someone can be tried for a crime. It cannot be the case, for that matter, that selecting only some such criminals, those who were protected by political forces, both is and is not discrimination against one group. We must, surely, choose between the formalism of the Hungarians or the determination to ensure substantive justice of the Czechs.

Or must we? There are those who would have preferred the Czech Court, if they felt obliged to allow the prosecution of political offenders from the past, to simply say that during a period of transition exceptions had to be made to the normal standards of a state governed by law, rather than to try to show that no breach of the standards being tolerated. There will be others who very much take the Czech point, and regard Hungarian formalism as dangerous because it insufficiently couples the

[52] Sólyom op. cit., n. 10, comes very close to using this form of argument to account for differences between various CEE states.

values of the new state to the formal idea of a law governed state. Which is the greater threat to liberal democracy? An over facile demonstration that something rather dubious is not only acceptable but characteristic of the new values, or an over willing acceptance that constitutions cannot be expected to provide substantive justice? Or does it not, in fact, matter? Perhaps the dichotomies set up above are false—maybe two conflicting definitions of legal certainty can be contained within one legal universe. Maybe that is what the classic "margin of appreciation" is all about. One might be happier were there cases to cite in which the court of the Czech Republic had slapped down its legislature over lustration issues. Because it is easy to show the Hungarian court, for all its formalism producing powerfully liberal decisions, sometimes supporting, sometimes negating the parliament: the history of its decisions over compensation for the past, which there has been no time to discuss, are to point out, but not exhaustive of such examples. And yet the powerful legal creativity summed up in the insight that there is something wrong with a doctrine on legal certainty that ignores value *discontinuity* is very attractive. Perhaps the contrast is, in the end, in itself a sign of legal intellectual health which can only benefit the rest of Europe. In a recent article Bernhard Schlink has likened the writing of legal opinions to the writing of a series of mysteries or love stories:

> Format, printing, and layout remain the same, the blurbs above the authors' names look similar, and the covers are designed to match. Some novels have the same author, and the reader recognizes the same writing. Some obviously belong to the same tradition or follow the same pattern. Others could hardly be more different from each other. Each novel tells a different mystery or love story. But all of the novels preserve the law of the genre.[53]

On that basis, the European genre has new authors, but law abiding ones.

---

[53] Bernhard Schlink, "Hercules in Germany", *International Journal of Constitutional Law,* 4:4 (2003), p. 610.

4. Citizens and Foreigners in the Enlarged Europe

Enrica Rigo

1. Introduction: Repositioning European Borders

The Eastern enlargement poses an essential challenge to the issue of European membership. The current process of repositioning European borders not only dramatically increases the population of the "new" Europe but also confronts the theory and practice of defining "European citizenship". During the past decade the debate about citizenship has largely been dominated by contending ideas of an exclusive Westphalian model of membership, based on nationality, versus an inclusive post-Westphalian model where the entitlement to rights is based on *personhood*.[1] In the case of Central and Eastern European countries this debate has been particularly polarized within normative discourses on "national values" and "national community," which have partially framed discussions about internal constitutional reforms as well as the depiction of a European post-national and potentially all-encompassing membership.[2]

The process which redefines citizenship in the context of European Union enlargement illustrates a more complex state of affairs. I will argue that the transformation of European borders creates a system of "differentiated" memberships which questions the normative assumption that post-national communities are potentially inclusive. My aim is not so much to investigate whether national values continue to permeate the concept of citizenship in Central and Eastern Europe but to critique the reification of the debate on EU enlargement into contrasting models

---

1 The literature on citizenship is extensive, for an overview see Stephen Castles and Alastair Davidson, *Citizenship and Migration. Globalization and the politics of belonging* (London: Macmillan Press 2000); for a critical approach on post-Westphalian citizenship, see Else Kveinen, "Citizenship in a Post-Westphalian Community: Beyond External Exclusion?", *Citizenship Studies*, 1 (2002), pp. 21–35.

2 On citizenship and constitutional reforms in Eastern Europe, see Ulrich K. Preuss, "Patterns of Constitutional Evolution and Change in Eastern Europe", in Joachim J. Hesse and Nevil Johnson (eds.), *Constitutional Policy and Change in Europe* (Oxford: Oxford University Press 1995), pp. 95–125; on contending models of citizenship in Eastern and Western Europe see André Liebich, Daniel Warner and Jasna Dragovic (eds.), *Citizenship East and West* (London: Kegan Paul International 1995); for a critical approach see Willfried Spohn and Anna Triandafyllidou (eds.), *Europeanisation, National Identities and Migration. Changes in Boundary Construction between Western and Eastern Europe* (London: Routledge 2003).

Wojciech Sadurski et al. (ed.), Spreading Democracy and the Rule of Law?, 97–119.

of membership. In particular I intend to concentrate on the limited inclusiveness of European citizenship revealed by the emerging practice of border administration. In fact, in order to account for the specificity of the European membership model(s), it is necessary to focus on the norms that identify boundaries at each level of the European polity. The signing of the Schengen agreements,[3] their incorporation in the Amsterdam Treaty through the creation of an area of "freedom, security and justice" and the enlargement process have determined structural changes in border control regimes. The common assumption that controls were subsequently relocated from national borders to the external frontiers of the European Union is only partially true. In reality, the very concept of borders has undergone deep transformation.[4] Borders are no longer dividing lines between distinct political territorial units with clearly defined sovereignties. On the contrary, they develop into areas where sovereignty is shared among different actors and is sometimes delegated to private agents. Borders delocalise governmental[5] policies over populations and individuals far beyond either the territory of national states or the territory of the European Union. At the same time, the legal institutions which define the status of aliens generate lines of continuity between external and internal boundaries: in other words they internalize borders in the form of diffuse mechanisms of control.

Present-day borders are products of modernity. With the birth of nation states, as Raimondo Strassoldo argues, "[w]hat was formerly a frontier area of expansion of European civilization, becomes a state, and therefore tends to harden, close and

---

3 "Schengen agreements" here refer both to the first Schengen agreement signed by Germany, France and Benelux on 14th July 1985, and the agreement of 19th June 1990 which applied Schengen I. All the member states with the exception of United Kingdom and Ireland have gradually joined the Schengen Agreements.

4 Elsewhere I have argued that frontiers between member states did not disappear following the implementation of the Schengen Agreements. Citizens of non-EU states are still subject to forms of internal border controls within "Schengenland". Sandro Mezzadra and Enrica Rigo, "L'Europa dei migranti", in Giuseppe Bronzini, Heidrun Friese, Antonio Negri and Peter Wagner (eds.), *Europa, Costituzione e movimenti sociali* (Roma: Manifestolibri 2003), pp. 213–231; Enrica Rigo, "Politiche di migrazione", *Derive Approdi*, 22 (2002), pp. 157–162.

5 The term "governmental" is used here with reference to Michel Foucault's analysis of the "art of government" which, according to the author, differs from sovereignty: "This means that, whereas the doctrine of the prince and the juridical theory of sovereignty are constantly attempting to draw the line between the power of the prince and any other form of power, because its task is to explain and justify this essential discontinuity between them, in the art of government the task is to establish a continuity, in both an upwards and a downwards direction", Michel Foucault, "Governmentality", in Graham Burchell, Colin Gordon and Peter Miller (eds.), *The Foucault Effect. Studies in Governmentality* (London: Harvester Wheatsheaf 1991), p. 91. On borders as dispositives of governmental policies see also William Walters, "Mapping Schengenland: denaturalizing the border", *Environment and Planning D: Society and Space*, 20 (2002), pp. 561–580.

control its boundaries."[6] This geopolitical understanding of borders and the role they have served for the construction of national identities, has often overshadowed other meanings of political and territorial boundaries. Firstly, borders not only divide but also link. As a consequence their main function is less concerned with "separation" than with "differentiation". This was emphasized by Niklas Luhmann who analysed territorial borders as system boundaries and considered them "means of production of relations"[7] which allow for increasing differentiation and complexity of modern societies. Secondly, territorial borders produce two combinations of political relations: those between distinct political systems and those between the political system and the world which limits the system itself.[8] In other words, they do not simply produce and regulate relations between states but also over the people who come from outside the political system. It is especially this relationship which reveals the characteristic asymmetry of borders: the fact that they perform diverse functions according to the side from which they are crossed.[9]

Migration movement challenges the territorial system of national states. However, when considering trans-national migration, sociological literature rarely takes into account the fact that migrants' flows are not *the only* variable. Territorial political and legal boundaries also move and transform themselves; continuously redefining the relation between citizens and foreigners. The process of European enlargement is a privileged field in which to analyse the transformation of national and supra-national borders and consider the system of differentiated European memberships. I will focus on changes that have occurred in post-communist legal systems in an attempt to incorporate candidate countries into a European area of "freedom, security and justice." Particular attention will be given to the legislation on aliens approved by parliaments of Central and Eastern European countries in order to meet the requirements of the Schengen *acquis*. The cases of Poland, Romania and Bulgaria will be used as exemplification. Poland is one of the countries where changes first occurred (largely as a result of its particular relationship with Germany) and where transformations in national legislation have been the most far-reaching. Romania and Bulgaria have been chosen with the purpose of comparing countries which will participate in successive phases of the enlargement. Moreover, these two countries hold a key position in relation to migration

6 Raimondo Strassoldo, "Boundaries in sociological theory: a reassessment", in Raimondo Strassoldo and Giovanni Delli Zotti (eds.), *Cooperation and Conflict in Border Areas* (Milano: Franco Angeli 1982), p. 259.

7 Niklas Luhmann, "Territorial borders as System Boundaries, in Raimondo Strassoldo and Giovanni Delli Zotti (eds.), *Cooperation and Conflict in Border Areas* (Milano: Franco Angeli 1982), p. 237.

8 *Id*, p. 236.

9 Ètienne Balibar, *La paura delle masse. Politica e filosofia prima e dopo Marx*, trans. Andrea Catone (Milano: Mimesis 2001), p. 210.

movements due to the fact that they are situated on transit routes for migrants entering Europe from Asia.

Poland has recently approved a new Act on Aliens in view of meeting the Schengen requirements (*Polish Act on Aliens* of 13 June 2003, *Journal of Laws* of 2003, No. 128, it. 1175). The first comprehensive legislation on aliens was passed by the Polish Parliament in 1997 (*Polish Aliens Law* of 25 June 1997) which was then amended in 2001 (Act of 11 April 2001). On the same date that it passed the *Act on Aliens*, the Polish Parliament also approved an *Act on granting protection to aliens within the territory of the Republic of Poland* (*Journal of Laws* of 2003, No. 128, it. 1176). This second law introduces new forms of legal status for aliens such as "tolerated stay" and "temporary protection". In December 2002 the Romanian government repealed the previous legislation on aliens and replaced it with a new body of rules approved through an *Emergency Ordinance on the regime of aliens in Romania* (*The Romania Official Journal* No. 955, 27 December 2002). The ordinance was approved on the basis of the provision in article 114(4) in the Romanian constitution which states that the government may adopt "in exceptional cases" emergency orders that need subsequent approval by the parliament. In 2002 Bulgaria also introduced amendments to legislation, although major changes to the first *Law on Foreigners in the Republic of Bulgaria* approved in 1998 had already been established in 2001.[10] The principle aim of the changes introduced by the three countries was to adapt the domestic normative framework to the new visa regulation imposed in view of future entrance into the Schengen Area. Nevertheless, these acts affect other aspects of the legal condition of aliens and reflect a progressive "Europeanization" of domestic legislation. To illustrate the consistency between external and internal boundaries I will focus on a range of legal institutions related to the detention and expulsion of aliens.

2. EUROPEAN POLICIES AND THEIR EASTWARD INFLUENCE

Before examining the recent transformations in legislation of Central and Eastern European countries and attempting to formulate some hypotheses about the actual and future implementation of laws, it is necessary to refer to the multi-level system of decision making established in the wake of the harmonization of immigration and asylum policies within the actual Member States of the European Union. Since the middle of the 1980s, European states have increasingly coordinated their immigration and asylum policies with the aim of combating illegal immigration and redistributing the burden of hosting asylum seekers. The first stage of co-operation coincided with the signing of intergovernmental agreements and conventions such as the Schengen agreements, which concerned the free movement of persons within

[10] The analysis of the legal acts approved in Poland, Romania and Bulgaria is based on official English translations provided by the OCSE Office for Democratic Institution and Human Rights, Warsaw, Poland.

the territory of member States, and the Dublin Convention, which determined which state was responsible for examining asylum applications. In 1997 the Amsterdam Treaty incorporated the Schengen Agreements into the Union's *acquis* and asylum and immigration policies were transferred from the third to the first pillar of the Union. This evolution is currently undergoing a transitional period of five years (which commenced following the entry into force of the Amsterdam Treaty in 1999) during which time major decisions taken unanimously by the Council are binding for all member states (with the exception of Ireland, United Kingdom and Denmark) and are introduced accordingly into domestic legislation.[11]

Both the Schengen Agreements and the Dublin Convention can be considered "laboratories" for European policies,[12] especially in the field of border management. Even though Eastern and Central European countries were not part of these two inter-governmental agreements, they were nevertheless affected by them. In order for their citizens to benefit from visa exemptions, candidate countries had to implement measures to prevent the transit of illegal migrants through their territory, guarantee the readmission of migrants returned from Member States and progressively implement a tighter system of visa regulation the basis of which had already been established within the Schengen framework. Moreover, the system set up by the Dublin Convention to prevent the repeated applications by asylum seekers arriving from countries considered "safe" forced Central and Eastern European Countries to shoulder a great part of the refugees who tried to enter member states overland. As a result of the Schengen Agreements and the Dublin Convention national borders have not simply been relocated at the external frontier of the Union but rather, neighbouring countries have become dynamic components of a new "communitarized" concept of a "border" which extends its influence throughout their territories.

During the entire accession process, issues of migration control and asylum policies have played a prominent role. As a condition of membership in the Union, applicant states have been required to fully implement the communitarian *acquis* in these areas before completion of their accession and despite the fact they took no part whatsoever in the negotiations and decision process.[13] Due to the multi-level system of decision-making outlined above and the different stages of its implementation, it is difficult to provide a straightforward account of the results and tendencies

---

11 For a recent and extensive analysis of the European decision-making system on immigration and asylum policies see Maria Fletcher, "EU Governance Techniques in the Creation of a Common European Policy on Immigration and Asylum", *European Public Law*, 4 (2003), pp. 533–562.

12 Jörg Monar, "The Dynamics of EU Justice and Home Affairs: Laboratories, Driving Factors and Costs", *Journal of Common Market Studies*, 39 (2003), pp. 747–764.

13 On this issue, with regard to Bulgaria and Romania, see Lora Borissova, "The adoption of the Schengen and the Justice and Home Affairs *Aquis*: The Case of Bulgaria and Romania", *European Foreign Affairs Review*, 8 (2003), pp. 105–124.

of European asylum and immigration policies. Besides European treaties, communitarian and national legislation, the *acquis* encompasses non-binding instruments, norms of general guidance and rules associated with European Union objectives.[14] In addition, it is essential to consider how domestic strategies of migration control lead to different kinds of bilateral agreements between member states and prospective countries as well as between prospective states and third countries. These include readmission agreements to facilitate the return of illegal migrants and cooperation agreements over the issue of border management.

Member and applicant states have played a different role in regional and subregional approaches to migration control according to their stronger or weaker influence in external relations. A typical example is the role played by Germany in influencing Polish and Czech policies, referred to sometimes as the "German factor."[15] However, migration policies have also been influenced by non-applicant countries, as in the case of recent Polish visa regulations for neighbouring countries which had previously been postponed due to the opposition of Russia, Belarus and the Ukraine. Indeed, the visa requirements to enter the EU—and now also applicant countries—have been recognized as one factor that fuels anti-EU sentiments among the populations of south-east Europe and the former Soviet Union.[16] In the specific case of the eastern Polish border, many commentators predict that the new visa regime will probably lead to the collapse of the cross-border trade (estimated in 2002 at 700 million euros) which in many cases constitutes a main source of income for sizeable part of the population in the region.[17]

---

14 Rosemary Byrne, Gregor Noll and Jens Vested-Hansen, "Western European Asylum Policies For Export: The Transfer of Protection and Deflection Formulas To Central Europe and the Baltics", in Rosemary Byrne, Gregor Noll and Jens Vested-Hansen (eds.), *New Asylum Countries? Migration Control and Refugee Protection in an Enlarged European Union* (The Hague: Kluwer Law International 2002), pp. 5–28. Examples of non-binding documents include various *Schengen Catalogues* on borders management and police co-operation and the *Green paper on a community return policy on illegal residents* (COM(2002) 0175 final, 10th October 2002).

15 Wlodek Aniol, *Poland's Migration and Ethnic Policies: European and German Influences* (Warsaw: Friedrich Ebert Foundation 1996), p. 10.

16 Milada A. Vachudová, "Eastern Europe as Gatekeeper: The Immigration and Asylum Policies of an Enlarging European Union", in Peter Andreas and Timothy Snyder (eds.), *The Wall around the West. State Borders and Immigration Control in North America and Europe* (Boston: Rowman and Littlefield Publisher 2000), p. 166.

17 Helmut Dietrich, "The new border regime at the Bug river. The east of Poland and the PHARE programmes" (Forschungsgesellschaft Flucht und Migration Working Paper 2002); available at http://www.ffm-berlin.de/english/publik/bug%20river.doc; Guy P. Chomette, "Alle Frontiere orientali dell'Unione Europea. Integrazione della Polonia, disintegrazione di Ucraina e Bielorussia", *Le Monde Diplomatique* (Italian version), March 2003. The decrease of the cross-border trade is positively considered by the Commission as a sign of the efficient implementation of the new visa regime (European Commission, *Comprehensive monitoring*

After the collapse of the "iron curtain" a new curtain of entry visas and administrative procedures has been erected with the purpose not only of limiting admission to European member states but also to candidate countries and therefore frustrating the promise of a freedom of movement that had only recently been acquired. The case of Kaliningrad is paradigmatic. As a result of the implementation of the Schengen *acquis* by Poland and Lithuania the inhabitants of the Russian enclave will need a valid passport to travel to the rest of Russia, which is actually in breach of the constitutional right of freedom of movement guaranteed to Russian citizens. During the enlargement negotiations, the Russian government pressed for a flexible application of the *acquis* by neighbouring countries, at least with regard to the inhabitants of Kaliningrad.[18] Although reasonable, this proposal has not been accepted because admission to the EU does not allow any form of flexibility with regard to "security" matters. The absolutist attitude held by present Member States highlights the unequal position of candidate countries and reflects a degree of "*hypocrisy*."[19] This is particularly the case if one considers that the Europe of Justice and Home Affairs is affected by a "variable geometry" arising from the different positions held by the United Kingdom, Ireland and Denmark which are not bound by the Schengen *acquis*.

The increasing relevance of borders is corroborated by the fact that they are becoming ever more autonomous objects of European policy-making and that permanent community structures are created in order to co-ordinate integrated strategies of border management. Already in May 2002 the Commission proposed the setting up of an "External borders practitioners' common unit"[20] which was endorsed by the Council in the *Plan for the management of the external borders of the Member States of the European Union* agreed on June 2002.[21] More recently the Commission presented a *Proposal for a Council regulation to establish a European Agency for the Management of Operational Co-operational at the External Border*.[22] While the competencies of the Common Unit regarding the strategic co-ordination of border management would remain, this new Agency would deal with operational tasks that, until now, have been left to the exclusive competence of national authorities. For instance, the Agency would be in charge of "co-ordinating and organising

report on Poland's preparation for membership, 2003; and European Commission, *Regular report on Romania's progress towards accession*, 2003).

18 For an extensive analysis of this issue see Olga Potemkina, "Some ramification of Enlargement on the EU-Russia Relations and the Schengen Regime, *European Journal of Migration and Law*, 5 (2003), pp. 229–247.

19 Neil Walker, "The Problem of Trust in an Enlarged Area of Freedom, Security and Justice: A Conceptual Analysis", in Malcom Anderson and Joanna Apap (eds.), *Police and Justice Co-operation and the New European Borders* (The Hague: Kluwer Law International 2002), p. 28, italics in original.

20 COM (2002) 233 final, 7th May 2002.

21 Doc. 1009/02 FRONT 58 COMIX 398, 14th June 2002.

22 COM (2003) 687 final, 11th November 2003.

return operations of Member States and identifying best practices on the acquisition of travel documents and removal of third country nationals from the territory of the Member States."[23] The Commission justifies the Agency's supplementary competences with the pretext that in most member states such tasks "fall under the competencies of the authorities responsible for controlling the external borders."[24] This extension of competences confirms, however, that the process of "communitarization" changes the object of border management: managing external borders is not limited to keeping unwanted foreigners out but to continue administrating their positions inside the territory. These positions are not at the exclusive disposal of the hosting state authorities but arise from the intersection of powers exercised by different national, trans-national and sub-national actors.

The words used in official documents to describe the tasks of the "Common Unit" well reflect the balance between decision-making at EU and national levels. The Common unit is defined as "acting as "head" of the common policy on management of external borders and as "leader' co-ordinating and controlling operational tasks."[25] On the one hand, this language echoes the fact that major policy developments have occurred outside the communitarian framework, and on the other, it mirrors the reluctance of states to relinquish sovereignty in matters of Justice and Home Affairs. One consequence of this is that policies related to internal security have been proceeded "by drift and reaction rather than by direction and design."[26] Another related consequence is that operational agencies and expertise groups proliferate to the detriment of transparency. The alarm raised over the lack of democratic accountability is compounded by the concerns over the limited judicial control of the Court of Justice. In fact various norms in European Treaties exclude the competence of the Court when "relating to the maintenance of law and order and the safeguarding of internal security" (Art. 68 II EC) and a similar provision has also been reproduced in the draft Constitution presented by the Convention. Bearing in mind that national legislation considers immigration and asylum policies as strictly related to the maintenance of "internal security" and "public order", operational tasks carried out by national police forces and administrative authorities are *de facto* barred from the control of the European Court of Justice.

3. THE EASTERN BORDERS OF EUROPE

Official documents of the Union declare that the enlargement poses new challenges for the protection of its external frontiers given the fact that future member states

---

[23] *Id*, p. 3.

[24] *Ibid*, at. 23.

[25] *Id*, p. 2. The Italian version of the document also utilises the term "*direttore d'orchestra*", orchestra conductor.

[26] Walker, above n. 19, p. 31.

will be largely responsible for the internal security of the Union.[27] However, the involvement of candidate countries in European policies on immigration control dates back to the beginning of the 1990s. The two main instruments through which present member states have unloaded part of their responsibility towards hosting migrants and asylum seekers are the "safe country principle" and "readmission agreements."

The "safe country principle" was introduced in the German Federal Constitution in 1993 with the aim of regulating the arrival of protection seekers from Poland and the Czech Republic. Asylum seekers entering Germany from a "safe country" would now be subject to denied entry or, if stopped and identified on German territory, to removal. Shortly afterwards, the "safe country principle" was adopted by the other European member states, and all countries bordering the Union were designated as "safe". This policy had the effect of transforming countries bordering the EU into "buffer zones" for asylum seekers and transit migration. Moreover, in order to maintain their good relationship with the EU, neighbouring countries were responsible for preventing transit migration from moving further west. The tightening of European migration and asylum policies has spread with a "domino effect" to Central and Eastern European Countries who, in turn, have modified their domestic legislation to declare neighbouring countries to be "safe" and have signed readmission agreements with migrants' countries of origin and transit states. Over the past decade some Central and Eastern European countries have amended their legislative framework on more than one occasion, and each time in an increasingly restrictive way. For example, according to art. 14 of the *Act on granting protection to aliens within the territory of the republic of Poland* of 13th June 2003, an alien arriving from "a safe country of origin or a safe third country" is refused refugee status as this is now regarded "[a] reason of manifestly unfounded nature of the application." In the previous *Polish Aliens Law* of 1997 the arrival from a safe country and the lodging of a "manifestly unfounded" application had to be both taken into consideration in order to refuse the refugee status.

Readmission agreements are the instruments which enable the actual removal of aliens from a state's territory and are therefore essential to the functioning of the "safe countries" policy as well as guaranteeing the return of illegal migrants. Once again, Germany acted as pioneer signing with Poland in 1993 the *Governmental Agreement on Co-Operation in matters Referring to Migration Movements*.[28] This agreement was a bilateral modification of a general document signed in 1991 between Poland and the Schengen States which had done little to limit migration, especially towards Germany. Since then most other European member states have concluded similar agreements with migrants' countries of origin and transit, and as

---

27 Doc. 1009/02 FRONT 58 COMIX 398, 14th June 2002.

28 Gregor Noll, "The Central Link: Germany Poland and the Czech Republic", in Byrne *et al. op. cit.* n. 14. p. 43.

Central and Eastern European states constitute the unavoidable overland route to Europe (as well as being the origin of migration movements) all candidate countries are presently bound by these readmission agreements. In turn, prospective member states have had to sign analogous agreements with countries of origin of migrants in order to return illegal migrants or refused asylum seekers, but also as a condition of complying with the Schengen *aquis*. Poland has concluded readmission agreements not only with Germany and the other Schengen states, but also with Bulgaria, the Czech Republic, Romania, Slovakia, the Ukraine, Croatia, Moldova, Hungary, Latvia, Lithuania, Estonia, Slovenia and Switzerland, while the transfer of people to Russia and Belarus is regulated under a Polish-CIS agreement. In the case of Romania, an example of a country that will participate in the second stage of EU enlargement, readmission agreements have been concluded outside the Schengen area with Hungary, India, the Czech Republic, Slovakia, Slovenia and Switzerland, while negotiations are underway with Estonia, Ukraine, Belarus, China, Bulgaria, Lithuania, Turkey, Latvia, Serbia and Montenegro, Lebanon and Iran.[29] Through readmission agreements the expulsion of aliens can be conceived of as a transnational system of concentric circles. Candidate countries function as stop-off points outside the core of actual member states, but the reciprocally binding effects of this system reach territories much further away.[30]

From a legal point of view, the readmission agreements have developed from rather general texts into detailed documents which also regulate the readmission of nationals of third countries who have entered or stayed illegally in the territory of one of the contracting parties before moving to the other. Whereas these initially took the form of bilateral agreements between individual states, the European Commission has recently started to insist that these readmission agreements be signed at the communitarian level, thus binding all actual (and future) member states, and that readmission clauses be introduced in other kinds of agreements. In addition, while previous agreements required proof of an alien's nationality (which was one of the main obstacles for the return of migrants), there has been a growing tendency to include clauses that widen the range of cases which constitute presumption of a person's nationality or evidence that they have stayed in a state's territory.[31] For example, in a note written by the General Secretary of the EU Council circulated to

---

29 For the latest developments in negotiations over readmission agreements with third countries see the annual Commission's *Regular Reports on Progress Towards Accession*, available for each candidate states.

30 According to Frank P. Weber, the historical precedents of readmission agreements were those signed by Germany in 1920–1921 with Poland, Russia, Latvia, Lithuania, and Estonia in order to facilitate mass deportation; Frank P. Weber, "Expulsion: genèse et pratique d'un contrôle en Allemagne", in Didier Bigo (ed.), *Circuler, Enfamer, Eloigner. Zones d'Attente et Centres de Rétention des Démocraties Occidentales* (Paris: L'Harmattan 1996), pp. 107–154.

31 Steve Peers, "Readmission agreements and EC External Migration Law", Statewatch analysis 2003; a full version of the paper is published in Steve Peers and Nicola Rogers (eds.), *EU*

council members regarding the introduction of readmission clauses in cooperation agreements with China, it was advised that "*no proof of identity shall be required in respect of persons to be admitted*."[32] By tracing out these readmission agreements one effectively produces a map of the "flows of expulsion." Thus, an Asian migrant expelled from Germany might pass through Poland and Romania before being "sent home" without necessarily his or her national identity ever being proven.

These examples illustrate the assertion that European borders do not coincide with the perimeter of the European Union territory nor with the territory of those states that will become EU members in the forthcoming "waves" of enlargement. Readmission agreements are dispositives of control over population movements which de-territorialize states' sovereignty and trace borders that cannot be represented as continuous dividing lines. Instead, they constitute administrative borders whose function is not simply to keep out those who are perceived as "trespassers" but, first and foremost, to govern populations both inside and outside a state's territory. This function of borders is highlighted by another principle of European migration policy; namely the principle of "conditionality" according to which quotas of legal entry are reserved for nationals of those countries which collaborate in combating illegal migration.[33] Readmission agreements also play an important role in implementing this principle, since collaborating in the combating of illegal migration primarily means accepting and facilitating the return of unwanted migrants from European member states. During the European Council held in Seville in June 2002, the principle of conditionality was defined as either "positive" or "negative". The former connotes positive sanction—such as the provision of higher quotas of entry—for countries whose commitment against illegal migrants is judged to be efficient. The latter implies negative sanctions for countries that do not collaborate which may consist of the suspension of economic aid. The "negative conditionality" was criticized by part of the Council and in the conclusive document it was decided that "negative" sanction could only be applied unanimously by the Council and not by singular member states.[34] Although presented as innovative in Seville, a form of *de facto* "conditionality"—both in its positive and negative designations—has long been common in migration policies. In fact, the signature and the implementation of readmission agreements have often been encouraged through the promise of economic aid, while their breach has been discouraged with the threat of suspending aid.[35]

Immigration and Asylum Law: Text and Commentary (The Hague: Kluwer Law International 2003).

32 Doc. 13206/01, 25th October 2001, italics in original.

33 On "conditionality" in migration policies, see the *Communication from the Commission to the Council and the European Parliament integrating migration issues in the European Union's relations with third countries*, COM(2002) 703 final, 3rd December 2002.

34 *Presidency Conclusion Seville European Council*, Doc. 02/13, 24th June 2002.

35 Weber, above n. 30.

Readmission agreements are not the only example of the deterritoralization of borders. Migrants seeking to legally enter the EU encounter the border when they first visit the embassy or consulate in their country of origin in order to apply for an entry visa. Didier Bigo and Elspeth Guild have recently used the term "*police à distance*"[36] to describe the Schengen system of visa regulation. According to these authors, the term designates the mechanisms of control which are exercised by "professionals" of security strategies which do not refer to national police forces but to diplomatic authorities and administrative bureaucracies. Therefore, the impact of the shifting of European borders is not limited to legislative changes. It also involves the constitution of new authoritative figures and forms of expertise involved in the implementation of new social practices. Besides candidate states, neighbouring countries are also affected. Legislation on aliens approved in Central and Eastern European countries in order to comply with Schengen visa regulation, for example, provide for the establishment of new consular offices in neighbouring countries.

The incorporation of candidate countries in the area of "freedom, security and justice" also implies the transfer of the notions of "national security" and "public order" that have been developed in the present member states. According to art. 5 of the Convention which applies the Schengen Agreements, in order to be admitted into the territory, an alien must not be considered dangerous to the "national security", the "public policy" and the "international relations" of *any one* of the member states. Usually the classification of a foreigner as an unwelcome migrant depends on her/his lack of fulfilment of national legislation requirements during a previous stay in a Schengen country. The criteria of data on "undesirable aliens" registered in the pan-European information system (SIS) are therefore defined at the national level and range from criminal offences to simple breaches of administrative rules. Due to the overlapping of the different conditions of entry into Schengen territory, the concepts of "security" and public "order" (or "policy") applicable in the area of "freedom, security and justice" are thus not the result of an autonomous elaboration but the sum of restrictions established in each country.

After the completion of the accession, therefore, any interpretation of migration laws approved in candidate countries will also need to take into consideration notions of "national security" and "public order" as defined by each member state. For instance, in the case of Poland, entry is barred to those foreigners whose data "has been recorded in the index of aliens whose residence on the territory... is undesirable" (*Polish Act on Aliens* art. 21(1)) and to any foreigner whose entry or residence "may constitute a threat to the state security and defence as well as to the

---

[36] Didier Bigo and Elspeth Guild, "La mise à l'écart des étrangers: la logique du visa Schengen", *Cultures and Conflits*, 49–50 (2003).

public security and policy or it would be in breach of the interests of the Republic" (*Polish Act on Aliens* art. 21(6)). In the case of Romania, entry is refused to aliens who represent a "threat for national defence and security, public order, health and moral probity" (*Emergency Ordinance on the regime of aliens in Romania* art. 6(1,f)[37]) or, in the case of Bulgaria, to those "included in the informational massif of the unwelcome foreigners in the country" (*Law on Foreigners* art. 10(14)). Although these norms refer directly to domestic criteria, their combination with art. 5 of the *Schengen Convention* extends the normative definition of "national security" and "public order" or "policy" in a manner proportional to the extension of the area of "freedom, security and justice."

The notion of "*police à distance*", as exercised by consular authorities, regards migrants who attempt to legally enter European member or candidate states. In the same way, a migrant who tries to enter the enlarged Europe, partially or totally avoiding the legal requirements, encounters its borders long before its territorial delimitation. They are encountered, for example, when the migrant uses transport companies to reach the European Union or applicant states. "Carriers", in fact, are required to make stringent checks for undocumented aliens to avoid running the risk of sanctions. "Carrier liability" clauses are contained in all aliens laws of European member states, and now they are also introduced in applicant countries' legislation so as to meet the Schengen *acquis*. Such clauses were first introduced in Poland with the *Aliens Law* of 1997. In the new *Polish Act on Aliens*, art. 138 states that "if the carrier [brings] into the territory of the Republic of Poland an alien who does not posses . . . the travel document and the visa required to cross the border, . . . an administrative fine in the amount of PLN equal to the sum not less than EUR 3000 or EUR 5000 for each person carried shall be imposed on the carrier." Comparable norms are also present in Romanian (art. 7 of the *Emergency Ordinance on the regime of aliens*) and Bulgarian legislation (art. 20 of the *Law on Foreigners* amended in 2001). In addition to administrative fines, Polish and Romanian acts oblige carriers to return aliens to the countries from which they were transported or to refund expenses sustained for their forced repatriation. As a result of such provisions, not only the state's typical function of border control but also the implementation of operational tasks concerning repatriation are delegated to private agents.[38]

37 The *Emergency Ordinance on the regime of aliens in Romania* also provides for a particular administrative measure of authority based on a declaration of undesirability which can be ordered "against an alien who performed, performs or there are strong evidence that he intend to perform such activities as to endanger the national security and public order" (art. 83(1)). An alien can be declared undesirable for a period from 5 to 15 years with the possibility of extending the term.

38 This state of affairs particularly jeopardizes the rights of protection seekers who normally do not posses entry visas or travel documents.

4. LEGAL BORDERS

European borders maintain many elements of "fortification" which characterized traditional national borders. Poland, for example, will preserve and even reinforce defensive tools of the old "iron curtain" that, through the PHARE programmes,[39] will be relocated along the eastern frontier:

> Unlike the German-Czech border, the demarcating barbed wire from the time before the collapse of the Warsaw Pact wall will not be removed. The fortified border watchtower, invented by the conquering and territorial sates, celebrates its resurrection here. Such towers are planned to being built every 15 to 20 kilometres, each equipped with the most advanced and expensive electronic and optical paraphernalia. Spying from above and hunting down units on the ground—with the border surveillance at Poland's eastern border, military and police units converge in new ways.[40]

Differing from conventional geopolitical borders, the new European external frontiers are not fortified against the threat of military invasions. As Helmut Dietrich points out: "The future border regime represents a socio-technological attack on the informal cross-border economy and on transit migration."[41]

Official documents and public discourse justify the fortification of European borders in view of combating illegal migration and the abuses of asylum requests. Nevertheless, the tightening of asylum and migration polices can also be seen to lead to a massive "illegalization" of movements.[42] In the case of asylum seekers, it has been underlined elsewhere that "persons who formerly sought protection would now regard illegal stay as the better option, avoiding any form of contact with authorities."[43] In the case of cross-border trade and transit migration, new visa requirements mean that movements of population which were formerly considered lawful have become illegal. In fact, until recently Central and Eastern European countries possessed relatively laissez-faire migration regimes. Even before the 1990s there was some form of mobility at least within national boundaries. In some of the countries of the former Soviet Union labour mobility, synonymous with social mobility, reached 15% of the active population.[44]

---

39 PHARE stands for *Pologne-Hongrie: Assistance à la reconstruction économique*. The project specification of the PHARE programmes for 2001 and 2002 also provides an insight into the modernization and extension of Polish eastern border.

40 Dietrich, above n. 17, p. 4.

41 *Id.*

42 Noll, above n. 28, p. 31.

43 *Id.*

44 Frank Laczko, Irene Stacher and Amanda Klekowski von Koppenfels (eds.), *New Challenges for Migration Policy in Central and Eastern Europe* (The Hague: T M C Asser Press 2002).

The process of "illegalization" of migration movements can be reconstructed by examining the changes that have occurred in domestic legislation of Central and Eastern European countries. Of particular significance are the conditions of detention and expulsion of aliens as these are the sanctions that legal systems typically reserve to illegal migrants. Under the *Polish Aliens Law* of 1997, for example, illegal entry *per se* was not formally sanctioned with expulsion. However art. 52 of this Act did put forward a general requirement stating that an alien who did not possess the requisites to entry and residence in Poland was liable to expulsion. The amendments introduced in the *Polish Aliens Law* in 2001 specified the procedures under which an alien might be obliged to leave (art. 51) or might be deported from the territory of the Republic of Poland (art. 52). Listing preconditions of the deportation orders, Art. 52 of the amended act also refers to the requirements of entry established in art. 13 which, in the new version, exclude the authorization of entrance to aliens who "crossed the border in defiance of the regulation" (art. 13(1) point 6). The *Act on Aliens* of 13th June 2003 substantially reiterates the same conditions of expulsion while introducing new cases of expulsion in view of Poland's future membership in the Schengen space and information system (art. 88(1) point 4 and point 5). However, the "Penal provisions" chapter of the new act states that whoever "resides on the territory of the Republic of Poland without the required authorization... shall be liable to a fine" (art. 148). The progressive "illegalization" of the movement of migrants is thus completed: an alien who resides in a territory without permit is not only subject to expulsion but also liable to a penal provision.

The progressive "illegalization" of previously lawful behaviours is made explicit in the Romanian legislation. Art. 79 of the *Emergency Ordinance on the regime of aliens in Romania* states that: "The competent authorities ... may take the measure of removal from the Romanian territory against the alien *whose stay in Romania has become illegal* or whose right to stay was revoked under the condition of this emergency ordinance, as well as against the alien *who has been decided to have entered illegally* the Romanian territory and, as the case may be, they can decide the interdiction of re-entering Romania for an established period of time" (emphasis added). In contrast with the cases of Poland and Romania, the *Law on Foreigners* amended in 2002 by the Bulgarian Parliament did not explicitly introduce major changes that would legally qualify in different terms the conduct of border "trespassers." The Bulgarian criminal code already included penal sanctions for illegal entry and stay. But, of course, the tightening of conditions for legal entry and stay widens the range of preconditions that qualify individual conduct as unlawful.

Both Romanian and Bulgarian legislation penalise the illegal crossing of borders with sanctions that include incarceration. In 2001, the Romanian government approved an *Emergency Ordinance on Romania's state border* according to which: "The entrance or exit of the country by illegal crossing of the state border is a criminal act and is punished with imprisonment from 3 months to 2 years" (art. 70(1) of the ordinance). Art. 279 of the Bulgarian criminal code provides for up to 5 years of imprisonment for persons who cross the borders without the required documentation. Paragraph 5 of the same article excludes punishment for those who enter the country to apply for asylum, although memoranda of nongovernmental human rights organizations have reported cases of asylum seekers being detained on the basis of the criminal code.[45] While this limitation of the rights of asylum seekers rightly raises humanitarian concerns, so the deprivation of migrants' personal liberty on the basis of simply crossing borders should be a cause for alarm. Such crimes are legislatively constructed. They do not offend pre-existing public or private goods, but changeable and, to a certain extent, imported concepts of "public order" and "security" which are the outcome of the "communitarization" of borders. As a result, there is little perception of such offences as anti-social by the "perpetrators" themselves.

Even when the formal sanction for migrants who enter or reside unlawfully in a national territory is a penal sanction, expulsion remains the ultimate punishment which characterizes their legal status. This form of punishment reserved to non-citizens may lead to consequences which are more severe than those established by penal provisions. As stated in Chapter 9 of the *Polish Act on Aliens*, expulsion may also be preceded by the "placement of an alien in the guarded centre or in arrest for the purpose of expulsion." According to the *Polish Aliens Law* of 25th June 1997 and its successive amendments, an alien could be detained for 48 hours prior to expulsion. The period could be extended to a maximum of 90 days under a court decision. The new *Act on Aliens*, besides reiterating such provisions, introduces a clause which states that: "the period of stay in the guarded centre or in the arrest for the purpose of expulsion may be prolonged for a specified period necessary to execute the decision of an expulsion, if that decision was not executed due to the aliens fault. The period of stay in the guarded centre or in arrest for the purpose of expulsion may not exceed one year" (art. 106(2)). This example illustrates how the same act of illegally entering or staying in Polish national territory leads, on the one hand, to a penal sanction of a fine (qualified as such under the "Penal provision" chapter), and on the other, to an administrative procedure that can end with the actual punishment of one year of detention. In other words, a serious limitation of individual freedom is based on an administrative, rather than criminal, procedure. Moreover, the phrase "due to the aliens fault" can be better understood by referring to other legislation which contains similar provisions. For example, according to the German law the detention period can be extended if the expulsion is not executed because the alien does not collaborate in providing the information or the documents necessary to her/his identification. Therefore, even if not formally defined as penal, such norms have a correctional function typical of the modern theory of punishment which also aims to direct individual behaviour.

---

45 International Helsinki Federation for Human Rights, *Annual Report*, 1999.

In the case of foreigners who do not fulfil the legal requirements for entry or stay in Romanian territory, the *Emergency Ordinance on the regime of aliens* distinguishes between the administrative measures taken for the "return of aliens" (art. 88–90) and for the "expulsion of aliens" (art. 91–92). Both measures may imply the physical deportation from the territory also against the alien's will. The difference between the two does not depend on the outcome, but on the fact that expulsion is reserved to the alien "who committed a crime on the Romanian territory" (art. 91(1)). The combined disposition of art. 92(2) and art. 15(1) excludes expulsion for aliens "charged or accused in a penal case [when] the prosecutor decides the implementation of the interdiction measure of leaving the town or the country" (art. 15(1a)) and for aliens "sentenced by a final court decision [when] they have to carry out a prison sentence" (art. 15(1b)). Although illegal entry is qualified as a criminal offence under Romanian law, the combination of the above norms does not result in "border trespassers" facing an ordinary criminal procedure unless they have already been sentenced or there is a prosecutor's order of interdiction to leave the territory. The ultimate punishment for illegal migrants remains expulsion rather than penal sanction, nevertheless the qualification of border crossing as a criminal act plays a powerful symbolic role in the criminalization of migrants.

Under the rubrics "Public Custody" and "Accommodation Centres" the Romanian legislation also provides for the administrative detention of foreigners. The measure regards aliens issued with either a return or an expulsion order. However, while the measure expires within 30 days in the case of aliens being returned (and can be extended for a maximum period of 6 months (art. 93(2)(6))), for aliens awaiting expulsion the law does not establish any temporal limitation. Besides leading to severe consequences for personal liberty, the qualification of the detention of aliens as an administrative measure of "public custody" allows *de facto* for the breach of general principles of criminal law which require the peremptory determination of penalties.

The Bulgarian *Law on Foreigners* provides for a wide range of compulsory administrative measures for aliens who do not fulfil the legal requirements of entry and stay: the "revoking the right of stay" (art. 39(1)); the "compulsory taking to the border" (art. 39(2)); the "expulsion" (art. 39(3)); the "prohibition to enter" (art. 39(4)) and the "prohibition to leave" (art. 39(5)) the country. While expulsion is imposed when the presence of the foreigner in the country "creates a serious threat for the national security or the public order" (art. 42(1)) and is always followed by a prohibition of entry for 10 years, in the case of an alien being compulsorily taken to the border there is no automatic prohibition of re-entering the country. As distinct from Polish and Romanian legislation, Bulgarian law does not include norms which provide for the administrative detention of aliens. Nevertheless, the preconditions listed for the application of the compulsory administrative measures overlap with conducts penalised by the criminal code. Aliens may thus be detained for illegal entry on penal grounds.[46] As a consequence the fate of "border trespassers" under Bulgarian law is ambiguous since in reality the outcome of their prosecution, as well as the entire penal procedure, may be overridden by the application of compulsory administrative measures.

These examples of the legal institution of expulsion and detention of foreigners bring into light the increasing intermingling between penal institutions and administrative procedures. This is a process which has characterized the evolution of migration laws of the member states and which is now influencing the changes to legislation of candidate countries. The fact that the Bulgarian law does not include the administrative detention of aliens is not the sign of a different political choice, but rather an indication of a lesser degree of "Europeanization" in domestic legislation. This is clearly apparent in the Commission's report on progress towards accession, which recommends Bulgaria construct adequate detention centres for illegal aliens in order to meet criteria necessary to enter the area of "security, freedom and justice."[47] Instead, the rising number of detained foreigners under the Polish law is judged by the Commission as a sign of its efficient implementation of Schengen standards,[48] while the PHARE programme for Romania provide considerable funds for the further construction of detention centres for migrants.[49]

In comparison with Romanian and Bulgarian legislation on immigration, Polish law is undoubtedly the one where the process of "Europeanization" has been the most far reaching. Administrative remedies prevail, while penal instruments mostly

---

[46] According to the International Helsinki Federation for Human Rights, it is standard practice in Bulgaria to detain asylum seekers and so called "bogus" asylum seekers in the transit zone of Sophia airport and in a centre in nearby Drujba. This practice often exceeds the maximum limit of 24 hours prescribed by the Ministry of Interior (International Helsinki Federation for Human Rights, *Annual Report 1999*).

[47] European Commission, *Regular Report on Bulgaria's progress towards accession*, 2003.

[48] European Commission, *Comprehensive monitoring report on Poland's preparation for membership*, 2003.

[49] PHARE 2001, *Strengthening the management of the migration phenomenon in Romania*, RO-0107.17. A recent plan presented by the British government considers the relocation of centres for the detention of aliens outside the territory of member states a strategy for the better management of protection seekers in order to avoid the risk of abuses of the legal framework of asylum. The project includes financial aid for the construction of Transit Processing Centres in the countries of origin of migrants and asylum seekers as well as in countries of transit. The intended function of such centres is to deter "those who enter EU illegally and make unfounded asylum applications". Furthermore, "it is for consideration whether the centre would also receive illegal migrants intercepted en route to the EU before they had lodged an asylum claim but where they had a clear intention of doing so" (New international approaches to asylum processing and protection, attachment to a letter from Tony Blair to Costas Simitis, 10th March 2003). Although the UK proposal has not been adopted by the European Union and has been contested by governments of other member states, it seems to be consistent with the tendency of pushing Europe's borders further east.

serve a symbolic role. In contrast, the Bulgarian legislation still maintains a strong penal character which is the legacy of the normative framework preceding the country's transition from communism. In all three countries, however, there is a clear tendency towards a progressive administrative treatment of the legal position of foreigners. This is to the detriment of the judicial control over the procedures carried out against them; a danger which is exacerbated by the limited jurisdiction of the Court of Justice at European level.

5. CITIZENS ACROSS EUROPEAN BORDERS

Borders not only have a physical dimension but also a temporal dimension which strongly affects the legal status of migrants. Their lives are marked by: the waiting period of obtaining the documents required to enter or reside in the host countries; the amount of time necessary to acquire a different legal status such as permanent residence; and the period of residence that national legislations impose to obtain naturalization.[50] More generally, migrants enjoy *pro tempore* rights conditioned by the persistence of their status as legal residents. The Algerian sociologist Abdelmaleck Sayad noticed that the legal systems of host countries always consider migrants in a transitory position which is intended to persist *indefinitely*.[51] This *indefinite* temporariness, which characterizes the structure of aliens' legal subjectivity, allows for the continual redefinition of the relation between citizens and foreigners. The physical and temporal boundaries of membership expand to include new categories of previous foreigners, while excluding others not only from the original polity, but also from the new extended boundaries which in the past they were allowed to cross.

The succeeding waves through which the enlargement process will take place highlight the diachronic dimension of the boundaries of European membership. Although exempt from visa requirements to enter the European Union, citizens of the candidate countries are currently subject to national legislations on immigration when hosted in present member states. Their right to reside and circulate in the area of "freedom, security and justice" is affected by measures analogous to those implemented by prospective member states to limit and regulate the accession of third country nationals, such as expulsion, administrative detention and work permits. The Commission's report on Romania's progress toward accession emphasises the

---

50 On the temporal dimension of borders see also Charles Westin, "Temporal and Spatial Dimension of Multiculturality. Reflections on the meaning of Time and Space in Relation to the Blurred Boundaries of Multicultural Societies", in Rainer Bauböck and John Rundell (eds.), *Blurred Boundaries: Migration, Ethnicity, Citizenship* (Aldershot: Ashgate 1998), pp. 53–84.

51 Abdelmaleck Sayad, *L'immigration ou les paradoxes de l'altérité* (Bruxelles: De Boeck Université 1992), p. 51. On the issue see also Federico Rahola, *Zone Definitivamente temporanee. I luoghi dell'umanità in eccesso* (Verona: Ombrecorte 2003).

considerable number of Romanian illegal migrants returned in 2003 from present member states and neighbouring first wave candidate countries.[52] These figures are considered a sign of Romania's success in implementing readmission agreements, as well as the efficacy of neighbouring countries in implementing Schengen standards of control. In addition, citizens of candidate states are affected by dispositions approved in their own countries which aim to prevent illegal migration to Europe. For example, according to an *Emergency Ordinance* approved in August 2001 by the Romanian government: "The entering or leaving a foreign state by the illegal passing of its borders, committed by a Romanian citizen or by a person without citizenship residing on the Romanian territory is considered as an offence and is punished with imprisonment from 3 months to 2 years."[53] Hence, a Romanian citizen (and also a future European citizen) who illegally crosses the border of the European Union or of a neighbouring country such as Hungary is liable, if caught, to be expelled from the host country, returned home and then prosecuted and punished as a "border trespasser."

Even after accession, citizens of the new member states will not immediately benefit from the Schengen lifting of national borders because workers will not be able to freely circulate during a transitional period which will last from two to seven years. During this time migration movements for employment purposes will be regulated according to communitarian and national policies, even though different conditions may be agreed on the basis of bilateral relations between singular member sates and candidate countries.[54] Although the greater possibility of mobility is regarded as one of the benefits of enlargement in the eyes of the populations of Central and Eastern European Countries,[55] accession to European citizenship will be restricted precisely with regard to those rights which characterised its most

---

52 European Commission, *Regular Report on Romania's progress towards accession*, 2003.

53 Art. 1(1), *Emergency Ordinance No. 112 referring to the punishment of some action committed abroad by Romanian citizens or by person without citizenship residing in Romania*, 30th August 2001.

54 European Commission, *Information note on the free movement of workers in the context of enlargement*, 6 March 2001. The entrance of workers will be subject to the "conditionality" principle which reserves quotas of legal entry to those nationals whose countries collaborate in combating illegal migration. The principle of "conditionality", which requires candidate states to meet the Copenhagen criteria for admittance to the European Union, has been widely considered in the debate about enlargement, unlike the "conditionality" principle of migration policies which does not officially relate to the enlargement process. Nevertheless, the accession of new EU citizens to present member states will also be regulated for a long period by this second principle. Accession of candidate states does not mean the automatic accession to a full European membership for their citizens. In other words, the same border produces different sets of relations for prospective member states on the one hand and for their populations on the other.

55 European Commission, *European citizens and freedom, security and justice, a qualitative survey of citizens of the 15 Member States and of the 13 applicant countries*, March 2003.

significant content: the freedom of movement and settlement in other member states. Nevertheless, visa exemption for citizens of candidate countries facilitate their accession to the informal labour market and assure them a privileged position in comparison to migrant workers of different origin. This phenomenon has already been analysed among migrants workers employed in agriculture in Southern Spain where Polish workers are a step ahead of their competitors coming from African countries.[56] Moreover, a *de facto* flexible application of measures such as expulsion and detention against nationals of countries candidate in the first wave of enlargement guarantees them advantages also in comparison to nationals of other candidate countries such as Romania.

The relocation of the European Community's eastern borders implies the fortification of boundaries that in the past were easily crossed by the inhabitants of Central and Eastern European countries and which, in some cases, did not even exist. The history of the region has been characterized by the re-drawing of national boundaries; the modifications which occurred after the collapse of the communist bloc being only the most recent case. As a consequence, many candidate states face the problem of ethnic nationals living in neighbouring countries. The case of Hungary is the most problematic as there are Hungarian minorities living in Slovakia, Romania, Ukraine and the former Yugoslavia. Although to a lesser degree, other candidate countries are affected by similar situations such as the Polish minority living in the Ukraine and Romanians living in Moldova. As has been underlined by the Romanian scholar Alina Mungiu-Pippidi, the sealing off of the borders of prospective member states "would sever minorities' connection with countries where the bulk of their culture lies, prompting illegal entrance and feeding resentment."[57] This has induced candidate countries to pass laws which entitle ethnic nationals who are citizens of other countries to a particular status of semi-citizenship. The best known case is the so-called *Status Law* which entitles Hungarian nationals to limited work-permits and other benefits. Following the example of Hungary, other countries approved legislations which give ethnic nationals comparable rights or decrease conditions and periods necessary to acquire citizenship, such as the Polish *Repatriation Act* of 9th November 2002, and the amendments introduced in 2002 in the Bulgarian law on citizenship. Such legislative acts have been criticised for basing the entitlement to rights on ethnic grounds and have thus been considered as nationalistic measures in breach of the universalistic principle which should ideally characterize European membership.[58] More simply they can be seen as a

---

56 Nicholas Bell, "The exploitation of migrants in Europe", contribution to the conference "Borders and Migration", Austrian League for Human Rights, Vienna, 29–30 October 2002.

57 Alina Mungiu-Pippidi, 'Europe's "Desert of Tartars, Challenge: The Borders of the Enlarged European Union," ' *Working Paper RSC* No. 2001/43, European University Institute 2001, p. 7.

58 For an extensive analysis of the Hungarian *Status Law* and of debates on similar acts under discussion in other countries, see Brigid Fowler, 'Fuzzing citizenship, nationalising political

partial solution to the problem of the mobility of ethnic nationals once these find themselves on the other side of the fortified borders of an enlarged Europe.

Focusing on the temporal dimension of borders illustrates how membership in an enlarged Europe is developing as a plurality of diachronically differentiated legal positions. Following accession, citizens of the new member states will enjoy a status of semi-membership in contrast to the one granted to the citizens of actual member states as their right of circulation and settlement for employment purposes will be limited. The same conditions will apply to the countries in the succeeding waves of enlargement reproducing a sort of waiting-room for future citizens. Nevertheless, citizens of prospective member states already enjoy a privileged status compared to non-Europeans. At the same time, new visa requirements applied by candidate countries in order to meet Schengen standards extends the restricted area for migrants arriving from third countries. This disparity will, to a certain extent, be mitigated for ethnic nationals of candidate countries living in third countries, as they will enjoy limited membership rights in new member states and second phase candidate countries. Each restriction to the freedom of movement and settlement of imminent and future citizens is also a limitation to their social mobility. Therefore, each differentiated status corresponds to a position in a hierarchical order of relations.

6. CONCLUSION

The context of enlargement is a useful framework in which to analyse the system of differentiated membership which result from the transformation and repositioning of European borders. From the point of view of membership, borders are first and foremost "biographical" borders encountered by migrants long before their arrival in the proximity of EU territory. As Elspeth Guild has underlined: "One important physical manifestation of borders results from attempts by individuals to move. The individual, through interaction with state and other actors over the granting or withholding of rights, activates the "border" and engages with the government regarding the position of the border."[59]

The role that political and territorial boundaries serve in producing relations of *difference* over foreigners, commences "outside" and continues "inside" in the form of diverse legal status ascribed to individuals. Clear lines of continuity can be traced between the externalization of border control through visa policies or readmission agreements and the internalization of borders resulting from the institutions of expulsion or the administrative detention of aliens. Legal borders have exactly the function of constructing boundaries of *difference* surrounding individuals. It is this

space: A framework for interpreting the Hungarian "status law" as a new form of kin-state policy in Central and Eastern Europe', Working Paper 40/02 published by the ESRC "One Europe or Several?" Programme, Sussex European Institute 2002.

[59] Elspeth Guild, "Moving the Borders of Europe", inaugural, lecture held at University of Nijmegen, 30th May 2001, quoted in Bigo and Guild, above n. 36, p. 4.

difference that matters, rather than the actual physical departure of foreigners from the territory, as it allows the implementation of "governmental" policies of border management directly over individuals.

At the same time, the enforcement of policies and orders over a territory no longer applies to the state but to a network of different actors and bureaucracies. Foreigners' positions are not ruled by law but are "administrated" in the name of a functionalistic principle of securitization. From the viewpoint of political and legal theory this process reflects a cleavage in the unity between law and sovereignty which has characterized the depiction of the modern state.In his essay on governmentality, Michel Foucault pointed out that law and sovereignty were absolutely inseparable: "On the contrary, with government it is a question not of imposing law on men, but of disposing things: that is to say, of employing tactics rather than laws, and even of using laws themselves as tactics—to arrange thing in such a way that, though certain number of means, such and such end may be achieved."[60] From the position of the individual, the cleavage between law and sovereignty corresponds to a fragmentation of its legal subjectivity.

Traditional representations of citizenship, even when based on contending grounds for membership, have been characterized by equality among citizens. Difference resids outside borders, whether they are the nation's or the community's boundaries, or those extended over an ideal *cosmopolis*. In contrast, as underlined by Étienne Balibar, the positioning and functioning of borders no longer regard the margin of Europe but its inner method of government.[61] Borders are dragged into the core of Europe because they follow the biographies of the individuals whose mobility is limited. Paradoxically the fact that the exclusive and discriminatory character of the "European fortress" not only lies at its perimeter but extends within and beyond the territorial delimitation of the EU also allows for a wider definition of its potential inclusiveness. This, however, does not derive from an abstract model of "post-national" membership, but from the fact that the fortified borders of Europe are violated and contested on a daily basis by people in movement. A consideration of these non-institutional aspects of membership and the everyday "practice of citizenship" demonstrates how the limits of inclusion coincide with those of exclusion and subsequently calls into question any rigid distinction between citizens and foreigners. The enlargement process challenges the theory and practice of defining European membership exactly because it brings into light how the deterritorialization and relocalization of the EU polity's borders leads to a fragmentation of the legal subjectivity of the *citizen*. In other words, any eastern border of Europe is a border drawn within Europe itself.

60 Foucault, above n. 5, p. 95.

61 Étienne Balibar, "L'Europa, una frontiera "impensata" della democrazia?", in Giuseppe Bronzini, Heidrun Friese, Antonio Negri and Peter Wagner (eds.), *Europa, Costituzione e movimenti sociali* (Roma: Manifestolibri 2003), pp. 231–244.

5. Sub-National Governance in Central and Eastern Europe: Between Transition and Europeanization

Gwendolyn Sasse, James Hughes & Claire Gordon

1. Introduction

The accession of eight Central and East European countries (CEECs) in May 2004 marked the beginning of a more direct and equal interaction between the political, economic and legal orders of the old and new Member States within the framework of EU policy-making.[1] It also shifted the emphasis to the implementation and sustainability of the institutions, rules and norms adopted over the last decade. Thus, the post-enlargement context added a new impetus to the discussion about the successful transition and consolidation of states, democracy and market economies in CEE. While the post-enlargement dynamics have to remain speculation at this stage, there is a clear need for empirical research into the impact of the EU on the candidate states so far. Such research will be the basis for a better understanding of the relationship between the processes of transition and enlargement. By analyzing the EU's role in shaping sub-national governance in CEE, this chapter aims to make a step in this direction. The locale, the sub-national arena of regional and local politics is of key importance for the interrelated processes of post-communist transition and EU eastward enlargement. For political and economic changes to become consolidated, they have to become ingrained at all levels of governance. Likewise, EU enlargement and integration reach beyond national elites and institutions. They affect—and are affected by—sub-national actors and institutions.

Four conditions frame the analysis of the trends of regionalization presented in this chapter. First, EU regional policy comprises one of the biggest incentive structures for the accession countries. The CEECs stand to benefit substantially from the EU's structural funds and regional and cohesion policy. The enlargement to the CEECs in 2004 have brought a sharp increase in budgetary subventions from the EU. The financial package agreed at the Copenhagen Council in December 2003 committed €40.8 billion to the ten new members in 2004–2006, over half of which amount (€21.7 billion) is to be spent on "structural actions."[2] The new

---

1 This paper is based on research conducted within the framework of the ESRC project, "Elites and Regional and Local Governance in Eastern Europe" (Award no. L213252030; ESRC Programme "One Europe or Several?").

2 See Annex I of the Presidency Conclusions, Copenhagen European Council, 12–13 December 2002.

Wojciech Sadurski et al. (ed.), Spreading Democracy and the Rule of Law?, 121–147.

member states are also expected to be the main beneficiaries of regional funds in the next budgetary cycle 2007–2013. This incentive structure, underpinned by the power asymmetry characterizing the relationship between the EU and the CEECs, left a considerable scope for EU conditions, rules and norms to shape institution-building, perceptions and practices in the transition countries. One could therefore expect a significant and detectable impact of the EU on sub-national governance in CEE as well as a degree of convergence in the institutional outcomes across the CEECs.

Secondly, despite the prominent role of regional policy within the EU, the institutional environment at this level of governance is flexibly arranged. Regional governance is a sovereignty issue of the member states, and the EU's emphasis in regional policy is on process and outcome rather than on particular institutional models. Accordingly, the *acquis* is very "thin" on regional policy. The divergent models inside the EU and the absence of clear legal requisites counterbalances the latitude for EU influence in the candidate countries. We can hypothesize that the impact of the EU has been constrained by the lack of institutional detail tied to conditionality in this policy domain.

Thirdly, the apparent thinness of the *acquis* in the field of regional policy contrasts with the centrality of this domain in EU policy-making and its budgetary implications. The lack of a complex set of explicit and codified institutional rules in the *acquis* and even the Structural Funds Regulations suggests a wider scope for implicit or "soft" conditions as well as individually tailored guidelines and pressure during the enlargement process. This setting increases the likelihood of inconsistency in the message communicated by Commission officials over time, resulting in weak institutional outcomes in the CEECs.

Fourthly, the pre-accession negotiations have exhibited a "regional deficit" in that they have been confined to the Commission on the EU side and national elites from the executive structures in CEE. The lack of involvement of sub-national actors in the preparation for EU regional policy suggests a cross-national preference for minimalist and formal rule adoption, including a bias against politically empowered regions. Moreover, one could expect disengaged sub-national elites to be more Eurosceptic than the acculturated "Europeanized" national elites.

2. EUROPEANIZATION AND CONDITIONALITY DURING ENLARGEMENT

"Europeanization" describes the diffusion of common political rules, norms and practices in Europe, but there are significant differences of opinion as to the substantive content of the concept and whether it has meaningful effects within national political systems.[3] Defined broadly, it denotes "ways of doing things" which are

[3] See Kevin Featherstone, "Introduction: In the name of Europe", in Claudio Radaelli and Kevin Featherstone (eds.), *The Politics of Europeanization: Theory and Analysis* (Oxford: Oxford University Press 2003), pp. 3–26; Tanja Börzel and Thomas Risse, "When Europe hits

first defined and consolidated in the making of EU decisions and then incorporated into "the logic of domestic discourse, identities, political structures and public policies".[4] Europeanization is thus understood as a top-down process of "institutional adaptation and the adaptation of policy and policy processes",[5] including "the penetration of national and sub-national systems of governance by a European political centre and European-wide norms".[6] Studies of "Europeanization" generally tend to emphasize one or more of three key dimensions: the source of "Europeanization" (although there is a lack of precision with regard to particular EU institutions), its impact on advancing the convergence of institutions and policies, and its role in the norm diffusion which forms the basis of a "European" identity.[7] Macro-analyses of political structures tend to detect lower levels of "Europeanization" and convergence than policy-level studies.[8] For some the variation simply reflects the fact that the process is "incremental, irregular, uneven over time and between locations, national and sub-national."[9] For others the "domestic impact of Europe varies with the level of European adaptation pressure on domestic institutions and the extent to which the domestic context (. . .) facilitates or prohibits actual adjustments."[10] The apparent weaknesses of "Europeanization" as a concept and an analytical tool are best summed up by Goetz's description of "a cause in search of an effect."[11]

Despite these weaknesses, the context of EU enlargement provides a novel testing ground for the notion of "Europeanization", given that the EU has a potentially strong instrument at its disposal—conditionality—through which to impose "European" rules and norms on the candidate countries. There are several reasons

---

home: Europeanization and domestic change", *European Integration online Paper (EioP)*, 4, 15 (2000), p. 2; Claudio Radaelli, "Whither Europeanization: Concept stretching and substantive change", *European Integration online Papers (EioP)*, 4, 8 (2000); Beate Kohler-Koch, "The evolution and transformation of European governance", in Beate Kohler-Koch and Rainer Eising (eds.), *The Transformation of Governance in the European Union* (London: Routledge 1999), pp. 14–35.

4 Radaelli, above n. 3, p. 3.

5 Featherstone, above n. 3, p. 5.

6 Johan P. Olsen, "The Many Faces of Europeanization", *ARENA Working Papers*, 2 (2002), p. 3.

7 Börzel and Risse, above n. 3, pp. 1–3; 268–270; Christoph Knill and Dirk Lehmkuhl, "How Europe Matters. Different Mechanisms of Europeanization", *European Integration online Papers (EioP)*, 3, 7 (2000); Claudio Radaelli, "How does Europeanization produce Policy Change? Corporate Tax Policy in Italy and the United Kingdom", *Comparative Political Studies*, 30, 5 (1997), pp. 553–575.

8 Olsen, above n. 6, p. 14; Radaelli, above n. 3, p. 19.

9 Featherstone, above n. 3, p. 4.

10 Knill and Lehmkuhl, above n. 7, pp. 1–2.

11 Klaus H. Goetz, "European Integration and National Executives: A Cause in Search of an Effect?", in Simon Hix and Klaus H. Goetz (eds.), *Europeanised Politics? European Integration and National Political Systems* (London: Frank Cass 2001), pp. 211–231.

why conditionality should be expected to operate as a strong force for "Europeanization" during the EU's eastward enlargement. The lack of alternative ideological or systemic paradigms for the CEECs, their institutional debilitation arising from the exit from communism and their preoccupation with political and economic transition, has made the elites in the CEECs structurally weak protagonists in the accession negotiations. Moreover, the adjustments to be made by the CEEC concern many 'new' policy areas for which there was no equivalent under the old regime. In the case of the transition 'laggards', where domestic political and economic decisions had not yet created lock-in effects, this scope for EU influence was potentially even higher. Additionally, the EU structured parts of the accession process like a race, particularly through the introduction of the "queuing system" for accession in 1997. The incentive for CEEC elites was to engage in a competitive emulation of 'Europeanness' and to cooperate with the Commission on a strictly bilateral basis. The compliance and commitment of the CEECs was regularly monitored by the Commission in the Opinions of 1997 and the subsequent annual Regular Reports, which maintained the momentum for adaptation and cross-country comparison.

The Copenhagen criteria of 1993 are the standard point of reference for studies about EU conditionality. Scholars of EU enlargement have matched macro-level national developments with the fulfilment of the broad normative goals outlined in the Copenhagen criteria.[12] More recent studies have acknowledged that the broader elements of the Copenhagen criteria are, in fact, largely politically determined by the EU.[13] The 'Europeanizing' effect of EU conditionality for eastward enlargement to the CEECs has so far been generally assumed rather than empirically investigated.[14] In principle, conditionality should be based on a catalogue of succinct criteria as well as clear benchmarks, enforcement and reward mechanisms to ensure credibility and consistency in its application over time. The Copenhagen criteria, however, do not define the benchmarks or the process by which EU conditionality could be enforced and verified. Furthermore, the 80,000 pages of the *acquis* are not uniformly conditional across policy areas. Some areas of the acquis are 'thicker' on regulatory content than others.

---

12 Karen Smith, 'The use of political conditionality in the EU's relations with third countries: how effective?', *EUI Working Paper*, 7 (1997); Heather Grabbe and Kirsty Hughes, 'Redefining the European Union: Eastward Enlargement', *RIIA Briefing Paper*, 36 (London: Royal Institute for International Affairs 1997).

13 Heather Grabbe, 'How does Europeanization affect CEE governance? Conditionality, diffusion and diversity', *Journal of European Public Policy*, 8, 6 (2001), pp. 1013–1031; Heather Grabbe, 'European Union Conditionality and the *Acquis Communautaire*', *International Political Science Review*, 23, 3 (2002), pp. 249–268.

14 For the first coverage of a range of policy studies within one conceptual framework, see the papers presented by Frank Schimmelfennig, Ulrich Sedelmeier *et al.* at the Workshop 'The Europeanization of Eastern Europe: Evaluating the Conditionality Model', EUI Florence, 4–5 July 2003.

This chapter explores the institutional and attitudinal dimensions of 'Europeanization' by means of a comparative case study of Hungary and Poland. Through process-tracking it first examines how EU conditionality has operated in practice and whether we can attribute to it any 'Europeanizing' effects in institution-building and convergence with regard to sub-national governance. Hungary and Poland have been selected because they have been among the most important candidates for EU membership from several viewpoints. They are two of the most powerful economies of the CEECs, they are generally regarded as having successful transition records, they were the priority focus of the EU's technical transition assistance programmes delivered by PHARE, and they were the among the most important core group of the CEECs during the enlargement process. They share certain additional key features that could influence regional reform. On the one hand, they both have a tradition of regional identities, while exhibiting a low salience of politically significant ethno-territorial cleavages that might have deterred regional reform. On the other hand, they have both experienced repeated changes of government across the left and right of the political spectrum during the 1990s, making institutional reform an issue of party politics and delaying its completion. Despite these commonalities, their institutional adaptation in the field of regional policy has been very different and illustrates the two trends of regionalization in CEE: administrative-statistical regionalization (Hungary) vs. democratized regionalization (Poland). Based on large-scale local elite interviews in Pécs (Hungary) and Katowice (Poland), the second part of this chapter tries to gauge the extent to which sub-national elite values and attitudes have become 'Europeanized' during the enlargement process. The research presented here demonstrates that EU conditionality not only escapes a narrowly positivist framework of analysis, but also that it is better understood in procedural rather than strictly causal terms. It involves formal and informal pressures arising from the behaviour and perceptions of the actors engaged in the political process of enlargement. It also puts the interaction between international incentives and pressures and the domestic political context of transition states at the heart of our understanding of EU enlargement as a whole.

3. Regional Administrative Capacity in a Legal Vacuum

While parts of the Commission seem to have been influenced by the ideal of "multi-level governance" and the desirability of "participation" at the regional level in the shaping of regional policy in the CEECs,[15] the accession negotiations have been confined to the Commission on the EU side and national elites from the core executive structures in the CEECs. Moreover, the Commission lacked a coherent institutional model of sub-national governance to draw on and project into CEE.

---

[15] See James Hughes, Gwendolyn Sasse and Claire Gordon, 'Conditionality and Compliance in the EU's Eastward Enlargement: Regional Policy and the Reform of Sub-national Governance', *Journal of Common Market Studies*, 42 (2004) 523.

Regional policy is overwhelmingly a competence of the Member States, and its institutional environment varies widely along a spectrum from unitary-centralized to federalized-decentralized states. Reflecting the Commission's limited remit in this policy area, chapter 21 of the *acquis* is concerned with procedural rather than institutional form. It requires Member States to have an "appropriate legal framework", an approved "territorial organization" based on NUTS classifications, "programming capacity" (including a development plan, procedures for multi-annual programming, the partnership principle which envisages the involvement of regional administrative, social and economic actors in the management of structural funds and ex-ante evaluation of the development plan), "administrative capacity" (defined as the clear definition of the tasks and responsibilities of all bodies and institutions involved in the preparation and implementation of Structural Funds and the Cohesion Fund and effective inter-ministerial cooperation) and sound "financial and budgetary management" (including control provisions and information on co-financing capacity and the level of public or equivalent expenditure for structural action).

The loosely defined legal and institutional provisions of chapter 21 are derived from the Framework Regulation (Council Regulation (EC) 1260/1999) on the Structural Funds, which in itself does not require transposition into national legislation. Chapter 21 has proved to be one of the most problematic areas during the negotiation process.[16] The structural thinness of the *acquis* in regional policy makes for an apparent conditionality gap during enlargement, which is only partly filled by the EU's Structural Funds regulations. The Regular Reports of 2001–2002 and the Comprehensive Monitoring Reports of 2003 made the most explicit use of the Structural Funds criteria for measuring progress, while putting the emphasis on the adoption and amendment of laws, regulations and regional development programmes as well as the establishment and reorganization of ministries and co-ordinating units.

While the adoption of the *acquis* was a fundamental condition tied to the Copenhagen criteria, the Madrid European Council (1995) introduced a supposedly clarifying condition to the effect that the candidate countries must have the "administrative capacity" to implement the *acquis*.[17] The terminology was restated in the Commission's report "Agenda 2000—For a Stronger and Wider Europe", the Commission's 'Opinions' on the candidate countries' readiness to join in July 1997. The Commission linked the call for "administrative capacity" to specific areas of the *acquis*, for example sectoral capacity, effective structures for coordinating the negotiation process, administrative and judicial reforms, and the preparation for

---

16 Among the CEECs the Czech Republic provisionally closed chapter 21 in April 2002; Estonia, Latvia and Lithuania followed in June 2002, Hungary, Slovakia and Slovenia in July 2002 and Poland in October 2002. Bulgaria and Romania have not yet closed chapter 21.

17 See Presidency Conclusions, Madrid European Council, 15–16 December 1995.

the implementation of structural policies.[18] The Commission adopted the baseline criteria for administrative reform developed by the SIGMA group of the OECD. These criteria focus on administrative reform generally, such as the establishment of an independent and professional civil service and judicial system, and do not contain detailed recommendations for the reform of sub-national governance.

Regional administrative capacity forms a fundamental part of the horizontal and vertical configuration of a country's administrative space. The Commission has tried to build administrative capacity in the candidate countries for the implementation of regional policy with the help of a number of pre-accession instruments (PHARE, Sapard and ISPA), specifically targeted projects and "Twinning".[19] The Regular Reports have routinely emphasized weak administrative capacity in relation to chapter 21, in particular at the sub-national level and in terms of the coordination between national and sub-national-level bodies. Even the Comprehensive Monitoring Reports of 2003 still point to the shortcomings in this area. Thus, the temporal correlation between the Commission's interventions and institutional reform is less clear-cut with regard to regional administrative capacity than in the area of national-level administrative reforms.[20] Moreover, as we will discuss below, the CEECs diverged significantly in their responses to the weakly defined call for "regional administrative capacity".

4. Reforming Sub-National Governance: The Impact of Transition and Enlargement

The reform of centre-regional-local relations in the CEECs has taken place in the double context of transition and EU enlargement. In many CEECs the reform of sub-national governance was an integral part of the post-communist transition and predated the beginning of the EU accession process. In formulating reform proposals domestic policy-makers have looked to their historical legacies, to the

---

18 Antoaneta L. Dimitrova, 'Enlargement, Institution-Building and the EU's Administrative Capacity Requirement', *West European Politics*, 25, 4 (2002), pp. 171–190.

19 Since the reorientation of PHARE in 1997 about 30% of the PHARE budget has been allocated to 'institution-building', defined widely as 'adapting and strengthening democratic institutions, public administration and organizations that have a responsibility in implementing and enforcing Community legislation'. 'Twinning' was extended to the regional level in the 2000 programming round.

20 The national public administrative space in CEE appears to converge more than within the EU itself. Moreover, the timing and nature of the civil service legislation passed in the CEECs after 1997 is clearly correlated with the Commission's increased emphasis on administrative reforms. See Attila Agh, 'The Reform of State Administration in Hungary: The Capacity of Core Ministries to Manage Europeanisation', Budapest Papers on Europeanisation, 7 (Budapest: Hungarian Centre for Democracy Studies Foundation 2002); Dimitrova, above n. 18.

transferability of governance models in Western Europe and beyond, as well as the incentives and pressures emanating from the Commission. Historical legacies have shaped, though not determined the perceptions and ideas about sub-national governance. The CEECs that were formerly part of the Austro-Hungarian Empire could draw on the experience of a system of self-government and autonomy dating from the mid-nineteenth century and enduring in some cases until the 1930s. The communist era, in turn, left a strong impression of disempowered local governments and a regional tier that served as a transmission belt for party control and patronage networks. While the former strengthened the rationale for local government reform after 1989, the latter fed into a widespread bias against regional governance. Nevertheless, communist era planning regions tended to provide a functional template for the NUTS classification required for EU regional policy.[21] Size has been an additional factor shaping the debate about sub-national governance. While ideas about regionalization found a natural sounding board in the larger candidate states, small countries like Slovenia and the Baltic states had little experience and functional need for regional governance, thereby adding to the challenge of addressing the EU's call for "regional administrative capacity". The regionalization processes in Hungary and Poland illustrate the two ends of the spectrum of institutional change in the CEECs. In both cases, however, the domestic political debate about sub-national governance formed part of the endogenous transition process. The EU accession process partly reframed this debate by adding new incentives and pressures. Hungary and Poland are instructive cases to evaluate the relative importance of the EU's impact compared to domestic political conditions and considerations.

4.1. Hungary: Administrative-Statistical Regionalization

In 1990 Hungary became the first post-communist country to introduce local self-government.[22] Reform plans had been discussed among academics and reformist members of the Hungarian Communist Party since the mid-1980s.[23] The drafters of the reforms looked to models of self-government in Western Europe, but also drew

---

21 The Regional Research Centre at the Hungarian Academy of Sciences, which was responsible for drafting Hungary's National Regional Development Concept, recommended the establishment of six regions corresponding to the six economic planning regions of 1971. See Brigid Fowler, 'Debating Sub-state Reform on Hungary's "Road to Europe"', *ESRC "One Europe or Several?" Working Papers*, 21 (2001), p. 32; Gyula Horváth, "Transition and Regionalism in East Central Europe", *Occasional Paper*, 7 (Tübingen: Europäisches Zentrum für Föderalismusforschung 1996), p. 28.

22 Kenneth Davey, "Local Government in Hungary", in Andrew Coulson (ed.), *Local Government in Eastern Europe* (Cheltenham: Edward Edgar 1995), p. 74.

23 József Hegedüs, "Hungarian Local Government", in Emil Kirchner (ed.), *Decentralization and Transition in the Visegrad Countries: Poland, Hungary, the Czech Republic and Slovakia*, (Macmillan, Basingstoke 1999), p. 133.

on Hungary's historical tradition of *megyek* (county) level governance.[24] There was little dispute over the necessity for decentralization to the local level as a fundamental part of systemic change. Almost any village or rural settlement was allowed to establish its own self-governing institutions which were granted a wide range of functions. This incentive structure led to a mushrooming of small governing units (to some 3,200 units) which often lacked the experience and financial basis to fulfil basic governing tasks.

The Hungarian Democratic Forum coalition government (1990–1994) held only 54% of the seats in parliament and was compelled to compromise with the opposition (Alliance of Free Democrats and Fidesz) over sub-national governance in order to secure the required two-thirds majority of the parliament for the passage of the new local self-government legislation. The essence of the compromise of 1990 was that county level governments would be indirectly elected by lower level local councils, thereby weakening their authority vis-à-vis the directly elected local governments. The local and county governments were supposed to co-exist in a non-hierarchical relationship. A novelty was the creation of eight regions, each of which was made up of two to three counties and overseen by a centrally appointed "Commissioner of the Republic."[25] These officials were appointed directly by the prime minister, and their main responsibility was to supervise the legality of the work of local governments.[26] This new structure, resulting from a political compromise, fell short of an effective system of checks and balances.

Hungary was awarded PHARE money as early as 1992 to assist in the country's regional development. The institutional framework enabling the government to decentralize the formulation and implementation of regional policy formed an integral part of this assistance.[27] The first post-communist resolution on regional development, passed by the Hungarian parliament in 1993, expressed a preference for "Europeanization" by recommending that the relevant institutions should correspond to

---

24 Hellmut Wollmann and Tomila Lankina, "Local Government in Poland and Hungary: From post-communist reform towards EU accession", in Harald Baldersheim, Michael Illner and Hellmut Wollmann (eds.), *Local Democracy in Post-Communist Europe* (Opladen, Leske & Budrich 2003), p. 94.

25 Tibor Navracsics, "Public Sector Reform in Hungary: Changes in Intergovernmental Relations (1990–1995)", in Attila Agh and Gabriella Ilonszki (eds.), *Parliaments and Organized Interests: The Second Steps* (Budapest, Hungarian Centre for Democracy Studies 1996), p. 305.

26 See Gábor Bende-Szabó, "The Intermediate Administrative Level in Hungary", in Eric Breska and Martin Brusis (eds.), *Central and Eastern Europe on the way to the European Union: Reforms of Regional Administration in Bulgaria, the Czech Republic, Estonia, Hungary, Poland and Slovakia* (Munich: Centre for Applied Policy 1999), pp. 23–41.

27 Peter Heil, *PHARE in Hungary: The Anatomy of a Pre-accession Aid Programme, 1990–1999*, unpublished PhD thesis (Budapest, CEU 2000), p. 43.

EU systems and practice.[28] The institutional design at the regional level, however, remained controversial in Hungary's transition politics. It was shaped by diverging and shifting interests. At the outset, the Hungarian Democratic Forum, the Hungarian Christian Democratic Party and the Smallholders' Party supported the revival of strong county government combining both self-government and state supervision offices. This was opposed by the Alliance of Free Democrats, the Hungarian Socialist Party and Fidesz which feared the continued control through state administrative offices as well as the domination of the counties over the localities.[29] In their 1994 election manifestos the Hungarian Socialist Party, the Alliance of Free Democrats and the Hungarian Democratic Forum had all voiced their support for the establishment of regional development bodies, but the views diverged regarding their composition and functions as well as the place of the counties within this structure. The Alliance of Free Democrats and Fidesz supported the maintenance of the county level governments as a forum of association for the local self-governments.[30] According to these proposals, the county councils were to continue to be made up of elected representatives from the municipal level without gaining any significant independent status.

The mushrooming of local governments resulted in confusion, authority leakage and inefficiency. The reluctance of these units to cooperate or merge paved the way for renewed centralization. Some 40 state administrative departments were deconcentrated to the sub-national level including key areas such as policing, taxation, education and public health.[31] As these central government organs at the local level proliferated, they created inroads for cronyism and corruption. The political cycles of transition exacerbated these tensions, namely through a polarization between the centre-right Hungarian Democratic Forum coalition government and the county and local governments many of which were dominated by members of the opposition parties Fidesz and the Alliance of Free Democrats.

Following the accession to power of the Hungarian Socialist Party in coalition with the Alliance of Free Democrats with a 72% parliamentary majority after the elections of 1994, a new reform attempt was launched. The institution of the Commissioners of the Republic and the newly created regions were abolished, and self-government at the county level was strengthened. The county councils were to be directly elected, and they were given key responsibilities for public services. In place of the Commissioners but with similar responsibilities, a new system of Public Administrative Offices (PAOs) was established at the county level. The basic

---

28 Gyula Horváth, "Regional and Cohesion Policy in Hungary", *Discussion Paper*, 23, (Pécs: Centre for Regional Studies of the Hungarian Academy of Sciences 1998), p. 20.

29 Fowler, above n. 21, pp. 11–14.

30 Ibid, at 24; Bende-Szabó, above n. 26, p. 16; Navracsics, above n. 25, pp. 289–293.

31 Bende-Szabó, above n. 26, pp. 6–7; Ilona Palne Kovács, "Regional Development and Governance in Hungary", *Discussion Paper*, 35 (Pécs: Centre for Regional Studies 2001), pp. 13–15.

structure of two tiers of non-hierarchical sub-national organs, has been maintained notwithstanding amendments in 1996 and 1999.

The political and institutional struggle over the fundamental structure of Hungary's sub-national governance arrangements had been largely settled by the time the process of EU accession intensified. Nevertheless, the question of how to best tap into future Structural Funds, together with pressures from PHARE, fuelled an ongoing debate among Hungary's political elites over the benefits of establishing a regional tier of administration. The influence of the EU on Hungary's regional policy was most pervasive through PHARE regional development programmes. PHARE was instrumental in the preparation of Hungary's administrative-statistical regionalization through the 1996 Act on Regional Policy and Physical Planning. This act provided for the voluntary establishment of so-called "development regions" and divided the country into statistical planning regions in compliance with the EU's NUTS II units and in consultation with Eurostat. Both "development" and "statistical" regions were to be based on groups of counties, although the economic logic for particular configurations was not always clear. Regional Development Councils (RDCs) were set up, composed of representatives of county councils, local government associations, social and civic organizations and officials from the Ministry of Environment and Regional Policy.

The establishment of RDCs remained voluntary under the 1996 legislation, and no agreement could be reached among the main political parties on the exact territorial division and allocation of powers. The governing coalition was itself split over the issue. Within the Hungarian Socialist Party there was support for large regions, whereas many deputies of the Alliance of Free Democrats favoured bottom-up regionalization based on groups of counties or local units.[32] The different preferences had informed the decision to establish two different types of regions—statistical planning regions corresponding to NUTS II units and "development regions" representing a proto-regional administrative structure. The Commission lauded Hungary's approach in its 1997 Opinion, placing it ahead of the co-applicants for EU membership: "Hungary is the first among Central European countries which adopted a legal framework closely in line with EU structural policy. Many sections of the new law have been drafted in perspective of taking over the acquis".[33]

In view of the expressed Commission preferences, the Hungarian government rushed through parliament the act on the National Regional Development Concept in March 1998, just prior to the elections. The Regional Development Concept established seven statistical planning regions.[34] However, as the "development

32 Fowler, above n. 21, pp. 34–36.

33 European Commission, *Opinion on Hungary's Application for Membership of the European Union* (1997), p. 90.

34 Author's interview with official in the Hungarian Mission to the EU, Brussels, 15 December 2000.

regions" were voluntary and lacked resources and powers, the county governments remained the dominant players in the preparation of development plans and the distribution of state and EU funding.[35] The 1998 elections brought to power a new centre-right coalition made up of Fidesz and the Smallholders' Party. It justified its policies on sub-national governance as a response to pressures from the Commission as part of the EU accession process.

By 1999 five RDCs had been established, covering virtually the entire territory of Hungary. However, the administrative organization, including staff and financial resources, remained skeletal.[36] Aside from EU funding, the RDCs had a very weak resource base and, as unelected quango-like agencies, they had difficulties in establishing themselves as effective and authoritative organizations. Although the Commission's Opinions had clearly welcomed the establishment of the seven administrative-statistical regions and the RDCs, subsequent Regular Reports criticized Hungary for the slow pace at which the RDCs were established, the fact that the councils at regional and county level were not fully operational and a general delay in the implementation of regional policy objectives.[37] Instrumentalising the EU pressures, Fidesz strengthened central government control of the RDCs, changed the status of the RDCs from voluntary to compulsory organs, and realigned the "development regions" to overlap with the seven statistical planning regions of 1998. In October 1999, the Law on Regional Development and Physical Planning was amended to put the RDCs at the NUTS II level on a statutory basis with guaranteed state funding, and to define their role in the programming and implementation of regional development. The legislative amendments helped to consolidate the new regional institutions, but RDC membership was now weighted in favour of central government appointees at the expense of sub-national representatives and civil society.[38] Thus, the independence of the RDCs and the government's commitment to the EU principles of "partnership" and "subsidiarity" were compromised.

The strengthening of the RDCs and the regions corresponding to the NUTS II level was welcomed by the Commission in its 2000 Regular Report. Concerns were raised, however, regarding efficient decision-making and programming at the regional level. Hungary was explicitly asked to clarify the role of the regions at NUTS II level.[39] In general, by 2000/2001 the primary concern of the Commission

---

35 Palne Kovács, above n. 31, p. 29.

36 Andrea Cziczovszki, "The Regional Problem in the Transition to Europe: The Case of Hungary", Paper presented at the BASEES Annual Conference, Cambridge, 2000.

37 European Commission, *Regular Report on Hungary's Progress toward Accession* (1999), p. 46.

38 Bende-Szabó, above n. 26, p. 7.

39 European Commission, *Regular Report on Hungary's Progress Toward Accession* (2000), p. 63.

in the field of regional policy is the capacity of regional structures to participate effectively in the management of funds. Accordingly, the Commission's emphasis was on central government control and efficiency.[40] In the meantime, the growing domestic political criticism of Fidesz's overly centralized approach and corruption generated demands from across the political spectrum (including both the Hungarian Socialist Party and the Alliance of Free Democrats) for the introduction of elected regional bodies. Moreover, Fidesz claimed to pursue a long-term policy of "double decentralization", which would eliminate the counties and replace them with state administrative supra-regions that would ultimately have elected assemblies.[41]

Hungary's regionalization has been characterized by two trends. In the first half of the 1990s regionalization was determined by internal transition politics, while the regional reforms in the second half of the 1990s were shaped by domestic politics situated in the context of EU accession (see Appendix 1). Despite the consensus among the main political parties about securing the country's membership in the EU as quickly as possible, the process of regionalization has been a cross-cutting issue. Through PHARE the EU had a direct impact on the number and shape of the "development regions". Perceived or "real" pressures from the Commission for institutional reforms going beyond compliance with the Structural Funds requirements were instrumentalised by domestic political actors, particularly by Fidesz. Overall, the accession process channelled and fuelled the domestic debate on sub-national governance, but at a time when the Commission appeared to favour decentralization it did not alter the decision against democratic regionalization which had been made before the beginning of the accession negotiations. Moreover, the EU accession process did not settle the domestic debate about regionalization. Hungary's latest reform plan of mid-2003 envisages regrouping local governments into economic and geographical regions, merging counties into larger regions and setting up regional public administration offices (on the basis of the current statistical-planning regions) and elected regional governments. Parts of the reform require a two-thirds majority in parliament, thereby aptly highlighting the lock-in effects of the early choices made during transition. For the time being, the plan is to finalize the reforms before the next general elections in 2006.[42] Some of the structures established during the accession process may become the starting-point for further reform. Thus, the dynamic interplay between the domestic and external incentives or constraints regarding sub-national reforms is set to continue.

---

40 Ibid, pp. 62–63; *Regular Report on Hungary's Progress Toward Accession* (2001), p. 75.

41 Fowler, above n. 21, pp. 41–42. So-called "small areas" were to be established at the level between the counties and local governments.

42 *Comprehensive Monitoring Report on Hungary's Preparations for Membership* (2003), p. 12.

4.2. Poland: Democratized Regionalization

Poland was the first CEEC to enact a democratizing reform of both regional and local governance. Decentralization quickly emerged as an integral part of Poland's transition to democracy. Sub-national reforms, including the establishment of a regional tier of government, had already been a crucial component of the Roundtable talks between Solidarity and the socialist government in the late 1980s. In contrast to Hungary, where there was an early political consensus against regional self-government, Poland's debate hinged on the shape of the reform, rather than on the principle as such. In the late 1980s the Communist Party supported the retention of the existing 49 regions (*województwa*) as part of a more centralized state structure, whereas Solidarity favoured a strongly decentralized government as a counterbalance to decades of communist centralism.[43] Persistent disagreements among the political parties about the design of the reform, in particular the number and functions of the new regions, together with a crowded transition agenda in the early post-communist period, led to an almost ten-year gap between the introduction of local self-government in 1990 and the institutionalization of regional governance structures in 1999. The 1990 local government reform preserved the 49 communist-era regions of 1975 as an unelected level of de-concentrated government. At the former *powiat* (district) level a tier of state administrative districts was established. The main democratizing element lay in the creation of self-governing local communes (*gminy*). As in Hungary, the rapid multiplication of under-funded local self-governing units stored up administrative inefficiencies. The 1990 legislation was conceived of as an interim solution, as there was a general political consensus on the need for further decentralization, including the introduction of a regional tier of self-government.[44]

Throughout the period 1990–1997 national-level policy issues dominated the transition agenda. Public administration remained centralized and fragmented by the communist-era legacy of industrial sectoral ministries. By the middle of the 1990s functional arguments came to the fore in Poland's debate about sub-national governance. There was a growing recognition of the shortcomings of a centralized system characterized by large numbers of uncoordinated state administrative offices, deficient public finances and a lack of transparency. Consequently, the reform of 1999 was driven by an economic logic to promote effective integrated regional development. The first serious proposals for regional administrative reform came from the regional level itself. The regional elite in Silesia, for example, increasingly voiced its frustration with the failure of the centre to facilitate regional economic

---

43 Wollmann and Lankina, above n. 24 , p. 101.

44 Wiktor Glowacki, "Regionalization in Poland", in Gerard Marcou (ed.), *Regionalization for Development and Accession to the EU: A Comparative Perspective* (LGI Studies, Budapest: Open Society Institute 2002), pp. 110–111.

restructuring, and Poznań *województwo* launched its own economic development programme.[45]

The regional government reform was stalled by the ruling coalition (1993–1997) of the Democratic Left Alliance (SLD) and the Polish Peasants' Party (PSL), despite the fact that the organizational and legislative preparations had been finalized by the short-lived coalition government under Hanna Suchocka (July 1992–May 1993), which consisted of seven post-Solidarity and centre-right parties. PSL leader and Prime Minister Waldemar Pawlak favoured a strong central government. Given that his party's political hold was strong in many of the regions, he opposed the dismantling of the existing 49 regional structures. In the 1993 parliamentary elections, the PSL had also performed well in a considerable number of the *województwa* and was intent on holding on to these gains by blocking an intermediary level of governance.[46] The PSL proposed the retention of the existing regions but with elected assemblies and a centrally appointed governor (*wojewoda*). The Democratic Left Alliance (SLD) supported the establishment of 12–14 large regions and self-government at the district (*powiat*) level. The issue divided not only the governing coalition but also the rest of the political spectrum. Principally, no reform occurred because the political priorities were focussed on other aspects of the transition.[47] The debates re-emerged upon the accession to power of the Solidarity Electoral Action—Freedom Union (AWS-UW) coalition after the elections in September 1997. Numerous proposals for the administrative sub-division of the country had been circulated among government specialists and academics in the early 1990s with the proposed number of regions varying from 6 to over 40. There was also an ongoing debate about the functions of the proposed regions and in particular the relationship between self-governing organs and state administrative offices within each territorial unit. The three main options which were put forward were: functional regions dominated by the central government; self-governing regions within a unitary state; and a federal structure modelled on the German Länder.[48]

---

45 James Hughes et al., "Silesia and the Politics of Regionalisation in Poland", in George Kolankiewicz (ed.), *Regional Issues in Polish Politics* (London: UCL Press 2004).

46 Jacek Zaucha, "Regional and Local Development in Poland", in Kirchner, above n. 23, pp. 53–79.

47 Wollmann and Lankina, above n. 24, p. 103; Jadwiga Emilewicz, and Artur Wolek, *Reformers and Politicians: The power play for the 1998 Reform of Public Administration in Poland, as seen by its main players* (Warsaw: Elipsa 2002), p. 109.

48 Harald Baldersheim and Pavel Swaniewicz, "The Institutional Performance of Polish Regions in an Enlarged EU. How much Potential? How Path Dependent?", in Michael Keating and James Hughes (eds.), *The Regional Challenge in Central and Eastern Europe* (Brüssel: Peter Lang 2003), pp. 69–88; Michal Illner, "Municipalities and Industrial Paternalism in a Real Socialist Society", in Petr Dostál et al. (eds.), *Changing Territorial Administration in Czechoslovakia: International Viewpoints* (Amsterdam: Universiteit van Amsterdam 1992), p. 15.

The reforms, prepared by AWS-UW, were passed as part of a larger package of structural reforms, including provisions on health care, pensions, education and the judicial system. Though the reforms were all interconnected, as a package they were overly ambitious and rushed, leaving in their wake a host of unresolved problems.[49] Given that AWS was itself an alliance of some 30 political organizations and parties, it is not surprising that differences emerged over the content of the reforms. The majority of "mainstream" Solidarity parties favoured the division of the country into 12–13 regions with both self-governing and state administrative structures. Nine cities were identified as meeting the necessary criteria to be strong regional centres; three cities in the poorer eastern part of the country were added to this list in order to achieve a balanced configuration of regions across the whole country. The members of the national-catholic wing of the AWS opposed the decentralizing reform altogether. Some AWS deputies argued that the reforms threatened the unity of the state.[50] The members of the ruling coalition compromised by agreeing to restrict the rights of the new self-governing regional governments, while increasing the supervisory powers of the central government representative (wojewoda).

On the opposition side, the Democratic Left Alliance (SLD) favoured a return to the pre-1975 division into 17 regions, while proposing an assistance programme for those cities faced with the loss of their regional status. The PSL continued to oppose the reform both at the *województwa* and *powiat* level, fearing a loss of support in the rural communities and existing regions. It argued in favour of a two-tier system based on the existing regional breakdown, with the current regions being transformed into self-governing entities.[51] There was also a certain amount of opposition from employees of central ministries and the local administration in those cities which feared to lose their regional status. In the end, the government and the opposition reached a compromise over a 16-region configuration similar to the pre-1975 communist system.

As a result of the 1999 reforms, Poland now has a three-tier sub-national self-governing system.[52] The basic units are the 2,489 municipalities (*gminy*) at the local level, 308 *powiaty* at the district level, 65 urban municipalities which have been granted *powiat* rights and the 16 *województwa* at the regional level. All three

---

49 See Jerzy Regulski, *Building Democracy in Poland, the state reform of 1998, Discussion papers*, 9 (Budapest: the Local Government and Public Services Reform Initiative, Open Society 1999).

50 Alexander Szczerbiak, "The Impact of the October 1998 Local Elections on the Emerging Polish Party System", *Journal of Communist Studies and Transition Politics*, 15, 3, (1999), p. 86.

51 Glowacki, above n. 44, pp. 110–111.

52 For details, including the debates in the *Sejm*, see Patricia Wyszogrodzka-Sipher, "The National and International Influences on the Reform of Polish Government Structures", Paper for the workshop "Europe, Nation, Region: Redefining the State in Central and Eastern Europe", London, Royal Institute of International Affairs (2000).

levels of governance have a democratically elected council. The regional level is characterized by a dual administrative structure—the *wojewoda* is appointed by the Prime Minister upon the nomination of the Interior Minister, and it is his/her responsibility to protect the interests of the state and to coordinate the administrative relations between the centre and the region. Each *województwo* council elects a chief officer, the marshal (*marszatek*), who is responsible for regional development under the Polish Agency for Regional Development. The key weakness of the reform lay in its failure to devolve sufficient fund raising powers to the regional level to enable the new governments to function effectively. Critics talk of a decentralization of competences without a corresponding decentralization of finances.[53]

The impetus for democratized regionalization predated EU enlargement conditionality in this policy domain,[54] but the timing and nature of the regionalization dovetailed with the ongoing preparations for EU membership (see Appendix 2). The 16 województwa correspond to the EU's NUTS II classification.[55] In the course of the Sejm debates on the new law, supporters of the regional reform maintained that strong, large regions were important if Poland was to benefit fully from its integration into the EU, thereby using the EU as a legitimating device to advance their preferences. Polish officials hoped that the responsibilities of the regional-level governments, such as the promotion of economic development; regional public services, environmental protection and the development of regional infrastructure would help to satisfy the EU's demand for "regional administrative capacity". Thus, the 1999 reform, supplemented by a law on regional development in May 2000 and the establishment of a Ministry of Regional Development in June 2000, were shaped by the criticism raised by the Commission in the 1997 Opinions and in the 1998 and 1999 Regular Reports. These reports asserted that Poland's regional administrative reform was "incomplete", complained about the lack of legal basis for the implementation of regional policy, and the absence of a mechanism of coordination of regional policy at the national level.[56] The Commission was, in fact, deeply concerned about the future management of Structural Funds, given the ambiguities in the division of responsibilities between centre and regions and by

53 Grzegorz Gorzelak and Bohdan Jalowiecki, *Analiza wdrażania i skutków reformy terytorialnej organizacji kraju, Raport końcowy* (An analysis of the introduction and results of the territorial reform of the state, Final report) (*Warszawa: Europejski Insytut Rozwoju Regionalnego i Lokalnego, Insytut Spraw Publicznych*, 2001).

54 In the sub-national discourse about regionalization the question of EU membership was rarely raised in the early to mid-1990s. See Tanja Majcherkiewicz, *An Elite in Transition: An Analysis of the Higher Administration of the Region of Upper Silesia, Poland 1990–1997*, Unpublished PhD Thesis, London School of Economics and Political Science (2001).

55 Andrzej Kowalczyk, "Local Government in Poland", in Tamas M. Horvath (ed.), *Decentralization: Experiments and Reform* (Budapest: LGI Publications 2000), p. 226.

56 European Commission, *Regular Report on Poland's Progress Toward Accession* (1998–2000).

the fact that the lack of a regional tax base severely constrained the capacity of the new *województwa*.[57]

In early 2001, having encouraged the development of regional structures at the *województwo* level to facilitate the management of Structural Funds, the Commission shifted its emphasis to the importance of continued central management and of ensuring the necessary administrative capacity at the centre.[58] The 2001 Regular Report on Poland illustrates this change by stating that despite previous progress Poland's preparations for the implementation of Structural Funds had stalled, particularly as regards programming at the national level. Poland was reminded that "a clear division of responsibilities must be established at the central level, between central and regional levels and at the regional level between the *Voivods* and Marshals". The Commission now argued that "the role of the regions in the management of the funds in the period up to end 2006 requires careful consideration."[59]

Hungary and Poland have adopted different approaches to the reform of subnational governance. While Poland introduced a democratically elected tier of regional government, Hungary has—at least for the time being—restricted itself to administrative-statistical regionalization. In both cases, however, the reforms were rooted in endogenous debates and political choices made during the early transition period. The bid for EU membership, PHARE and the Commission's emphasis on regional administrative capacity influenced the shape and timing of the reforms, but mainly by crystallizing, reinforcing and fine-tuning existing trends defined by the transition process.

5. EUROPEANIZATION OF ELITE ATTITUDES

While emphasizing organizational structures, the Commission's call for administrative capacity included references to the recruitment and training of staff. For the *acquis* to be implemented, the newly established structures have to be staffed with personnel who are imbued with the appropriate norms and knowledge. Some aspects of the enlargement process were explicitly concerned with this transfer of norms and knowledge. The "structured dialogue" of the early 1990s and the accession negotiations themselves, for example, helped to acculturate the post-communist CEEC national elites into the "European" elite discourse. The rapid increase in elite interactions between the EU and the CEECs,

---

57 Authors' interview with a senior official in DG Regional Policy, European Commission, Brussels, 28 March 2001.

58 Authors' interview with an official in charge of regional policy negotiations, Polish Mission to the EU, Brussels, 28 March 2001.

59 European Commission, *Regular Report on Poland's Progress Toward Accession* (2001), p. 79.

whether channelled through the inclusion of the CEEC national elites in EU fora and activities, through EU instruments that involved sub-national elites such as PHARE, SAPARD, ISPA, scientific and educational exchanges or "twinning", contributed to this "socialization". The accession negotiations were supported by a broad national elite consensus in the CEECs on the desirability of EU membership. Given the small size of the circle of national elites involved in the negotiations, we should not assume that the sub-national elite attitudes concur with those of the national elites.

The attitudes of sub-national elites are significant for three key reasons. Firstly, one of the aspects of institutional debilitation during transition is that political parties are organizationally weak, particularly as regards their penetrative strength from national to local level. Consequently, the importance of regional and local elites as gatekeepers and mediators between national elites and public opinion is enhanced. Secondly, sub-national elites occupy a central position regarding the successful implementation of the *acquis* and EU policy in the post-enlargement era. Thirdly, the regional and local elites are of normative political importance for the EU, as the notions of "partnership", "subsidiarity" and "multi-level governance" suggest.[60] A significant divergence of norms, knowledge and attitudes between national and sub-national elites is obviously not conducive to institutional and policy coherence. The structure of the accession process allows us to predict a disjuncture between the more "Europeanized" attitudes and norms of the acculturated national elites and the largely disengaged sub-national elites.

5.1. The Relevance and Meaning of the EU at the Sub-National Level

Elites that are embedded in EU policy transfer or policy learning processes can be expected to have good knowledge about the activities of the EU in their own spatial or functional domain and higher levels of commitment to membership.[61] Although most aspects of local and regional governance will be affected by European regulation as a result of accession, our research reveals that low levels of engagement with and poor knowledge about the European Union prevailed among the sub-national elites in the CEECs in 1999–2002.[62] Our elite interviews in regional cities

60 See Liesbet Hooghe and Gary Marks, *Multi-Level Governance and European Integration* (Lanham: Rowman & Littlefield 2001), p. 102 and European Commission, *White Paper on European Governance*, COM (2001) 428.

61 For an empirical proof of this hypothesis, based on research into the attitudes of Czech civil servants, see Petr Drulák, Jiří Česal and Stanislav Hampl, "Interactions and identities of Czech civil servants on their way to the EU", *Journal of European Public Policy*, 10(4), (2003), pp. 637–654.

62 Our research comprised 66–76 elite interviews in Cluj (Romania), Pécs (Hungary), Katowice (Poland), Maribor (Slovenia) and Tartu (Estonia).

show that EU enlargement was not a salient issue for the sub-national elites who were primarily concerned with the social and economic problems arising from the domestic transition process. In the case of Pécs (Hungary) only 4% considered EU enlargement to be an important issue; in Katowice (Poland) less than 2.5% thought so. The focus on domestic socio-economic policy issues is understandable given the scale of the post-communist transition, but it seems to go hand in hand with a lack of recognition that EU assistance could play a role in alleviating the local problems of transition, in particular through PHARE or Structural Funds. Knowledge about local EU-funded projects serves as a proxy to gauge the level of awareness about EU activities.

Respondents were asked: Can you name (up to) three (or more) current (wholly or partly) EU-funded projects in your city? Answers were coded "good" if respondents were able to name projects and the source of funding; "poor" if respondents were unable to name any projects or sources of funding; "limited" if respondents showed knowledge of projects, but were unable to identify the source of funding (see Figure 1).

In Katowice, 55% had poor or limited knowledge of city-based EU programmes; in Pécs, the equivalent figure was 63.5%. This lack of awareness suggests that there has been a major communication and recognition problem with the way that EU programmes have been delivered at the local level. The exception to this trend were

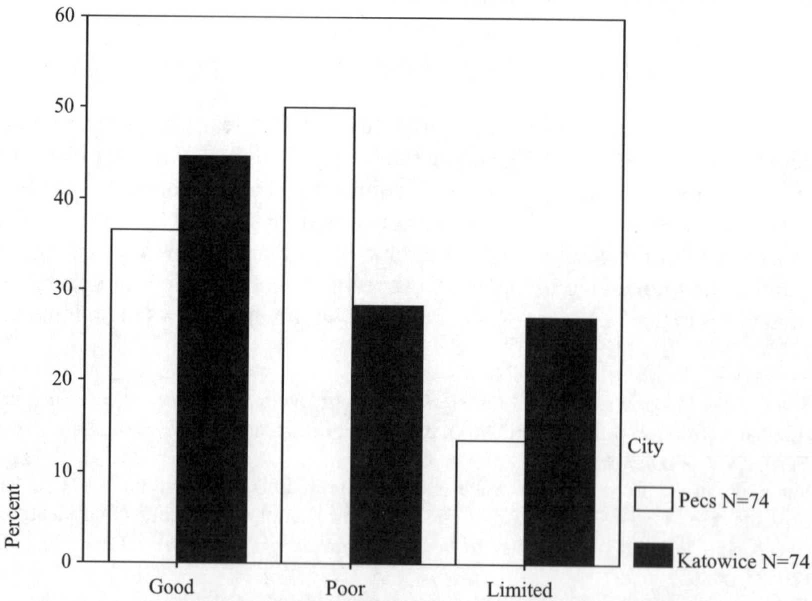

Figure 1

EU funds for major infrastructural projects, for example, new roads or waste water treatment plants. The fact that EU aid, including PHARE, is organized and funded through central ministries and rarely delivered on a territorial basis partly explains this low level of recognition. The level of correlation between the EU financial assistance that has gone into specific cities or regions and the level of elite knowledge about EU programmes is difficult to assess accurately, as the Commission does not keep records of the amount of EU aid dispersed to particular cities or regions. The somewhat higher level of elite knowledge exhibited in Katowice suggests an institutional explanation: the domestic consensus on democratic regionalization appears to have acted as an institutional vehicle for connecting the sub-national elites to the wider political process, including EU accession.

Elite attitudes towards the EU are connected to perceived benefits (or costs) of membership. In most cases, the local elites in CEE saw the benefits of EU membership accruing to the national level rather than the sub-national levels. The gap between the perceptions of the benefits of enlargement at the national versus the local level was most pronounced in Pécs: 93% of the members of the local elite thought that Hungary benefited "significantly" or "moderately" from its relationship with the EU, whereas only 20.5% felt that Pécs was benefiting "significantly" and 36% thought that Pécs was benefiting "minimally" or "not at all" from this relationship. The local elites did not seem to be aware of the potential economic benefits that the EU could bring. In Katowice this trend was reversed: 54.3% of the respondents thought said that Katowice would benefit "significantly" (as compared to 34.2% for Poland as a whole). In the next category the results were inverted, with 53.4% thinking Poland benefits "moderately" from its relationship with the EU, as compared to 37.1% describing the benefit of Katowice as "moderate".

Theory suggests that greater connectedness to EU activities promotes norm diffusion, acculturation and the formation of a "European" identity. To gauge the level of identification with Europe among the sub-national elites in the CEECs, our respondents were asked to select and rank their identity from a list of options, including Europe, Central Europe, their country, the region, and the city. 27% of respondents in Pécs opted for "European" as their primary identity compared to 17% in Katowice. This result shows that the degree of identification of sub-national elite members with "Europe" is not necessarily indicative of their level of connectedness with the "EU", as demonstrated through the awareness of and perceived benefits connected to EU membership. In Katowice, where the elites are among the most positively predisposed towards the EU, regional identity ranked second after a strong sense of national identity. The case of Katowice suggests a link between democratized regional government, regional identity and positive attitudes towards the EU during the accession process. Some 25% of respondents in Katowice chose the locale (whether regional or city) as their primary identity. Only 6% chose the regional identity as their first preference in Pécs (Baranya county).

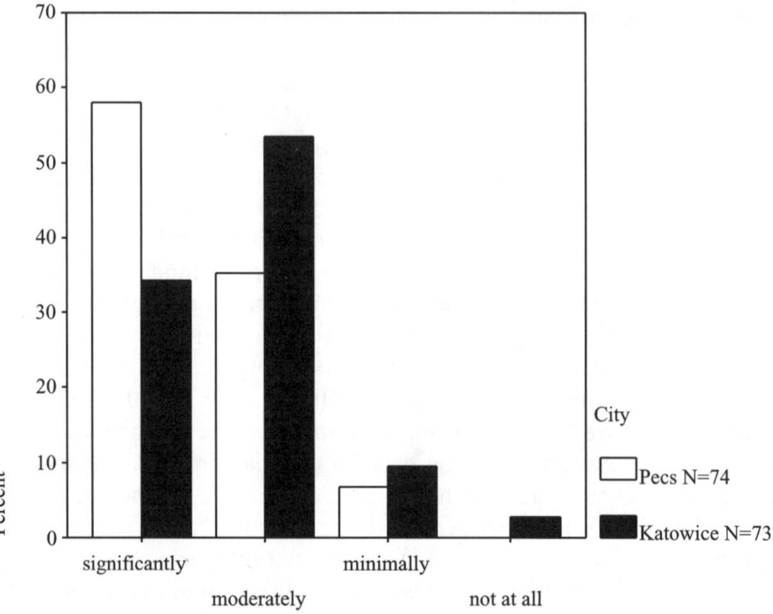

Figure 2

The latter result sits oddly with the much-trumpeted "thousand year history" of the county level in Hungary (see Figure 3).

The empirical evidence does not suggest that the sub-national elites are hostile to the EU or the process of accession. Rather as a result of their exclusion from this process, they were poorly informed about its details and implications. Despite this lack of awareness, they were in general positively predisposed to the economic benefits of membership of the EU at the macro-level. These elites have been pragmatic rather than actively Eurosceptic and are, therefore, potentially open to a greater level of engagement and connectedness with the EU. The elites generally expressed a consolidated view about the EU, with large majorities seeing the future of their country closely tied to the EU. In the cases of Pécs ($N = 74$) and Katowice ($N = 75$), 82.3% and 81.3% of respondents saw their respective country's future most closely tied to the EU (see Figure 4).

6. CONCLUSION

The institutional design of regional governance in the CEECs is best understood as a development influenced by the interaction of a country's domestic political trajectory of transition (including its historical legacies) and EU conditionality

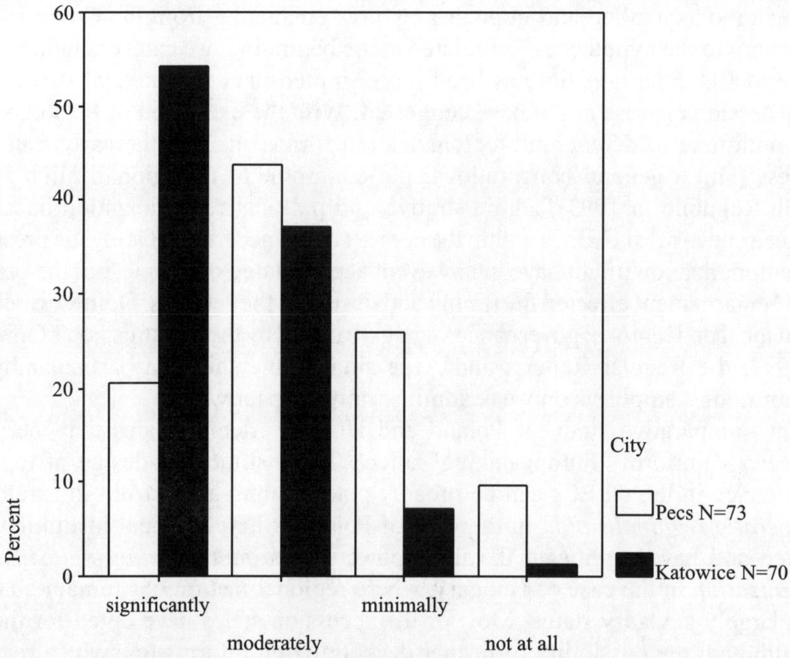

Figure 3

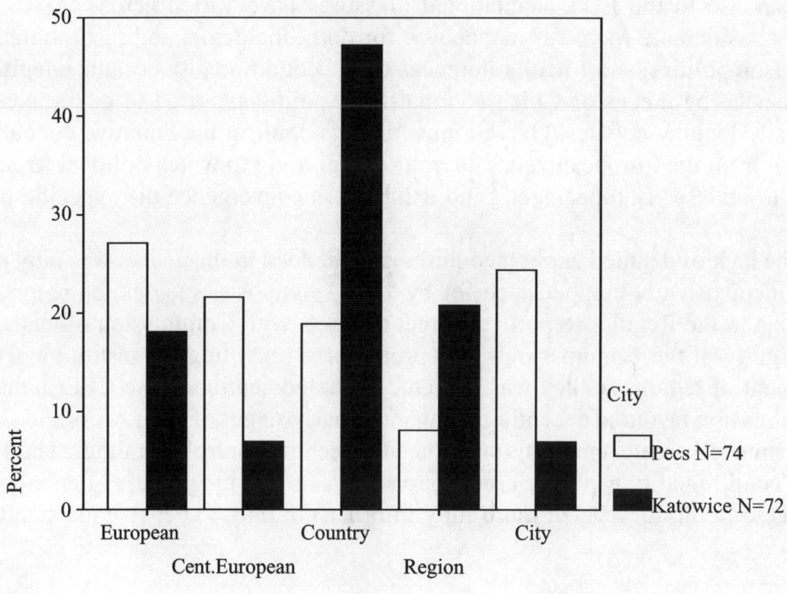

Figure 4

(understood as explicit and implicit pressures emanating from the Commission). Returning to the hypotheses formulated at the beginning, we can conclude that the scope of EU conditionality has been more limited than the unequal structure of the accession process might have suggested. With the exception of Poland, where a commitment to democratic regionalization formed part of the early transition process (and a general constitutional pre-commitment to regionalization in the Czech Republic in 1993), administrative and political regionalization became a salient issue in most CEECs within the context of EU accession. Domestic pressures for regionalization might have in any event accumulated over time, but the process of EU enlargement affected the timing and design of the reforms. Domestic debates about local and regional governance were galvanized by the Commission's Opinions of 1997, the Regular Reports and Accession Partnerships, in particular by the Commission's emphasis on weak administrative capacity.

Our comparative study of Poland and Hungary demonstrates that there has not been a uniform "Europeanizing" effect. The institutional design of regional governance in the CEECs can be broadly placed along a spectrum illustrated by *democratic regionalization* in the case of Poland, where regional institutions are elected and have significant devolved powers, and *administrative-statistical regionalization* in the case of Hungary, where regional institutions remain quangos with largely advisory status. Most of the accession states have opted for the latter, although the possibility of further decentralizing reforms to create a regional governance tier continues to be discussed in some of the candidate countries (including Hungary). As in the old Member States, the domestic institutional changes in response to the EU's adaptational pressures have varied across the CEECs, with considerable room for manoeuvre for domestic actors and institutions.[63] In domestic politics, short-hand references to EU conditionality became a legitimating device by means of which national-level politicians tried to circumvent potentially lengthy debates. Overall, our findings confirm the tentative conclusions drawn from the Europeanization literature, according to which political structures tend to be less "Europeanized" and exhibit less convergence than specific policy areas.

The lack of detailed explicit conditions embedded in the *acquis* was only partly and inconsistently compensated for by "soft" signposts, such as the recommendations in the Regular Reports or direct contacts with Commission officials. The ambiguity of the Commission's own preferences regarding the institutional environment of regional policy was reflected in the perception in the CEECs that the Commission favoured decentralization in the early stages of the process and shifted over time to a greater emphasis on the need for central control over funds. The apparent "conditionality gap" in a crucial area suggests that the process of enlargement needs to be disaggregated more fully in order not only to better understand how

[63] See Börzel and Risse, above n. 3, p. 11; Olsen, above n. 6, p. 16.

relevant EU conditionality is to specific policy domains, but also to demonstrate the interaction between the domestic political agendas and the EU. Ultimately, domestic political conditions and choices made during the early transition period were the basis of a certain resistance to Europeanization.

The lack of political mobilization among regional actors in most CEECs limited the need for national-level elites to consider models of democratic regionalization. The accession process also did not provide sub-national actors with any immediate political leverage. As yet it is unclear to what extent the current governance arrangements reflect sub-national preferences. The overall weak connectedness of the sub-national elites in the CEECs to the EU points to a shallow level of attitudinal "Europeanization". EU accession has been perceived as a national-level elite project, leaving sub-national elites disengaged though not actively Eurosceptic. Despite the weak attitudinal "Europeanization" of sub-national elites, their position and functional importance guarantees their involvement in key policy areas, thereby raising doubts about effective implementation of EU policy, at least in the short- to medium-term.[64] It is conceivable that in the medium- to long-term sub-national actors in CEE will follow the example of the current Member States and increasingly use EU channels to influence policy-making at the domestic and the EU-level. As we know from the experience of the current Member States, Structural Funds are managed in a variety of ways. Thus, ultimately, the extent to which the gap between the values of national and sub-national elites in the area of regional policy will close in the CEECs, depends on the organizational structures for the management of Structural Funds and the investment of the new Member States in building capacity at the sub-national level of governance.

The decisional calculus of sub-national elites in accession states has been dominated by their focus on managing the immediate problems of transition rather than a strategic vision of European integration. The normative gap in "Europeanization" at the sub-national level did not appear to have significant ramifications for the referenda on EU accession, but we cannot similarly discount its impact on the prospects of "deep" integration. It is striking that among the elites in Katowice the evidence for the normative gap was consistently weaker. This suggests that democratic regionalization that involves significant regional self-government may *inter alia* foster a higher level of attitudinal connectedness of elites with the EU and have concomitant knock-on effects in promoting cognitive change to a higher level of commitment to European integration.

APPENDIX 1.

Openness to EU Influence on Sub-National Reforms (Pécs 1999)

Respondents were asked: Do you agree with the proposition that traditional administrative boundaries should be redrawn, if necessary, to comply with EU funding criteria (see Figure 5)?

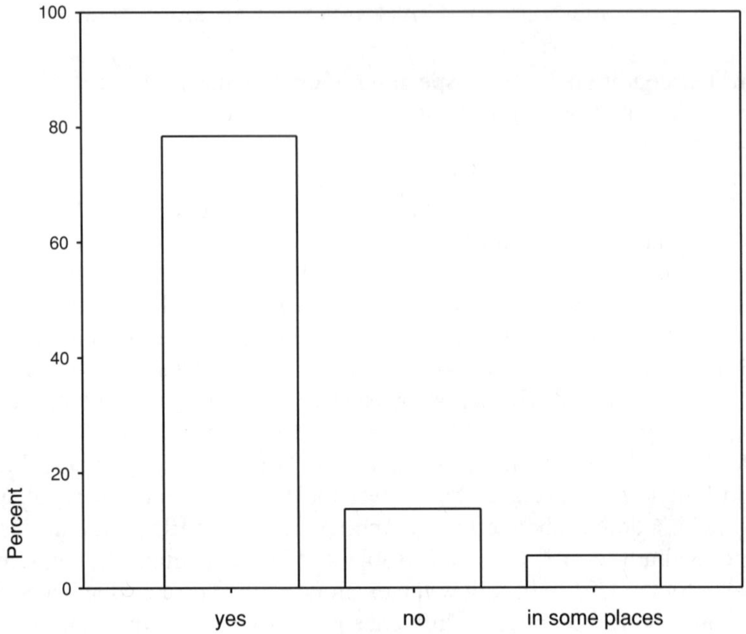

N = 72

Figure 5

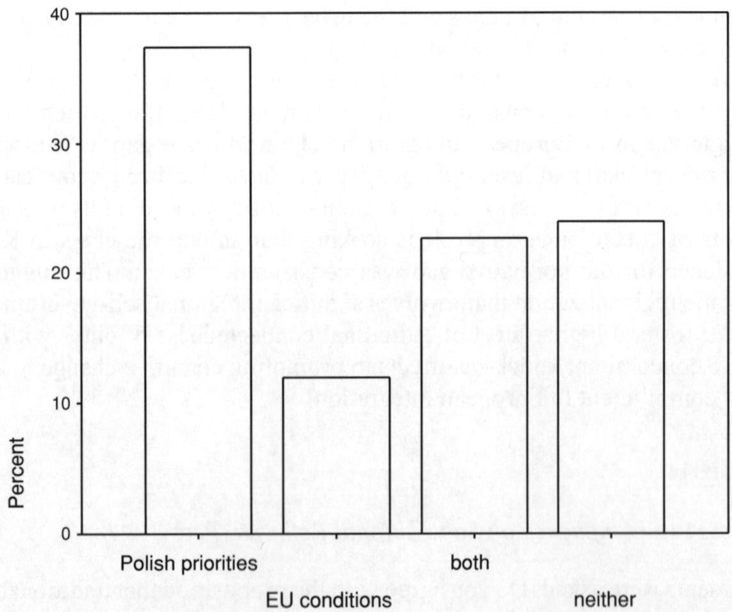

N = 72

Figure 6

APPENDIX 2.

Perceptions of the Impact of the EU on Sub-National Reforms (Katowice 2000)

Respondents were asked: Do you think that the reform of regional and district governance structures in Poland in 1999 was on the whole the result of 1. Polish priorities; 2. EU conditions; 3. both; or 4. neither (see Figure 6)?

6. The Copenhagen Criteria and the Evolution of Popular Consent to EU Norms: From Legality to Normative Justifiability in Poland and the Czech Republic

Dionysia Tamvaki

1. INTRODUCTION

The Copenhagen European Council on 13 December 2002 brought the eastward enlargement full-circle, by concluding negotiations in the city where the membership conditions were first set nine years ago. The passage from Copenhagen 1993 to Copenhagen 2002 puts the final touches in a protracted period of political and economic transformation in Central and Eastern Europe, which has envisaged to bring the "novices" closer to the EU ways of acting. In that sense, the current wave of EU widening assumes the characteristics of a socialization process, through which Western Europe diffuses its shared beliefs and institutional practices to the "untrained" East. Socialization, hence, becomes the buzzword of my choice for explaining enlargement and emphasis is given on the causal mechanisms that bring European norms and democratic practices in the domestic political arena.

While reviewing the EU socialization process, I first touch upon the Copenhagen Criteria and explain how they set the rules of the accession game. To ensure, nevertheless, not just the formal transposition of EU membership rules in the domestic sphere but also their gradual internalization into the value repertoire of state actors, persuasion and argumentation are needed as intermediary steps. Consequently, all persuasion and argumentation tools forming part of EU's pre-accession strategy enter into this research equation. The effectiveness of EU socialization tools, in turn, is being tested by assessing the progress Polish and Czech state actors make in adapting domestic institutional structures to EU democratic political criteria. Such longitudinal evaluation is made possible using the Commission's Regular Reports of 1998 and 2000 as well as the comprehensive monitoring reports issued in November 2003.

Nevertheless formal institutionalization of EU democratic norms does not constitute the end point of my inquiry. Rather, the crucial question to be addressed in this paper is whether domestic institutionalization influences the evolution of popular consent to EU norms and institutional standards. Direct popular EU legitimation is treated as the most significant socialization by-product, because if it is absent the EU of the future, of the 28 member states, will be unable to sustain among its population a generalized willingness to comply. For this reason I take

Wojciech Sadurski et al. (ed.), Spreading Democracy and the Rule of Law?, 149–171.

recourse to Eurobarometer surveys conducted in the candidate countries and trace the degree of popular habituation to the EU cause.

Such a choice, however, brings forth a methodological pitfall; an inter-level fallacy to be acknowledged right from the beginning and it will be better understood by reviewing the sequence of my argumentation. Put simply, the questions raised in this paper are ordered as follows. What are the EU socialization tools employed for all CEE candidates and do they affect, in a similar manner, formal elite-driven adaptation of EU institutional practices? Then, is the degree of formal institutionalization reflected in popular habituation of EU beliefs and practices? If that is the case, what can the EU do so as to further improve elite institutionalization and through it popular habituation to EU norms? In other words, in this paper I shift from the elite to the popular level and the argument I ultimately make is correlational rather than explicitly causal. This is so, because I do not delve into the domestic socialization process that starts from the elites and addresses the wider public. Such a process is subject to entirely different dynamics and would be better assessed by tracing the "teaching" of state elites effectuated via the local press. For the time being, however, I will limit the discussion to a comparative assessment of formal elite-driven institutionalization and popular habituation of EU democratic beliefs and practices, as influenced by EU socialization attempts.

2. Defining Socialization: a Macro and Micro Perspective in Unison

Before delving into the particularities of EU socialization, it would be useful to conceptually unfold socialization. In general terms, it could be defined as "a process by which social interaction leads novices to endorse expected ways of thinking, feeling and acting".[1] Such a broad theorization would indeed satisfy the various disciplines encompassed in the literature of socialization. Conceptual precision, nevertheless, is essential for both a meaningful theoretical debate and defensible empirical work. Hence, socialization from a political scientists' point of view would be more accurately defined as a process "resulting in the internalization of norms so that they assume their *taken for granted* nature", defining the identities, interests and social realities of either states or distinct individuals—depending on the targeted level of analysis (macro or micro).[2]

In this respect, socialization acquires both a macro-international and micro-national dimension. In the first case, international organizations take an active stance in disseminating their constitutive beliefs and practices to the contracting

[1] Alastair I. Johnston, "Treating International Institutions as Social Environments," *International Studies Quarterly*, 45 (2001), pp. 487–515.

[2] Thomas Risse, "Let's Argue: Communicative Action in World Politics," *International Organization*, 54 (2000), p. 28. See also Frank Schimmelfennig, "International Socialization in the New Europe: Rational Action in an International Environment," *European Journal of International Relations*, 16 (2000), p. 111.

states. In the second case, state actors transpose the new normative standards to the domestic arena seeking to alter the intersubjective understandings of the wider public. In this paper both the international and national dynamics of socialization will be catered for with a view to identify the crucial effect EU conditionality has had not only on the formal state structures of CEECs but also on the wider population at large.

The preceding reflections on the dual aspect of EU socialization point to a temporally separate top–down diffusion mechanism. First, CEE decision makers get exposed to the prescriptions embodied in EU norms as the accession negotiations progress. EU supranational institutions act as "teachers" who define the "lesson plan" for the CEE pupils. Subsequently, the socialized state agents instruct the masses in the new intersubjective understandings with a view to successfully complete EU socialization. Most of the scholarly literature on the subject matter, however, focuses on the international aspect of social learning while the internalization of EU norms by the public is taken for granted or is even ignored. For example, drawing upon the work of Schimmelfennig, one does not fail to notice such bias in favor of the international aspect of EU socialization.[3] CEE countries, their domestic structures' readiness to adopt liberal norms and the attitudes of their political elites towards the diffusion of Western European values constitute his main explanatory variables in assessing the success of top down EU socialization. Similarly, Checkel assumes a statist approach even though there is nothing about the logic of socialization and elite social learning that would lead one only to state centrism. Given the centrality of popular consent, however, for the legitimation of EU power and the perpetuation of the European cause, the top-down dissemination of EU norms from the national elites to the masses will also enter into this research equation.[4]

3. SOCIALIZATION: A PURE CONSTRUCTIVIST ENTERPRISE OR A QUASI-RATIONAL GAME?

Prior to an investigation of the socializing power of EU institutions, as reflected on both the formal structures of the aspiring entrant states and the wider public

---

[3] Frank Schimmelfennig, "The Community Trap: Liberal Norms, Rhetorical Action, and the Eastern Enlargement of the European Union," *International Organization*, 55 (2001), pp. 47–80. See also Frank Schimmelfennig, "The Impact of International Organizations on the Central and Eastern European States," in Linden Ron (ed.), *Norms and Nannies: The Impact of International Organizations on the Central and Eastern European States* (Lanham: Rowman and Littlefield, 2002).

[4] Jeffrey T. Checkel, "Bridging the Rational-Choice/Constructivist Gap? Theorizing Social Interaction in European Institutions,"*ARENA Working Papers* WP 00/11(2000). See also Jeffrey T. Checkel, "International Institutions and Socialization in the New Europe," *ARENA Working Papers* WP 01/11(2001).

opinion, it would be useful to theoretically define socialization. Hence, switching to a more analytic mode, I shall review constructivist work on norm compliance due to the perfect compatibility of "socialization" with this research project. Sociological constructivists, such as Emanuel Adler, explore the nature of the reconstitution of actors' identities via the impact of international norms.[5] For them, it is mainly the social construction of reality that generates new intersubjective understandings and such changes in the normative environment, in turn, precede and define changes in the material world. Similarly, Peter Katzenstein and the contributors to his volume take the debate a step further and show how useful the constructivist perspective can be in explaining the politics of national security.[6] Hence, given the centrality of norms and intersubjective cognitions for the constructivist school, it is no wonder that "socialization" permeates the constructivist epistemology explaining how social structures transform actors' identities and interests and why individual actors behave in line with institutionalized beliefs and practices.

Building on socialization and theories of learning, constructivism addresses the problem of agency and manages to overcome its structuralist bias. Simply put, the causal effect of social structures, on shifts in state behaviour is no longer taken for granted. Rather, the "socialization" mechanisms by which international organizations manage to teach their normative underpinnings to the contracting states bring agents back to the constructivist ontology. Hence, it is not just social structures that constitute agents and social practices. Agents too, far from being "structural idiots", amalgamate social reality on the basis of their collective beliefs, ideas and interpretations about the world.[7] The reconstitution of agency has obviously reversed the traditional causal arrows between agents and structures, showing that they can have a combined effect. What is more important though is that socialization, by overcoming the ontological primacy of structures has also introduced a thin rationalist logic into the normative content of constructivist thinking. More specifically, in EU socialization what matters is not just that shifts have occurred in CEE state behaviour and whether such shifts should be attributed to the EU as a socially constitutive structure. Rather, the mechanisms by which the EU manages to "teach" its normative underpinnings to the aspiring entrants come at center stage in the "agency driven" approach of EU socialization. EU political agents are thought to act purposively on the basis of their collective meanings and assumptions

5 Emanuel Adler, "Seizing the Middle Ground: Constructivism in World Politics," *European Journal of International Relations*, 3 (1997), pp. 319–363.

6 Peter Katzenstein, "Introduction: Alternative Perspectives on National Security," in Peter Katzenstein (ed.), *The Culture of National Security: Norms and Identity in World Politics* (New York: Columbia University Press, 1996), pp. 1–32.

7 Martha Finnemore, *National Interests in International Society* (Ithaca: Cornell University Press, 1996), p. 25. See also Jeffrey T. Checkel, "Norms, Institutions and National Identity in Contemporary Europe," *ARENA Working Papers,* WP 98/16 (1998), pp. 2–3.

about what is to be a member of the Union and thereby generate changes in the social structures and practices of the candidate countries. Hence, in examining the effect EU socialization has had on CEE applicants, I shall dismiss the age-old controversy between radical variants of rationalism and constructivism and adopt a new trend in political science that favours a both/and conceptualization of social reality.[8]

More specifically I shall abide by a synthetic model, put forward by March and Olsen, according to which actors enter into new relationships with a view to maximize their own utility, but develop identities shaped by shared norms and values as a result of accumulated experience. These experiences socially constitute agents and provide them with the impetus and direction for action. In this sense, self-interested modes of action are "self-limiting" while norm based modes are "self-reinforcing", thus demonstrating to EU political agents what is called for when admitting new Member States and making such "teaching" effective in the long run for CEE state actors.[9] In this process of social interaction between old and new Member State actors instrumental action gradually gives way to norms and rules that reshape fundamental agent properties in both sides and therefore "socially constitute" the things they do.

4. SOCIALIZATION IN CENTRAL AND EASTERN EUROPE: DO EU IDEAS MATTER ALL THE WAY DOWN?

Moving the debate to the dynamics of EU socialization in Central and Eastern Europe, I will identify, with greater precision, how the interplay between rationalism and constructivism manifests itself in the socialization strategies the EU employs. In describing the process of socialization, I shall abide by the three causal mechanisms Risse, Ropp and *Sikkink* advocate.[10] Namely, the first stage in the socialization process involves strategic bargaining and instrumental behaviour. Argumentation and persuasion come next, while institutionalization and habituation mark the final steps in the whole process.

---

8 Markus Jachtenfuchs, "Deepening and Widening Integration Theory," *Journal of European Public Policy*, 9 (2002), p. 654.

9 James G. March and Johan P. Olsen, "The Institutional Dynamics of International Political Orders," *ARENA Working Papers*, WP 5 (1998), p. 13. For a postmodern constructivist approach see Richard Ashley, "The geopolitics of geopolitical space: Toward a critical social theory of international politics," *Alternatives*, 12 (1987), pp. 403–434. For a neoliberal-rational approach see Robert O. Keohane, *After Hegemony* (Princeton: Princeton University Press 1984).

10 Thomas Risse, Stephen Ropp and Kathryn Sikkink (eds.), *The Power of Human Rights: International Norms and Domestic Change* (Cambridge: Cambridge University Press 1999).

4.1. Copenhagen Criteria: Setting the Rules of the Socialization Game

To begin with, one can readily identify the Copenhagen Criteria as an embodiment of the superior bargaining power the EU possesses.[11] Admittedly, the unprecedented challenge the latter pose to Central and Eastern European candidates, is indicative of the tenacity of materialist assumptions of rationality. Conditions to accession are not an entirely novel procedure as the EU has repeatedly shown a preference for using "carrots" in its relationship with third countries. However, the prerequisites set for previous enlargements only affect the conditions of accession, not the beginning of negotiations nor the very chance of joining. In addition, the vague wording of the first two Copenhagen conditions and their qualitative nature point to the asymmetries in the bargaining power of the negotiating parties, which ultimately constrain any accommodation of CEECs' preferences.[12]

Alternatively, one might feel tempted to perceive this first stage in the CEE socialization process as inherently normative, treating the Copenhagen criteria as an embodiment of the EU's constitutive beliefs, centered on the notion of democracy and market economy. More particularly, one could argue that the Copenhagen conditions are but a concise summary of the normative standards set out in the EU Treaties, and in other important instances of EU discourse, such as the conclusions of successive European Council summits.[13] Arguing along these lines, it is difficult to deny the normative content of the Copenhagen conditions. What nevertheless proves the tenacity of the rational assumptions listed above is that the criteria do

---

11 In June 1993 The European Council in Copenhagen, established the accession of the CEECs as an EU objective provided that they ensure: (a) stability of institutions guaranteeing democracy, the rule of law, human rights and the respect for the protection of minorities; (b) the existence of a functioning market economy and the capacity to withstand competitive pressure and market forces within the Union; (c) the ability to take on the obligations of membership, including adherence to the aims of political, economic and monetary union.

12 Heather Grabbe, "European Union Conditionality and the *Acquis Communautaire*," *International Political Science Review*, 23 (2002), pp. 251–256. See also András Inotai, "The CEECs: From Association Agreements to Full Membership?," in John Redmond and Glenda G. Rosenthal (eds.), *The Expanding European Union: Past, Present, Future* (London: Lynne Rienner Publishers 1998), pp. 159–160.

13 Article 2 of the Treaty of Rome provides that: "The Community shall have as its task, by establishing a common market and an economic and monetary union... to promote throughout the Community a harmonious balanced and sustainable development of economic activities... raising social cohesion." The element of effective market economy is therefore combined with that of social solidarity for these two are indispensable to pluralist democracy. Community language officially extends to liberal democratic principles only later on, in the Copenhagen European Council of 1978, where a summary list of democratic standards is set out. Furthermore, in Article 6 of the Treaty on European Union states that: "The Union is founded on the principles of liberty, democracy, respect for human rights and fundamental freedoms and the rule of law, principles which are common to the member states".

not simply constitute a declaration of what "good Europeans do". Rather, accession is made conditional on meeting these prerequisites. Hence, the Copenhagen conditions assume the character of rules that take the form "Do X to get Y", rather than the form "Good people do X" that corresponds to norms.[14]

The legality aspect assigned to EU membership conditions is not only meant to guide CEE applicants, but also reassure reluctant Member States that any disruption risks emanating from enlargement would be minimal. Only conformity to the established Copenhagen rules authorizes accession to the EU club. In this sense, the EU is not just a rational actor but a sovereign authority whose rulings are acknowledged as final. By making the Copenhagen criteria strictly enforceable, the EU successfully takes the first step in the socialization of the newcomers. Yet the rules on their own do not essentially result in the internalization of EU beliefs and practices which is the desired outcome of socialization. To reach that end, argumentation and persuasion are needed as intermediary procedures. The latter prepare the ground for a passage from "legality" and mere rule following to "normative justifiability" that is justification of the EU rules by means of shared beliefs and cognitive understandings.[15] To put it in March and Olsen's terms, argumentation and persuasion signal a transitional phase from the logic of consequentiality to the logic of appropriateness. This means that state actors no longer abide by the rules of the EU game simply because they want to maximize their individual utility. Rational cost benefit calculation gradually gives way to principled beliefs, which turn rules into behavioural standards that are both desirable and appropriate to follow.[16]

4.2. EU Socialization Tools: Argumentation and Persuasion—Preparing the Passage from Legality to Normative Justifiability

In translating argumentation and persuasion into something concrete and measurable, special attention shall be given to the various accession instruments employed by the EU while preparing CEE applicants for admission. Before proceeding, nevertheless, it is important to clarify the conceptual definitions adopted in this paper for these two socialization micro-processes. For some, argumentation is synonymous with persuasion, as a process of communication, which aims at changing people's attitudes, beliefs or behaviour through structured debate rather than overt coercion. While this holds true for argumentation, the process of persuasion described here is subject to rather different dynamics. More particularly, persuasion is not devoid of conflict involving besides reasoning, sanctions and positive incentives to the

---

14 James D. Fearon, "What is Identity, as we now use the word?," Stanford University, Draft manuscript (1997).

15 David Beetham, *The Legitimation of Power* (Atlantic Highlands: Humanities Press International 1991), pp. 16–17.

16 March and Olsen, *op. cit.* n. 9, pp. 8–12.

addressees of socialization, so as to abstain from defection.[17] Moving the debate to the EU level, one comes to realize that argumentation is not the preferred EU strategy towards the CEE aspiring entrants. Rather, considerable weight is given to persuasion which seems to be prevalent in the pre-accession instruments employed by the EU (see Figure 1).

4.2.1. "Coercive Persuasion" Tools

The first persuasion instruments to be singled out of the set of EU pre-accession tools are the "Europe Agreements" (EA). These were signed bilaterally with each applicant from 1991 onwards and they constitute a set of formally structured trade relations containing both political and economic provisions that would eventually entrust the CEECs with a free trade area over a 10-year period. The general framework of political and economic cooperation envisaged by the EAs also included the approximation of legislation, thus starting the process of introducing the *acquis* to the applicants. It becomes apparent therefore, that the Agreements could possibly persuade the CEE to consolidate all three EU rules subsequently spelled out in the Copenhagen criteria. The learning pressure was determined by

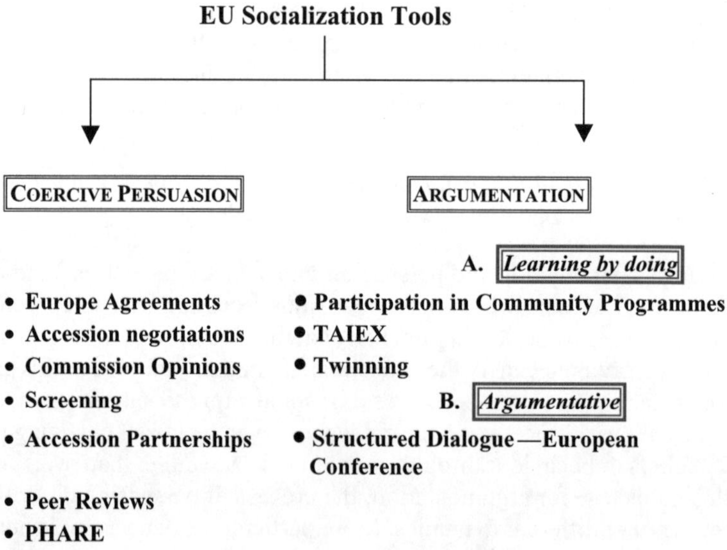

Figure 1 EU Socialization Tools.

[17] David Black, "The Long and Winding Road: International Norms and Domestic Political Change in South Africa," in Thomas Risse, Stephen Ropp and Kathryn Sikkink (eds.), *The Power of Human Rights: International Norms and Domestic Change* (Cambridge: Cambridge University Press 1999), p. 103. Regarding persuasion see: Johnston, *op. cit.* n. 1, p. 490.

the desire of the CEECs to reap the benefits of a liberalized trade area. Given, nevertheless, that the final outcome did not meet the initial expectations of the applicants, I ought not overstate the efficacy of Europe Agreements in bringing the applicants closer to the normative standards of the EU.[18]

Moving away from this first attempt to induce the applicants into the EU practices, I shall rather turn to a more promising instrument of persuasion: The accession negotiations between representatives of the Council and members of the applicants' governments at various levels.[19] Accession negotiations, as Avery and Cameron point out, "[are] not aimed at an agreement between the Union and an external partner... as is the normal case in international negotiations, but with the way in which an applicant country will function as a member. [They are] concerned with how the 'external' becomes 'internal'".[20]

Building upon their claims, one might assume that negotiations have a predominantly argumentative character. There is no true deliberation though, because the accession negotiations involve no concessions and counter concessions with the goal of reaching an agreement. Rather, the applicant has to abide by the EU membership rules if it wishes to join the institutional structures of the Union. The only issues up for negotiation are (i) the length of time, allowed to fully implement the acquis and (ii) the amount of financial support to implement it. Hence, the persuasive role of accession negotiations cannot be questioned for they attempt to change the behavioural standards of CEE applicants by using both positive incentives (aid) and sanctions (postponement of accession).

Accession negotiations opened formally on 31 March 1998 under the British Presidency, after the publication of the Commission's Opinions (*avis*) on the applicants and the Conclusions of the Luxembourg European Council in December 1997. In its ten *avis* published as part of Agenda 2000 in July 1997, the Commission recommends that negotiations should start with five countries (The Czech Republic, Estonia, Hungary, Poland and Slovenia) while the rest should be excluded on economic grounds, with the exception of Slovakia that is turned down due to its failure to meet the political conditions. The persuasive power of the "Opinions" is established in the conclusions of the Luxembourg Council, where the recommendations

---

[18] Their effectiveness was reduced by the EU's inability to provide comprehensive and unconditional market access. The Community offered faster import liberalisation on the EU rather than on the CEE side and the degree of market opening on offer in agriculture, iron, textiles and steel was unsatisfactory. For further details on Europe Agreements see Alan Mayhew, *Recreating Europe: The European Union's Policy Towards Central and Eastern Europe* (Cambridge: Cambridge University Press, 1998).

[19] The Commission is a very important interlocutor between the Union and the candidates and assumes a substantive role in preparing the ground for the negotiations, despite the fact that it formally takes a secondary role in the negotiating process itself.

[20] Graham Avery and Fraser Cameron, *The Enlargement of the European Union* (Sheffield: Sheffield Academic Press, 1998), p. 33.

of the Commission are carried out to the letter. Even though it is stated that formal accession negotiations will open simultaneously with all ten CEE candidates, the substantive negotiations open on 10 November, with the five CEECs mentioned above, plus Cyprus. These six applicants constitute the "ins" while the rest fall in the category of "pre-ins".[21]

As against this argument one might claim that since the dynamics of EU accession conditionality changed, in December 1999, by means of the Helsinki European Council and an "inclusive accession process" was preferred to the old strategy distinguishing between two waves, it becomes clear that the Commission's *avis* bear little weight and cannot function effectively as persuasion tools. However, a convincing counter claim can be found in the Commission's first Regular report published on 4 November 1998. This document highlighted the progress made in Latvia, Lithuania and Slovakia and made recommendations to promote individual CEECs to a faster track. Such a recommendation was taken further in the Commission's Composite paper issued in October 1999 where it was mentioned that full accession negotiations should start with the other five CEECs, as well. In that respect the Helsinki Council is but a strong proof of the persuasive vigor Commission's Opinions possess, as they determine applicants' access to negotiations.[22]

The socializing effect of the EU on CEE applicants can be also traced in two other persuasion mechanisms that have a monitoring effect: namely, "screening" and "Accession Partnerships". Screening, is a detailed presentation and explanation by the community experts on each of the 31 chapters of the *acquis* to all candidates. It also identifies the legislative gaps and institutional weaknesses in each applicant country and thereby determines the speed with which it shall progress in the negotiations. Accession Partnerships, introduced in 1998, are more technically oriented setting out a list of policy priorities that have to be implemented within the year or in the medium term. Given that the Commission subsequently reports on the candidates' progress in meeting each policy priority in the autumn of the year, and publishes revised Accession Partnerships, if necessary, it is not difficult to grasp the power this monitoring tool has in convincing the applicants to gradually change their institutional standards.[23]

An enhanced monitoring action that complements the ongoing monitoring process, focusing only on areas of particular concern identified either by the Regular Reports or proposals for revised Accession Partnerships, is known as "Peer Reviews". The latter involve experts from the Member States and the Commission

---

[21] Helen Wallace and Ulrich Sedelmeier, "Eastern Enlargement," in Helen Wallace and William Wallace (eds.), *Policy Making in the European Union* (Oxford: Oxford University Press 2000), pp. 449–450.

[22] Heather Grabbe, "How does the EU Measure When the CEECs are Ready to Join?," in Charles Jenkins (ed.), *The Unification of Europe: An Analysis of EU Enlargement* (London: Centre For Reform 2000), p. 40.

[23] Grabbe, *op. cit.* n. 12, pp. 257–258.

who evaluate the administrative capacity of the candidates. The coercive nature of Peer Reviews ensures that the applicants will not go back on their commitments to build up adequate administrative capacity. Hence, they also contribute to the successful transposition of EU administrative practices in CEECs.[24]

The monitoring mechanisms described so far, control not only the access of candidates to more advanced stages in the negotiations but also determine their access to financial aid administered via the PHARE programme. PHARE, with an annual budget of 1.5 billion Euro co-finances institution building together with associated investment in the infrastructure, for the implementation of the *acquis*. From 2000, the Commission has doubled its assistance to over 3 billion Euro. The two new sources of aid complementing the PHARE are ISPA (Pre-Accession Structural Instrument) and SAPARD (Structural Adjustment Programme for Agriculture and Rural Development) which prepare candidates for the structural funds.[25] Financial and technical aid of this sort is a persuasive "carrot" that CEE actors cannot ignore if they wish to overcome the considerable onus political and economic transformation has imposed on their societies.

Arguing along these lines, a mix of persuasion and rational adaptation to the EU membership demands seem to be the driving mechanism behind EU socialization efforts. Nevertheless, if we subscribe to the writings of Ikenberry and Kupchan exogenous material inducements lead over time to the internalization of norms once adopted for instrumental reasons. Translating their claim to CEE reality, we may argue that access to accession negotiations initially functions as a rational mechanism constraining the utility maximizing behaviour of the CEE actors, who would like to enter the Union making the least possible concessions and effort. In the long run, however, this coercive socialization process preparing CEECs' admission to the EU club may have a constitutive effect on their identities leading to shared cognitive understandings with the rest of the EU members.[26]

4.2.2. Argumentation Tools

The EU socialization tools that prepare the ground for such greater normative convergence between the Union and the applicants are not of the same kind as the pure persuasion instruments listed above. Some have an argumentative character and are based on an exchange of views, while others have a more practical side and promote the internalization of EU norms using a "learning by doing" approach. The latter,

---

24 Commission of the European Communities, *Making a Success of Enlargement: Strategy Paper and Regular Reports from the Commission on Progress Towards Accession by Each of the Candidate Countries* (Brussels, 2001), p. 24.

25 Commission of the European Communities, *Enlargement Strategy Paper: Regular Reports from the Commission on Progress towards Accession by each of the Candidate Countries* (Brussels, November 2000), p. 7.

26 John G. Ikenberry and Charles Kupchan, "Socialization and Hegemonic Power," *International Organization*, 44 (1990), pp. 290–292.

correspond to three Community actions, namely: (a) Participation in Community Programmes, (b) TAIEX (Technical Assistance Information Exchange Office) and (c) Twinning. More specifically, the participation of the CEECs in Community programmes and agencies contributes to their effective integration in the institutional beliefs and practices of the current EU Member States. The e-Europe initiative and national employment strategies have already been extended to the candidates through "e-Europe plus" and the "Joint Assessment of Employment Policy Priorities". In addition, pre-accession economic programmes have also introduced the CEECs to the context of EMU. In the same direction are also aiming the two PHARE instruments, TAIEX and twinning. The first provides practical support, making experts available for short-term advice on improving the administrative capacity of the CEECs. The second involves the long-term secondment of officials from Ministries, regional bodies, public agencies and professional organizations in the Member States to corresponding bodies in the candidate countries. All these Community initiatives do not simply transfer technical and administrative know-how but progressively induce the candidates into the ways of EU thinking and acting.

Two pure argumentative tools that have been employed as part of the EU socialization strategy are the Structured Dialogue and the European Conference. The structured dialogue formed part the first pre-accession strategy launched at the Essen European Council in December 1994. It was intended as a forum for multilateral discussion of issues, moving away from the bilateral scheme of agreements with the CEECs that had so far prevailed. The Structured Dialogue was meant to function as a genuine argumentative instrument fostering contact and exchange of views among the Member States and the applicants. Nevertheless, its lack of decision making power and its lack of focus on specific subjects gave it secondary importance and few EU members bothered to attend these multilateral meetings. Hence, in order to overcome the dead-end, the structured dialogue gave way to the European Conference during the Luxembourg European Council in December 1997. The European Conference is yet another multilateral forum for consultations between the EU and the applicants mainly in the areas of CFSP and JHA. It involves annual meetings at heads of government and foreign minister levels and it is an important step in producing higher normative allegiance to the EU because it addresses issues of general concern to the participants, which may even grow beyond the above mentioned fields, so as to broaden and deepen cooperation.[27]

All in all, the socialization tools employed by the EU are meant to guide CEE countries towards membership. In their vast majority they create incentives and judge the progress of the candidates in transposing EU political and economic practices in the domestic sphere. In other words, coercive persuasion prevails over

---

27 European Parliament, *The European Conference and the Enlargement of the European Union*, Briefing No. 18 (2003), http://www.europarl.eu.int/enlargement/briefings/18al_en.htm.

pure argumentation with a view to ensure rapid alignment with EU standards among all candidates. The EU, by applying the same socialization mechanisms to all candidates seems to be imposing a single EU model in their domestic institutions and policies. At the same time, no specific model of western liberal democracy exists and thus the candidate states are supposed to follow vague templates. More specifically, it is up to the candidates to socialize themselves. The EU simply sets the conditions to be met and provides information and expert knowledge on how to fulfill such requirements. It prefers to keep a reactive than proactive stance to CEE socialization by deciding not to directly intervene in the external states to transform their domestic institutions. Meeting the EU criteria is up to the CEECs, if they want to be entitled to the benefit of aid and later on to accession.[28] The implications of such coercive but reactive approach to CEE socialization is to be tested against the end product of EU socialization efforts, i.e. the internalization of EU norms.

4.2.3. *The Internalization of EU Norms and Institutional Practices in CEE: Mission Accomplished?*

The third step in the socialization of CEE applicants is the internalization of EU norms, a process that involves two levels. Initially internalization takes place at the corporate level and brings about changes in the formal operating procedures of domestic institutions. Change in the individual belief systems comes only later and ensures the norm conforming behaviour of states at large.[29] Nevertheless such procedure of habituation, through which EU norms assume their "taken for granted" nature, does not solely affect the identities and cognitive structures of state actors. Rather, habituation as opposed to institutionalization is expected to go beyond individual decision-makers and reach the public. If that is not accomplished then the long-term effectiveness of socialization cannot be guaranteed, because it is not just the State that constitutes the people. The people, in turn, form the State, and their readiness to abide by the new norms determines state actors' future behaviour in the international arena. Before estimating the degree of public habituation to EU norms in CEECs it would be more appropriate to evaluate the degree of effective formal institutionalization.

5. AN ASSESSMENT OF POLISH AND CZECH CANDIDATES POLITICAL FIT FOR THE EU

As much as I would like to engage into an evaluation of all CEE applicants, for reasons of space and time that is not possible. Instead a commentary will be provided on the degree of institutionalization achieved by two countries, Poland and the Czech Republic, using the conclusions of the 1998 and 2000 Regular Reports as

28 Schimmelfennig, *op. cit.* n. 2, pp. 126–127.
29 *Ibid*, at 118–119.

well as the 2003 Monitoring reports as a reference guide. These may not constitute a representative sample of all candidate countries, however, I have chosen to dwell upon them because they have always been among the front-runners in the accession process.

Drawing upon all six Regular Reports that have been issued by the European Commission since 1998, one can plausibly argue that the institutionalization of EU democratic beliefs and institutional practices is a matter of degree as it comprises seven dimensions along which Polish and Czechs do not score evenly. More specifically, in order for a candidate country to achieve "stability of institutions guaranteeing democracy, the rule of law, human rights and the respect for the protection of minorities" it should (a) establish a *parliament*, (b) have a well functioning *executive*, (c) build up its *judicial system*, (d) adopt *anti-corruption measures*, and finally (e)ensure for its citizens *civil and political rights*, (f) *economic social and cultural rights* as well as (g) *minority rights and protection of minorities*.

Overall, the causal force of EU democratic beliefs and institutional practices cannot be denied as one tracer the evolution of political life in both the Czech Republic and Poland. All the formal procedures are now in place to guarantee a democratic government, from free and fair elections to separation of powers, although not all procedures have been fully implemented. There is no doubt that both the Czechs and the Poles, like all ten applicants of EU membership, have "passed the point of no return to Communism."[30] Nevertheless, there is diversity in how fully they have broken their ties with past patterns of governance and in how far they can incorporate the democratic practices of existing EU members into their own institutions. Hence, formal institutionalization varies as Tables 1 and 2 indicate, and along with it the success of EU socialization mechanisms in these two countries. Even though the tools that have been used are the same, it is important to note that the response has been different, which implies that the EU should carefully reconsider its socialization practices and adjust them to the needs of each candidate.

Apparently, the Czech state actors have been more receptive to EU ideas. Even though in 1998 the positive institutional developments in the two countries coincide numerically, in 2000 the Czech Republic demonstrates a slight comparative advantage in the number of positive comments it attracts. Put more clearly, in the last monitoring report the Czech state actors prove their willingness to fully abide by the rules of the EU accession game. The executive was the only area that gave cause for concern, since the Civil Service Act had not entered into force before 1 January 2005,[31] which means that the Czechs were admitted to the EU without having reformed their central administration. Of course the judicial structures too have still a long way to go before fully meeting western democratic standards, but

30 Heather Grabbe and Kirsty Hughes, *Enlarging the EU Eastwards* (London: The Royal Institute of International Affairs, 1998), p. 44.

31 This is due to the financial burden caused by the floods of 2002.

Table 1 Poland—progress in meeting the political criteria

RR	*PAR*	*EXEC*	*JUD*	*AC*	*CPR*	*ESCR*	*MR*
1998	+	−	−	−	+	(−)	+
2000	+	+	−	−	−	−	+
2003	+	−	−	−	+	+	+

Note. RR, Regular Reports; PAR, Parliament; EXEC, Executive; JUD, Judiciary; AC, Anti-Corruption; CPR, Civil and Political Rights; ESCR, Economic Social and Cultural Rights; MR, Minority Rights.
+: overall positive comments, −: overall negative comments, (−): negative comments on a par with positive.
Source. Commission, Regular Reports, 1998, 2000 and Monitoring Reports, 2003.

there are numerous trends in the right direction. In addition, the Czech political authorities have to cope with the hurdles the communist past imposes on their fight against corruption. The latter is almost taken for granted and public officials find it difficult to adapt to the post-communist political ethos, according to which personal favours from governmental and private sources are no longer acceptable.[32] In overall terms, however, the progress of the Czechs is seen as satisfactory, not just because an anti-corruption commission has been established by the Ministry of the Interior, but also due to the fact that a special telephone hotline and e-mail address have been inaugurated with a view to enable citizens to launch complaints of corruption.[33]

While the Czechs are simply advised to consolidate reforms and maintain their effort to fully respond to EU membership demands, the Poles are strongly rebuked by the Commission in the last monitoring report issued on 5 November 2003. Given that the Commission singles out only three areas, which give cause for alarm, one might think that Poland has successfully internalized EU institutional norms and practices. However, one should bear in mind that typically the political conditions of membership have been met by all applicants, and the monitoring reports only deal with the judiciary, the executive and anti-corruption measures because they are important for the implementation and enforcement of the acquis. Hence, the conclusion to be drawn is that the Polish record in EU membership socialization faces a downward trend in recent days. More specifically, in public administration,

---

32 Karen Henderson, "Reforming the Post-Communist States: Meeting the Political Conditions for Membership," in Charles Jenkins (ed.), *The Unification of Europe: An Analysis of EU Enlargement* (London: Centre For Reform, 2000), p. 32.

33 Commission of the European Communities, *Comprehensive Monitoring Report on the Czech Republic's Preparations for Membership* (Brussels, 5 November, 2003), pp. 10–14.

Table 2 Czech Republic—progress in meeting the political criteria

RR	*PAR*	*EXEC*	*JUD*	*AC*	*CPR*	*ESCR*	*MR*
1998	+	(−)	−	−	+	+	−
2000	+	−	−	−	+	+	(−)
2003	+	−	(−)	(−)	+	+	+

Note. RR, Regular Reports; PAR, Parliament; EXEC, Executive; JUD, Judiciary; AC, Anti-Corruption; CPR, Civil and Political Rights; ESCR, Economic Social and Cultural Rights; MR, Minority Rights. +: overall positive comments, −: overall negative comments, (−): negative comments on a par with positive.
Source. Commission: Regular Reports, 1998, 2000 and Monitoring Reports 2003.

the Commission bluntly admits that "most of the structures dealing with European Integration issues need further strengthening and some will have difficulty being fully capable of dealing with these new duties in an efficient, timely and professional manner by the date of accession".[34] In the field of the Judiciary, the Commission argues that the wide interpretation of penal immunity of judges is "alien to other legal systems in Europe and is not in itself a guarantee of independence". The Commission's criticism, nevertheless, reaches its peak in the field of corruption, which is said to "affect all aspects of public life."

Moving beyond institutionalization, as demarcated along the seven dimensions singled out in the Regular and Monitoring reports, there are two further reasons for which the Poles rather than the Czechs have acquired a reputation of constant "heel dragging" on EU membership. To begin with, the Czech state actors skillfully managed their way through the exigencies of democratic change, despite the fact that democratic transition in Czechoslovakia was abrupt, and the democratic reformers were neither numerous nor prepared.[35] In Poland, political transition did not have the same point of departure as it came out of a political compromise agreement between the opposition (Solidarity movement) and the communists. The Solidarity Trade Union Movement of 1980–1981 did not only give the Polish Revolution an early start but also established the foundations of a civil society indispensable to the growth of democratic institutions. Furthermore, Solidarity gave a formative

[34] Commission of the European Communities, *Comprehensive Monitoring Report on Poland's Preparations for Membership* (Brussels, 5 November 2003), pp. 13–14.

[35] David M. Olson, "Democratization and Political Participation: The Experience of the Czech Republic," in Karen Dawisha and Bruce Parrot (eds.), *The Consolidation of Democracy in East-Central Europe* (Cambridge: Cambridge University Press, 1998), p. 154.

experience to the new governing elite that would take over in 1989.[36] For these reasons one would expect Poland to absorb easily the values of Western democratic societies and be in the avant-garde of "EU socialized states".[37] Of course building upon differences in historical legacies and political culture, as well as on differences in domestic political structures one could explain in greater detail why some candidates have been more responsive than others to the causal effect of EU socialization mechanisms. My present effort is aimed at mapping such differences in elite-driven institutionalization and provide evidence to invite a great deal more exploration.

The differences in the degree of institutionalization of EU democratic values among the Czech and Polish state actors do not constitute a sound proof of their socialization success or failure unless the habituation of state actors enters into this analytical picture. Given the difficulty of obtaining data on elite attitudes that would help me trace the degree to which EU constitutive norms have penetrated and modified the value repertoire of CEE state elites, I shall rather turn attention to the habituation of the public into the EU ideal. In other words, the focus will be on public opinion polls directly, recognizing the fact that by doing so I am subject to an inter-level fallacy, because popular socialization is a process subject to different dynamics than elite socialization. Opinion polls, however, will help me gauge the attitudes of the mass public and see whether their habituation to EU norms and practices is analogous to the institutionalization inflicted by state elites.

In addition, if I abide by Schimmelfennig's writings the prevalence of popular over elite habituation becomes apparent. More specifically, Schimmelfennig argues that

> The socialization of states as corporate actors does not necessarily require personal internalization at the level of policy makers if the beliefs and practices in question are sufficiently institutionalized in domestic decision-making process and effectively protected by domestic sanctioning mechanisms.[38]

---

36 For further details on regime change and democratisation in Poland see: Marjorie Castle, and Ray Taras, *Democracy in Poland* (Oxford: Westview Press 2002), pp. 63–94. See also: Bernhard Wessels and Hans-Dieter Klingemann, "Transformation and the Prerequisites of Democratic Opposition in Central and Eastern Europe," in Samuel H. Barnes and János Simon (eds.), *The Post-Communist Citizen* (Budapest: Erasmus Foundation and Institute for Political Science of the Hungarian Academy of Sciences, 1998), pp. 1–34.

37 Andrew A. Michta, "Democratic Consolidation in Poland after 1989," in Karen Dawisha and Bruce Parrot (eds.), *The Consolidation of Democracy* in*East-Central Europe* (Cambridge: Cambridge University Press 1998), pp. 74–75. See also John Fitzmaurice, *Government and Politics in the Visegrad Countries: Poland, Hungary the Czech Republic and Slovakia* (London: MacMillan Press, 1998), pp. 23–27.

38 Schimmelfennig, *op. cit.* n. 2, p. 112.

Put simply, it is mainly the formal adaptation that matters at the elite level. If elite institutionalization is not accompanied by gradual popular habituation to the new institutionalized practices, it is not hard to imagine how hard it will be for state elites to keep EU institutional patterns and beliefs unchallenged mainly in the national but also in the supranational sphere.

6. PUBLIC OPINION IN CEE AND THE NORMATIVE JUSTIFIABILITY OF EU MEMBERSHIP

Wishing to monitor Czech and Polish citizens' attitudes towards EU across time, namely, before the 1998 regular report, a few years after (2001) and finally at a more recent date (2002), I had difficulties locating a set of comparable survey questions. Only the Eurobarometer (EB) and World Value Surveys' (WVS) data sets the regular repetition of key questions establishing long and short-term trends and thus the possibility for time series. The WVS results for the period 1999–2002, were not available at the time of writing so I focus instead on EB questions only.

Given my interest in normative justifiability, i.e. the extent to which the EU has infiltrated the value repertoire of both Czech and Polish citizens, I shall be looking at peoples' affective allegiance to the EU and the democratic principles it propagates. The operationalization of affective support for the EU is a hard task to undertake and the scarcity of sufficient comparative data for CEE, even in the Eurobarometer surveys, further confound my measurement effort.[39] There are, however, two broad questions that have been asked consistently over the period 1996–2002 and shall be used to construct the index of "diffuse" popular support for the EU. I will employ one question regarding the image of the EU in the candidate countries and another one measuring the respondents' voting intentions on a referendum about EU membership.[40] The vagueness of these survey items suggests that they can load on both a utilitarian and affective dimension of EU support. Put simply, a Czech or a Polish citizen can have an overall positive impression of the EU, and express an intention to vote for membership not just because he/she has started to identify with the EU and its constitutive principles, but rather due to an egoistic calculation of material self-interest. Nevertheless, such a combination should not affect the validity of my measurement, because as David Easton posits "diffuse support" arises not only from a normative process of identification but also from accumulated

[39] I shall be using both Central and Eastern Eurobarometer (CEEB) and its successor, the Candidate Countries Eurobarometer (CCEB).

[40] The exact wording of these questions is as follows: A. As you know 15 states of "Western Europe" form together the "European Union". Would you say that your impression of the aims and the activities of the EU is generally 1. positive 2. neutral or 3. Negative? B. On the whole are you very satisfied, fairly satisfied, not very satisfied or not at all satisfied with the way democracy is developing in our country?

Table 3 Positive image of the European Union

	1996		1997		2001		2002
Czech Republic	33	100	34	103	46	139	NA
Poland	58	100	56	96.5	44	76	NA
CEE total	49	100	50	102	52	106	NA

Source. Central and Eastern Eurobarometer Nos. 7 and 8, Candidate Countries Eurobarometer 2001, 2002 (first results).

positive utilitarian appraisals, which become, in time, dissociated from performance and get transformed into generalized attitudes of affective allegiance.[41]

In overall terms, the data presented in Tables 3 and 4 appears to support the claim that formal transposition of EU norms to CEE elites can influence public habituation to EU ideas and practices because the normative identification of Czech and Polish respondents with the Union is analogous to the degree of institutionalization achieved in the domestic sphere. How can such a conclusion be drawn? Before proceeding with the analysis, allow me to make a preliminary note concerning the presentation of the collected survey material. Apart from the percentage of those who have responded positively to the above-mentioned survey items, I have chosen to standardize my data to 100, taking as a starting point a period two years before the first Regular Report issued in 1998. This is done not only with a view to ensure consistency and clarity of presentation. Rather, what is more important is registering the change in popular identification with the EU, in both the Czech Republic and Poland, as time goes by. And I have deliberately chosen to make the 1996 percentages my starting point, because this is a period in which popular perceptions of the EU start to grow in maturity moving beyond the revolutionary

Table 4 Vote for EU membership in upcoming referendum

	1996		1997		2001		2002	
Czech Republic	43	100	49	114	54	126	50	116
Poland	70	100	63	90	54	77	61	87
CEE total	61	100	60	98	65	107	69	113

Source. Central and Eastern Eurobarometer Nos. 7 and 8, Candidate Countries Eurobarometer 2001, 2002 (first results).

41 For a detailed analysis of the notions of "diffuse" and "specific" support, see David Easton, "A Re-Assessment of the Concept of Political Support," *British Journal of Political Science*, 5 (1975), pp. 435–457, as well as David Easton, *A Systems Analysis of Political Life* (New York: Wiley, 1965).

euphoria of 1991 when the motto "return to Europe" had almost intoxicated the public.

Turning now to the central theme of my inquiry that is the evolution of normative justification for the EU among the public and whether it varies depending on the degree of domestic institutionalization. I shall juxtapose the Czechs with the Poles while evaluating their score in both questions constituting the index of EU affective support (i.e. habituation to EU norms). Looking closely at the standardized figures of Table 3, one does not fail to detect a significant upward trend in positive popular perceptions of the EU among the Czechs. Even though the initial percentage of those who would attribute a positive image to the Union (33%) is well below the CEE average in that period (49%), still positive EU conceptualization grows steadily over the years, reaching the level of 39 points above the 1996 measurement. On the contrary, the figures tapping positive perception of the EU among the Polish public progressively recede. The high percentage (58% = 100) of respondents, who would have a positive "impression of the aims and activities of the EU" in 1996, gives way to a rather disappointing figure 24 points below the initial measurement (that is 44%). Furthermore, such a decline in the image of the EU among the Poles does not reflect a general trend among the CEECs because the CEE total figure is subject to a small but steady increase over the years.

Similarly, the standardized figures in Table 4 register slow but substantive progress in popular approval for EU membership among the Czech public, while in Poland the prospect of joining the EU does not find the degree of ardent popular support it would enjoy in 1996, two years before the opening of accession negotiations. Looking closely at the Czech score, one cannot deny the evolution in popular allegiance to the EU as the initial level of respondents who would vote for EU membership (45% =100) grows by 26 points in 2001, and despite the decline registered in 2002 percentages, it is still 16 points above the initial measurement. By contrast, the trajectory of public support for accession to the EU has been generally falling in Poland, apart from a small gain in 2002 (from 54 to 61% = 87) which is still 23 points below the wide support of 70% (=100) registered in 1996. Even though in 2002, the average level of popular support for EU membership is higher among the Poles than the Czechs by 11 percentage points, the overall progress of Poland does not follow the upward trend in average support for accession, registered among the total of CEECs.

7. AN OVERVIEW OF THE OPINION POLLS AND CONCLUDING REMARKS

Overall, comparing the results obtained by opinion polling in Poland and the Czech Republic, with Tables 1 and 2 presenting the degree of domestic institutionalization, one does not fail to notice that popular habituation to EU norms and actions can be influenced by formal elite institutionalization. The logic of this discussion suggests that the normative justifiability of EU power is substantially determined by the formal transposition of EU beliefs and actions in domestic institutional practices.

In Poland, the slow process of adaptation to the demands of liberal democracy, matched by the growth in corruption, give rise to public discontent and trigger the so called "impact of waiting", since people coming out of "the dramatic fast-forward of revolution" want drastic, transformative results.[42] Hence, people's impression of the aims and activities of the EU does not improve in the course of time. In addition, the Poles' positive disposition towards EU membership should no longer be taken for granted because it is subject to decline as time goes by. In the Czech Republic, the slow but steady progress in the institutionalization of EU democratic standards has given a favourable push to popular habituation with the EU and the prospect of joining its institutional structures. The percentages indicate, though, that there is still room for improvement. There is no doubt that the Czechs open up to the EU, as the state actors incorporate the EU democratic lessons in the daily experience of domestic institutions. Nevertheless, the Union is still far from having won the hearts and the minds of the Czechs.

Building upon such evidence, the EU should reassess its socialization practices and leave aside coercive persuasion focusing rather on argumentative and "learning by doing" instruments. As the accession negotiations have been successfully concluded with all ten CEE applicants and the day of admission comes closer, it is time for EU actors to show confidence in the CEE "pupils" and gradually enculturate those into the liberal democratic practices without using the socialization "sticks" that only help euroscepticism grow. Instead of taking recourse to exceptional criticisms of the new Member States launched either via Commission written reports or through statements in the media, the EU should rather strengthen its advisory role, better co-ordinate its "learning by doing" tools, and enhance the status of the argumentative mechanisms. The use of "learning by doing" tools, more specifically, should be reinforced in the countries lagging behind in terms of formal transposition of EU membership demands and participation could be encouraged by applying the same tools not just to CEE candidates but even to current Member States. If the socialization mechanisms apply to all members, both old and new, that should increase the credibility of EU socialization efforts in the candidate countries and subsequently the willingness of state actors to move along with formal institutionalization.

Of course I do not dismiss monitoring altogether, as it can still provide the CEECs with useful guidelines on how to successfully assume the responsibilities of membership. Monitoring after accession, nevertheless, would be more effective if conducted under a more argumentative prism, like the one offered by the European Conference, where political consultation becomes more important than mere exposition of the weaknesses of the new members.[43] In this manner, monitoring

---

42 Timothy G. Ash, *History of the Present: Essays, Sketches and Dispatches from Europe in the 1990s* (Allen Lane: The Penguin Press, 1999), p. 43.

43 In the Comprehensive Monitoring Report issued by the Commission in 2003 it is mentioned that monitoring after accession will not diminish but rather follow different procedures and

will deepen co-operation among member states and shall have a constitutive effect upon the identities of state actors involved. After all, only through genuine dialogue will the EU patient be able to recover the shock the European Constitution failure caused in December 2003, spreading doubts as regards the successful socialization of new Member States in general and Poland in particular.

European heads of state, instead of abandoning negotiations, should rather put all the cards on the table and discuss, at length, if it is possible to find a way out of the impasse characterizing current EU affairs. Deliberation is not a panacea but it will definitely assist in the establishment of common grounds among the new Europe of 25 Member States. The Brussels IGC on 12 December 2003 only proved that in the absence of dialogue, EU solidarity that has so far driven the process of integration, gives way to a "grocers' mentality" by means of which disagreement over the reweighting of votes in the Council becomes an insurmountable obstacle. European leaders did not take time to exchange views on the subject matter that would help them reach a compromise of some sort. As a Greek newspaper would point out, they only convened for an hour and after a 20-hour break they would discuss for a few minutes before deciding to interrupt the workings of the IGC.[44] Even the new Constitutional Treaty that finally emerged from heated intergovernmental debate on 18 June 2004, was not precisely the outcome of consensual deliberation, where argumentation supplements bargaining over pre-given national preferences. Rather, it was the product of intense interstate negotiations surpassing the initial deliberative character of the Convention that had been responsible for its drafting. As such, there is great uncertainty over the eventual ratification of the Constitutional Treaty by all member states having taken part in its rational bargaining.

On the basis of structured dialogue, however, co-ordinated by EU hierarchy if necessary, i.e. the Commission president, current and new EU members should be able to understand each other better and set in motion the political integration engine. Such co-operation at state actors' level may also prove useful in inspiring EU citizens to enlarge their national identity by adding to it a European dimension of common political fate. So far, the imposition of EU beliefs in the form of membership conditionality did not help all candidates to successfully "digest" the EU lesson. Neither will the imposition of economic sanctions help appease elite and public discontent in the new Member States, that wish to be treated on an equal

---

manifest itself differently, e.g. using the "internal market scoreboard" on the transposition of internal market directives instead of "regular reports". Where possible it will be based on the ongoing pre-notification of the transposition of directives through the TAIEX office. The Commission will assume its normal task of enforcing the acquis and, where necessary, will take administrative and legal action.

44 Γιώργος Δελάστικ, "Η Διεύρυνση της Ε.Ε Εφερε Μεγάλη Κρίση" [EU Enlargement Brought about an Unprecedented Crisis], Η Καθημερινή 21/12/2003, p. 16.

basis after all these years of waiting for EU to open its doors.[45] This time the EU should take recourse to argumentation that will bring the "new" Europe closer to the "old".

Last but not least, the EU should underlie the need for state actors to reach out to the wider public and restore the linkages that have weakened over time. Of course the challenge of public opinion is something that must be met on the local and national level. The EU should nonetheless reinforce national communication strategies, not just reminding but also supporting politicians and decision-makers in other sectors of society, in their effort to bring the citizen closer to the European cause. Promising steps have been taken in this direction via the Commission's "Communication Strategy for Enlargement" adopted in May 2000. That is an action meant to improve public knowledge of the EU in the candidate countries, to explain the implications of accession for each country and hence help the citizens to overcome misperceptions that give rise to fears and concerns in the public sphere. Current Member States are also involved with a view to achieve an improved understanding of the enlargement process among the wider public. After all, accession is "a new contract between citizens and not merely a treaty between states" as the heads of state and government vociferously argued while signing the accession Treaty on 16 April 2003. However, co-ordinated efforts of this sort should be maintained even after accession with a view to promote dialogue at all levels of society between policy-makers and the public on the role of the EU in their daily life.

45 After the Brussels IGC the six net contributors to the EU budget (Germany, France, the United Kingdom, the Netherlands, Sweden and Austria) sent a letter to the Commission President, Romano Prodi, letting him know that they would "freeze" their contributions to the EC budget to 1% of the current EU GDP for the period 2007–2013.

Part II: Constitutionalism

7. Becoming "Europeans": The Impact of EU "Constitutionalism" on Post-Communist Pre-Modernity

András Sajó

1. Introduction

One of the persistent fears in the European Union is that the accession countries will be unable to catch up with the prevailing practices of constitutionalism and the rule of law that supposedly ground the common tradition of Europe. This fear is rationalized when considering that unbridled nationalism necessarily impacts upon territorial stability. There are other concerns regarding the weakness of democratic tradition especially after the years of totalitarian rule. It is believed that the institutional systems in place for enforcing the rule of law[1] merely exist in a formal sense rather than in terms of self-sustaining value commitments. The scope of this chapter does not allow for an analysis into the truth of such assumptions. It is undeniable that extremist nationalism is not absent in the rhetoric, and sometimes actual policies, of Eastern European political elites who in turn find popular endorsement for their nationalistic campaigns.[2] These nationalistic sentiments will be echoed once the population of new member states will be confronted with negative experiences as a result of them being unable to successfully articulate their special interests in a great "empire"; unfavorable comparisons of "Brussels as the new imperial power" with the "yoke of the Soviet empire" has already been made in many former communist countries.

One of the striking features of East European nationalism is that it is embedded in a value system that is (at best) indifferent to modernity as it grounds itself in past (ascribed and mystical) national glory. This belief does not generate much interest in the ethics of modernity as put forward in the rule of law (rational accountability for

---

1 In fact, both new and old member states confront, with some difficulty, the aggressive enforcement of bureaucratic (excessively bounded) rationalism that relies on Union supremacy to the detriment of nation-state level constitutionalism. For the old member states see, e.g., the *Alcan* decision: Case C 24/95, *Alcan* II [1997] ECR I-1591 [German rule of law concept disregarded by the ECJ].

2 The Summer 2003 Gallup poll indicates that although many Hungarians and Estonians identify themselves as citizens of the nation-state *only* (39%) this is not particularly high compared to Great Britain (64%). However, there was no Hungarian who would have identified himself/herself as "European only". Hungarian identity correlates with age but not with party affiliation.

Wojciech Sadurski et al. (ed.), Spreading Democracy and the Rule of Law?, 175–192.

one's acts, transparency, predictability through formalism, etc.). Modernists (modernizers) argue that accession will change attitudes toward modernization among large segments of the population. However, given the process of accession and the way the new Union is shaped, firm, popular commitment to an efficient democracy as well as the belief in popular self-government, such an efficient responsive and responsible modern institutional system has limited opportunities to prevail beyond the institutional façade. Citizens of the new member states might become *Zwangsdemokraten* (forced democrats).[3] This is problematic because so long as the new European constitutional identity remains an unfinished and uncertain project (an imposed mask) only a limited modernizing identity will be offered. It is also true that the Eastern European political elite seems to have a very instrumentalist disregard[4] for the rule of law even though formal legalism is at least accepted. (Even Meciar accepted unfavorable decisions of the Slovak Constitutional Court.)

Instrumentalism and the hidden contempt of the rule of law and constitutional values in general are confronted with a normative commitment to constitutionalism and the rule of law which programmatically exists in the "older" member states. So long as "European solutions" are felt as being imposed and detrimental to local self-interests, "modernity" (i.e. efficiency considerations and pragmatism in decision-making, irrespective of traditional values and communitarian sentiments) will be detested. However it could be that those national institutions beyond national democratic control and interrelated with European institutional networks may create institutions within the traditional national(istic) states that serve democracy.

It is believed, and in many regards rightly so, that accession to the Union will push Eastern Europe towards the values and institutional settings of modernity. Modernity, in allowing for interest group collective action, can be considered a mixed blessing. Interest group politics behind European centralization is neither particularly conducive to a robust republican design of democracy nor does it contribute to fairness with regard to the protection of minority and other vulnerable groups.[5] As a result of these shortcomings relating not only to the process but

---

3 The term was used by a German journalist with regard to the late Bavarian Prime Minister Franz-Joseph Strauss. Of course, given certain historical circumstances the progress to genuine democracy might lead through imposed democracy.

4 It is quite telling that the Hungarian Government's chief delegate to the European Convention who joined the overwhelming majority of the delegates signing a document proposing that the new Constitution should be adopted by national referenda, stated in Hungary that he does not deem it appropriate to call a referendum; his signature was added as part of the horse trading that took place at the negotiations. This is a telling, though not unique, example of the understanding of the binding force of contracts, both in the public and among the political elite.

5 On the new European constitutional design as a project of centralization related to special interest group interest representation where they are loosing at the national level, see Michele Ruta, "The Allocation of Competencies in an International Union: A Positive Analysis," http://www.ecb.int/pub/scientific/wps/author/html/author222.en.html

also the political, historical and cultural consequences of accession, the effect of modernization might, in the short term, be limited and perhaps even quite the opposite. Furthermore, the ambiguities of the European project could reinforce pre-modern values within acceding states. The current practices of constitutional public politics are limited to electoral participation of limited relevance for decision-making. In other words, the rational discourse that allows for intellectual formation, the acceptance of governmental decisions and a more engaging decision-making process is absent.

In this chapter, I will look at the present impact of "Europeanization" on public understanding of constitutional democracy and the institutional structures put in place within new member states. I will then briefly consider the foreseeable impact of the European Constitution on the constitutional structures (the new checks and balances) of new member states. Due to the scope of this chapter, I will not address the human rights dimension of constitutionalism. I will consider, in particular, the formation, and distortion, of constitutional democratic politics in the accession process particularly with regard to the referenda and the constitutional structures that have emerged thus far in the new member states. The politics of accession and other governmental practices remain highly instrumentalist. Such instrumentalism diminishes the likelihood that the general public will cherish the virtues of deliberative democracy and tempered majoritarianism.

Relying primarily on the Hungarian experience I will analyze the potential changes in the democratic and constitutional ethos as a result of the emerging allocation of powers in the new Union. The constitutionalist inspiration that transpires from the debate on the European Constitution as well as the draft itself is highly problematic as a blueprint for "transformative constitutionalism".[6]

My first claim is that the accession process as well as the drafting of the European Constitution has reinforced the irrelevance of constitutional democracy in the eyes of the public who continue to see it as a matter of majoritarianism. It remains to be seen how the emerging European Union model of pluricentric separation of powers ("network constitutionalism") will be understood and used democratically by the citizens of the new member states.

My second claim is that, outside of the genuinely free elections firmly entrenched within new member states, certain patterns of state socialism are going to be reinforced through membership to the Union. Democratic politics is understood for many people as a tool of maintaining free public services, irrespective of contribution or need (except the needs of service providers). Such trends might be

---

6 Transformative constitutionalism is about openness to the future and it is based on a critical relationship to the past. In the distinction of preservative and transformative constitutions I follow Cass Sunstein, *Designing Democracy. What Constitutions Do* (New York: Oxford University Press 2001), p. 67. On the pre-modern traditionalism of post-communist constitutions see András Sajó, "Preferred Generations: A Paradox of Restoration Constitutions", *Cardozo Law Review*, 14 (1993) pp. 847–864.

reinforced whist converting local constitutional politics to the European level. The experiences of the accession process indicate that democratic participation and parliamentarism are often quite formal. Instead of genuine participatory politics and accountability, democracy becomes an opportunity to influence politics in order to maximize welfare services. *Union law and policies reinforce the welfare entitlement attitudes of the East European public*. The Union has its own social welfarist value system (or routine) which reinforces the inherited welfarist expectations in the new member states. In these countries, the use of resources for the maintenance of European Union type welfare systems might be counterproductive and contribute to the difficulty in creating a robust democratic and constitutional culture.

2. CONSTITUTIONAL STRUCTURES AND THE THINNING OF MAJORITARIAN DEMOCRACY

2.1. "Europe Clauses"—Preservative Constitutionalism

Eastern European accession countries have recent constitutions that were created after the collapse of communism.[7] The Estonian Constitution (1992) (Art. 1)[8], and the Czech and Slovak constitutions (1992) declare the respective countries to be *sovereign*, while Poland (1997), Hungary (1990 amendment), Latvia (1992), Lithuania (1992) and Slovenia (1991) refer to *independence*. Lithuania's Constitution also states that people's sovereignty cannot be limited. Even in cases where the Constitution is less unequivocal (as in Hungary) prevailing national sentiment is well represented in the jurisprudence of the Constitutional Court. Here a very traditional concept of sovereignty (see below) has been agreed upon which in turn has resulted in the restrictive wording of the Europe clause in Hungary. The transfer of public powers is not possible. Only the transfer of the right to exercise certain powers is allowed since such a transfer cannot be based on the ultimate source of sovereignty—the Hungarian people.[9]

This concern with *state* sovereignty as a basis for independence is remarkable when compared with Western European constitutions where the matter is either not discussed at all, or is not made explicit (see e.g. Austria[10], Belgium), or is

7 The Hungarian Constitution is technically the Constitution of 1949 but it was fully amended in 1989 with several additional revisions since then.

8 "Estonia is an independent and sovereign democratic republic wherein the supreme power of the state is held by the people." The formulation follows closely Article 1 of the 1938 Estonian constitution which is the basis of the adoption by referendum of the 1992 constitution, as expressly stated in the Preamble of the 1992 Constitution.

9 See for example Olivér Várhelyi, "Hungary" in Andrea Ott and Kirstyn Inglis (eds.), *Handbook on European Enlargement* (The Hague: T.M.C. Asser Press 2002), p. 264.

10 The Austrian Constitution states (Art. 1) that her legal order originates in the people. This, of course, can be seen as a reference to sovereignty.

referred to in the context of the source of sovereignty: Italy, Art. 1; France, Art. 3—where sovereignty pertains to the people; Spain Art. 1.2—where the people are the depository of sovereignty; Portugal is one of the few exceptions where there is direct reference to state sovereignty.)

Since EU membership affects sovereignty, and arguably the independence of Eastern European states, it is understandable that the independence and sovereignty clauses are therefore seen as obstacles, to integration. The importance of these provisions is increased not only because they touch upon foundational issues but also as a result of the pro-independence public sentiment. The population in nation-states with newly recognized or regained sovereignty is understandably sensitive to issues of independence. Opposition politicians are ready to bring up the issue hoping for increased popularity in a society where popular culture traditionally honors (unsuccessful) heroes of independence. Moreover, the cultural and the legal elite are often keen to emphasize independence as a fundamental constitutional principle (because of the constitutional wording and independence dreams in their legal traditions). Both the general public sentiment and the ongoing political conflicts explain why constitutional amendments intended for accommodating the operations of the Union are sometimes rather narrow.

By way of comparison it is worthwhile noting that the various approaches of transferring competence within the Europe clauses are essentially compatible with the prevailing continental constitutional solutions that emerged in the post-Maastricht context. The East European accession countries have carefully considered the constitutional solutions adopted in the Member States after Maastricht. The EU made it a priority to provide a knowledge base of expertise in this area. Given the increasing uncertainty of the nature of the Union, its identity, mission and decision-making powers at the time the accession clauses were being written into the respective constitutions, it is understandable why some accession countries were reluctant to take a final position on the transfer of powers and competencies to the Union. The Latvian amendment, for example, expressly considers the accession to be subject to revision by way of a referendum that can be initiated by the people. Lithuania's amendment of Art. 136 also contains a safeguard clause: "The Republic of Lithuania participates in international organizations if such participation does not contradict interests of the state and its independence." However, the Europe clause states that it expressly "transfers to the EU the competencies of the national institutions in the fields foreseen in the Founding Treaties of the EU, so that it shall be entitled to implement common competencies with other EU member states in those fields."

2.2. Referendum—Instrumentalism and Lack of Deliberative Democracy

Given the concern with independence and (popular) sovereignty and because of the fundamental changes that would result from accession, all the Eastern European countries concerned opted for a referendum to sanction accession (or the accession treaty). This was irrespective of whether this form of popular support is prescribed by the constitution or not as was the case of Hungary until the 2002 amendments, or Poland (where this is a matter of choice). Indeed, some of the constitutions were amended so that they include the requirement of confirmation by referendum. It would be expected that those firm believers in popular sovereignty (i.e. that sovereign power resides in the people) would welcome this position. However, with the significant exception of Lithuania,[11] the Eastern European accession countries (which do constitutionally and doctrinally endorse the position of popular sovereignty) have been keen to avoid referenda and plebiscite. For instance, even in the case of the dissolution of Czechoslovakia there was no referendum. Mobilizing support in a referendum has always been a problem because of the quorum difficulties. Hungary barely satisfied the 50% participation requirement in the case of the Hungarian NATO accession referendum. All previous referenda ended unsuccessfully in Slovakia where the law on referendum requires (as was the case in Hungary) that voter turn-out must be higher than 50 percent of all registered voters in order for the referendum to be valid. Also many previous attempts at holding a referendum were perceived by the Eastern European political establishment as populist attempts to undermine the parliamentary constitutional order. (For the actual destabilizing effects of the use of referenda, see its use in the power struggles between the Parliament and the President of Ukraine and similarly in Moldova.[12]) It is quite telling that the Hungarian Constitutional Court, although in principle a protector of the individual political right to referendum, systematically restricted the applicability of referendum declaring various initiatives to be disguised attempts at amending the Constitution. The Hungarian Constitution was amended in 1997 with the effect of curtailing the use of referenda as a device of change.[13]

On the one hand a theory of constituent power that denies the right of popular initiative in this context is perhaps an odd one, but on the other hand, it is quite understandable with regard to constitutional stability: a value that was considered crucial in the early formative years of the new democracies.

---

11 The Lithuanian constitution stresses the constitutional and constituent importance of referendum from its moment of creation. Art. 9.1 provides that on matters of fundamental importance affecting the population or the country that a referendum be held. Note that the independence of Lithuania was restored through a 1991 referendum that was the culmination of mass resistance to Soviet rule.

12 For a review of the use of referenda see Norman Dorsen, Michel Rosenfeld, András Sajó and Susanne Baer, *Comparative Constitutionalism: Cases and Materials* (St. Paul, Minnesota: West Group, 2003), Ch. 3.

13 The amendment was adopted by the socialist-liberal coalition ruling at the time, which disposed of a parliamentary supermajority sufficient to constitutional amendment. The provision became an obstacle in 2003 for the same coalition which currently has only a narrow majority. Because the socialist-liberal coalition restricted the use of referendum they could not and will not be able to bypass the resistance of the opposition in accession matters by calling a referendum (where they probably would have a clear majority); the special terms of the one time referendum on accession required the consent of the opposition.

Notwithstanding the lack of constitutional positions, and the remarkable legitimacy of the available specific parliamentary process,[14] the political elites of all East European countries sensed (without any specific discussion) that accession needs a plebiscite-like popular endorsement. In a way, a referendum is not the preferred constitution amending procedure in the case of these easy-to-amend constitutions, neither is the tool of referendum intended to become the choice even after the current round of amendments. In fact, in most countries, the mechanism foreseen to handle future constitutional amendments resulting from EU developments excludes the referendum (although Estonia and Latvia are somewhat ambiguous exceptions). The desire of governments for popular legitimation resulted in one-off solutions regarding referenda, yet exceptionalism in constitutional matters is always a cause for concern.

It is possible that the use of a referendum will create certain expectations with regard to future constitutional amendments and EU constitutional changes. The prevailing anti-referendum constitutional pattern seems, however, unchanged. Indeed, at least in Hungary (but not in the Czech Republic) the political elite finds that there is no need to accept the European Constitution via referendum because low level endorsement would be seen as a vote of no-confidence in the government; a referendum would provide additional opportunities for the parliamentary and extra-parliamentary opposition to impose its will on the government. Such considerations are clearly pragmatic and instrumentalist. Of course, within the Union, as the 2002 Irish referendum indicates, allowing a referendum remains an important popular control device over executive activities. "It is clear that retained powers of the people may force government to bring about greater domestic scrutiny of EU legislative proposals in advance of the referendum."[15] Without such a device the executive will gain further powers.

2.3. A New Separation of Powers in the Union: Further Loss of Popular-Democratic Control

The most fundamental (substantive and procedural) changes in the Eastern European constitutional systems, laws, institutions, and societies will occur in the coming years immediately proceeding accession. It is only during this time

---

14 Miroslaw Wyrzykowski, "European Clause: Is it a Threat to Sovereignty?", in M. Wyrzykowski (ed.), *Constitutional Cultures* (Warsaw: Institute of Public Affairs 2000), at 278 indicates that a large coalition is needed for ratification. The Polish Constitution is prudent enough to enable parliamentary majority to go to the country via referendum in order to circumvent stalemate and opposition blackmail. The Hungarian socialists, when in power, ruled out that possibility through a constitutional amendment. That possibility, of course, determines the opportunistic behavior of the parliamentary opposition of the day.

15 Gerard Hogan, "European Union Law and National Constitutions: Ireland" (FIDE XX Congress London 2002), www.fide2002.org 24.

that an entirely new institutional mechanism will redefine these relations. Most of these changes will not be reflected in the constitutions unless there will be fundamental changes in the Union itself through the emerging constitutional framework. The interpretation of the constitutions and the extra-constitutional interpretation of sub-constitutional laws and institutions in political practices will, however, reflect these changes.

The constitutions of the new member states so far poorly reflect the shifts in decision-making. The current amendments address the role of the legislative branch in the formulation of future European policies and legislation in a minimalist way, allowing in practice an increase in the power of the executive. The amendments were adopted following instrumentalist considerations and as part of ordinary party politics. The prevailing solution limits the role of national Parliaments in the shaping of European decisions to that of a consultative body.[16]

In fact the powers of most parliaments will diminish and in some respect the powers of the executive will further increase especially in the case of those Eastern European countries where the matter is simply pushed under the carpet. However because of the current cabinet dictatorship in most Eastern European countries the legislative branch is already weak by design. The emerging new division of powers takes away Parliament's legislative powers in matters that are of Union competence and renders unclear those legislative powers related to implementing legislation, that is if such powers will be retained by the national Parliament at all. In addition the present constitutionally provided control powers of parliament (relating to fundamental rights protection that require some form of supermajority in some East European countries) will erode. These developments will contribute to an increasing sense of loss of popular control over the nation's destiny and the irrelevance of constitutional institutions.

2.4. Does the European Constitutional System Provide Constitutionalism for the New Member States?[17]

The lack of transparent popular representation may not be the ideal beginning for the people of the new member states about to set foot on a common European

---

[16] The model of consultative status for national Parliaments in EU decision-making relies on the German model. Today many observers find this to be an insufficient solution for a parliamentary representative democracy, although contrary to Hungary or the Czech Republic, the German government is subject to more stringent control, given the structure of joint-decision making in certain federal areas. In other words, because of the federal structure there is more power retained by Land legislative bodies, including through the Bundesrat. Of course, the Bundesrat does not genuinely fit the model of an elected representative body, since it is composed of non-elected Land government representatives.

[17] I am not considering here the rule of law and human rights enhancing contribution of the Union to the new member states—here the advantages are more obvious.

path that is leading to a partially uncharted European decision making process without full representation (or with a new complex representative system based on partial representation). The representative element of the concept of the representative government is at stake. It is unlikely that people will be compensated for this loss of representative democracy by direct elections to the European Parliament. The further diminished importance of the national parliaments fits into an existing European trend. Weiler refers to a "flexible" Europe with a "core" "at its centre" that "will actually enable that core to retain the present governance system dominated by the Council—the executive branch of the Member States—at the expense of the national parliamentary democracy. *Constitutionally, the statal structure would in fact enhance even further the democracy deficit*."[18] The national legislative branches are the losers. Given the current constitutional arrangements, namely the lack of competence and information in national Parliaments as well as parliamentarians' defective capacity to handle the issues that are to be determined by the Council, Parliaments will not be able to defend the subsidiarity principle even if there were national or Union powers to that effect in the future. On the other hand, the national executive will be in the position to push through policies in the Council that it would not be able to push through its own Parliament because of opposing public opinion, or majority (or coalition) party interests, or supermajority requirements would present insurmountable obstacles.[19]

Given that alternative forms of democracy are rather weak in East European civil societies, the European "democracy deficit" will be reproduced (in different forms) locally. However, this negative consequence might be countered by other consequences of membership. Furthermore, given that European integration "has been, historically, one of the principal means with which to consolidate democracy within and among several of the Member States, both old and new, with less than perfect historical democratic credentials,"[20] accession may well have a beneficial overall effect on the quality and strength of the kind of democracy, or at least rule of law and political civility, practiced in the countries to join.

The transfer of powers from national Parliaments to the Council reshapes the fundamental relations among the branches of power in the respective member states without any public participation or even any public cognition of the new development. One may argue that in the parliamentary systems that prevail in Eastern Europe the separation of powers does not offer much protection against abuse of power anyway. Parliamentary systems per se are weak substitutions of the working

---

18 Joseph H.H. Weiler, "Conclusions", note 4, Conference paper, Europe 2004—Le Grand Débat: Setting the Agenda and Outlining the Options (Brussels, 15 and 16 October 2001), emphasis added.

19 Consider, among others Ingolf Pernice, *Der Parlamentarische Subsidiaritätsausschuss*, (Walter Hallstein-Institut WHI—Paper 11/02. Berlin, September 2002), www.whi-berlin.de/pernice-psa.htm.

20 Weiler, above n. 18, p. 220.

model of a robust democracy based on long standing traditions. Therefore there is not much to lose in the Europeanization process. However, the constitutional performance of the new states was surprisingly good in the last decade. Even if parliamentary representation and traditional checks and balances are weakened, there are other sources of legitimacy such as government efficiency. The above concerns are motivated by abstract principles of the theory of democratic representation. To use normative claims is perhaps somewhat misguided in this case. After all, the existing parliaments have never had a decisive influence on the executive but have merely served as transmission belts that convey the results of popular elections through the mechanism of the formation of the cabinet.

It can certainly be said that from a constitutionalist perspective, and contrary to a democratic theory perspective, the new "allocation of powers" is not objectionable per se. In fact the likelihood of power concentration within a single hand is further diminished. The arrangement, however, does not automatically increase the power of the people via improved self-determination. Given these preconditions and because of the fact that the constitutional amendments on accession did *not* arise as the consequence of a crisis, one should not expect more robust national Parliaments debating European issues. The trends that emerged in the Nation State (the domination of the executive in the welfare administrative state) were not challenged through the process but were able to determine the constitutional regime of accession. A Constitutional safeguard of efficient governmental information to Parliaments and people regarding pending EU decisions, or lack thereof, makes no difference here.

The consequences of the constitutionalization of accession do not necessarily enhance constitutionalism. The whole process is marked by ad hockery and most steps taking the new member states into the Union remain within the ordinary and quite open horse trading between opposition and majority. The political elites of Eastern Europe opted for an accession referendum. This looks like a gamble: the issue is not popular deliberation but demonstration of loyalty via plebiscite. The legal discussion is primarily about the expediency of the procedure (see Slovenia), and political discourse is replaced by guesswork about quorum and majorities. This is hardly an example of taking people seriously.

At first glance it seems that national parliamentarism, the quintessential form of democratic government in the public imagery and a bulwark against executive tyranny, is going down the drain. However, this is not necessarily the message coming from the European Union. In view of the EU Treaty Parliaments remain important:

- in exercising political scrutiny of the positions adopted by their respective governments within the Council;
- in establishing cooperative relations with other parliaments in the EU;
- in drafting and implementing EU law.

In addition, the draft EU Constitution provided for additional opportunities and powers to national Parliaments. These new opportunities would have included direct and (more or less timely) notification regarding planned European legislation and opportunities of recourse, formally independent of the national executive in matters of abuse of the subsidiarity principle. One could argue, however, that these possibilities are not genuine possibilities for national parliaments as the identifiable instruments of representative government. The direct impact of national representative governments on the European Parliament (through national delegates of Parliaments who might have binding mandate) disappeared with the system of direct elections. The proposal to create a second chamber representing national Parliaments has never been popular. It is true that there is a certain sentiment that national Parliaments deserve special attention in the European legislative process for reasons of democratic representation, "being close to citizens"[21] rather than for reasons of national sovereignty. But the prevailing understanding is that powers in the Union emanate from the EU Constitution, even with regard to constitutionally established matters of subsidiarity.

Even with improved possibilities of early warning of Parliaments (as suggested in the European Constitution) one cannot take for granted, in the light of past experience, that national Parliaments will make use of these opportunities. Moreover, given the remaining opportunities of national parliamentary involvement, the position of the parliament might be that of defensor of national interests. Especially in case of the subsidiarity recourse it might be embarrassing for the majority to endorse a position against the one that the executive has endorsed. On the other hand, and with particular relevance to new member states which are in the shadow of suspicion of being inculcated by nationalism, the opposition of the day might be inclined to castigate the majority and the government for giving up the national interest by not taking a clear position against a Commission position or a piece of European legislation that might be challenged on subsidiarity grounds. In this scenario national Parliaments may become the forum of nationalism.

Of course, the demise of national parliaments, even if it occurs, does not rule out alternative forms of parliamentarism, and more broadly, a deliberative democracy. The European Parliament offers a form of expression of popular will. How deliberative the European legislative process will be is a matter to be seen. What is more obvious is that the European parliamentarism, deliberately and to a great extent, offers representation for the European identity of their electors, as the system allows for less effective national interest representation (in the sense of primordial national interest).

Certain features of the European Parliament might have negative impacts on the public in the new member states. For representatives coming from smaller countries there is little they can do about the nationalistic sensibilities of their electors. For small states the elected representatives will have no chance to represent

---

21 See e.g. French Convention representative, Hubert Haenel, http://european-convention.eu.int/docs/wd4/3640.pdf.

successfully nationalistic interests. As they join big pan-European factions where blocs of larger countries dominate they will be dissolved and disappear in this distant formation. It is unlikely that the activities of the Parliament will satisfy the nationalistic expectations of the public in a small country. This might increase a sense of abandonment of national interests and add to the feeling that there is no genuine representation at the European level.

One could argue that Senate members in the US are also popularly elected in their state constituency without losing their state-interest representation capacity. But the differences are formidable both in terms of the constituency and the way the representation is organized in the two systems. The constituency difference can be explained by reference to the motto of the European Constitution: representation in Europe is about unity in diversity; in the US it is diversity within unity that prevails. As to the constituency, the European MP represents a nationality—his electors are mostly of the same nationality, and of the same state. All US Members of Congress are elected by Americans, who might have local (state or substate level) interests or ethnic affiliation. A congressman elected in a predominantly black, Jewish or Irish district (and most districts do not have such a profile) will represent Americans first, with some ethnic positions on a few issues. This is not the case in Europe where the districts create clearly national constituencies, however, the representatives are forced to abandon this implicit mandate where it is dictated by (party) ideology, by European party discipline, and, most of all, by sheer numbers.

The logic of European legislation satisfies certain conditions of deliberative democracy, not necessarily because of the dialogue within the Parliament but because of the inter-institutional dialogue. Unfortunately this discussion is likely to remain non-transparent. Furthermore one cannot take for granted that the system has the potential to remedy the problem of bureaucratic-administrative homogeneity that characterizes executive legislation[22] and that is a major problem at the national level with regard to the implementation of European law (directives being implemented via executive regulation bypassing legislation). The problem of administrative homogeneity ("like-mindedness") remains where the interaction is between central (European) administrators and likeminded national administrators. (These latter are "like-minded" because of a pro-European training.) And even where there is interaction with the elected European or even national Parliaments these might share the administrative European ethos too. (See the impact on legislation and robust democracy of the composition of the legislature in Germany where civil servants are elected to Parliament in great numbers.)

The nature of European Union law further diminishes the positive impact of the inter-institutional dialogue as fundamental problems are left unsettled, either because of subsidiarity or due to unprincipled political, intergovernmental, or

[22] Executive legislation in the administrative state runs the risk "of a situation in which like-minded people are pressing one another toward an unjustifiable position", Sunstein, *op. cit.* n. 6, p. 141. Sunstein argues that control of delegated legislation is a remedy.

inter-institutional compromises that leave matters unresolved or decision-making at the national level, which often means exclusively executive legislation, to the detriment of public deliberation. Politically uncontrolled executive regulation means that the implementing regulation is prepared and enacted within the civil service. It is here that the insufficient constitutional/rule of law experience and the interest in democratic control will impose a high cost on the new member states. It is likely that in these countries there will be no public or institutional insistence that regulatory matters, other than dealing *directly* with *fundamental constitutional* rights restriction, be regulated in parliamentary processes. At least the Hungarian draft law on the legislative process prepared by the Ministry of Justice in 2003 intends to further restrict the domain of parliamentary law, enabling the executive to write the implementing legislation. One can already foresee the nature and qualities of regulations written by overwhelmed bureaucrats whose main concern is to have the norm pushed through without conflicts, and irrespective of constitutional, rule of law, or efficiency considerations. Of course, there are important reasons for this avoidance of Parliament: namely the dangers of delay and overpoliticization. But given the lack of commitment in the public bureaucracy to constitutional/rule of law values it is at this deeper level that the fears regarding insufficient commitment to the rule of law seem appropriate. The political elite is not ready (yet?) to reshape the procedure allowing for more costly, rule of law committed procedures, partly because the same elite has an instrumental attitude to law: it is satisfied with the semblance of due process etc. This is a political elite that looks at politics as a matter of interest-based horse trading, where principled positions are laughed at.

Note further that the East European civil service is not responsive to the public. Its leaders are not elected and for good reason. Such arrangements contribute to diminished democratic accountability. Such trends might be reinforced in the environment of the European administrative state. The European administrative state has to work as an impartial entity (with regard to national interests). A democratically elected executive that controls the administrative structures would politicize the whole Union. The legitimacy of the civil service is unrelated to the democratic legitimation of the leaders, both at the European and member state level. The contrast is clear with the United States.[23] National courts have no power to review the implementing legislation as it is a matter of community law.

Notwithstanding the above, the long term perspectives are not hopeless for constitutionalism in the new member states. After all, the emerging supranational

[23] The prevailing US doctrine that allows administrative discretion is formulated in *Chevron USA* vs. *Natural Resources Defense Council* 467 U.S. 837 (1984). Agencies are authorized to interpret ambiguous legislative terms as they think it fit, as long as the interpretation is reasonable. Courts are expected to defer to the administrative interpretation of statutes. However, unlike Europe, the American executive is popularly legitimated. The European and member state bureaucracies are without any popular legitimation.

separation of powers adds to what remains of a separation of powers at the national level. With regard to restricting the chances of elected dictatorship the changes are favorable to constitutionalism. It will take time to learn to live with, use, and perhaps appreciate the new constitutional arrangement where the traditional branches of power operate within (and complement) networks of interest representations which have limited democratic legitimation and partial representativity. It is possible that these alternative interest representations will operate as new checks and balances: it certainly does not satisfy traditional expectations of democracy and popular representation but may perhaps provide counterbalances and at the same time contribute to a more efficient steering of the European administrative state. To the extent the Union is indeed an administrative state (with an overloaded bureaucracy composed of generalists) it does not presuppose much democratic control through national parliaments, and even through a Union level parliament.

3. WELFARISM AND THE PERPETUATION OF THE STATE-SOCIALIST ENDOWMENT EFFECT

Given that citizens of the new member states have limited political and practical opportunities as well as material and intellectual means to determine their own fate, and that this limitation is neither disguised nor regretted in prevailing Eastern European political cultures, the traditional patterns of a welfare dependent, anti-modernist *complaint-subject* might be reinforced. By “complaint-subject” I mean citizens who behave like subjects of a paternalist state, who refuse to take responsibility for their fate through democratic participation, and whose “voice” (Hirschman) remains limited to complaints. People complain about their personal bad luck and the bad luck of their national history, and about mistreatment by insensitive politicians, and lack of honesty and decency of other people, in particular of those who appear to be successful. Political attitudes and action of the East European citizen remain one of complaint (hence the pattern of protest vote). The complaints include dissatisfaction with welfare provisions. It should be noted that welfarism is particularly present in Hungary with a 54% rate of welfarist redistribution (that is 54% of the GNP). Similar problems and welfarist-populist resistance to or reluctance to reduce welfare spending on the middle class is present in the Czech Republic and Poland. These three largest accession countries face considerable budget deficits.

As mentioned above, popular democratic control in the post-communist countries will not be enhanced after accession. Moreover, and partly related to the emerging European decision-making process, the legacy of state socialism will be reinforced; namely socialist welfare dependence will be reinforced by the prevailing solidarity culture of the Union. The Union is programmed to promote welfare as the source or precondition of European homogeneity. This will have perverse effects in many new member states. The prevailing inherited attitude of the majority of the population in the new member states is that the State should provide all sorts of services for free, irrespective of individual contribution and need assessment. (Needless to say this may not correspond to the principle of social solidarity even though it may not be in conflict with the European practices that emerge in the name of social solidarity). Most political parties and governments have subscribed to this popular/populist attitude. This primitive theory of entitlements has been elevated to a theory of "subjective rights" in Hungary; that "theory" is voiced by government and opposition and sanctioned by the decisions of the Hungarian Constitutional Court.[24] Social rights serve as the basis of government provided services, which are taken for granted for all citizens. The attitude is inherited from socialism—the state socialist system provided all sorts of services in exchange for political loyalty and to a great extent irrespective of merit and economic inefficiency consequences. The resulting inefficiencies made the state socialist system unsustainable. However, the welfare expectations continued to operate in conformity with what one could expect on the basis of the endowment effect. People are generally inclined to ask much more for selling a good they possess than they are ready to pay, if asked to buy it. People estimate very highly the services which were already provided, although they would be reluctant to pay for such services. Such attitude is generally quite irrational, especially where it helps to maintain very inefficient and costly bureaucracies, as it is the case in the post-communist countries (see, in particular the healthcare system).[25]

Endowed welfarism has proven to be quite popular. This popularity is not limited to Eastern Europe although richer countries may afford it more. It is a typical middle class attitude that favors, among others, the maintenance of universal services. The attitude was masterfully summarized in a dissenting opinion of Justice Kilényi of the Hungarian Constitutional Court.[26] Justice Kilényi argued that social rights are to be understood in conjunction with the constitutional right to social security. Social security is far more than the right to a social existence minimum (i.e. subsistence support). It is a constitutional right that pertains to *all* (individuals and families), "irrespective of differences in wealth." It includes the obligation of the state not to interfere with the material conditions of the citizens in a way that imposes on the masses of citizens burdens that are disproportionate and exceed their possibilities. At the beginning of 1995 the Hungarian Constitutional Court repeatedly protected existing, non-contribution based social services as statutory entitlements amounting to acquired rights that cannot be repealed, at least not until

---

24 Likewise the Polish Tribunal, in the Pension cases. For Hungary, see A. Sajó, "How the Rule of Law Killed Welfare Reform," *East European Constitutional Review*, 5 (1996) pp. 31–41.

25 Posner argues that endowment effects are rational if the disparity reflects the unique character of the goods in question—unique in the sense of lacking close substitutes. This is certainly not the case of the welfare services which are (or would be) available on the market. Richard Posner, *Economic Analysis of Law* (5th edn.), (New York: Aspen Law & Business 1999), p. 95.

26 26/1993 (IV.29.) AB hat, [annualized increase of pensions below inflation upheld].

the recipients had sufficient time and opportunity to find alternative protection. The Court and, increasingly, most political parties accepted that general entitlements, unrelated to needs assessment are "subjective rights" and pertain to all.

The social welfare dependency that is rooted in the endowment effect had dramatic fiscal consequences. Universal services that were inherited from socialism were of a nominally high quality. As a result of different populist-electoral policies, at least some of these services were further extended after the collapse of state socialism. The state could not sustain these services, or their level (quality), except at the price of excessive taxes with negative impact on investment and increasing government debt that imposed increasing fiscal burden on economic development. At the moment when the requirements of the Stability and Growth Pact became a concern to the new member states and the governments, certain governments attempted to reduce the budget deficit. There was a general public outcry against any attempt to move towards a needs assessment based welfare system. It has to be admitted that the gross income of the population is HUF 1,1 m (4,000 Euro) with an average of 28% income tax and approximately another 11% social security tax. Only 4% of the taxpayers reported more than HUF 4,000.000 annual gross income. As long as the tax remains high (40% above the 4,000 Euro bracket) there is no disposable income for social services and the population is not in a position to make informed choices, even though, in the given system, the level of services deteriorates.

It is likely that the welfare expectations attitude will be reinforced ideologically in the Union. Further, to some extent, such tendencies might be reinforced on the basis of the specific rules of the secondary legislation of the Union that reflect welfarist concerns but correspond to the possibilities of much more affluent societies. (It is a matter of conflict for the future how the new member states will satisfy the budget deficit, and national debt reduction, etc. requirements of the Euro zone.) The solidarity-inspired and other socialistic provisions of the Treaty/Constitution will enhance the attitude of middle class welfare dependence.

The European attitude is exemplified in the Constitution that continues to enhance the idea that a high level of health protection is to be provided under nationally determined systems as promoted by Union policies.[27] To the extent that this points to an all-European standard, the pressure on the weaker national economies to maintain free, or below market price services will continue. Note that per capita health care spending in Germany exceeds at least sevenfold Hungarian per capita expenditure, though in terms of the respective percentages of the national budgets the

---

[27] Article II-35: Health care:

Everyone has the right of access to preventive health care and the right to benefit from medical treatment under the conditions established by national laws and practices. A high level of human health protection shall be ensured in the definition and implementation of all Union policies and activities.

two countries are not fundamentally different. However, the Hungarian expenses are almost exclusively covered on the basis of a national insurance system that runs a major deficit, covered by the budget.[28]

I would like to illustrate the welfarist burden on the new member states (with the already mentioned consequences of welfare dependency reinforcement and negative impacts on economic development) with a more specific example that originates in the secondary legislation on commercial activities. Directive 2002/22/EC of the European Parliament and of the Council of 7 March 2002 on universal service and users' rights relating to electronic communications networks and services (Universal Service Directive) requires that universal services be made available at an "affordable price" (Article 3(2)). Annex IV specifies that such a duty implies averaged prices or the provision of specific tariff options for consumers with low incomes. The resulting loss to the operator has to be recovered from contributions from the other undertakings (who will charge more to their users). I am sure that even Adam Smith would offer some arguments for such arrangements referring to public goods; modern economists would talk about positive network externalities. Further, solidarity might provide additional justification for such arrangements. For example, emergency calls will be available to all. However, what are the implications of such logic where large numbers of the population have low incomes? The affected companies (sectors) will lose their competitiveness.

Welfarist provisions in European Union law, similar to the above mentioned examples, are of considerable importance for reinforcing socialist mentalities of endowment and post-socialist welfare institutions with all the inherent inefficiencies, unfairness (middle class bias) and non-sustainability that it entails.

After all, the quoted welfarist provisions of European Union law seem to reflect the same welfarist perspective that the national parliaments have inevitably accepted in response to democratic pressure. Such language and policies might be attributed to the self understanding of the administrative welfarist state. The Union's institutions and networks are not catering to welfarism and function to some extent as buffers against the self-destructive welfarism of democracy at the national level. Nevertheless, the comprehensive language of the Union seems to mimic what would have resulted from traditional popular representative democracy. This may not be decisive where particular policies are left to independent networks without a welfare-oriented redistributive mission. It should be added quickly that all this is intended to indicate a possible trend only, a trend that at this moment is undermined by at least three facts. Firstly, the Union does not have much power of direct reallocation as this remains within the budgetary powers of national parliaments.

---

[28] The health care expenditure looks non-sustainable in its present system of administration based on an allegedly "acquired right". Attempts to reform the system run into the resistance of the well organized medical profession and the pharmaceutical industry, supported by the opposition of the day, claiming that any reform imposing direct costs on the population violates people's rights.

Secondly, the transfers of the Union are certainly and perversely redistributive (see CAP). Thirdly, there are genuine efforts to recreate representative government or a network of representative governments at the Union level that might respond to (or resist) the same redistributionist democratic impulses that characterize national parliaments.

8. Happy Returns to Europe? The Union's Identity, Constitution-Making, and its Impact on the Central European Accession States

Jiri Priban

1. Introduction

This chapter addresses the problem of political identity within the ambit of the post-war European integration process as well as the recent Constitution-making efforts. It focuses on the distinction between civic and ethnic political identity within the framework of the European Union and in the context of the Central European accession states. The first section analyses the problem of ethnicity in modern European history drawing on the role of the EU as a neutralizing force of ethno-national divisions, tensions and conflicts. The following section deals with the enlargement process, paying particular attention to policies set up by the EU to contain ethno-political conflicts emerging in Central Europe after the collapse of communism. The final section is a discussion of the European Union's political symbolism premised on the possibility of a potential European *demos.*

The crux of the argument lies in comparing two models of constitution-making: the Hobbesian vertical versus the Lockean horizontal version of the social contract. I shall argue that the vertical constitutional model does not allow for the political ambitions of a European Federation or a Europolity to be met due to the notable absence of a European People as the Constitution's constituent power. The vertical, authority-promoting model may have been beneficial to the accession countries were it applied during the Convention's deliberation. Conversely I aim to demonstrate that the horizontal constitutional model, as presented in the Convention's Draft Treaty, has great potential for creating a Constitution which embraces a European identity premised on the tension between civil democratic virtues and old national loyalties.

2. Constitution-Making and Political Identity in Post-Communist Central Europe: Preliminary Remarks

Most of the countries which joined the European Union in 2004 are experiencing a unique movement related to their constitution-making. After the fall of communism in the late 1980s and the early 1990s, former communist countries such as the Baltic States, the Czech Republic, Hungary, Poland, Slovakia and Slovenia reinvented

Wojciech Sadurski et al. (ed.), Spreading Democracy and the Rule of Law?, 193–218.

their national sovereignty by introducing and cementing the liberal democratic rule of law into their new constitutional systems. The constitution-making processes, typical of the political climate in the early 1990s, were part of the juridification of emerging democratic politics and human rights culture in post-communist countries.

The constitution-making process in Central and Eastern Europe in the 1990s was heavily influenced by the political motivation to accede to the European Union. Under the "Return to Europe" slogan, former communist countries opened a complex process of negotiations with the EU which resulted in the enlargement of the Union from its existing 15–25 Member States. The enlargement process began at the EU Copenhagen summit in June 1993, continued at the EU Amsterdam summit in 1997 where the process of negotiations commenced, was formally recognised at the EU Nice summit in 2000 where the accession countries were invited to participate in the Convention's constitution-making, and was completed at the EU Copenhagen summit in December 2002 when the Central and East European countries concluded negotiations on the EU accession.

National sovereignty achieved after the fall of communism was used as a political instrument to negotiate new forms of integration and limitations to sovereignty. The revival of the Nation-State in post-communist Europe was transitional in bringing those nations into the "postnational constellation" of the European Union. The symbolic and somewhat vague claims of integration were gradually converted into pragmatic policies of the institutional and structural accommodation of democratic government, the civil rights based rule of law, and the market economy. The consolidation of these democratic regimes and their accession negotiations were taking place simultaneously. The integration process was part of the post-communist state-building and constitution-making exercise due to its symbolic power of bringing together the region with the liberal democratic and prosperous Europe (symbolic rationality) on the one hand and its pragmatic effect on political, economic and constitutional transformations (purposive rationality) on the other hand. The European Union was the main "focal point"[1] which had a profound effect on the quality of the political process and the nature of the self-reflection of collective political identity in those countries. For many Czechs, Hungarians and Poles, this development was merely a restoration of the region's historical and cultural unity with the West. Despite the resurgence of historical nationalist movements, ethnic tensions, xenophobia and other transient "turbulence", the general support of this integration policy has remained solid over the last 15 years.[2]

---

1 J. Elster, C. Offe and U.K. Preuss, *Institutional Design in Post-communist Societies: Rebuilding the Ship at Sea* (Cambridge: Cambridge University Press, 1998), p. 188.

2 For a detailed analysis, see annual reports of *Central and Eastern Eurobarometer General Public Opinion Surveys*, and more recently (since 2001) *Candidate Countries Eurobarometer General Public Opinion Surveys*.

3. EUROPEAN CONSTITUTION-MAKING: THREE ARGUMENTS

By trading their national sovereignty in favour of European integration, the Central and Eastern European countries are partaking in the constitution-making process at the European level. Within this 15 year period therefore, these countries have experienced two fundamental constitution-making processes: from building national sovereignty to building supra-national sovereignty.

Prior to analysing the role of the EU's institutional framework in these processes, it is worthwhile summarizing the major arguments in favour of the current European constitution-making efforts which began with the work of the Convention and subsequently were transferred to the Intergovernmental Conference in October 2003 and signed in Rome in October 2004. We may divide these arguments into the following three categories: the functionalist argument, the democratic renewal argument and the identity argument. The functionalist argument primarily uses the language of globalisation to demonstrate that the shape of the European political map must change since European nation states can no longer regulate the global economic, environmental and political processes effectively. Global communication and economic exchange exceed the power of nation states.[3] The modern state can neither promote nor benefit from national economic development alone. The mobility of capital fundamentally affects the labour markets of wealthy post-industrial societies and their social welfare systems. According to the functionalist argument, state administration is too weak to cope with the disappearance of national economies. As a result the progress of the European integration process into a tighter, constitutionally entrenched, political model appears to be a direct consequence of economic and political global trends.

Following the functionalist argument, the European Union has to be constructed as a supranational political agency which would be able to address the challenges of the existing monetary union and denationalised European market. For instance, Jürgen Habermas demands the "overcoming" of the nation-state in the post-Maastricht Europe when he states:

> [F]or the present, a politics still operating within the framework of the nation-state limits itself to adapting its own society in the least costly way to the systemic imperatives and side-effects of a global economic dynamic that operates largely free from political constraints. But instead it should make the heroic effort to overcome its own limitations and construct political institutions capable of acting at the supranational level.[4]

---

3 K. Ohmae, *The End of the Nation State: The Rise of Regional Economies* (New York: Free Press, 1995).

4 J. Habermas, *The Inclusion of the Other: Studies in Political Theory* (Cambridge: Polity Press, 1999), p. 124.

According to Habermas, tighter political and administrative integration is considered to be the only anti-dote to the erosion of social solidarity, the welfare state and the public sphere. One does not have to be a hero politician to see the political challenges of economic globalisation, yet all attempts to reconstruct and strengthen the European political system in order to respond to the developments in the European and global economic systems have received rather mixed and mostly lukewarm reactions.

Political building of the "ever closer union" had been mentioned already in the 1957 Treaty of Rome and Jean Monnet, one of the European "founding fathers", advocated the process of institutionalisation which, although not an end in itself, might result in the tight-knit political entity of the United States of Europe.[5] The object of post-war European integration was the fostering of peace, prosperity and liberty where the building of a democratic community was left to the nation states.[6] Nevertheless, the permanent shift in power to the European level puts further pressure on overcoming the democratic deficit of the Union's institutions within the spheres of authority, representation and accountability. The European Union has to deal with its own democratic deficit and therefore needs to "democratize" the system of its administrative institutions. It cannot be a union merely based on functional integration[7] by harmonizing its political institutions with economic developments as a result of reactive strategies.[8]

This argument of democratic renewal has been the most common source of criticism of the European Union. It treats European politics as the politics of a "confused empire" in which the proliferation of offices obfuscates the political rule.[9] A critique of the pathological nature of current European politics is the starting point of this argument with the aim of strengthening the weak democratic legitimacy of EU institutions. The Union obtains its legitimacy through the previous and therefore indirect legitimacy of the member states.[10] The People of Europe do not identify themselves with, and take very little interest in, European politics which is an issue that needs to be tackled through the constitution-making process. An expansion of democratic legitimacy and its incorporation into formal constitutional

5 J. Monnet, *Memoirs* (London: Collins, 1978), p. 520ff.

6 G.F. Mancini and D.T. Keeling, "Democracy and the European Court of Justice", 57 *Modern Law Review*, 2 (1994), pp. 175–90.

7 For the concept of "functional integration", see especially H.P. Ipsen, *Europäisches Gemeinschaftsrecht* (Tübingen: Mohr, 1972).

8 W. Wallace and J. Smith, "Democracy or technocracy? European integration and the problem of popular consent", 18 *West European Politics 3* (1995), pp. 137–157.

9 For the term, see P. Sloterdijk, *Im selben Boot. Versuch über die Hyperpolitik* (Frankfurt: Suhrkamp, 1993), Chapt. 3.

10 See, for instance H. Wallace, "Deepening and Widening: problems of legitimacy for the EC", in S. Garcia (ed.), *European Identity and the Search for Legitimacy* (London: Pinter, 1993), pp. 95–105.

rules of the EU is therefore being requested in order to promote the regulatory power of European institutions.

This idea of dealing with democratic deficit by reducing the constitutional deficit of the Union is closely related to the outcome of the third identity based argument. While the democratic renewal argument demands democratisation of the political bodies of the EU in order to legitimate them, the identity argument builds upon the successful historical achievements of the European integration process thus far. It is premised on the primary function of the European integration process of neutralising nationalist tensions. Taming *ethnos* in European nation states has always been considered to be the primary purpose of both economic and political integration. European popular identity is constructed as the reverse of modern nationalism and its political myths. This creation of a civil European *demos* is contrasted with different ethnic pre-political identities of peoples of Europe and its symbolic power is supposed to keep *ethnos* on the sidelines of European politics. *Ethnos* is treated as a mere structural excess of post-nationalist European politics. Within the process of European integration a common European people is to be invented and given a voice which adheres to the principles of democratic government. The identity argument accommodates the notion of cosmopolitan citizenship and invents the *demos* as democracy's subject which is extended from the boundaries of the nation-state to those of the supra-national level.[11] Nevertheless, this effort is rendered more complex by the fact that European integration runs two different courses. On the one hand, an intensive process of transferring power from national to European institutions is occurring and on the other hand, an extensive process of the incorporation of the new member states to the European Union is also taking place.

4. TAMING *ETHNOS* AND ITS SYMBOLIC POWER FOR THE NEW MEMBER STATES

The first argument could only affect the post-communist accession countries indirectly since they are just opening their markets to the forces of globalisation. The second argument could have no impact until the acceding states are informed that they are to become "members of the EU family." Unlike the first two, the identity argument has played an essential role in the national constitution-making in Central and Eastern Europe in the 1990s. It has also formed an important part of the public discourse of the accession states.

Modern European states were created as institutions of both liberal democratic hopes and exclusive political identity of an ethnically integrated community. Romantic nationalism resulting in the creation of modern nations often initiated the transformation of the early modern states into democratic and republican regimes.

---

11 See, for example, D. Beetham, *Democracy and Human Rights* (Cambridge: Polity Press 1999).

The nationalist discourse therefore provided a very effective symbolic universe which facilitated a more abstract form of the social integration of populations in modern political societies.[12] The nation as an ethnic community of common language, tradition and ancestry represents the collective identity even for the modern European states that are premised on principles of democracy and liberal republicanism. This duality of civic and ethnic collective identity and the institutional framework of modern politics "leads to a double coding of citizenship, with the result that the legal status defined in terms of civil rights also implies membership in a culturally defined community."[13] In this respect, Habermas summarizes that "[T]he tension between the universalism of an egalitarian legal community and the particularism of a community united by historical destiny is built into the very concept of the nation(al) state."[14]

The European Union has been symbolically constructed as a civil alternative to the ethnically burdened nation states. Taken from the historical point of view, the European integration process is a post-1945 attempt to successfully answer the "German question" and its ethnic extremism of *Volk* politics which continues to haunt modern European history. The question of whether the people constitute an ethnic or civic community has also been central in all Central European states. The Union's recent policy of promoting regionalism only strengthens its civic image because it delimits administration to the units beyond the institutional framework of a sovereign state. The modern administrative and redistributive roles of a nation state are weakened by the two opposite trends in the shifts in power. While the first trend delimits more power to "smaller" regions of the EU member states, the second one shifts more power to the "bigger" European Union. The Union has thus been perceived as an organisation able to promote the values of cosmopolitan republicanism and civic virtues and curb the risks arising from ethno-nationalism. The modern state is an institution affected both by the ideals of a republican political society and the vices of ethnic communitarianism. The struggle between society and community, so central in the modern sociological paradigm, finds its reflection in the symbolic political language of European integration. The EU represents itself as a cosmopolitan civil society which is ready to recognise ethnic communities at the regional level, but which confronts the residual ethnic nature of its member states.

The political dualism of community versus society may be far from the reality of EU politics yet it plays a significant role in its legitimation. This argumentation has also played an essential role in the mandates of pro-EU campaigners in the former Central and East European countries. This strategy should come as no surprise when considering the recent history of Central and Eastern states and in particular the

---

12 H. Schulze, *Staat und Nation in der Europäischen Geschichte* (München: C.H. Beck, 1994).

13 J. Habermas, *The Inclusion of the Other: Studies in Political Theory* (Cambridge: Polity Press 1999), p. 113.

14 *Ibid*, at 115.

shocking example of Yugoslavia disintegrating into isolated islands of ethnic hatred and violence. The "Europeanization" of the Central and Eastern European countries was perceived as the best scenario for the region since the post-communist political reconstruction of democratic institutions and economic reforms could be backed by the "grand design" of the European Union.[15] The strong involvement of "patron power" guaranteeing the peaceful nature of post-communist transformations and the enforcement of democratization by internationally recognised standards had been favoured because of its ability to curb the growing threats of political authoritarianism, nationalist factions and other disturbing consequences of the post-1989 political changes.[16]

5. THE COPENHAGEN CRITERIA AND BEYOND: THE UNION'S *ETHNOS*-ORIENTED STRATEGIES IN CENTRAL EUROPE

Central European states formally started the process of the EU integration after the Copenhagen summit of 1993 which set up conditions for the accession states. In June 1993 in Copenhagen, the European Council specified the following criteria which individual states had to meet: the stability of institutions guaranteeing democracy, the rule of law, human rights and respect for and protection of minorities (political criterion); the existence of a functioning market economy as well as the capacity to cope with competitive pressure and market forces within the European Union (economic criterion); and the ability to take on the obligations of membership including adherence to the aims of political, economic and monetary union (criterion concerning adoption of the Community *acquis*). These accession conditions are very general and vague but their meaning could largely be extracted from the existing institutional frameworks and practices in the EU and its member states. However, these frameworks and practices were changing as a result of the transformation of the EU itself during the 1990s.[17] For the accession states, the Union became a fluid goal which was yet to be achieved. While the Union was progressing in its political debates during the 1990s and proposed fundamental constitutional changes, the accession talks were driven by clear reference to the status quo of the 1993 Copenhagen criteria. The enlargement process required compliance and stabilisation whereas the Union's stability was non-existent.

Furthermore, these conditions even expand the EU frameworks and practices as in the case of ethnic and national minority rights. Although the EU regulations dominated the list of conditions, the conditionality policy was not necessarily limited to the Union's own standards. The Union could demand extra conditions only

---

15 A. Agh, *The Politics of Central Europe* (London: Sage, 1998), pp. 43–44.

16 See, for instance, C. Offe, "Capitalism by Democratic Design? Democratic Theory Facing the Triple Transition in East Central Europe", 58 *Social Research*, 4 (1991), p. 889.

17 See, for instance, C. Jenkins (ed.), *The Unification of Europe: An Analysis of EU Enlargement.* (London: Centre for Reform, 2000).

because the European integration was such a high political priority for all accession states. This asymmetrical patron relation between the EU and the accession states and the Union's superiority was typical of the enlargement process, often described as the "learning process."[18] The conditions were even expanded after 1997 when the Commission introduced annual reports and elaborate monitoring of economic and political institutions and their transformation in the accession countries. The process of approximation of laws, which was not originally perceived as a legal condition for accession, eventually became a central activity of the legislative bodies and governments in all accession countries. The harmonisation of the EU and national legal systems of the accession countries seriously affected the quality of democratic deliberation in those countries because national parliaments favoured a smooth integrative process and mechanically, without an adequate political debate, enacted most of the proposals harmonising national laws with the EU legal framework. This practice was possible due to the fact that the Copenhagen principle of conditionality set up standards for those aiming at becoming the Union's members and assumed that meeting these standards would automatically open the Union's gates. The accession states even raced to be first to knock on those gates![19]

With regard to the identity argument, European integration has nevertheless always proceeded as a neutralising force in the ethnically and politically diverse regions of Europe and its positive effect therefore should not be underestimated. The Copenhagen special minority rights criteria were part of this force. The *neutralisation function* was emphasised, for instance, in post-1989 tensions between Hungary and Slovakia regarding the policy of ethnic and national minority rights in both states. Hungary's attempts to veto Slovakia's accession to CSCE following the split of Czechoslovakia in 1992 and abstention at the admittance of Slovakia to the Council of Europe in 1993 worsened diplomatic relations between the two countries. In order to reduce the growing tension, the European Union launched its first Joint Action of the EU Common Foreign and Security Policy—"the Balladur Plan" based on the idea of preventive diplomacy.[20] The Balladur Plan drafted by the French government pursued the idea of a stability pact cemented by bilateral agreements on ethnic and national minority problems arising between neighbouring countries and threatening their peaceful coexistence and political stability. Supported by the Recommendation 1201 of the parliamentary Assembly of the Council of Europe on minority rights, this plan led to the successful

18 See M. Marescеau, "Pre-accession", in M. Cremona (ed.), *The Enlargement of the European Union* (Oxford: Oxford University Press, 2003), p 22.

19 This race was inspired by an enlargement strategy *Agenda 2000* published by the European Commission on 15 July 1997. The document was published together with individual reports on the applicant countries and outlined detailed assessments of each state.

20 For further details, see L. Valki, "Hungary: Understanding Western Messages", in J. Zielonka and A. Pravda, eds., *Democratic Consolidation in Eastern Europe, Volume 2: International and Transnational Factors* (Oxford: Oxford University Press, 2001), pp. 304–6.

Hungarian-Slovak "Treaty of the Republic of Hungary and the Slovak Republic on Good Neighbourliness and Friendly Cooperation".[21] Although one must not overestimate the role of the treaty in sensitive diplomatic relations between Hungary and Slovakia and its impact on the Meciar government in Slovakia (1994–8) or the Antall and Orbán governments (1990–4; 1998–2002) in Hungary, this diplomatic effort certainly reduced the risk of both countries escalating their nationalist policies which would lead to international crisis and possibly violent conflict.

The Union's policy of active involvement is even more striking in its treatment of the Mečiar government in Slovakia between 1994 and 1998. After the split of Czechoslovakia, Slovak foreign policy was focusing on its European integration and the government pledged to fulfil the requirements formulated at the 1993 Copenhagen and the 1994 Essen EU summits. However, the nationalist, populist and authoritarian Mečiar government which came to power in 1994 gradually steered the country toward international isolation which resulted in the elimination of Slovakia from the list of first round candidates of the NATO membership in Madrid in 1997 and EU refusal to continue the integration process with Slovakia. The government's foreign policy used the self-perception of the Slovak nation as having a unique strategic position on the map of Europe and being constantly threatened by its neighbours and international "big powers" and consequently strengthened its cooperation with Russia.[22] The collapse of Slovakia's European integration policy in 1997 and severe criticism of governmental policies by the Union's representatives subsequently affected the victory of political opposition in the 1998 parliamentary elections and helped to restore liberal democratic politics in the country.[23] The combination of diplomatic pressure and local liberal democratic aspirations thus worked as a mechanism of curbing the worst scenario of violent outbreak of nationalist populism and collapse of liberal democratic politics. The Union's executive power supported the principles of parliamentary democracy and constitutionalism in Slovakia by reporting and expressing concerns over the power abuses of government and its attempts to undermine the role of parliament.[24] The EU thus played a fundamental role in the consolidation of democracy in Slovakia in the second half of the 1990s.

Another example of the Union's active policy of containment of ethnic divisions and nationalism was the role of the EU Enlargement Commissioner Gunther

---

21 Signed in Paris on 19 March 1995.

22 See I. Samson, "Slovakia: Misreading the Western Message" in J. Zielonka and A. Pravda, *Democratic Consolidation in Eastern Europe Volume 2: International and Transnational Factors* (Oxford: Oxford University Press, 2001), pp. 376–80.

23 See, for example, EU Commission, "Commission Opinion on Slovakia's Application for Membership of the European Union", *Bulletin of the European Union*, suppl. 9 (1997).

24 See G. Pridham, "The European Union's Democratic Conditionality and Domestic Politics in Slovakia: the Mečiar and Dzurinda Governments Compared", 54 *Europe-Asia Studies* (2002), pp. 203–227.

Verheugen during the negotiations with the Czech Republic regarding the controversial issue of the Beneš Decrees that legalized the expulsion of Sudeten Germans from Czechoslovakia after World War II. In the final stage of negotiations, the Austrian government, the government of the German state of Bavaria, and the Hungarian Prime Minister Orbán repeatedly called for the repeal of the decrees. In the heated atmosphere of the 2002 parliamentary elections in the Czech Republic, Germany and Hungary, Verheugen managed to assure the Czech government that the decrees would not be a bar to accession while suggesting that a symbolic moral gesture recognizing the injustices of the expulsion would be helpful. Apart from its symbolic role in the modern political history of a collective guilt, the EU Commission was reluctant to open the issue because it was closely linked with property restitution, family law issues (the decrees provided a basis for divorce), and compensation.[25] Furthermore, similar decrees had been issued in other countries such as Poland and Denmark and the specific character of the Czechoslovak decrees would therefore necessarily have broader international legal consequences.[26] The carefully crafted strategy of keeping the legal *status quo* and promoting the culture of moral "collective repentance", which started with Havel's apology in 1990 and was incorporated into the 1997 Czech-German Joint Declaration of Parliaments, was the only possible option in the critical situation in which the Czech government and parliament made it clear that any EU annulment demands would effectively put an end to accession talks.[27]

The last and probably most persuasive example of the Union's promotion of civil society oriented politics and the protection of minority rights is the protection of minority rights of the Roma populations living in the region. Roma living in Central and Eastern Europe are one of the most vulnerable minority groups subject to individual and institutional racism and discrimination. The EU set up national action plans for the candidate states with sizeable Roma communities and provided funding for their implementation. These programmes were intended to address

---

[25] For instance, a Christian Democratic Union member of Bundestag (German Parliament) and President of the Association of Expelled Germans (Bund der Vertriebenen) Erika Steinbach, who is famous for radical ethno-nationalist views, said that the British and American reluctance to support German restitution demands meant acceptance of the genocide of 15 million Germans after 1945 and accused the European Commission of ignoring the laws depriving Germans of their rights in four future member states of the EU (the Czech Republic, Poland, Slovakia and Slovenia). Quoted from an analysis of the Czech diplomat Jiří Šitler, "Že by mi vrátili tu mou almaru?" (Would they return my cupboard?), published in *Lidové noviny*, Orientace, 3 January 2004.

[26] For further details, see "Constitution Watch", 11 *East European Constitutional Review*, No. 1–2, Winter/Spring 2002, pp. 14–15; "Constitutional Watch", 11/12 *East European Constitutional Review*, No. 4, No. 1, Fall 2002, Winter 2003, p. 19.

[27] See, for instance, *The Declaration of the Assembly of Deputies of Parliament of the Czech Republic*, of 24 April 2002.

discrimination issues as well as to promote Roma cultural and ethnic identity.[28] It is also noteworthy that similar policies of promoting the national and ethnic integration and diversity were encouraged by the European Commission in the Baltic States with large Russian-speaking minorities.[29]

6. TIMING THE FUTURE IN PROCESS: "IMAGINED EUROPE"

Focusing on the symbolic power of constitution-making and the role of European integration, the effect of "imagined Europe" was essential in building the collective identity of Central European political societies. Europe's symbolic value was given by its temporal orientation. It was always a future oriented political goal for politicians and populations of post-communist countries which helped to contain political myths of the national past threatening to reinvent nationalist politics based on historical and ethnic claims of "blood and soil."

The collectivist communitarian temptation to perceive political communities as transcendental entities entrenched in their traditions is part of political romanticism which led to the worst disasters in modern Europe. Similarly like romantics, communitarians believe that history and human traditions are sources of true collective nature of a nation and its present identity has therefore to be derived from its past. According to this view, collective identity should be the "gravitational field" of a constitution because it reflects communal values superior to liberal individualism.[30] However, this politics of "historical future"[31] turns out to be politically very dangerous because it draws on the system of historical pre-political identity and transforms particular traditions and national myths into political symbols. Communitarian critics of liberalism are legitimately concerned about the similarity between their position and fascist ideology.[32] Politics of primordial attachments[33] is constituted by beliefs in the shared customs, blood-ties, language and tradition of a political community, which are normatively binding for its members. Nationalist sentiments are presented as "natural" and historically "inevitable". This

---

28 For many valuable details and analysis, see *Monitoring the EU Accession Process: Minority Protection, Volume I: An Assessment of Selected Policies in Candidate States* (Budapest: Open Society Institute, 2002).

29 See, for instance European Commission, *2001 Regular Report on Estonia's Progress Toward Accession*, Brussels, 2001, p. 24.

30 G. Walker, "The Idea of Nonliberal Constitutionalism", in I. Shapiro and W. Kymlicka (eds.), *Ethnicity and Group Rights (NOMOS XXXIX)* (New York: New York University Press, 1997), p. 169.

31 H. Joas, *The Creativity of Action* (Chicago: University of Chicago Press, 1997), p. 250.

32 G. Walker, "The Idea of Nonliberal Constitutionalism", in I. Shapiro and W. Kymlicka (eds.), *Ethnicity and Group Rights (NOMOS XXXIX)* (New York: New York University Press 1997), pp. 169–70 and pp. 177–8.

33 See C. Geertz, "The Integrative Revolution: Primordial Sentiments and Civil Politics in the New States", in C. Geertz (ed.), *Old Societies and New States* (London: Free Press, 1963).

legitimation by "natural history" facilitates the normative force of these sentiments, makes people attached to their ethnically marked political community, and delineates the limits of community membership.[34]

As a result of such politics, constitutions would become mere symbolic expressions of mythical history of a nation and a powerful technique of constructing its modern political myths. Instead of rational decision-making, constitutions would become a source of the nationalist magic which had turned out to be so disastrous in the modern history of Europe. In a comment, reiterating Max Weber's distinction of charismatic and legal rational domination, Ernst Cassirer mentioned that "[T]he modern politician has had to combine in himself two entirely different and even incompatible functions. He has to act, at the same time, as both a homo magus and a homo faber."[35] Drawing on this comment, one can say that communitarian politics of the reinvention of historical ethnic roots would result in the ethnic re-enchantment of modern political world and the leadership of *homo magus*.

In comparison to this politics of historical future, politics recalling a common post-1945 European identity has been driven by the opposite temporal logic which might be called the "future in process." Unlike the historical future, the future in process is not primarily legitimated by past experiences and therefore must be modelled in a more abstract way. The primary political goal of the future in process is to unify the heterogeneous groups and individuals who share a common political life. From the very beginning, the process of European integration was a project of building a supranational community which would need to emerge in order to minimise particular nationalisms and maximise the integrative power of political culture of civil rights and parliamentary democracy. The supranational ideal of the Union's citizenry is to prevent the nationalist abuses of the state power in the future and defuse nationality as the principal reference of democratic politics. This ideal has always been present in the European politics as an aspiration and purpose of unification. It has a dual nature of its origin and *telos*.[36] It therefore permeates both the symbolic and purposive rationality of European politics. The concept of a European citizenry operates as a point of reference of the "ever closer union" and opens possibilities of future decision-making at the European level.

The primary effect of such a complex concept of the European identity on the nations of post-communist countries was "negative": it protected them from falling into the abyss of history-oriented nationalism and ethnically based political identity. Nationalisms, which falsely call for the awakening of nations to self-consciousness

---

34 M. Nash, *The Cauldron of Ethnicity* (Chicago: University of Chicago Press, 1989).

35 E. Cassirer, *The Myth of the State* (New Haven: Yale University Press, 1946), p. 282.

36 Z. Bankowski and E. Christodoulidis, "The European Union as an Essentially Contested Project", 4 *European Law Journal*, 4 (1998), p. 347.

and "invent nations where they do not exist",[37] certainly played a significant role in the post-1989 Central and Eastern Europe but they never transformed into politics of state and tribal violence like in the Balkans in the 1990s. Due to this external "European identity" influence, re-awakened nationalisms could influence only some political decisions and legislation but, with the exception of Slovakia between 1994–8, they never fully determined the course of national politics in the accession countries.

The European constitution-making process has been based on the "future in process." This future in process was typical, for instance, of the attempt at formulating an identity basis for the process of European unification in the *Declaration on the European Identity* signed by the then nine member states of the European Community.[38] It states that the member states shared "the same attitudes to life, based on a determination to build a society which measures up to the needs of the individual." In the process of the European integration, the "historical future" has mainly been constructed as a negative element in the whole symbolic structure of the EU, which represented the history of nationalism, ethnic hatred, racism and anti-Semitism. The historical trauma and reflection of modern political disasters such as the Holocaust and the two world wars in the last century can have an educative and unifying effect for Europeans, both "old" and "new" joining the Union in 2004, and eventually lead to the self-identification of a new European citizenry.[39] The historical future accepted by European constitution-making was the republican history of cosmopolitan demos which was always confronted by the destructive power of nationalist political myths. The dream of "everyone's Europe" of the future announced by the President of the European Commission Romano Prodi was described as a gift "we owe to future generations."[40] In his address, the cosmopolitan political programme was almost meeting a utopian dream of ultimate inclusion of all people which would leave nobody out. It is this language of the future in process and not the historical future which has had formative power in recent European constitution-making.

The 1992 transformation establishing a single market and the *Single European Act* were driven by the ideology of European ascendancy and people in the member

---

37 E. Gellner, *Thought and Change* (Chicago: University of Chicago Press, 1964), p. 169. For a similar definition of "the invention of the nation", see also B. Anderson, *Imagined Communities: Reflections on the origin and spread of nationalism* (London: Verso, 1983); E. Gellner, *Nations and Nationalisms* (Oxford: Blackwell, 1983).

38 Commission of the European Communities, *Declaration on the European Identity*, 1973 Bull. EC 12, Cl. 2501, pp. 118–27.

39 See, for instance, J. Habermas, *The Inclusion of the Other: Studies in Political Theory* (Cambridge: Polity Press 1999), p. 152.

40 R. Prodi, "Shaping the New Europe", Prodi's speech in the European Parliament delivered on 15 February 2000. Here quoted from I. Ward, "A Decade of Europe? Some Reflections on an Aspiration", 30 *Journal of Law and Society*, 3 (2003), p. 236.

states were "successfully called to rally behind and identify with a bold new step toward a higher degree of integration."[41] The European market's purposive rationality was to be fortified by the symbolic rationality of political culture, ethos, and ideology. Europe as unity was a slogan of the 1990s and the original EU integration goal of limiting state sovereignty[42] was progressing through ever closer economic integration with the hope that full political union of federal Europe would follow. Herder's concepts of primeval cultural bonds and the spiritual, social and political homogeneity of ethnically defined nations as the main characteristic of the sovereign people were dismissed as damaging the endeavour of the European political integration and democracy. Doctrines of political and social homogeneity of the sovereign people were criticised as invoking the metaphysical concept of *Volk* hiding behind the *demos* and contradicting the democratic and multicultural ethos of a common European state "composed of a plurality of nations and yet founded on a *demos*, deriving its legitimacy from consent rather than descent and its chances of survival from civil rather than primordial loyalties."[43]

The European polity brought gradually into being by the 1957 Treaty of Rome and subsequent integrative efforts was believed to be in need of its democratisation and Euro-federalists started arguing strongly in favour of the case for common statehood in the 1990s. However, the federalist model reveals an obvious problem: this *demos* may exist as a utopian fantasy and political project, yet it does not exist in the everyday reality of European politics. Advocates of cosmopolitan democracy and citizenship failed in their attempts to reduce the juridical and representative role of the nation state.[44] Democracy has not been successfully extended from the nation state framework to the Union and its population as a whole. The peoples of Europe and their democratically elected representatives at the national level even regularly criticise the European Union for the lack of democratic legitimacy and accountability. The European sense of belonging, solidarity, and identity is much weaker than the identification of people with their region, country and nation.[45]

---

41 See J.H.H. Weiler, *The Constitution of Europe: "Do the new Clothes have an Emperor?" and Other Essays on European Integration* (Cambridge: Cambridge University Press, 1999) p. 89.

42 The strategy of limiting the nation-state had been present already in the 1950 Schuman Declaration and the 1951 European Coal and Steel Community Treaty. See Schuman Declaration of May 9, 1950 and the preamble to 1951 Treaty of Paris.

43 See G.F. Mancini, "Europe: The Case for Statehood", 4 *European Law Journal,* 1 (1998), p. 35.

44 See D. Held, *Democracy and the Global Order* (Cambridge: Polity Press 1995); D. Archibugi, D. Held and M. Koehler (eds.), *Re-imagining Political Community* (Cambridge: Polity Press, 1998).

45 See, for instance, D. Beetham and C. Lord, *Legitimacy and the European Union* (London: Longman, 1998), p. 46.

European federalism may be supported by different local and national elites, yet it still lacks solid democratic consent.[46]

Instead of representatives of the "imagined" European nation, it is representatives of the member states, middle-range European officials and a variety of private advisory bodies agents who sit on different committees exercising administrative and regulative functions. This "comitology"[47] inevitably suffers from the deficit of legitimacy and strengthens the perception of the Union as driven by the elites and their conceptions of the emerging polity. The committee based form of European governance is neither constitutional, nor unconstitutional. It is beyond the reach of the constitutional discourse because it exceeds its concepts of different branches of government, checks and balances, principles of delegation and separation of power etc.[48] The expansion of government by committees contradicts the proclaimed ascendancy of a common European citizenry and its ethos of public control and political accountability. It is much closer to the decisionist concept of law and state elaborated by Carl Schmitt in his critique of the liberal democratic rule of law.[49] The democratization of the Union by constitution-making, which involves the attempt to establish the European demos, has thus to primarily be taken as a process attempting to reduce its decisionist character and make it more adjustable to Kelsen's concept of constitutionalism based on the concept of *Grundnorm* (basic norm).[50] The Union's decision-making agencies are to be provided with normative legitimation by a constitution.

Furthermore, the search of the European people was intensified by the fact that the Union has already been *de facto* building its constitutional order by decisions and practices of its administrative and judicial bodies. The doctrine of the European Court of Justice holds that European law constitutes a new legal order which is neither a sub-ordinate sub-system of the legal systems of member states, nor merely

---

[46] See L.K. Hallstrom, "Support for European Federalism: an elite view", 25 *Journal of European Integration*, (2003), pp. 51–72.

[47] The term used in R. H. Pedler and G.F. Schaefer (eds.), *Shaping European Law and Policy—The Role of Committees and Comitology in the Political Process* (Maastricht: European Centre for Public Affairs, European Institute of Public Administration, 1996). See also K. Bradley, "The European Parliament and Comitology: On the Road to Nowhere?", 3 *European Law Journal* (1997), 273; P. Craig and G. de Búrca (eds.) *The Evolution of EU Law* (Oxford: Oxford University Press, 1999).

[48] See J.H.H. Weiler, *The Constitution of Europe, op. cit.* n. 41, p. 98.

[49] C. Schmitt, *Verfassungslehre* (Berlin: Humblot, 1983, orig. 1928).

[50] This "symbolisation" of the current constitutional dilemmas in the "Kelsen vs. Schmitt" jurisprudential divide has become quite popular in recent debates. See J.H.H. Weiler, "In defence of the status quo: Europe's constitutional *Sonderweg*", in J.H.H. Weiler and M. Wind (eds.), *European Constitutionalism Beyond the State* (Cambridge: Cambridge University Press, 2003), p. 12.

part of international law.[51] National legal systems of member states consequently contain two distinct "basic norms", one coming from the national constitutional order and the other from the European law.[52] For instance, the response of the German Federal Constitutional Court to this doctrine denied that the Court of Justice could have the so-called *Kompetenz–Kompetenz* to determine the final scope of European law in relation to national law and sovereign state.[53] One of the main reasons stated by the German Constitutional Court was exactly that the Union did not have a *demos* and its legislation could not therefore claim supremacy. This famous "no demos thesis" and resistance to the European Court of Justice limiting national judicial and constitutional authority only revealed competing and conflicting visions of both jurisdictional and political authority of the European institutions in relation to the member states. National constitutional courts therefore do not necessarily support the emerging transnational European legal order, but often defend national democratic constitutionalism against "illicit encroachment from Brussels."[54]

Challenged or supported by systems of justice of member states, it is obvious that European constitutionalism had been practiced long before the Convention started its constitution-making job. The existence of a "constitution in practice"[55] reflects the fact that practical constitution-making and formation of a political community have been existing for long time and alongside conceptual, theoretical and normative debates of the Convention and inter-governmental conferences. It consists of daily practices and decisions of the EU institutions which are shaped into the form of the *acquis communautaire.* The efforts to invent the European people thus did not have only the symbolic function of giving priority to demos

---

51 See N. MacCormick, "Sovereignty, Democracy and Subsidiarity", in R. Bellamy, V. Bufacchi and D. Castiglione (eds.), *Democracy and Constitutional Culture in the Union of Europe* (London: Lothian Foundation Press, 1995), p 100.

52 This structural division in national legal systems invokes the idea of constitutional and legal pluralism. See, for instance, N. Walker, "The Idea of Constitutional Pluralism", 65 *Modern Law Review* (2002), p. 317.

53 See, for instance, J.H.H. Weiler, U.R. Haltern and F.C. Mayer, "European Democracy and Its Critique", in J. Hayward (ed.) *The Crisis of Representation in Europe* (London: Frank Cass, 1995), pp. 4–39, at 9–23.

54 See J.H.H. Weiler, "In defence of the status quo: Europe's constitutional *Sonderweg*", in J.H.H. Weiler and M. Wind (eds.), *European Constitutionalism Beyond the State* (Cambridge: Cambridge University Press 2003), pp. 7–23, at 16.

55 See J. Shaw, "Process and Constitutional Discourse in the European Union", 27 *Journal of Law and Society* (2000), No. 1, pp. 4–37, at 18. On the other hand, Dieter Grimm criticizes this thesis of "constitution in practice" as self-contradictory when he says that "... [T]he call for a constitution would be void from the outset if European legal scholars' assumption that the missing constitution already exists were right. In that case one could certainly talk about improving it, but hardly about creating." See D. Grimm, "Does Europe Need a Constitution?", 1 *European Law Journal*, No. 3, November 1995, pp. 282–302, at 284.

over ethnos in the "unification dream" decade of the 1990s. The invention of the European demos was also to affect all three spheres of democratic legitimacy of the European institutions and practical rationality of decision-making: authorisation, accountability and representation.

7. SPACE VARIETIES: TWO MODELS OF THE EUROPEAN CONSTITUTION-MAKING

Europe's search of its people and constitution-making are examples of a historically unique and paradoxical situation in which the "constitutive power" is desperate to constitute its "constituent power" (*pouvoir constituant*). The existing EU institutions decided to create a special agency—the Convention—which was expected to outline a new political structure and institutional framework inspiring the constitution of Europe's constituent power—the people. Concrete political actions and decisions were to be taken in two separate steps: the first one was to create the Convention while the second one was to create the Constitution. This gradual work of the EU agencies was then expected to transform the Union's political and legal structural framework and inspire the creation of the European democratic citizenry. While actions and decisions determined the structural transformation in the first part of the plan, the expected transformation was to inspire the creation of a new agency in the second part. This political structuration[56] would be a common social process if there were not a paradoxical expectation involved in the whole business: a new-born agency was to retrospectively legitimise the transformed political structure which made its creation possible. The constitution-making process would thus have serious political and cultural implications for all European nations involved and it is therefore not surprising to see that the whole nature of the process was questioned and re-designed by its agents.

The whole business of constitution-making and search of the European collective political identity has been undoubtedly risky like any sort of political constructivism. Apart from institutional and procedural aspects of power and obedience, it involves problems of moral commitment and cultural identity. No wonder that endless debates regarding the Draft Constitutional Treaty were regularly addressing the issues of cultural self-understanding of "Europeans" and the Philadelphia Convention was used as a decisive inspiration for the coming European democratic citizenry.[57] Despite such an overarching moral and cultural discourse, critics have often warned against possible destructive effects which the current process may have on democratic politics at the national level. According to these views, the imposed idea of a non-existing European citizenry may result in the weakening

---

56 For a general sociological account of "structuration", see A. Giddens, *The Constitution of Society* (Cambridge: Polity Press, 1984).

57 See, for instance, a speech delivered by the Convention's President Valery Giscard D'Estaing, "The Preparation of the European Constitution", *Second Annual Henry Kissinger Lecture*, Library of Congress, Washington, 11 February 2003.

of democratic legitimacy at the national level while having no real effect on the quality of European politics and its legitimacy. Other voices acknowledge the real achievements of the European integration, but want to keep it at the level of purposive legitimacy by common interests instead of symbolic legitimacy by a common people.[58] The main message of these pro-European, yet anti-federal, warnings is that it would be dangerous to instigate political identity where a political community does not exist. Instead, these voices propose that liberal democracy should rather be cultivated at the national level with the European constitution-making merely confirming the existing level of integration and thus reducing the potentially growing deficit of democratic legitimacy.[59]

Any sort of the European constitution-making, which would be based on the post-Maastricht European sovereignty claims and the notion of the supremacy of European law,[60] cannot pass the Hobbesian test of political order. According to Thomas Hobbes, it is the threat of anarchy and violence what makes the establishment of political order necessary. One can ask in a similar manner: "Why does Europe need a sovereign constitution when its political order is not threatened by anarchy and violence?" It may be distrusted by many European inhabitants, yet has been largely beneficial to most of them. Despite politically disruptive effects of government by committees, there is no imminent threat to its stability and the main driving force behind current changes therefore has been political ambitions to stretch further the existing levels of integration and build a federal Europe. Economic challenges and achievements of the common European market and currency were to be cemented by political ambitions to constitute a federal European polity. Federalism has been taken as a rich political tradition and practice which should be exploited by the EU policy-makers and constitution-makers in order to construct the Union as a federal polity.[61]

If the enlargement policy was driven by the logic of *conditionality* set up at the Copenhagen summit, the progressive political integration was typical of the logic of the "constitutional *finality*" of a European Federation.[62] For instance, the German foreign minister's finality principle included a stronger bicameral European Parliament representing both the citizens and the nation states and basic human

---

[58] H. Lübbe, *Abschied vom Superstaat: Vereinigte Staaten von Europa wird es nicht geben* (Berlin: Siedler Verlag 1994).

[59] D. Grimm, *op. cit.* n. 55. pp. 282–302.

[60] N. MacCormick, "The Maastricht-Urteil: Sovereignty Now", 1 *European Law Journal*, 3 (1995), pp. 259–266.

[61] R. Koslowski, "A Constructivist approach to understanding the European Union as a federal polity", 6 *Journal of European Public Policy*, Vol. 4, Special Issue (1999), pp. 561–578, esp. at 568–570.

[62] For this view, see especially the Germany Foreign Minister J. Fischer, "From Confederacy to Federation: Thoughts on the Finality of European Integration", speech delivered on 12 May 200 at the Humboldt Universitat, Berlin.

and civil rights enforceable at the European level. According to these federalist views, enlargement is taken as one of the reasons why political integration should speed up its progress. It has been argued that European institutions should get more decision-making powers in order to avoid possible political chaos and instability. Nevertheless, the enlargement process has eventually proved to run according to a very different logic which was incommensurable with the finality argument.[63] The Hobbesian finality argument could not be accommodated in the constitution-making process seeking to reconcile both visions of tightening and widening the European Union.

Nevertheless, the argument of fear as the most important cause of individual and collective violence which needs to be eliminated by a political sovereign, first made in Hobbes's *Leviathan*, had a formative effect in the pro-European discourse in former communist countries exposed to threats of nationalism and "new tribalism."[64] Although the Union could hardly be perceived as a sovereign power, it was nevertheless portrayed as a safe haven curbing all nationalist animosities and protecting the member countries from regress to an earlier state of ethnically defined politics and traditionalism. Europe was expected to act as *quasi-Leviathan* that promotes the virtue of civil unity and protects national politics from the risks of secessionist movements and nationalist separatism. Expectations of the Union's constraining power in the field of ethnic politics, including minority rights and political self-determinations, were indeed very high in the ethnically divided region of Central and Eastern Europe. The Copenhagen conditionality policy could therefore successfully use the Hobbesian model of political stabilization.

Although the Hobbesian model had a positive external effect on the accession states, its internal effect would be much more negative and harmful. The Convention's constitution-making therefore eventually involved many elements different from Euro-federalist aspirations and their Hobbesian logic of state building as power providing security for its subject citizens. It resembled the social contract a lot more in the sense of an alliance of the involved parties that have mutual responsibilities and rights. The dominating logic was that of John Locke's "horizontal" version of the social contract and not its "vertical" version formulated by Hobbes.[65] After the struggle between federalists and anti-federalists, the Convention presented a draft of the social contract between the peoples of Europe politically organised in their democratic nation states. At the same time, it drafted some institutional

---

63 Compare, A. Wiener, "Finality vs. enlargement: constitutive practices and opposing rationales in the reconstruction of Europe", in J.H.H. Weiler and M. Wind (eds.), *European Constitutionalism Beyond the State* (Cambridge: Cambridge University Press 2003), pp. 160–165.

64 The term used, for instance, by Michael Walzer. See M. Walzer, "Notes on the New Tribalism", in C. Brown (ed.), *Political Restructuring In Europe: Ethical perspectives* (London: Routledge, 1994), pp. 187–200.

65 For the distinction, see for instance H. Arendt, *Zur Zeit* (München, Deutscher Taschenbuch Verlag, 1989), pp. 145–146.

and structural preconditions of the federalist model of the Union, but without the concept of the European people legislating the constitution for itself. The preamble of the draft "treaty establishing a constitution for Europe" read:

> [C]onvinced that, while remaining proud of their own national identities and history, the peoples of Europe are determined to transcend their ancient divisions and, united ever more closely, to forge a common destiny. Convinced that, thus "united in its diversity", Europe offers them the best chance of pursuing, with due regard for the rights of each individual and in awareness of their responsibilities toward future generations and the Earth, the great venture which makes of it a special area of human hope.[66]

While a common identity is yet to be shaped and has been postponed for future-building, the reference to national identities includes both their positive and negative political consequences in European history. The unifying role of negative historical experience should work as a mechanism of enhancing the unification process. At the same time, the Union selects its "positive past" when it committed itself to respect cultural diversity and protect its cultural heritage in Article 1(3) of the draft treaty.

The heavy weight of regulatory politics, comitology and institutional framework of the European Union thus did not eventually result in the historical "awakening" of political societies of participating states and their integration into a civil European nation. In the current situation, the search of the European demos would resemble far too much the undesired Hobbesian model because it would be a search of the sovereign political power legitimating the federal transformation of political power in Europe. The recognition of sovereignty of member states has been reflected in the description of the draft as a "treaty" which means that it, like any other international treaty, would have to be ratified by national governments. The horizontal version of the contractual act forms a "pact" of the parties which reflects the original agreement, consent, and freedom of political will. The principle of negotiations and multilateral agreements between the member states has remained decisive in the Union's future constitution-making.

The fact that a constitution for Europe is to be enacted by the member states exercising their treaty making powers in the sense of international legal order is of vital importance. The will and capacity of the citizens of Europe is lacking and the operative constitutional framework therefore cannot be treated as a true constitution. "Europe's constitutional architecture"[67] is fundamentally different from models of national constitutions because its authority derives entirely from the member states, and not from the citizens of Europe. For this simple reason, the

---

66 See The European Convention document CONV 820/03, *Draft Treaty establishing a Constitution for Europe*, pp. 4–5.

67 See J.H.H. Weiler, "A Constitution for Europe? Some Hard Choices", 40 *Journal of Common Market Studies* (2002), pp. 567.

kind of constitutional authority and discipline in the Union will be different from any concept of statehood and a sovereign constitutional order. The constitutional language of statehood symbolism, which was typical of the Laeken Declaration of December 2001, has lost its momentum and "the current situation of massive enlargement brings back elements derived from the logic of international law."[68]

The EU enlargement fundamentally affected the constitution-making process because the Convention realised that it would be very hard to go both deeper and wider in shaping the future of Europe at the same time. The accessing countries have enormously benefited from this limitation of political ambitions because they were: a) treated as equal partners of constitution-making debates; b) not forced to renounce too much of their recently re-established national sovereignty. These countries experienced solidarity with other European nations, the sense of belonging to a common political network and being "one of us", when they were invited to participate in the Convention and the following Intergovernmental Conference.[69] They could build on the symbolic image of the enlargement as a process of the reunification of Europe and "the real end of World War II"[70] and incorporate it into the image of the Convention's constitution-making. It was also important that the preamble of the Convention's draft reflected it in its phrase of "reunited Europe."[71] New and fragile national democracies thus did not have to confront the public dilemma of "selling out to Brussels" at even a larger scale than during the enlargement negotiations and incorporation of EU law into their national legal systems.

The European integration process was thus typical of a mixture of both the Hobbesian and the Lockean model. While the first one was applied by the Union for instance in the Copenhagen criteria, the second one was applied by the Convention in its constitution-making and extended to the accession countries. As mentioned above, the Copenhagen criteria was a fascinating example of the Union's "double standards" policy setting certain political and constitutional conditions for the accession states which had been part of neither the Union's legal system, nor national legal systems of the member states. This double standards approach was striking in the field of minority rights protection which was expected from the

---

68 A. Wiener, "Finality vs. enlargement: constitutive practices and opposing rationales in the reconstruction of Europe", in J.H.H. Weiler and M. Wind (eds.), *European Constitutionalism Beyond the State* (Cambridge: Cambridge University Press 2003), pp. 159–160.

69 A concrete example of this participation was, for instance, an informal consultative Prague meeting of 15 states demanding further changes in the draft Treaty and better balance of power in favour of the smaller member states before the opening of the Intergovernmental Conference in October 2003. See the "Prague Memorandum" of 1 September, 2003.

70 M. Walker, "Enlargement of the European Union: How New EU Members Will Change the Shape of Europe", in R.J. Guttman (ed.), *Europe in the New Century: Visions of an Emerging Superpower* (London: Lynne Rienner Publishers, 2001), p. 58.

71 The European Convention's document CONV 820/03, *Draft Treaty establishing a Constitution for Europe*, p. 4.

accession states, yet ignored by some member states. Central and East European countries joining the EU were demanded to enter "with a clean slate in respect of their minorities" because "then there will be no need for the European Union itself to modify its "agnosticism" in respect of minority protection *inside* the Union."[72] The Union's external demand to deal with minority rights in the accession states before joining the EU was to help keep the whole constitutional and legal agenda of minority rights protection outside the gates of the Union's law.

While the Copenhagen criteria were based on the Hobbesian model, the contractual model of the Union's "Constitution in waiting" draws rather on the vision of a horizontal community of states which goes far beyond the conceptual framework of international law based on principles of state sovereignty, independence, neutrality, autonomy, national power and self-interest. The European Union has been designed as a community of states and peoples sharing political ethos, principles of government, human values and aspirations. Although it builds on the principle of "divided sovereignty" in growing number of policies and economic and administrative interdependence, it is based on the principle of balance between the interests of a member state and the interests of the community. It thus constitutes itself as a political and legal hybrid exceeding the territory of international law, yet without the coherence of a federal state.[73] This development leads to the European political and legal practice "beyond the sovereign state"[74] which, nevertheless, remains unsupported by the sovereign federal Union.

8. CONCLUSION: THE DILEMMATIC EUROPEAN IDENTITY AND CONSTITUTIONAL MARGINALISATION OF *ETHNOS*

The contractual model may be despised by federalists, but it has strong symbolic value especially for the new member states. It strengthens their European identity exactly because of the constitution's recognition of the diversity and heterogeneity of voices speaking through different national representations in common Europe. The legitimating force of a Constitution drafted as a treaty can be arguably stronger

---

72 B. De Witte, "The Impact of Enlargement on the Constitution of the European Union", in M. Cremona (ed.), *The Enlargement of the European Union* (Oxford: Oxford University Press, 2003), p. 239.

73 Despite the proposed principle of the Union's legal personality in Article 6 of the draft Treaty, it cannot be considered a sovereign state in the sense of international law which would exercise greater power over the member states. The proposed common foreign policy in Article 11(4) shows signs of external sovereignty of the Union toward the outside world and enhances mutual interdependence and closer cooperation between the member states. However, it is an example of divided sovereignty because sovereignty of the member states has not been lost, but rather subjected to a number of decision-making processes combining the power of the European institutions and the member states.

74 N. MacCormick, "Beyond the Sovereign State", *Modern Law Review* 1 (1993), pp. 1–19.

because it shows reciprocal influence and agreement between equal political democratic nations of Europe. Despite its character, it may still be perceived as the historical expression of an abstract beginning of the European polity based on the principles of equality and diversity.

Furthermore, the covenantal nature of the Convention's deliberation and the final draft inspired the civil virtues of equality, respect and agreement. They represented the Union's formative constitutional experience and the concept of constitutionalism which builds on procedural elements, conversation and dialogue, and equal treatment of all parties. This positive experience was possible only after resorting to the plan of strong European nation-building. In this light, the failure of the Brussels summit in December 2003 appears to be a positive formative moment which reveals a central role of negotiations and compromise and makes the constitution-making process a much more European public issue.

Nevertheless, it became obvious that the strong concept of political identity was not useful in the covenantal form of constitution-making. The identity of the European *demos* would be too difficult to formulate by the concepts of nationhood, sovereignty, and democratic state. Weiler speaks even about impossibility when he comments on the process of European state and nation building:

> It would be more than ironic if a polity with its political process set up to counter the excesses of statism ended up coming round full circle and transforming itself into a (super)state. It would be equally ironic that an ethos that rejected the nationalism of the Member States gave birth to a new European nation and European nationalism. The problem with the unity vision is that its very realization entails its negation.[75]

In his polemic with Grimm, Habermas, who has always been a strong proponent of the idea of a common European people, also recognizes troubles with the European identity and statehood and introduces a new project of a "heterogeneous" people which would have to replace old "homogenous" concept of the people in order to provide a legitimation framework for federal Europe:

> [O]f course, the argument that there is no such thing as a European people, and thus also no force capable of generating a European constitution, only becomes a fundamental objection through a particular use of the concept of "a people." The prognosis that there cannot be any such thing as a European people remains plausible only if "the people", as a source of solidarity, actually depends on some corresponding community as a pre-political basis of trust, which fellow countrymen and women inherit as the shared fate of their socialization.[76]

---

75 See J.H.H. Weiler, *The Constitution of Europe*, *op. cit.* n. 41. p. 94.

76 J. Habermas, *The Postnational Constellation: political essays* (Cambridge: Polity Press, 2001), p. 100.

The European identity lacks a common language, shared tradition and customs, yet it can draw on common culture and both historical negative and positive experiences. However, history cannot glue a political community. Habermas and other Euro-enthusiasts therefore call for a political identity established by European law, politics, the public sphere and civil society institutions. According to this view, a European citizenship is incompatible with the exclusionary nature of nationalist sentiment.[77] Nevertheless, the main source of this identity will have to be the language of law and the European constitutional guarantees of civil rights because the European public sphere, political parties and civil society do not exist.

Unlike the utopian image of one European people, the European identity is most likely to be constructed as a hybrid mixture of common civil ethos and persisting different national loyalties. It will be the *dilemmatic identity* which will be impossible to consolidate at the symbolic level. European identity and legitimacy will thus remain an open-ended process of the symbolization of the common social, cultural and political space. However, this process will have to exceed the common understanding of democratic legitimacy based on the question of who constitutes the people to which there must exist a mutually agreed and settled answer.[78] Post-communist experiences of the accession countries show that the identity dilemma had an enormous impact on constitution-making and political processes which could be stabilised externally by the symbolic power of the European Union as a supra-national structure representing the political virtues of civility. The choice between ethnic and civic identity was often reduced to the choice between authoritarian nationalism and democratic liberal politics. Inside the Union, the European civil identity has been a major constitutional tool for responding to the democratic legitimation gap at the Union's level and connecting with democratic politics of the ethnically consolidated Member States. In this context, it has not been a dilemma of clear alternatives but rather of supplementing and expanding one form of political identity over the other.

Despite their persistence, the building of a new European political identity will proceed as further marginalisation of the ethnically established loyalties and traditional communal identities. This marginalisation is part of an internal logic and constitution of the European Union in which *demos* was supposed to substitute *ethnos* and diminish its impact on political decision-making processes. This logic is an answer to modern European history, its nationalism and ethnically incited political violence. Furthermore, unlike civil rights and virtues, local ethnic identities are not sufficiently flexible for contemporary globalized societies of Europe. Local identity of ethnicity is too rigid and "thick" in the sense of its normative binding power. It is far too limited to cultural particularity. Unlike local ethnic

---

[77] N.W. Barber, "Citizenship, nationalism and the European Union", 27 *European Law Review* (2002), June, pp. 256–7.

[78] See, for instance, R. Dahl, *Democracy and its Critics* (New Haven: Yale University Press, 1989).

identity, purposive rationality of general economic and legal networks produces social flexibility, has power to expand social communication, and transcends local limits. However, these networks can lead to the establishment of merely "thin" identity[79] based on specified costs and benefits.

European constitution-making is therefore accompanied by multi-dimensional identity which is disentangled from the traditional concepts of solidarity, community, and face to face relations.[80] Cultural rigidity is replaced by flexibility of social networks and multiplied personal choices. The Union has already extended civil rights enforcement beyond the nation-state and thus effectively put an end to the modern limitation of rights to the boundaries of a state sovereign power. The emergence of a minimum common identity through the network of European constitutional law is well documented in the concept of the European citizenship. The original Maastricht citizenship provisions incorporated in Article 8 of the Maastricht Treaty have been elaborated in Article 8 of the draft of the Constitutional Treaty and declare that "[e]very national of a Member State shall be a citizen of the Union. Citizenship of the union shall be additional to national citizenship; it shall not replace it." Although national citizenship is not affected, this provision clearly makes citizens of EU member states the subject of rights and entitlements provided at the European level. This trend of directly granting the rights at the European level weakens old communal loyalties, but it does not mean a full decoupling of national and European citizenship. It is still member state nationality which opens the way to the rights guaranteed for European citizens.[81]

The primary source of European identity will be the emerging constitutional framework, which may gradually establish a common "thin" constitutional identity based on the principle of universality of rights and its political benefits to European citizens.[82] The systemic logic of European constitutional law will be enforcing rights and protecting civil liberties of individuals and various groups. The Kantian republican cosmopolitanism will have to be mediated by the established systemic logic of European constitutional law. So far, it cannot be mediated by a common civil ideology and political ethos because the European public sphere does not exist as an effective communicative network and basis of democratic will-formation.

---

79 See D. Beetham and C. Lord, "Legitimacy and the European Union", in A. Weale and M. Nentwich, *Political Theory and the European Union: Legitimacy, constitutional choice and citizenship* (London: Routledge, 1998), p. 22.

80 D. Beetham and C. Lord, *Legitimacy and the European Union* (Longman: London 1998), p. 44.

81 See, for instance, J.H.H. Weiler *et al*, *op. cit.* n. 53, p. 21.

82 See, for instance, K.O. Apel, "Das Anliegen des anglo-amerikanischen 'Kommunitarismus' in der Sicht der Diskursethik. Worin liegen die 'kommunitaeren' Bedingungen der Moeglichkeit einer post-konventionellen Identitaet der Vernunftperson?", in M. Brumlik und H. Brunkhorst (Hg.), *Gemeinschaft und Gerechtigkeit* (Frankfurt: Fischer Vlg. 1993), p. 172.

Inside the Union, the systemic language will necessarily continue to prevail over the language of political morality and the public sphere. It is false to assume that this "thin" sense of European identity could eventually support the establishment of the "thick" European people supporting the idea of the European federal statehood. The European citizenry will hardly transform into a sovereign with both symbolic and real power to support the establishment of supreme political and legislating authority in federal Europe. The system and networks of the EU cannot inspire such identity and its constituted protection of civil rights is far too weak to create political solidarity and the "we-feeling" of a "thick" political community.

The European Union and identity are "essentially contested projects"[83] and have to be perceived as open-ended processes which are principally future-oriented and must respect the continent's pluralistic nature together with a complicated system of hierarchies which exceed the scope of the member states. The European identity can emerge only as a symbolic space of heterogeneity, permanent contestation of existing practices, compromise-oriented negotiations and the conversational model of politics. In this model, the Kantian abstract ideas of cosmopolitanism and universal republicanism must be accompanied by political realism inspired rather by the philosophy of David Hume and based on the recognition of existing political practices, beliefs and customs. Drawing on these two intellectual legacies, it is possible both to keep the vision of a European political community identified with the concepts of civil rights and democratic virtues and respect political and cultural diversity of the continent.

---

[83] See Bankowski and Christodoulidis, *op. cit.* n. 36, p. 341.

9. An Evolutionary Approach to the Constitutionalism of an Enlarged EU: Why will Cognitive and Cultural Boundaries Matter?

*Daniela Piana**

> "Laws, in their most general signification, are the necessary relations arising from the nature of things. In this sense all beings have their laws ... We must therefore acknowledge relations of justice antecedent to the positive law by which they are established: as for instance if human societies existed it would be right to conform to their laws."[1]

1. Introduction

Several different perspectives have been put forward in order to reach a better understanding of European constitution making and, at the same time, of constitution making processes that have occurred in the Central and Eastern European countries (CEEC). In this chapter, I will address the impact enlargement has had on the European constitution-making process by analyzing three main issues.[2] The first relates to questioning the empirical adequacy of models provided by the social sciences to study the interaction between constitutionalisation and the enlargement of the EU. The second is concerned with the capacity of these very models to grasp the essence of the normative validity of constitutional rules. I will argue that the models proposed are inadequate in explaining and shaping (through policy making and the institutional building in the CEECs) the constitutional rules of new Member States. I will propose a mode of analysis which, in my view, transcends the limitations of the above mentioned models, as it is better equipped to detect the

---

* I am very grateful to W. Sadurski for his remarks on a draft version of the chapter. The seminars in legal and political theory, organized in Paris in 2002, and directed by Jon Elster, have been very enlightening about the processes of institutional building.

1 Charles de Secondat Montesquieu, *De l'esprit des lois* (1748) (Paris: Flammarion, 1979), p. 4.

2 For an overall analysis of the impact of the various normative sources on domestic systems see Rein Mullerson *et al* (eds.), *Constitutional Reform and International Law in Central and Eastern Europe* (The Hague: Kluwer Law International, 1998) and, for a more specific view on enlargement, Alfred Kellerman *et al* (eds.), *EU Enlargement. The Constitutional Impact at the EU and at the National Level* (The Hague: Asser Institute, TMC, 2001).

Wojciech Sadurski et al. (ed.), Spreading Democracy and the Rule of Law?, 219–235.

complex interplay between the multiple sources of norms within the constitutional game in CEECs, on the one hand and, the impact of enlargement on the meaning that constitutionalism would have in the future Europe, on the other. I will take an evolutionary approach to the constitution making processes and will highlight how, in this evolutive process affecting the scope and the meaning of the constitutional rules, cognitive and cultural factors matter. This analysis should be considered as a preliminary assessment of the approach which is mainly used here to make the point about its advantages and adequacy. A further and more detailed empirical research on the issues touched in this chapter will be required in the future.

2. BUILDING AN ENLARGING EUROPEAN CONSTITUTION: WHERE DOES THE RATIONALE COME FROM?

Following a classic distinction introduced by Friedrich von Hayek, two main traditions can be distinguished. The first "constructivist" tradition is based upon a strongly rationalist view of social orders. The second "evolutionary" tradition assumes that social orders are created through spontaneous processes where human rationality does not constitute the absolute and sufficient reason of their existence.[3] With specific reference to the CEECs' application to enter the constitution making processes, I would state—following Hayek—that the first view holds that constitutions are designed and implemented according to some rational procedures. Whereas the second claim affirms that constitutions are spontaneous orders which can be explored and discovered.[4]

The constructivist perspective relies upon three main premises. The first relates to the (rational) capacity of agents to shape their social rules according to a given set of preferences and interests. The second affirms that rules bind rational actions because they have an impact on the pay-offs of the alternatives.[5] The third premise assumes that it might be possible to design a social, decisional procedure that transmits (once rational agents decide to adopt institutions to solve their social dilemmas) the initial normative meaning, attributed by the individual to the preferred alternative, to the final outcome of the collective choice.[6] Put simply, social orders are held to be rational and, therefore, valid from a normative point of view because they have been chosen according to a social decision making process which is neutral with regard to the decision makers' interests, with regard to the alternatives and those problems faced by the collectivity. In the case of the constitutional choices, the constructivist view says that constitutions, because they are

3 Friedrich von Hayek, *Law, Legislation and Liberty* (London: Routledge, 1982), Chap. 1.
4 *Ibid.*
5 Kenneth George Binmore, *Game Theory and Social Contract* (Cambridge: MIT, 1994).
6 James Colomer, *Political Institutions and Social Choice* (Oxford: Oxford University Press, 2001).

born from rational and formally valid collective decision making, are legitimate.[7] This view is represented by the contractualistic perspective[8] which states that the procedure to create a legitimate constitution is a contract among free and rational citizens:[9] "the rules of political order can legitimately be derived only from the agreement among individuals as members of the policy."[10] In this perspective, the legal orders—and *a fortiori* constitutional ones—are held to be structures, fixed in time. Therefore, the contract is held to able to organize *ex nihilo* a social system, a social community.

The empirical adequacy of this framework to explain the process of European constitution making turns out to be too narrow and inadequate. As a matter of fact, the constitutional norms of the EU have not been intentionally agreed anywhere, nevertheless, their existence and validity has been extensively argued. It is much more likely to interpret the process of the constitutionalisation of the EU in a completely unintentional perspective where the choices made by institutional agents—the European institutions and the states—have to interact with a wider, broader and diffuse process of evolution of the European legal order.[11] This process has partially occurred outside the scope of the interests and the intentions rationally and strategically pursued by actors through explicit agreements. As it has finally been highlighted, the constitution of the EU is much more of an overlapping structure where the rationale cannot be ascribed to an initial constitutional choice. It is true that the European constitution determines the main axes of the political structure of the EU, while the policies and the social processes originated by them are dynamic and changing in time. But it is also true that many feedbacks turn out to affect the validity and the meaning of the constitutional rules. If this is the state of the art then some critical assessments can be put forward about the framework adopted to shape the guidelines of the pre-accession strategy. In effect these guidelines follow the constructivist vision where the constitutional norms of the EU could be transferred as a packaged out system of data.[12] They have been held to transmit normative content that, once integrated in the legal orders of

---

7 Geoffrey Brennan and James Buchanan, *The Reason of Rules: Constitutional Political Economy* (Cambridge: Cambridge University Press, 1996).

8 For a critical assessment of the contractualist theories, *see* Christopher Morris, *The Social Contract Theories: Critical Essays on Hobbes, Locke and Rousseau* (Lanham: Rowman Littlefield, 1999).

9 See for a criticism of this view Russell Hardin, "Why a Constitution?", in Bernard Grofman and Donald Wittman, eds., *The Federalist Papers and the New Institutionalism* (New York: Agathon Press, 1989), pp. 100–101.

10 Brennan and Buchanan, *op. cit.* n. 7, p. 26.

11 Bruno De Witte, "The closest thing to a constitutional conversation in Europe. The semi-permanent treaty revision process", in Paul Beaumont, Carole Lyons and Neil Walker (eds.), *Convergence and Divergence in European Public Law* (Oxford: Hart, 2002).

12 Lykke Friis, "Conceptualising Enlargement", paper prepared for the workshop "Governance by Enlargement", Darmstadt, 23–25 June 2000, and Anna Murphy, "The European Union

the new Member States, could transform them into *European States*. The implicit hypothesis within this policy is a rationalist one which assumes that social orders can be created through a well-designed institutional change. The criteria adopted to assess the impact of the transfer of norms to the candidate countries have been targeted according to a frozen idea of the European constitution as well.[13]

However, this framework would have been rejected from an evolutionary perspective. Actually, the divide between the constructivist and the evolutionary perspective is threefold. The first concerns the limited rationality ascribed to agents. Constitution makers do not forecast the outcomes of their choices, neither are they allowed to govern the process of implementation of the set of the institutional tools which they have opted for. Furthermore, the evolutionary perspective holds the causal mechanisms at the origin of the emergence and stabilisation of a constitution to be close to those mechanisms that are at the origin of the natural and cultural evolution. Therefore, this view tries to figure out patterns for the introduction of novelties, for the selections of variations and for the transmission of these novelties that make sense in the social orders. The outcomes of these mechanisms are over and above human intentions, in the sense that the content of a constitution can't be reduced to the intention of a human player. In fact, since human minds are naturally and intrinsically bounded and subject to failure,[14] the rules composing a stable constitution go far beyond the rules that could be created with what can be called "one shot choices"—as it would be an intentional agreement.[15] Thirdly and consequently, the rationality of a constitution can be assessed only through a dynamic perspective, looking at its capacity to cope with the changes and the new issues that come out from collective actions.[16]

The advantage of this second view follows from its greater empirical adequacy, with regard to the real capacity of people to shape reality through institutional design. Moreover, it is a perspective that is closer than the constructivist one to the on going process linked to the use of rules. Evolutionary scholars have pointed out that norms change because of an internal process of change. This change is the outcome of interpretative actions and impinges upon the scope and the social impact of the norms themselves. Therefore, behind the intentional selection of

---

and Central and Eastern Europe: Governance and Boundaries", *Journal of Common Market Studies* (37) (1999), pp. 211–232.

13 Elena Iankova, "Governed by Accession. Hard and Soft Pillars of Europeanization in Central and Eastern Europe", *East European Studies, Occasional papers*, 2001.

14 Friedrich von Hayek, *Scientism and the Study of Society* (1942–1944), in *The Counter-Revolution of Science. Studies on the Abuse of Reason* (Glencoe: The Free Press, 1952), pp. 13–102 and 207–221.

15 Friedrich von Hayek, "The Use of Knowledge in Society", *American Economic Review* (35) (1945), pp. 519–530.

16 Viktor Vanberg, "Institutional Competition Among Jurisdictions: An Evolutionary Approach", *Constitutional Political Economy* (5) (1994), pp. 193–219.

norms—that is represented for example by the statutory acts of the legislative or of the government—a widespread and incremental process of change affects the meaning of the constitutional rules and renders them to be effective.[17] Furthermore, the interpretation of the norms is strongly related to the values that social actors attributed to them. Since constitutions are very general rules governing the abstract relationship between citizens on the one hand, and between citizens and the State on the other hand, their normative value is not only related to the specific, punctual outcomes reached through their implementation, but also the general meaning that is attributed to them. This meaning is determined by cognitive and cultural factors shared by a collectivity.[18]

This twofold composition of the mechanism of change that impinges upon constitutional rules is very pertinent if we look at the constitution-making process of an enlarged Europe. In fact, the normative validity of the legal order of a future Europe will go beyond the normative contents of the Treaties and beyond the normative content that has been intentionally transmitted and intentionally adopted by the candidate countries. The outcome of enlargement and the European process of constitution making can be grasped only if we account for the widespread interactions among several normative sources of constitutional principles and constitutional rules that have participated in this process. Therefore, it seems that to grasp the dynamics of constitution making, a set of evolutive mechanisms should be created in order to come to terms with the puzzle of the constitutionalisation of an enlarged Europe. Such mechanisms should enable us to understand not only the changes in the legal systems, but also—I would argue this to be the most important aspect in this context—the micro-changes in the scope of the norms following from their *interpretation*.

3. ENLARGING THE RULE OF THE LAW OR CHALLENGING THE NORMATIVITY OF LAW: A COMPLEX EVOLUTIONARY APPROACH

If we take the points stressed in the last paragraph, the events that have characterized the recent history of the new Member States seem to have a wide and unpredictable impact on the overall political and legal order of the future Europe Union. In order to have an insight into the weight of, and the meaning of, enlargement on the constitutionalisation of the EU, the effects born from the interaction of the various sources of norms that have played a role in shaping post-communist constitutions[19] have to be accounted for. For instance, it should be considered that in the first period

---

17 Robert Alexy, *A Theory of Legal Argumentation: the Theory of Rational Discourse as a Theory of Legal Justification* (Oxford: Clarendon, 1989).

18 Donald Davidson, *Subjective, Intersubjective and Objective* (Oxford: Clarendon, 2001).

19 Friedrich Kratochwil, *Rules, Norms, and Decisions. On the Conditions of Practical and Legal Reasoning in International Relations and Domestic Affairs* (Cambridge: Cambridge University Press, 1989).

of the democratic transition some international economic institutional players—namely the World Bank and the IMF—have contributed to enhancing the liberal imprinting of the economic constitutions of the CEECs.[20] Moreover, the Council of Europe has pushed towards a very pervasive and punctual monitoring of the integration of the provisions held to be able to enforce the protection of human rights in CEECs. With regard to the domestic sources, the democratic transition has represented, on its own, a process of creation, selection and retention of norms adopted and used by the CEECs to shape their constitutional structures. Therefore, once the pre-accession strategies for the candidate countries have been adopted, their processes of constitution making have already begun. This means that the transfer of the "European" constitutional principles and norms, which have been governed through the pre-accession strategy by the European Commission, have crossed the outcomes, more or less consolidated, of the democratic transition.[21] As a result, domestic solutions to constitutional problems, historical traditions making sense of the identity of candidate countries and legal cultures[22] shared by domestic legal experts have been deeply exploited to shape the new states. Once accession to the European Union has been negotiated, the normative contents of the constitutional rules, the structure of the State and relationship between the legislature, the executive and the judiciary has been affected again. The *repertoire* of values and principles that are expected to be respected, enforced and protected in the CEECs have been integrated in the *repertoire* of the national constitutions.[23] The equilibrium among the different branches of the State has also been touched. Legal cultures have been influenced through an intensive contact with problems strictly related to the *European* dimension of the legal issues.

How should the feedback that the outcome of this complex process will have on constitutionalism of the EU be understood? The scientific literature developed to study democratisation turns out to be deficient when it faces the puzzle of the constitution making of the CEECs. The analysis of post-communist democratisation has been biased since the consolidation of democracy has represented a sort of rupture with the past and, therefore, the democratisation of Central and Eastern Europe will create a reality that is more or less similar to democratic regimes existing in Western Europe.[24] Since history is constituted by change and tradition, by novelties and memories, it is also reasonable to assume that people have learnt

---

20 Geoffrey Pridham *et al* (eds.), *Building Democracy? The International Dimension of Democratisation of the Eastern Europe* (London: Leicester University Press, 1990).

21 Andrew Janos, "Continuity and Change in Eastern Europe: Strategies for Post Communist Politics", *East European Politics and Society* (8) (1994), pp. 1–31.

22 Detleft Pollack, *Political Culture in Post Communist Europe* (Aldershot: Ashgate, 2003).

23 Carlo Gialdino, "Some Reflections on the *acquis communautaire*", *Common Market Law Review*, 32 (1990), 5, pp. 1089–1121.

24 Adam Fagin, "Democratisation in Eastern Europe: The Limitations of the Existing Transition Literature", *Contemporary Politics* (4) (1998), 143–159.

something useful, and helpful in the reconstruction of their political life,[25] even from their experiences under the communist regimes—in the negative or in the positive sense of the word. In other words, it seems that the term "transition" has been used too easily to refer to a rupture or a radical change, without questioning if some outcomes of the historical past of communist regimes have been maintained as reference points in the post-transition stage.[26] This idea not only forms the basis of democratisation studies but has somehow been accepted within European political discourse relating to enlargement.[27] In fact, when the pre-accession strategy was conceived, Western States agreed on core principles held to be the crux of a good and efficient democratic regime.[28] Somehow, it seems that the theory used to explain how transition has occurred has (supposedly) negatively influenced the discourse on the constitutionalization of the EU.[29] From an empirical perspective, the enlargement of the EU—in particular with regard to the pre-accession strategy and the transfer of a huge set of norms and procedures to the CEECs over the past decade[30]—has been governed by a rationale that is totally disjointed from the rationale of European constitution-making. This is not only limited to the policy strategy adopted,[31] but has also been extended to the theoretical frameworks used to grasp the logic of enlargement and the constitutionalization of the EU. To put it into dramatic terms "can we identify theoretical and substantial linkages between the dynamics of enlargement, pan-European politics, regional developments, and domestic politics within EU Member States?".[32] In more constructive terms, it can be questioned whether it is possible to integrate, in an enlarged "constitutional discourse",[33] the meaning that constitutionalism has in the European Union as well

---

25 James Gregor, "Constitutional Factors in Politics in Post-Communist Central and Eastern Europe", *Communist and Post Communist Studies* (29) (1998), 147–166.

26 Milada Anna Vachudova, "Are Transitions Transitory? Two Types of Political Change in Eastern Europe since 1989", *East European Politics and Societies* (11) (1997), pp. 1–34.

27 Lykke Friis, *op. cit.* n. 12.

28 European Commission, *Explaining enlargement*, http://European.Eu.int/comm/enlargement, 2002.

29 See Grzegorz Ekiert and Jan Zielonka, "Introduction: Academic boundaries and Path Dependencies Facing the EU's Eastward Enlargement", *East European Politics and Society* (17) (2003), pp. 7–23.

30 Lykke Friis, "The End of the Beginning of Eastern Enlargement—Luxembourg Summit and Agenda Setting", *European Integration Online Paper* (27) (1998), http://eiop.or.at/eiop/texte/1998-007a.htm.

31 Antje Wiener, "Finality vs. Enlargement. Constitutive Practices and Opposing Rationales in the Reconstruction of Europe", *Jean Monnet Working Papers* (8) (2002), http://www.jeanmonnetprogram.org/papers /02/020801.html.

32 Grzegorz Ekiert and Ian Zielonka, *op. cit.* n. 29, p. 8.

33 The choice of this unity of analysis implies a specific methodological perspective, namely relying upon discourse analysis. See Michel Stubbs, *Discourse Analysis* (Chicago: Chicago University Press 1983). See also Daniela Piana, "Constructing the European Constitutional

as in the CEECs, through the very complex historical processes that have characterized their recent histories. I would argue that this is only possible if the existence and the relevance—both at the descriptive and at the normative level—of the cognitive and cultural boundaries that pre-structured the set of normative solutions to the constitutional problems are taken seriously. Therefore, we come back to the first premise of the evolutionary approach, namely the hypothesis concerning the role played by norms in coordinate collective actions. In the specific case represented by constitutional norms, the analysis should aim to understand how different normative sources can interact in shaping constitutional solutions to collective problems, which are essentially *constitutional*. This interaction is held to be created through the use of normative sources in shaping the argumentations that actors would put forward when speaking about constitutional issues.

I have already stressed that from an evolutionary perspective, the concept of legal order is meant to refer to a process rather than to a system. In this sense, the very nature of the order and its interaction with other social or political orders that exist in social reality is conceived as an on going process instead of a match of structural properties. The dynamic dimension of social order depends on the essential and crucial character that social orders have within themselves. Since they come up from the existence of norms governing the relationship among social actions, the character of social order is strongly liked to the essence and the nature of these norms. Norms, as it has been argued, have an open semantic, in the sense that they are applied only once their semantic has been narrowly defined in a somehow conditional definition that makes the norm pertinent for a specific case.[34] To put simply, the practical consequences of norms,[35] when they are used by people to shape argumentations and to justify their choices and their actions are not simply deducted from the norms themselves. A fundamental intermediate step occurs in the middle between the existence of a norm and its use. This step is represented by their interpretation. Because of the structural character of the norms, social orders are opened to novelties and changes coming from the inside.[36] An external change to the norm is not needed in order to introduce novelties in these orders. A new interpretation of an old norm is enough to reach the same result. In this sense, an evolutionary approach to legal orders should integrate some analytical tools that enable researchers and experts to detect novelties and changes occurring inside the

---

Discourse? Arguments for Common Values in the European Convention", *South European Society and Politics*, 9 (2004) 24.

34 Daniela Piana, *Rappresentazione cognitiva delle norme sociali ed effetto framing*, in Rosaria Egidi e Massimo dell'Utri (eds.), *Normatività, fatti e valori* (Macerata: Quodlibet, 2003), pp. 335–343.

35 Michael Bratman, "Cognitivism about Practical Reason", *Ethics* (102) (1991), pp. 117–128.

36 James March and James Olsen, *Ambiguity and Choice in Organisations* (Bergen: Universitätforlagt, 1979).

system. These changes are caused by the interpretation that people, moving within the system, attribute to the norms.[37] In fact, from an evolutionary point of view, the change in scope and meaning of the rules does not happen by fiat, in just one shot.[38] As Hayek puts it, the changes of rules and institutions cross the social and political contexts where they are used and interpreted.

Once applied to the empirical field of constitution-making of the CEECs, the evolutionary approach implies that researchers and scholars should pay attention to the use and the interpretation adopted to make sense of the constitutional discourses of these countries. Two main dimensions should be considered in order to grasp the logic at the basis of the use of the norms. The first one is represented by the constraints that exist inside the constitutional discourse. I call these constraints "cognitive boundaries" because they are related to the categories used in the constitutional debate and in the constitutional texts.[39] The second one is represented by the constraints that are outside the constitutional discourses, *stricto sensu*. I refer to the collective beliefs and the historical traditions shared in these countries and call them "cultural boundaries." They are linked also to the previous experimented solutions and the previous consolidated equilibria discovered to cope with collective action problems.[40] Institutional legacies, political praxis and social capital[41] are the main empirical fields to which the research should be addressed.

So, when new norms—for instance European norms—have been introduced in these legal orders they have interfered with the cognitive and cultural boundaries. This interference has determined different outcomes according to the different contexts in which it has taken place.

4. Cultural and Cognitive Boundaries in East-European Constitution Making

When collective bodies or communities take decisions with regard to their own organization and their own finalities, they adopt rules and accept them on the basis of certain grounds that are said to constitute "good reasons". These reasons

37 Here again the intuition of Friedrich von Hayek, *op. cit.* n. 3, p. 52, is perfectly pertinent.

38 Jon Elster, "Coming to Terms with the Past. A framework for the Study of Justice in the Transition to Democracy", *Archives Européennes de Sociologie* (39) (1998), pp. 7–48.

39 Peter Häberle, "Constitutional developments in Eastern Europe", *Cahiers de Philosophie Politique et Juridique*, 24 (1993), pp. 127–157 and Wolf Heydebrand, "The Dynamics of Legal Change in Eastern Europe", *Studies in Law, Politics and Society* (15) (1995), pp. 263–313.

40 Elinor Ostrom, *Governing the Commons: The Evolution of Institutions for Collective Actions* (New York, Cambridge: Cambridge University Press, 1990).

41 Kathleen Dowley, "Social Capital, Ethnicity and Support for Democracy in the Post Communist States", *Europe Asia Studies* (54) (2002), pp. 505–527.

depend on the framework the community has adopted to make sense of its social dilemmas. In a sense, it is because of these reasons that the rules adopted have some normative value.[42] This is a kind of "cement"[43] that exists at the backdrop of the diversity and fragmentation within societies and makes possible some implicit consensus about a core of collective values. These values are also at the basis of the collective meaning attributed to constitutional principles and norms. There might be a differentiation in the practical consequences that actors, placed within different strategic or cognitive contexts, can draw from these principles.[44] But this contextual disagreement does not dismantle the fundamental consensus about the core values that should be protected in the constitutional game. Disagreement can enter the game when the values have to be mutually balanced and then applied to practical decisions.

In this work, we would look at the constitutional discourses and the constitutional cultures of the CEECs with regard to three points. The first one is concerned with the meaning that is attributed to the concept of being a "right-holder" in a legal and political order. Who are acknowledged as right-holders? Which properties make an individual a right-holder in a specific legal order? In which legal orders would CEECs citizens like to be recognized as right-holders?

The second point relates to the argument put forward to justify the legitimacy of the actions accomplished by public authorities. Are they related to the common aims of the communities living in a state? Or are they based on a more instrumental and functional conception of the state? These arguments have been used in shaping constitutional discourses in order to define a legitimate space where public authorities can use their power. There is a relationship between the reasons to believe in the legitimacy of the public action of the state and the reasons that people are disposed to endorse the limitations of individual rights due to that public action. This is actually what happens when individual rights—protected before the rule of the law—have to be balanced with the need to achieve collective aims and to provide public goods.

The third point relates to the relationship between national identity and transnational identity of right-holders. This is crucial to the mutual relationship that will emerge between the national level and the European level of the identity of European citizens. The collective answers formulated in the CEECs are very much influenced by the institutions or the traditions that people recognize as the normative sources from which values and principles of action are created.

---

42 Raymond Boudon, "The Cognitivistic Model. A Generalized 'Rational-Choice' Model", *Rationality and Society* (8) (1996), pp. 123–150.

43 Jon Elster, *The Cement of Society: a Study of Social Order* (Cambridge: Cambridge University Press, 1989).

44 Raymond Boudon, "Local versus General Ideologies: A Normal Ingredient of Political Life", *Journal of Political Ideology* (4) (1999), pp. 141–161.

It is noteworthy that these three points have not been extensively developed in this chapter since a detailed and multi-disciplinary empirical research is needed to achieve such a complex analysis. Still, I would argue that it is worth beginning the analysis by highlighting some aspects that could immediately impact upon the overall meaning that constitutionalism will have in the enlarged EU.

With regard to the first point, one of the most striking features of the constitution making process of the CEECs is represented by the interaction between the construction of a legitimate national sovereignty and the bargaining and the sharing of such a sovereignty at the transnational level. Actually, the CEECs have been integrated in a transnational order where the European Union is only one of the main sources of norm.[45] Both international law and community law—in particular at the level of the protection of human rights—have created a common legal grounding where national states share common rules. But this has also created a differentiation in the legal orders where individual rights can be expected to be enforced.[46] As a result, this could weaken or, at the very least, bind the legitimacy and strength of states in creating effective and reliable laws for sensitive policy fields. In other words, it is likely that the existence of alternative levels of seeking protection will become an opportunity to address the demands of justice differently, according to the respective right at stake.

Since the post-communist states have a weakened credibility in the protection of human rights—in particular with regard to minority rights—it might be that the protection of human rights will be framed within the transnational legal order rather than the national one. With specific regard paid to minority integration into the political and social order of the post-communist states, Popovic[47] talks about ethnic nationalism, on the basis of a comparative analysis of the perception that Central and Eastern Europeans have. He underlines that ethnic nationalism is not only present in constitutional texts, but also within administrative practices as well as day-to-day life.[48] If these elements are taken into account, it could be argued that social cognition[49] and collective representations of the relationship existing

---

45 Karen Henderson, *Back to Europe: Central and Eastern Europe and the European Union* (London: UCL 1999). See also Anneli Albi, "Postmodern Versus Retrospective Sovereignty: Two Different Discourses in the EU and in the Candidate Countries", in Neil Walker (ed.), *Sovereignty in Transition* (Oxford: Hart, 2003).

46 Christophe Bertossi, *Les Frontières de la Citoyennété en Europe: Nationalité, Residence, Appartenance* (Paris: L'Harmattan, 2001).

47 Dejan Popovic, *Les Ambiguités de la Conception Postcommuniste de l'Etat-nation. Fondements Constitutionnels de l'Etat-nation*, in Slobodan Milacic (ed.), *La Réinvention de l'Etat* (Bruxelles: Bruylant, 2003), p. 74.

48 Lorent Licata *et al*, "Driving European Identification through Discourse: Do Nationals Feel more European when Told they are all Similar?", *Psychologica Belgica* (43) (2003), pp. 85–102.

49 Albert Bandura, *Social Foundations of Thought and Action: A Social Cognitive Theory* (Englewood Cliffs, NJ: Prentice-Hall, 1986).

between the national and the transnational defence of the citizenship rights will matter in the construction of a European demand for justice. While in the Western tradition individual rights are strongly linked to the status of citizens, and thus defended by the State, this is not the only option contemplated in Central and Eastern Europe. Since the State hasn't fulfilled its function of defending individual rights in the past, people either do not consider it a particularly reliable source, or see it to be less reliable than more cosmopolitan or trans-national political entities.[50] In these two cases, theoretical conceptions, classifications and cognitive tools with which people commonly talk about common problems have been created in a historically determined context. The conception of what is a good political system is situated, and makes sense, only in the context where it is endorsed. This is also due to the fact that Eastern Europeans think more in terms of ethical categories and divisions from belonging to linguistic, ethnic, religious, regional minorities[51] than Western Europeans. While national citizenship—Polish citizenship, Hungarian citizenship, etc.—impose divisions that distinguish between the society and the communities in an artificial way, European citizenship can, in some sense, solve those cognitive boundaries within the more general framework of the European community. I would argue that the legitimacy of the European Constitution depends on its evolutive, adaptive capacity. This means that the European Constitution will settle a long standing set of norms if it is able to cope with new conflicts and new coordination problems that may occur through social and economic interactions. This will also entail the capacity to provide an answer to the different demands of justice that will come out of a different social identity.

In some sense, the game "we *versus* the others", which is played in the Central and Eastern European countries amongst minorities, ethnic groups, etc. can be solved on a more general platform, where there is a "we", *European*, even if differences in culture, language, etc. are preserved.[52] Therefore, the constitutionalization of the enlarged EU can create the space for some of their social groups or communities that do not recognize themselves in the dimension of the national state, and therefore provide a new opportunity to address their demands and have their identity recognized.[53]

---

50 Daniele Archibugi and David Held, *Cosmopolitan Democracy: An Agenda for a New World Order* (Cambridge: Polity Press, 1995). See also Robert Cooper, *The Post-Modern State and the World Order* (London: Demos, 1996).

51 Clifford Geertz, "The Integrative Revolution: Primordial Sentiments and Civil Politics in the New States", in Clifford Geertz (ed.), *Old Societies and New States* (London: Free Press, 1963).

52 About the search of a constitutional justice in the CEECs see Herman Schwartz, *The Struggle for Constitutional Justice in Post-Communist Europe* (Chicago: Chicago University Press, 2000).

53 Stephane Pierré-Caps, *L'Etat Postcommuniste entre Identité Nationale et Intégration Supranationale*, in Slobodan Milacic (ed.), ibid. *op. cit.* n. 47, pp. 37–53.

With regard to the second point, namely the reasons why democracy is held (or not) to be a legitimate collective procedure to solve social conflicts, a crucial issue should be mentioned. The CEECs have been shaped by the pre-accession strategy in a way strongly addressed to make them *European democracies*. As long as the communist regimes have been held to be *anti-democratic* and, accordingly, *incoherent* with the rule of the law, the political and the institutional legacies of the communist regimes have not been taken into account after all by the Western debate, neither when the pre-accession strategy was conceived nor when the European Convention began to work out its proposals. So, the main idea was that they should have been transformed and that the best way to do it was to transfer the *acquis communautaire* into them.[54] Sociological and historical research has, nevertheless, shown that a debate on democracy and the theory of a state had been developed throughout the years of the regime. These concepts were further exploited when, after the fall of communism, CEEC's faced the main hurdle of building up a political system. Several studies stress the fact that the constitutions created in those countries after 1989 were embedded in a long-standing debate which was also present during the regime.[55] In other words, people, in particular intellectuals and the political elite, in CEEC's continued to consider the conditions needed to be fulfilled for a political system to be *good*, despite the fact that the theoretical and the practical references were clearly distinct from those used in Western Europe. The first element is represented by the comparison with the recent past. Jon Elster[56] has stressed that the constitutions have not been created *ex nihilo*. He has clearly argued that the evaluation of the options taken into account by policy makers were based on different criteria, which include not only the cost-benefit analysis, but also a comparative criterion.[57]

People who lived within communism have collective preferences about what they do not want in a new political system. This idea was often stronger than a clear idea about what they want.[58] It has been shown that the Marxist ideology has been represented by a strong negative reference, in particular, with regard to the role of public authority. The idea that the state can be used as an instrumental organisation to realize private, partisan ends has been maintained in those countries. In some sense, the main frame to build a good government is related to the exploitation of shared universal principles, instead of being related to the application of the

54 Carlo Gialdino, *op. cit.* n. 23.

55 Jon Elster (ed.), *The Roundtable Talks and the Breakdown of Communism* (Chicago: Chicago University Press, 1986).

56 For a theoretical view Jon Elster, *Ulysses Unbound* (Cambridge: Cambridge University Press, 2000).

57 Jon Elster, "Rebuilding the Boat at the Open Sea: Constitution Making in Eastern Europe", *Public Administration* (71) (1993), pp. 169–217.

58 John Dryzek and Leslie Holmes (eds.), *Post Communist Democratisation: Political Discourse Across Thirteen Countries* (Cambridge: Cambridge University Press, 2002).

"art and the craft"[59] of politics. Even if socialist law has been perceived as a false story—since it was always possible to by-pass it in order to take decisions favourable to the party—it is nevertheless believed that the Law can be over and beyond the State. So the actors involved in the enforcement of the rule of the law should be empowered due to their ability to protect citizens against the state.[60] For these people it is not so important which group or lobby has power. The real concern is to what extent this power is used arbitrarily in the political game and against the citizens.[61] In this respect, the entrenchment of norms that can bind the discretionary power of political actors is a very important element to legitimate the democratic game.[62]

According to Milacic the channel of communication between civil society and the rule of the law has by passed the level represented by the State, whose legitimacy and functional capacity has been conceived as being strongly linked to the constitutions. Dreams and expectations have been moved from the level where political power is managed to the level where the rights of citizens are protected against this political power. In other words, people are able to perceive within constitutional rules the crucial mechanisms to create a good political system, much more so than to debate the specific organisation of the model of democracy they could adopt.

This is the reason why the debate on the kind of democracy characterising the EU is of central importance to Western Europe, whereas the debate on the role of the charter of the fundamental rights in the constitutional discourse is most crucial to the new incoming states.[63]

The third point I wish to stress is the relationship between national and European identity of the CEECs' citizens. Here, the differences in the historical conditions matter too. In contrast with the official assumption of the western institutions according to which the most prominent features of the candidate countries were common features—for example they do not have democratic assets, they have limited reliable bureaucracies, their market economies are not well-functioning, etc.—it could be argued that the most important elements in this context are represented by

---

[59] Aaron Wildavsky, *Speaking Truth to Power: The Art and the Craft of Policy Analysis* (New Brunswick: Transaction Publishers, 1987).

[60] Slobodan Milacic, *Les Ambuiguïtés du Constitutionnalisme Postcommuniste*, in Jean-Claude Colliard and Yves Jegouzo (eds.), *Le Noveau Constitutionnalisme. Mèlanges en l'honneur de Géranrd Conac* (Paris: Economica, 2001), pp. 339–356.

[61] Lorent Licata, "Representing the future of the European Union: consequences on national and European identification", *Papers on social representations* (5) (2003), http://www.psr.jku.at/psrindex.htm.

[62] William Mishler and Richard Rose, "Trajectories of Fear and Hope: Support for Democracy in Post Communist Europe", *Comparative political studies* (28) (1996), pp. 553–581.

[63] Wojciech Sadurski, "Constitutionalization of the EU and the Sovereignty Concerns of the New Accession States: The Role of the Charter of Rights", *EUI Working Paper*, LAW 2003/11 (Florence: European University Institute, 2003).

the different features that these countries have, depending on different historical traditions. Furthermore, the transition from the communist regime to the democratic and constitutional regimes has differed from one country to the next. Therefore, these different transitional patterns are likely to be crucial for the integration and the application of the norms coming in the domestic systems. The differences in the transition matter also in the way citizens' identities have been shaped through that transition. The participation in the transition itself and the ideas put forward to oppose the communist regime have been represented as the first social ground upon which to build a collective identity.

Although communist regimes have generally pursued similar social and economic policies, the effects of communist rules have varied among countries and have contributed to different national patterns of post-communist political change. At each stage in the transition from communism, the course of events has been shaped by the strength of the ruling elite *vis-à-vis* political opposition, and by the relative strength of groups hostile to compromise and those favouring compromise for the sake of peaceful change. The dynamics of change have also been affected by the presence or the absence of a vigorous dissent movement which has sometimes exerted an indirect, but powerful long-term influence on both elite and mass attitudes towards democratisation.[64] According to Milacic, it is not by chance that Romania and Bulgaria have adopted new constitutions by fiat, while in the Czech Republic and in Hungary a process of revision of the previous constitutions has been preferred. In Hungary policy makers have decided to go on through amendments, basing their decision on the common feeling that that the previous constitutional apparatus was enough to be used to modify by an inside-procedure the organisation of the state.[65]

The experience of the constitutionalization of Poland is quite interesting too. The constitutional debate has been animated by several proposals of constitutional treaties (after the 1991), both by political parties and by the constitutional committee of the senate. In 1992, the *Little Constitution* was adopted. One of the main issues in the debate, opened after the adoption of that constitution, concerned the role of the Church in the organisation of Polish society and more generally the weight of the catholic values in the constitution. Even if the constitutional asset chosen at the end of the debate seems to favour the *status quo*, allowing an incremental process of change, the debate has nevertheless manifested the core of values of Polish society.[66] The debate has also been so extended and animated because at

64 Mary Kaldor and Ivan Vejvoda, *Democratization in Central and Eastern Europe* (London: Pinter, 1999).

65 Slobodan Milacic, *La Démocratie Constitutionnelle en Europe Centrale et Orientale. Bilans et Perspectives* (Bruxelles: Bruylant, 1998).

66 See the position of Poland in the IGC related to the integration of Catholic values in the Constitutional Treaty of the EU. See the Polish government's website where the forum on the IGC was organized http://www.futurum.gov.pl/futurum.nsf/main

the basis of the discourse some common rules and ideas resulting from a historical process that began long before communism "grew up." In Poland democracy has been viewed as part of the country's historical legacy dating back to the Commonwealth of Poland-Lithuania of the 16th to the 18th century and to the experience of the Second Republic between the two World Wars. It has often been synonymous with Polish aspirations to rejoin the West. For the majority of Poles, economic prosperity was also associated with democratic institutions. The Poles have regarded democracy as the culmination of their historical struggle for self-determination and independence. The Third Republic has been seen as the direct progeny of the sixteenth to eighteenth century Polish-Lithuanian Commonwealth and the Second Republic of 1918–1939, though in fact, it is quite different from both. More importantly, the Poles have regarded the establishment of democracy as the prerequisite for becoming a "normal state", that is, one built on the systemic principles derived from the West and forming the necessary preconditions for joining western political, economic[67] and social institutions.[68]

For the CEECs, the development of a democratic culture depends not only on the presence of democratic institutions and the rise of civil society, but also on the willingness of citizens to view the emerging democratic framework as historically legitimate. This legitimacy is based on the reconstruction of a common identity, which will be a condition that the Europeanization of the New Members can affect, but not totally abolish or neglect. The cognitive and the culture boundaries determined by the meaning that common identity has for the citizens of CEECs will interfere with the meaning that common identity has for European citizens. This interference will turn out to be an innovative process, in the sense that it will take place in a different manner and with different outcomes, along the differences that the history of democratic transition has in each of these countries.

5. CONCLUSION

I have tried to show how the constitutional discourses of new Member States will have an impact on EU constitutionalism. The chapter has discussed why an evolutionary approach is better equipped to understand the rationale of the constitutional discourse of the enlarged EU. Taking this approach, scholars and policy makers should pay attention to the value attributed, through the interpretation and the use of norms and principles, to the different normative sources they have within a European legal order. Therefore, I have introduced the idea that the meaning of

---

67 Stephen Whitefield and Geoffrey Evans, "Attitudes towards the East, Democracy and the Market", in Jan Zielonka and Alex Pravda (eds.), *Democratic Consolidation in Eastern Europe*, Vol. 2 (Oxford: Oxford University Press, 2001), pp. 231–253.

68 Andrew Michta, "Democratic Consolidation in Poland after 1989", in Karen Dawisha and Bruce Parrott, *The Consolidation of Democracy in East-Central Europe*, Vol. 1 (Cambridge: Cambridge University Press, 1997), p. 69.

constitutionalism in an enlarged Union can be understood only in accounting for the impact that the normative frameworks of new Member States will have in the EU on the whole. This is the reason why the normative value—namely the legitimacy and the normative meaning actually reached in social situations—of the European constitutional principles will be discovered step by step, as the constitutional discourse of the enlarged EU will be faced with new types of problems and situations. Along this path, constitutional principles and values will be assessed against their contextual pertinence in solving social conflicts and against the legitimacy they have for citizens as well.

In this view, the differentiation and the pluralism coming from the new Member States could present an opportunity rather than a challenge to the constitutionalization of the EU. This joins, in some sense, the position taken by Montesquieu when talking about norms. If every society has its own norms that make social coordination possible, then the legal order that might be introduced into a society will make sense only matching the conditions and the boundaries that people draw from norms and principles—even implicitly—shared.

10. Constitutional Tolerance and EU Enlargement: The Politics of Dissent?

*Miriam Aziz**

1. Introduction

The successful conclusion of accession negotiations at the Copenhagen summit in December 2002 meant that ten countries joined the European Union (EU) in the biggest wave of enlargement it has ever witnessed after which the Union now contains 25 members. The accession Treaty, which is the legal basis for enlargement, was signed on 16 April 2003 under the Greek Presidency in Athens after which the Member States and the candidates undertook to ratify the Treaty in order to enable the accessions to proceed as planned on 1 May 2004. EU enlargement, the increasing drive towards constitutionalization of the Union as promoted *inter alia* by the European Convention[1] and the entering into force of the Nice Treaty on 1 February 2003 have generated considerable innovations to the institutional architecture of the Union and the values contained therein,[2] latterly embodied in the Draft Treaty establishing a Constitution for Europe delivered to the European Council meeting in Thessaloniki on 20 June 2003 and later submitted to the President of the European Council in Rome on 18 July 2003.[3] A number of theories have been canvassed as to why the Draft Constitutional Treaty initially failed. Ostensibly, however, the disquiet over voting rights in the Council in the period of

---

* I wish to thank James Hughes and Neil Walker for their comments concerning earlier versions of this paper as well as the participants to the *Sovereignty and the Constitutional Dimension of Enlargement* Workshop held at the Robert Schumann Centre for Advanced Studies of the EUI on 27 May 2002. Further thanks goes to the participants of a conference held at the European Centre Natolin, Warsaw, Poland on 31 January, 1 February 2003 entitled *Enlargement and the European Constitutional Process*. The usual disclaimer applies. This research was financially supported by the Marie Curie Fellowship which is financed by the European Commission's Framework 5 Programme. An earlier version of this article appeared in the *Annual of German and European Law*, 2003.

1 Established by the Laeken Declaration on the Future of the European Union, available at http://european-convention.eu.int/pdf/LKNEN.pdf. See generally J. Ziller, *La Nouvelle Constitution Européene* (Paris: La Decouverte 2003).

2 See Neil Walker, 'Constitutionalising Enlargement, Enlarging Constitutionalism', (2003) 9 *European Law Journal* 365.

3 CONV 820/03. This text was revised twice. (CONV 820/1/03 REV 1, CONV 820/1/03 REV 2). See also CONV 847/03, CONV 848/03.

Wojciech Sadurski et al. (ed.), Spreading Democracy and the Rule of Law?, 237–261.

post-accession obstructed the adoption of a unanimous consensus regarding the Treaty. Among the main "dissenters" was one of the new Member States, namely Poland, presumably because of the malaise which it has felt at being treated as a "second class citizen", a sentiment which is shared by some of the other new Member States.

A new enlargement creates tensions given the challenge of incorporating and assimilating legal systems and cultures of former socialist economies and societies into the EU; which the EC, as it was then, experienced in previous waves of enlargement (as in, for example, the case of Spain and Portugal); but never on such a vast scale. The question of the *viability* of the adoption of the *acquis communautaire*, or what is now referred to as the *acquis de l'Union* which extends to approximately 80,000 pages,[4] and modes of implementing the rights arising therefrom through law and governance is of a particular relevance for the transformation of the societies, legal systems and administrative practices, economies and polities of the new Member States. Moreover, issues of implementation arise in ways from which lessons may be learned by all of the EU Member States which are faced with the double challenge of Europeanization and transition.[5] This topic is particularly relevant as regards contemporaneous developments in the EU such as the Convention on the Future of Europe, the subsequent Intergovernmental Conference in 2004 and further Treaty revisions.

The purpose of this chapter is to address the issue of legal norms and the adaptive capacity of Central and East European Candidate Countries (CEECs) for enlargement. There is a need to distinguish between the formal process of implementation (the adoption of the *acquis*) and the legal norms and legal culture which will inform the implementation of the *acquis* in the day to day process.[6] One way of looking at this issue is to consider the nature of the legal norms, the legal cultures and traditions which inform the constitutional practice in existing Member States. It is arguable that unless these can be defined, that we cannot really say much about the adaptive capacity of the candidates. Raising this issue appears simple enough. The difficulties arise when one starts to address it, particularly as the question would appear to presuppose the existence of a unified legal culture in the current Member States of the Union. As regards constitutional practice in the face of the challenge posed by European Union law, it is clear that one ignores the importance

4 Which have been divided into 31 Chapters for the purpose of the negotiations.

5 See Miriam Aziz, *The Impact of European Rights on National Legal Cultures* (Oxford: Hart 2004).

6 See generally the Commission White Paper on the Preparation of the associated countries of Central and Eastern Europe for integration into the internal market of the Union, COM (95) 163. For a general overview of the process of adoption of the *acquis*, see Andrea Ott and Kirstyn Inglis (eds.) *Handbook on European Enlargement*, (The Hague: Asser Press, 2002).

of differentiation at one's peril.[7] This question has a corollary in the context of enlargement of the EU, namely, should one not also differentiate between the legal norms and cultures of the respective CEECs? The purpose of this article is to explore this issue by using the German experience concerning the juridical challenge to state sovereignty posed by European law in view of its history and the special position occupied by sovereignty in its legal order, but also given the influence the German legal order has had on the legal systems of those of the CEECs.[8]

2. DIFFERENTIATED AND NON-DIFFERENTIATED APPROACHES TO THE CEEC'S

A common general EU trend is to talk about the candidate countries as a bloc. At the same time, the European Commission negotiates with each of the candidate countries separately.[9] The concept of differentiation in this respect is difficult to analyze as the negotiations are not transparent. We can only assume that the terms of reference of the negotiations with the CEECs are roughly the same, relatively speaking. A consequence of a non-differentiated approach as regards law and legal culture is that the CEECs are viewed through the prism of their communist legacy as though there was only one legacy. Even if it is accepted that communism provided a sort of "shared legacy", it is clear that regional experiences differed markedly,[10] particularly as regards sovereignty.

2.1. The CEECs and the Legacy of Communism on the Sovereignty Debate

As regards the legacy of communism, each CEE has its own story to tell which influences *inter alia* the respective approaches and indeed the position of sovereignty in the constitutions of the CEECs.[11] Within the communist systems in Eastern

---

7 See generally Anne-Marie Slaughter, Alec Stone Sweet and Joseph H.H. Weiler (eds.), *The European Court and National Courts-Doctrine and Jurisprudence. Legal Change in Its Social Context*, (Oxford: Hart 1998).

8 As in the case of Hungary, for example, and the Czech Republic. See, for example, Ian Slosarcik, 'The Reform of the Constitutional Systems of Czechoslovakia and the Czech Republic in 1990–2000', *European Public Law* 7 (2001), pp. 529, 534.

9 According to Article 49 of the Treaty of European Union (TEU) accession of new members to the EU requires the unanimous approval of the Council and an absolute majority of the European Parliament. The Opinion of the European Commission is pivotal in assessing whether a candidate country meets the requirements for membership.

10 See Report of the Reflection Group on The Political Dimension of EU Enlargement: *Looking Towards Post-Accession*, The Robert Schuman Centre for Advanced Studies, European University Institute with the Group of Policy Advisors (2001), p. 55.

11 See Anneli Albi, 'Postmodern Versus Retrospective Sovereignty: Two Different Discourses in the EU and the Candidate Countries', in Neil Walker (ed.), *Sovereignty in Transition*, (Oxford: Hart Publishing 2003), 401.

Europe, communism operated differently and was received differently by elites and populations, while relations between these countries and the Soviet Union also varied. Countries like Hungary after 1956, Czechoslovakia after 1968, Poland from 1945, the German Democratic Republic (GDR), Romania and Bulgaria were all distinct in the way in which the communist system(s) operated, the way they were perceived by elites and populations and the way these communist states interacted with the Soviet Union. They were all sovereign states but subject to limited sovereignty by virtue of the *Brezhnev* doctrine.[12]

Briefly stated, the *Brezhnev* doctrine was embedded in Article 30 of the 1977 Soviet Constitution (the so-called "*Brezhnev* Constitution"), which committed the Soviet Union to "friendship, cooperation and comradely mutual assistance" in accordance with the principle of "socialist internationalism" and also to participate in "economic integration". Accordingly, important principles of equality, territorial integrity, independence, non-interference in domestic affairs were subject to particular interpretation in the interests of "fraternal assistance" towards other Eastern bloc countries. In other words, support for Soviet interventionism was justified on the grounds of the need to protect the socialist community of states. This self-imposed limitation on state sovereignty in the socialist bloc was a device to cloak Soviet interventionism to sustain its hegemony in Eastern Europe, and in particular its military occupation of the German Democratic Republic.[13] The Soviet Union, as its interventions in Hungary and Czechoslovakia illustrate, was unable to accept a "national" form of communism. To do so would have called into question its hegemony over the socialist bloc and even its leadership of the Warsaw Pact.[14] Consequently, in the aftermath of the crushing of the Hungarian revolution of 1956, the Soviet Union imposed a doctrine of limited sovereignty on the socialist bloc of

---

[12] For a discussion of the Brezhnev doctrine and its demise under Gorbachev see Charles Gati, *The Bloc that Failed Soviet-East European Relations in Transition*, (Bloomington: Indiana University Press, 1990) at pp. 71–79. For an exposition of the doctrine in Brezhnev's own words see the extract from his "Speech to the Fifth Congress of the Polish United Workers Party" (November 12, 1968), *Current Digest of the Soviet Press* 20 (46), 1968 at pp. 3–5.

[13] The Soviet military interventions in Hungary in 1956, Czechoslovakia in 1968, Afghanistan in 1979, and the pressures on Poland in 1980, were seen as legitimate measures to defend the socialist bloc. Those socialist states which did not accede to the hegemony of the Soviet Union, such as Yugoslavia (which broke with Moscow under Tito in 1948) and Albania, were isolated on the grounds that they had pursued the road of "nationalism"—the ultimate form of deviation from the socialist cause. Note that a "special relationship" which was maintained until the end as the discussions between Gorbachev and Honecker illustrate. See Daniel Küchenmeister (ed.), *Honecker-Gorbatschow. Vieraugengespräche*, (Berlin: Dietz 1993) at pp. 92–93. See also Hagen Schulze, *Staat und Nation in der Europäischen Geschichte*, (München: Beck 1994), at p. 323.

[14] *Ibid*.

states, which was referred to as "proletarian internationalism".[15] Thereafter, any development of national forms of communism which was perceived to threaten Soviet hegemony was met with the "fraternal assistance"[16] of military intervention, as the Warsaw pact invasion of Czechoslovakia in 1968 demonstrated. This so-called *pax sovietica* was also secured by a process of integration in the socialist bloc whereby ruling elites (the communist party nomenklatura), economies, militaries, and national interests were locked into Soviet controlled supranational organizations such as Comecon and the Warsaw Pact.

It is of interest to note that a model for the special relationship or the "fraternal assistance" between the countries of the Soviet bloc and the Soviet Communist party was never explicitly addressed nor was it developed. In the case of the German Democratic Republic, for instance, it was placed on a legal footing in a 1964 Treaty[17] which dealt with the event of any attack of force by another country.[18] Indeed, the Treaty goes further in providing that if any state which was a signatory to the Warsaw Pact had come under attack, the others were obligated to give immediate support[19] to each other through economic aid and the exchange of economic and technical know-how. The relationship between the GDR and the USSR is viewed in the West as one of forced dependency or a *Zwangsverhältnis*. The relationship was not regulated by transparent legal norms or the courts, but by non-transparent formal and informal agreements of communist party leaderships.

Some countries had room for maneuver under the shadow of the *Brezhnev* doctrine which others did not. The three Baltic States (Latvia, Lithuania and Estonia) were units in the Soviet Federation after their annexation. The reality was that there were important differences regarding how the Soviet Union treated them and the other members of the Soviet bloc in terms of their sovereignty. Poland, for example, had privatized agriculture (other Communist countries had socialized

15 As proclaimed in Moscow in October 1957 in the declaration of the communist parties in power to commemorate the 40th anniversary of the October 1917 Russian Revolution. The full text of "the twelve" is reproduced in *The Communist Manifesto and Related Documents* in Dan N Jacobs (ed.), 2nd edn., (New York: Harpertorch Books 1962) at p. 176.

16 Referred to as "comradely cooperation" in the Czechoslovak Constitution (article 14 (2) at 145), "friendship and cooperation" in the Polish Constitution (article 6 (2)) and "friendship, cooperation, and mutual assistance" in the Bulgarian Constitution (article 3 (1) *supra* n. 15).

17 Vertrag über Freundschaft, gegenseitigen Beistand und Zusammenarbeit zwischen der Deutschen Demokratischen Republik und der Union der Sozialistischen Sowjetunion vom 12 Juni 1964 (GB1. IS. 132).

18 *Ibid*.

19 See Article 5 of the Vertrag über Freundschaft, gegenseitigen Beistand und Zusammenarbeit zwischen der Deutschen Demokratischen Republik und der Union der Sozialistischen Sowjetunion vom 12 Juni 1964 (GBl. IS. 132).

collective farming),[20] the Catholic Church in Poland operated in a less constrained way than Orthodox or Protestant churches elsewhere. Indeed, the legacy of the Catholic Church's political leverage during communism is still felt today as the discussions concerning abortion and the EU Charter of Fundamental Rights in Poland testify. From the early 1960s, Hungary was allowed to introduce into the socialist market limited decentralized reforms in the economy and privatization. The country whose sovereignty was most limited was that of the (GDR) which was a country under military occupation[21] thereby illustrating the extent to which the Soviet Union both adopted and implemented a differentiated approach.[22]

It would be as erroneous to view the CEECs in a non-differentiated manner under the mantle of communism, and what came next, the period of transition which arose as a consequence of post-communism after 1989.[23] Indeed, the transition period was also differentiated, as illustrated by, for instance, the diverse and respective experiences of the roundtable talks between regimes and oppositional groups that took place in 1988 and 1990.[24] In the case of the GDR, for example, the very existence of the state was at the heart of the deliberations.[25] This was in direct contrast to the position of the other countries involved in roundtable talks. The Baltic States, for their part, claimed independence and, in terms of sovereignty, aspired to a return to the status quo which existed prior to 1946. In the case of Poland, the agenda of the initial talks did not include a revision of the constitution or the introduction of political democracy.[26]

The formation of a market economy necessitates the implementation of certain preconditions—both institutional and extra-institutional. The experience of the relatively quick transition of Spain, Portugal and Greece provide useful examples, although of limited use as analogies.[27] As regards the CEECs, this has involved a complete and systematic overhaul of *inter alia* regulations, the way in which

---

20 See David Stark, 'Path Dependence and Privatisation Strategies in East Central Europe', *East European Politics and Societies*, 6 (1992), p. 17 for an excellent typology of Central and Eastern European privatization strategies.

21 See Miriam Aziz, "Sovereignty Über Alles: (Re)Configuring the German Legal Order" in Walker, above n. 11 at p. 279.

22 See generally Gianmaria Ajani, *Diritto Dell'Europa Orientale*, (Torino: Unione Tipografico-Editrice Torinese 1996).

23 See Jon Elster, Claus Offe and Ulrich K. Preuß (eds.), *Institutional Design in Post-communist Societies: Rebuilding the Ship at Sea* (Cambridge: University Press 1998).

24 Jon Elster (ed.), *The Roundtable Talks and the Breakdown of Communism*, (Chicago: University Press 1996).

25 See Ulrich K. Preuß, "The Roundtable Talks in the German Democratic Republic" in Elster, *op. cit.* n. 24 at pp. 99–134.

26 Instead, the idea was to obtain official recognition of Solidarity in exchange for Western Aid and Solidarity's support of the economic reforms that the government deemed necessary.

27 See the Country Reports for Spain, Portugal and Greece in Luca Mezzeti (ed.), *Costituzione Economica e Libertà di Concurrenza*, (Torino: G. Giappichelli Editore 1994).

the system of law operates, reforms of the administrative structure of the state, changing the structure of ownership and so on. I say extra-institutional as the change in attitude to the law of both its political and legal elites and ordinary citizens is pivotal.

2.2. Sovereignty and the Age of Post-Transition

In the period of "post-transition", the importance of differentiation is borne by the fact that while all these countries are regarded as democracies and market economies within the Copenhagen criteria,[28] they are all different in terms of their constitutional architecture. What are the criteria or "markers", so to speak, of differentiation?[29] The distinction between unitary states and federal states[30] arguably serves as a useful line of departure, but in a way which must be qualified. Speaking in terms of constitutional systems, distinctions must be drawn between plurality elections or proportional representation, a presidential or parliamentary system, a federal or a centralized system, judicial review or lack thereof and so on, all of which vary significantly in terms of their operation, particularly as regards the system of proportional representation which have generally been held to be capable of "infinite variation".[31]

Although all of the CEECs are unitary states, the qualification which must be made is that one can also distinguish between states which are strongly centralized and states which are strongly regionalized. Together with the categories of Unitary/Federal, Centralized/regionalized, differential institutional arrangements also arise as a consequence of Presidentialism, semi-Presidentialism and Parliamentarism. These criteria of differentiation, so to speak will no doubt represent a considerable challenge to the implementation of the *acquis de l'Union* and will give rise to a similar—but not the same—tension which was experienced during the transition period. It is not my intention, however, to address these criteria here except to make the following point: it would not be useful to regard the legal systems of the CEECs as representing one homogenous unit as it would not be useful to presuppose that the legal systems and cultures of the Member States of the EU are homogenous. This has clear implications for the enlargement research agenda. Legal research has much to learn from political science in terms of the importance of empirical research: what is needed is empirical work on the transformation of legal systems and legal cultures as a consequence of enlargement, with particular emphasis on

28 That is to say the political and economic conditions for EU membership established at the Copenhagen European Council of 21–22 June 1993 (*Bull. EC* 6-1993, I.13.).

29 See generally Mark Tushnet, 'The Possibilities of Comparative Constitutional Law', *Yale Law Journal*, 108 (1999), at p. 650.

30 Note that the only two Central European federal states, namely, Yugoslavia and Czechoslovakia, collapsed as part of the transition process.

31 See Robert Dahl, below n. 40 at p. 44.

administrative law.[32] This includes observing the behaviour of the constitutional courts, the administrative courts and the lower courts, the reforms to legal education as well as informal changes to the respective legal cultures of the CEECs. It must be stressed, however, that this is more than a mere exercise in legal pathology. The aim of such research should be targeted to the reception of EU law into the national legal systems of the CEECs with the thoroughness and erudition which has informed examinations of the status quo in current EU Member States[33] whilst allowing for, and acknowledging, the particular characteristics of the legal systems and cultures of the CEECs. The prospective burden which local and regional administrative authorities will be facing post-accession has already been recognized in the case of, for example, the implementation and enforcement of EU Environmental Policy in the Candidate Countries.[34] Indeed, some financial provision has been made to facilitate this process from pre-accession instruments.[35] The budgetary impact of compliance is considerable. In the case of EU Environmental Policy, for example, it has been estimated as constituting approximately 80–110 billion Euro.[36]

The "language of post-accession"[37] must be framed not only in terms of questions of what are the criteria for a "good" or "bad" fit but also what in terms of an evaluation of the process of *how* a "good" or "bad" fit has and is taking effect within the respective constitutional orders of the CEECs and impact post-accession.[38] This raises the issues commonly associated with constitutional "borrowing" or

---

32 This argument has, as yet, only been made in relation to the current EU Member States although it may, and indeed must, be made as regards the potential Member States. See generally Carol Harlow, 'European Administrative Law and the Global Challenge', in Paul Craig and Graínne de Búrca (eds.), *The Evolution of EU Law*, (Oxford: Hart Publishing 1999), at p. 270.

33 See, for example, Karl-Heinz Ladeur, 'Conflict and Co-operation between European Law and the General Administrative Law of the Member States', in Karl-Heinz Ladeur (ed.), *The Europeanisation of Administrative Law. Transforming National Decision-Making Procedures*, (Dartmouth: Ashgate 2002) at pp. 1–13.

34 See Press Release DN:IP/03/81 published on January 21, 2003, European Commission on Track to Ensuring an Enlarged Europe is a Greener Europe.

35 Namely, PHARE which supports priority measures related to the adoption of the Community *acquis*, the instrument for Structural Policies for Pre-Accession (ISPA—Finances infrastructure in the environment and transport sector and SAPARD Finances measures to support agriculture and rural development).

36 This includes the implementation of the Urban Wastewater Treatment Directive (over 25 billion Euro), the Landfill Directive (10–12 million Euro). See Press release, above n. 34.

37 Referred to by Helen Wallace at the Journal of Common Market Studies Conference, April 13, 2002 at the European University Institute, Florence.

38 See generally Wojciech Sadurski, 'Conclusions: On the Relevance of Institutions and the Centrality of Constitutions in Post-communist Transitions', in Jan Zielonka (ed.), *Democratic Consolidation in Eastern Europe, vol. 1 Institutional Engineering*, (Oxford: Oxford University Press 2001), p. 455.

lending and the exportation of "western" legal norms whilst not overlooking their significance as essential preconditions for economic development,[39] for which there are a number of competing models.[40]

This also raises the issue of the exercise of tracking the changes of the adaptive capacity of the legal systems of the CEECs which includes the adoption of the spirit of the *acquis* by the legal elites and how they regard the challenge of EU law to their legal orders and its concomitant challenge to their loyalty.[41] This may not necessarily require the legal elites of the CEECs to become "EU-enthusiasts." The implementation of the *acquis* will, however, necessitate the co-operation on behalf of these elites in order to accept the consequences of EU membership for the legal systems which they serve. Indeed, the role of the legal elites is crucial in the process of consolidation of the European legal order in the CEE states. Not only must the knowledge of EC law be imparted and disseminated, but the elites must be persuaded to apply them and moreover recognize that it is in their own interest to apply them, a particularly difficult task if one bears in mind that sovereignty post-1989 has been a highly constrained and contested concept. If one can legitimately speak of "desiring sovereignty" in the context of the CEECs, then it makes sense to distinguish two forms of aspiration: either, a longing for that which was once possessed but which was lost, or a longing for that which was never possessed. Either way, sovereignty has traditionally been aspired to by constitutional lawyers, who regard it as the quintessential pre-requisite to independent state formation.[42]

The inroads made into the state sovereignty of the CEECs by the strident pace of Europeanization as part of the enlargement process are considerable. Indeed, the ambit of the obligations of the CEECs to approximate their laws is incredibly far reaching which serves as a useful reminder of the extent of the remit of EC law over the national legal orders. Thus, article 69 under Chapter III of Estonia's Europe Agreement, for example, lists the areas to which the approximation of laws shall extend to. They include customs law, company law, company accounts and taxation, banking law, intellectual property, financial services, rules on competition, protection of health and life of humans, animals and plants, protection of workers including health and safety at work, consumer protection, indirect taxation,

---

39 See David M. Trubeck and Mark Galanter, 'Scholars in Self-Estrangement: Some Reflections on the Crisis in Law and Development Studies in the United States', *Wisconsin Law Review*, 4 (1974), at p. 1062.

40 See Robert A. Dahl, 'Thinking About Democratic Constitutions: Conclusions from Democratic Experience', in Ian Shapiro and Robert Hardin (eds.), *Political Order* vol. XXXVIII, (New York: New York University Press 1996), at p. 175.

41 A point made in relation to administrative law in terms of "dual loyalty". See Mario P. Chiti, *Diritto Amminstrativo Europea*, (Milan: Giuffrè 1999) at Chapt. 7.

42 See generally Michael Stolleis, *Geschichte des öffentlichen Rechts in Deutschland*, (München: C H Beck 1992).

technical rules and standards, nuclear law and regulation, transport, telecommunications, environment, public procurement, statistics and product liability.

One is inclined to wonder whether any areas of law remain untouched by the adoption of the *acquis*. The potential for dissent is considerable, such as in the case of competition law, which for many CEECs will be the first encounter of EC law with the law of the CEECs.[43] Thus, the Hungarian Constitutional Court has already taken a firm stance in this matter, stating that competition law is under the exclusive jurisdiction of state sovereignty which it interprets as signifying that the state may dispose of its sovereign rights in its international relations.[44] A similar tension may arise in relation to social solidarity. Here too, the Hungarian Constitutional Court has dug its heels in, in an attempt to protect welfare rights and institutional services inherited from state socialism.[45] In the so-called *Hungarian Benefits Case*[46] Zlinszky J held as part of his concurring opinion that,

> The Constitutional Court does not wish to tie the hands of the legislature in the search for the appropriate solutions, but in a form more express than that incorporated in the Decision, the Court must call [to] the attention of the legislature that it can expect the agreement and co-operation of society, which is the necessary precondition of the success of the reforms, only if it chooses and requires restrictive solutions which meet the moral perceptions and sense of social justice of society.

A central element of the Court's reasoning is that the transition period provided by the law in question was inadequate. However, the underlying *ratio* is one which is embedded in the thorny issue of values, that is to say those values which underwrite a constitutional order, values which may be at odds with those contained in other constitutional orders, particularly those which are supra- and international.

In the case of Poland, for example, abortion provides a further bone of contention. At the end of January 2003, Poland had put forward a request to the EU to include a declaration safeguarding Polish laws on the "protection of human life", a request which was made rather late in the days of the drafting stage of the accession treaty. Poland may be granted the possibility to have a unilateral declaration on this issue

---

43 See Janos Volkai, *The Application of the Europe Agreement and European Law in Hungary: the Judgment of an Activist Constitutional Court on Activist Notions*, available at http://www.jeanmonnetprogram.org.papers.

44 See Volkai, *ibid.*, who cites Judgment 4 of 22 January 1997 (the so-called "Preliminary Issues Judgment") and Judgment 30 of 25 June 1998 which dealt with the merits of the submission (the so-called "Europe Agreement Judgment").

45 See Andras Sajo, "How the Rule of Law Killed Hungarian Welfare Reform", *East Constitutional Review*, 5 (1996) at p. 31.

46 43/1995 (VI.30) AB (Constitutional Court of Hungary), 4 E. Eur. Case Rep. Const. L. 64 (1997) (English translation) reproduced in Vicki Jackson and Mark Tushnet (eds.), *Comparative Constitutional Law*, (New York: Foundation Press 1999) at pp. 1452–1475.

attached to the Treaty, similar to the position of Ireland. Nevertheless, the Polish church has expressed doubts over the clause. According to Archbishop *Tadeusz Goclowski*, the declaration approved and put forward by the Polish government did not fully meet expectations as bishops had asked clearly for human life to be protected from conception to natural death and a definition of marriage as a legal union of a man and woman. The original proposal for the text put forward by the Polish government which was submitted for consideration reads as follows:

> The government of the Republic of Poland understands that none of the provisions of the Treaty on European Union, or in the Treaties establishing the European Communities, or in the Treaties or Acts modifying or supplementing those Treaties, shall disturb the right of the Republic of Poland to regulate on issues of moral importance and concerning the protection of human life.

Malta, another country which joined the EU in 2004, managed to obtain a protocol on abortion which was annexed to Malta's Accession Treaty to the EU, which would give legal certainty that EU law, present or future would not be able to change Maltese law on abortion. However, the Greek Presidency sent a clear message to the 10 acceding states that there would be no re-opening of negotiations before the completion of the accession treaty in early February 2003 which was signed on 16 April 2003 under the Greek Presidency. This may, however, be left up to the constitutional courts further down the line in the period of post-accession.

It is clear that judges of the constitutional courts of the CEECs will have to come to terms with what has been referred to as "constitutional tolerance", that is to say, the allowance for, and indeed the acceptance of, the spirit of the *acquis* by constitutional court judges.[47] Weiler was addressing his remarks to constitutional court judges of the Member States of the EU. His notion could also, however, be extended to constitutional court judges of the CEECs. What these judges will have to come to terms with, is the fact that in the period of post-accession, they will serve a reconfigured legal order, which they may regard as one or two legal orders. It is the latter which is more problematic as regards the implementation of the *acquis* where lawyers in the future Member States could elect to view EC law as constituting an international legal order. And if exclusively so, this could affect the respect of the rule of law as laid down by the EU Treaty in Article 6 and could indeed mean that EU citizens' rights are respected in a different manner as well as to a lesser extent than their counterparts in the old Member States. Integration clauses of the constitutions of the CEECs are particularly telling. Thus, in Poland, for example, Article 90 (1) of the constitution provides that, "The Republic of Poland may, on the basis of an international agreement, transfer to an international organization or international institution the powers of organs of the state authority in

47 See Joseph H.H. Weiler, *The Constitution of Europe*, (Cambridge: Cambridge University Press 1999), in the Foreword.

certain matters." Neither the words "European Union" nor "European Community" are used. Nor, however, are they used in some of the constitutions of the current Member States. In short, an association with a supranational organization is referred to without taking into account the fact that the EC legal order operates both within and without the borders of the state. Indeed, it is part and parcel of a state's legal order. Viewing it in terms of an international legal order only, is not only analytically erroneous but has concrete consequences for the addressees of the rights contained therein.[48] Whilst it is conceded that in some countries, the position of international law is taken very seriously indeed by being governed, as in the case of the Polish constitution,[49] by the principle of direct applicability, one wonders whether this will provide an adequate legal mechanism whereby jurists can give full effect to EC law norms.[50] In other words, the way in which jurists perceive the European Community Legal order is of paramount importance. By jurists, it is important to stress that I mean all jurists in the CEECs, that is to say, judges, practitioners and legal practitioners alike who participate in the juridical debate concerning the impact of the *acquis* on their legal orders.

2.3. *The Impact of the European Community Legal Order on National Legal Systems and Cultures*

Law is a normative order which is traditionally both perceived and conceived of in terms of a hierarchy.[51] In the German case, for example, the prevailing hierarchy is constituted by the Basic Law, Federal Law and State Law (or the law of the *Länder*). European Community (EC) law may also be understood according to a hierarchical model to the extent that it prevails over national law[52] and consists of primary and secondary sources of law (such as Regulations and Directives) arranged according to a hierarchy of precedence.[53]

---

48 Indeed, Professor Miroslaw Wyrzykowski, a judge of the Polish Constitutional Tribunal stated at a conference held at the European Centre, Natolin in Warsaw, Poland on January 31–February 1, 2003, *Enlargement and the European Constitutional Process*, that many constitutional lawyers regarded EC law in terms of international law.

49 See Article 91, para. 1 of the Polish Constitution in conjunction with article 9.

50 See generally Stanislaw Biernat, 'The Constitution of Poland and European Integration' in Giuliano Amato, Guy Brabant and Evangelos Venizelos (eds.), *The Constitutional Revision in Today's Europe*, European Public Law Series, Vol. XXIX at p. 439 et seq.

51 Through, for example, the doctrine of precedent housed in the English legal system or the *Anwendungsvorrang* in German law. See Hans Kelsen, *The Pure Theory of Law* (trans. M. Knight) (Gloucester: Peter Smith 1967).

52 Case C-6/64 *Costa v. ENEL*, 1964, ECR 585. However, this principle has been qualified by the *Maastricht* judgement of the German Constitutional Court. See 89 BVerfGE 155.

53 Although this has been under review by the Laeken Convention Working Group chaired by Giuliano Amato on Simplification which has suggested reducing the number of legal instruments to four.

The Nation State is central to the legal reasoning upon which the reception of EC law into the jurisdictions of the Member States is based. The underlying tension is as follows: either a state's membership of the EU entails categorical acceptance of the supremacy doctrine, which is in itself, an endorsement of the hierarchical model of law. Alternatively, the state retains the right, in certain cases, to set the supremacy doctrine aside, as has been effected by the German Constitutional Court. Thus, even if it is accepted that the sovereignty of a Member State has been qualified by its membership to the EU, it is a form of qualification which is by no means unconditional arguably giving rise to a hierarchy of qualifications. These two positions represent two versions of events, so to speak, of the relationship between EC law and national law and constitute competing schools of thought in the legal communities of some of the current EU Member States, such as Germany. To what extent, can we expect the emergence of a tension of this nature in the CEECs?

The creation of the European Convention has established two classes of members.[54] Briefly stated, the Declaration of Laeken in December 2001 established a Convention as a framework for dialogue on the Constitution of the European Union the work of which was concluded by an Intergovernmental Conference in 2004. In short, it was the European Convention's mandate to underwrite the Union with a dose of constitutionalism.[55] Candidate countries did not enjoy the same standing in the EU's "constitutional moment"[56] as the current Member States, a situation which has been reproduced at the level of the Inter Governmental Conferences.[57] The contribution of the CEECs was constrained by this power asymmetry which in turn more than hints at the presence of "empire and coloniality" in the process of "eastern enlargement" as a whole.[58] As regards the CEECs, it is clear that the tenor of the debate of the Convention set a tone for the period of post-accession, which is why it is arguably unsurprising that it was one of the new Member States which initially "defeated" the adoption of the Draft Constitutional Treaty which arose out of the Convention.

---

54 See Krassimir Y. Nikolov, "The Convention and the Accession States: Where Do We Stand? Where Do We Sit?", an abridged version of which is reproduced in the January 2002 issue of the electronic journal, *Challenge Europe of the European Policy Centre (EPC)* in Brussels, Belgium, http://www.theepc.be/challenge/.

55 See Laeken Declaration on the Future of the European Union, available at http://european-convention.eu.int/pdf/LKNEN.pdf.

56 Term borrowed from Bruce Ackerman, *We the People*, (Cambridge: Harvard University Press 1999).

57 See Bruno de Witte, "The Closest Thing to a Constitutional Conversation in Europe: The Semi-Permanent Treaty Revision Process", in Paul Beaumont, Carol Lyons and Neil Walker (eds.), *Convergence and Divergence in European Public Law* (Oxford: Hart Publishing 2002), at p. 39.

58 See Jan Böröcz and M. Kovács (eds.), *Empire's New Clothes. Unveiling Eastern Enlargement Central Eastern Review* (2001), available at http://www.ce-review.org.

The hypothesis being advanced is as follows: if the contribution of the new Member States to the framing of the constitution is marginalized from the outset, a commitment problem down stream is created. In other words, if they are not in at the rule making stage, how can they be expected to adhere to the rules later on? The CEECs do have participatory rights in the Council as a consequence of the accession Treaties, a position which also existed during the accession of Spain and Portugal. Casting our minds back to a previous wave of enlargement serves as a useful reminder of how quickly this process can occur. Spain and Portugal, for example, took part in the Inter Governmental Conference leading up to the adoption of the Single European Act in 1985 prior to having become full members. All that was done was that their signatures of the SEA were postponed until they acquired full membership. However, distinctions between old and new Member States were not made during the course of the IGC.[59]

Be that as it may, what is still unclear for many in the aftermath of the European Convention is what sorts of problems European constitutionalism must tackle and which problems it must leave to be resolved by the respective constitutional courts of the Member States. What can be accepted by the constitutional courts in certain cases can, however, be rejected in others, particularly in the face of the "moving target", so to speak of the competence question in the EU[60] and the eternally thorny issue of the corresponding division of powers between the EC and the Member States.[61] An example of dissent on behalf of the Hungarian Constitutional Court has already been cited in relation to competition law. However, the Hungarian Court has also been willing to consider international conventions as a constitutional obligation,[62] which have, as a result, repeatedly influenced its decisions such as those in the death penalty, agricultural land, the punishability of communist crimes and the statute of limitation, public data and information cases, to mention only a few.[63] The picture which begins to emerge is one where the issue of human rights

---

59 I am indebted to Professor Giuliano Amato for drawing my attention to this point at a conference held at the European Centre Natolin, Warsaw, Poland on January 31, February 1, 2003, entitled *Enlargement and the European Constitutional Process*.

60 See Gràinne de Bùrca and Bruno de Witte, 'The Delimitation of Powers between the EU and its Member States', in Anthony Arnull and Daniel Wincott (eds.), *Accountability and Legitimacy in the European Union*, (Oxford: Oxford University Press, 2002).

61 See the tobacco advertising ruling judgment of the European Court of Justice; Case C-376/98 *Germany* v. *European Parliament and Council* 2000, ECR-I-8419.

62 See article 7(1) which provides that, "The legal system of the Republic of Hungary accepts the universally recognized rules and regulations of international law and harmonizes the internal laws and statutes of the country with the obligations assumed under international law".

63 See generally I. Vörös, *Contextuality and Universality: Constitutional Borrowings on the Global Stage—the Hungarian View*, available at http://www/upenn.edu.

serves as a litmus test of adaptive capacity[64] despite the "stop valve" provided by the principle of subsidiarity now contained in article 5 (2) of the EC Treaty.[65]

3. CONSTITUTIONAL TOLERANCE

The experience of the constitutional discourse between the courts of the current Member States and the European Court of Justice has been varied. Whilst some constitutional courts have embraced a judicial dialogue underlined by mutuality, co-operation and co-ordination, as in the case of The Netherlands,[66] we have witnessed a number of voices of dissent, such as in the cases of the respective constitutional courts of Italy, Denmark and Spain.[67] The notable example is the German Federal Constitutional Court's jurisprudence concerning the impact of European integration on the German legal order in which the Federal Constitutional Court (FCC) has carved out a role for itself as guardian not only of the German constitution, but also of the identity—or "distinctiveness" of the German constitution and the human rights protection contained therein, which provides a useful case study of diversity and its impact on the constitutional cultures at the macro-level of the existing EU Member States.

3.1. Sovereignty, Rights and Macro-Diversity

In its *Solange I* decision,[68] the German Federal Constitutional Court (FCC) held that so long as ("*solange*") the EC did not provide adequate protection of basic rights, the (FCC) remained the ultimate arbiter concerning issues of human rights and would assess the level of protection afforded to human rights in *specific*[69] cases. In *Solange II*,[70] the EC was held to protect human rights in line with the protection of fundamental rights enshrined in the German Basic Law enabling the FCC to

---

64 See generally Thomas King, 'The European Community and Human Rights in Eastern Europe', *Legal Issues of European Integration*, 23(1996), at pp. 93–125.

65 Taken in conjunction with Protocol 30. See generally Antonio Estella, *The EU Principle of Subsidiarity and Its Critique* (Oxford: Oxford University Press 2002).

66 Monica Claes and Bruno de Witte, "Report on The Netherlands" in Weiler *et al.*, *supra* n. 7 at pp. 171–194.

67 For a general discussion of these cases see Franz Mayer, *Kompetenzüberschreitung und Letztentscheidung: Das Maastricht-Urteil des Bundesverfassungsgerichts und die Letztentscheidung über Ultra vires Akte in Mehrebenensystemen. Eine rechtsvergleichende Betrachtung von Konflikten zwischen Gerichten am Beispiel der EU und der USA* (München: C H Beck 2000).

68 BVerfGE 37, 271.

69 Author's own emphasis. This next section draws on the author's own contribution to the *Columbia Journal of European Law*, "Sovereignty Lost, Sovereignty Regained? Some Reflections on the Bundesverfassungsgericht"s Banana Judgment", 9 *CJEL* (2002), at p. 109.

70 BVerfGE 73, 339.

relax its jurisdictional hold over questions of basic rights. Accordingly, as long as the general level of protection was secured by the European Court of Justice, the FCC would not review the level in specific cases. The fundamental rights issue was not directly relevant for the *Maastricht*[71] judgment[72], however, one reading of the case[73] is that the FCC reaffirmed the position it adopted in *Solange II*, that is to say that the FCC would only look at general cases in the event of a decrease in the general level of human rights protection. It was this interpretation[74] of the *Maastricht* decision which was of particular significance regarding the FCC's most recent installment in its jurisprudence concerning European integration, namely, the *Banana* case[75] which was based on a challenge made by a group of third country banana importers[76] before a Frankfurt Administrative Court regarding the constitutionality of the conditions of trade for third countries imposed by virtue of an EU Regulation.[77]

According to the FCC in this case, fundamental rights in the European Communities, as the ECJ's decisions indicate, are sufficiently protected.[78] Moreover, this protection is commensurate with the protection guaranteed by the provisions of the German Basic Law. As long as this continues to be the case, the FCC shall not exercise its jurisdiction concerning the applicability of secondary EC law. The FCC shall therefore not review secondary EC law[79] unless the ECJ fails to protect fundamental rights to the degree envisaged in *Solange II*.[80]

The FCC's judgment was consistent with the provisions of the Basic Law. An amendment to the Basic Law (Article 23 (1) Sentence 1),[81] which was enacted

---

[71] BVerfGE 89, 155 or *Brunner v. European Union Treaty*, [1994] 1 Common Market Law Reports 57.

[72] It is important to point out that the *Maastricht* decision was based on arguments concerning democratic legitimacy and competence-competence. The human rights nexus of the case is *obiter dicta* only.

[73] Indeed, there are several. See, for example, Paul Kirchhof, 'The Balance of Powers Between National and European Institutions', *European Law Journal* 5 (1999), at p. 225.

[74] A plethora of interpretations of the effect of the *Maastricht* decision were offered as regards the human rights issue.

[75] Decision of June 7, 2000—2 BvL 1/97.

[76] Referred to as the Atlanta Group.

[77] In Germany, prior to the enactment of the regulation, the majority of the bananas on the market emanated from third countries.

[78] The FCC was thereby reaffirmed its *Solange II* decision. See BVerfGE 73, 378–381.

[79] Or "Solange dies so ist, wird das BVerfG seine Gerichtsbarkeit über die Anwendbarkeit von abgeleitetem Gemeinschaftsrecht nicht mehr ausüben. Vorlagen von Normen des sekondären Gemeinschaftsrechts an das BVerfG sind deshalb unzulässig." Here the court cross referred to its Solange II decision. See BVerfGE 73, 339.

[80] Above n. 79 at para 60.

[81] As amended on 21 December 1992. Article 23 (1) of the Basic Law provides that, "(1) To realize a unified Europe, Germany participates in the development of the European Union which is bound to democratic, rule of law, social, and federal principles as well as the principle

prior to both the *Maastricht* decision and the ratification of the Maastricht Treaty, provides constitutional limits to European integration. Thus, the EC Treaties and any secondary legislation arising therefrom should be read in the light of other provisions of the Basic Law, such as the provisions falling under the so-called "eternity clause"[82] which contains a reference to human dignity and the value of human life[83] as well as to the federal, democratic and social principles upon which the Federal Republic of Germany is founded.[84] The eternity clause provides that these principles may not be set aside by the legislature.[85]

The questions addressed in the *Maastricht* decision do, to some extent, overlap with those raised in the *Banana* case. The judgments are, however, by no means interchangeable. *Maastricht* concerned the issue of competence of the German state, under its constitution to ratify the Maastricht Treaty. By contrast, the *Banana* case was based on the issue of fundamental rights. Whereas these issues are substantively different, they both raise the question of the ultimate arbiter and by implication, the doctrine of sovereignty. It is of interest to note that the ease with which the FCC dealt with the human rights issue in a case which was essentially based on competence—albeit *obiter dicta*—was noticeably absent in the *Banana* case.[86] That is to say, that it elected not to address the issue of competence by way of *obiter dicta* in a case based on fundamental rights, a move which would have been in line with the tactics it adopted in its *Maastricht* decision.

What begins to emerge is a picture of the Court's power of definition in both framing and interpreting the central feature of the case.[87] Thus, whilst explicitly addressing fundamental rights protection, it has also implicitly developed its

---

of subsidiarity and provides a protection of fundamental rights essentially equivalent to that of this Constitution. The federation can, for this purpose and with the consent of the Senate, delegate sovereign powers. Article 79 (2) & (3) is applicable for the foundation of the European Union as well as for changes in its contractual bases and comparable regulations by which the content of this Constitution is changed or amended or by which such changes or amendments are authorized."

82 Article 79 (III) of the Basic Law.

83 Article 1 of the Basic Law.

84 See Article 20 of the Basic Law.

85 In the event of conflict, the competing constitutional principles must be balanced in accordance with the principle of maximum effectiveness or "practical concordance". See Konrad Hesse, *Grundzüge des Verfassungsrechts der Bundesrepublik Deutschland* (20th edn.) (Heidelberg: Müller 1995), at pp. 28,72. For a succinct yet informative outline of the applicability of Article 23 of the Basic Law, see Christoph Schmidt, 'From Pont d'Avignon to Ponte Vecchio: The Resolution of Constitutional Conflicts between the European Union and the Member States through Principles of Public International Law', in Piek Eeckhout and Takis Tridimas (eds.), *Yearbook of European Law*, 18 (1998), 415, 418–419.

86 See also BVerfG NJW 2000, 3124 and BVerfG EuZW 2001, 255.

87 An issue which I have drawn attention to elsewhere. See "Sovereignty über Alles: the (re) configuration of the German Legal Order", in Neil Walker (ed.), n. 11 above at 279.

"sovereignty jurisprudence" so to speak, based on a vision of itself as the ultimate guardian of the unity of the German state. The "Euro" decision is a further case in point[88] of a tactic which would be surmised thus: *sovereignty by any other name*. Interesting historical parallels arise, such as the German general strategy in 1948–1949 to regain full national sovereignty within parameters framed by military occupation by the Allies in which tactics were adopted to preserve as much national unity of the country as possible.[89] It is arguable that similar voices of dissent are likely to emerge post-accession, albeit in different contexts and within different legal cultural frameworks during the ongoing period of constitutional adjustment. The tension will possibly be accentuated by the power asymmetry which existed during the accession negotiations and which is again witnessed by the position of the CEECs in the Convention. Indeed, this is an issue which has been addressed in the context of referenda and the ratification of EU Treaties in the CEE. What is clear is that some issues may affect the CEE's more stringently than is the case for the current Member States, such as the case of minority rights.[90] Indeed, the issue of rights also provides a useful illustration of the issue of double standards in relation to the policy of political conditionality which exists between the EU and the candidate countries, the effect of which can be divisive.[91] Thus, for example, whereas the protection of minority rights was initially upheld in the Copenhagen criteria, it does not appear in article 6 (1) of the EU Treaty, giving rise to the situation where the CEECs have a more difficult and indeed more onerous burden to displace *vis-à-vis* human rights than the current EU Member States.[92] The Copenhagen criteria illustrate the phenomenon of human rights conditionality as a whole according to which the EU has compelled states to comply with procedural requirements such as human rights clauses which constitute a non-negotiable part of negotiating directives for Community agreements with third parties.[93]

---

88 *Id.*

89 See Edmund Spevack, *Allied Control and German Freedom: American Political and Ideological Influences on the Framing of the West German Basic Law* (München: LIT Verlag 2001), at pp. 322–323.

90 See generally Wojciech Sadurski, 'Charter and Enlargement', *European Law Journal*, 8 (2002) 340.

91 See Andrew Williams, 'Enlargement of the Union and Human Rights Conditionality: a policy of distinction?', *European Law Review* 25 (2000), at p. 601.

92 See Bruno de Witte, 'Politics versus Law in the EU's Approach to Ethnic Minorities' in Jan Zielonka (ed.), *Europe Unbound. Enlarging and reshaping the boundaries of the European Union*, (London: Routledge 2002), at p. 137.

93 See, for example, the European Community's development relations with the Lomé countries (the Asian, Caribbean and Pacific or ACP countries) as originally established by Part IV of the Treaty of Rome whereby ACP products are granted preferential access to the Union on a non-reciprocal basis. The Contonou Agreement signed on 23 June 2000, which is the successor of Lomé IV, is a useful illustration of the increasing trend to include human rights clauses as part of the EU's external relations. See O.J. 2000 L 317/3 at Articles 8 and 9 and

This has been extended to formulating human rights as a precondition for EU membership.[94]

3.2. Sovereignty, Rights and Micro-Diversity

The challenge mounted by diversity must be regarded as being mainly two-fold. First, there is the *external* challenge of diversity which the CEECs face on joining the EU and the multiplication of legal fora which accompanies membership. Secondly, there is the *internal* challenge of diversity on the candidate countries. This entails *inter alia* an assessment of how different bundles of norms and regulations which protect ethnic minorities, such as the EU, the OSCE, the Council of Europe and the UN come into play giving rise to what I term "multi-jurisdictionality". The issue concerning the extent to which multi-jurisdictionality provides a means of coming to terms with the complex reality of communities divided along ethnic, religious and linguistic lines in the light of the challenge posed by EU enlargement must operate from a clear empirical basis in order to address the central question: can constitutionalism meet the heavy demands made upon it by diversity, particularly given that one of state constitutionalism's heavy biases is the drive of homogeneity and what James Tully has called the "Empire of Uniformity"?[95] The implications for individual functional fields such as Justice and Home Affairs, Immigration and ethno-linguistic minority rights issues as regards the viability of the EU constitutional framework are considerable, particularly concerning coming to terms with the fragmentation which diversity engenders.[96] Indeed, the impact of EU enlargement is predicated on the reconfiguration of law and politics through models of decentralization, for which state fixated accounts of constitutionalism arguably master neither the grammar, nor the language nor the nuance.[97]

4. ENLARGEMENT AND MULTI-LEVELED CONSTITUTIONALISM

Implementation of the *acquis* has a considerable impact on regions, in particular, administrative institutions such as, for example, local administrative courts which

also Mielle Bulterman, *Human Rights in the Treaty Relations of the European Community*, (Antwerp: Intersentia 2001).

94 See Manfred Nowak, 'Human Rights "Conditionality" in Relation to Entry to, and Full Participation in, the EU', in Philip Alston, Mara Bustelo and James Heenan (eds.), *The EU and Human Rights* (Oxford: Oxford University Press 1999), at p. 687.

95 See James Tully, *Constitutionalism in an Age of Diversity* (Cambridge: Cambridge University Press 1995) at Chapt. 3.

96 Without, at the same time, sidestepping complexity through somewhat hackneyed recourse to conceptualizations of the Empire: Michael Hardt and Toni Negri, *Empire*, (Cambridge: Harvard University Press 2000).

97 See Neil Walker, 'The Idea of Constitutional Pluralism', *Modern Law Review*, 65 (2002), at p. 317.

act as its gatekeepers. The recognition of rights which arise as a consequence of EC law is dependent on knowledge of EC law as well as the willingness of these judges to apply it, both of which are essential as a means of ensuring meaningful access to EC law. The experience gained in some current Member States is sobering with reports of both knowledge and access being poor which has culminated in an appeal for judges and for legal practitioners to acquaint themselves with the EC treaties.[98] Can we expect the same trend in the CEE states post-accession? Support has been construed as depending on a level of awareness. This requires what has been referred to as *cognitive mobilization*, namely, whereby a citizen is integrated into modern organizations and extensive communication networks through social learning,[99] of which there is, as yet, little sign in the case of local and regional elites in the CEECs.[100] The higher the awareness, the more supportive a citizen becomes of the dominant values, expectations and institutions of a political community. Case studies of the preliminary reference procedure (art. 234 EC Treaty) such as the one conducted by Stone Sweet[101] are essential in order to track the process of constitutionalization, which is jeopardized by threats to uniform application of EU law in the face of decentralized Community courts where the conditions under which national courts must refer preliminary questions are too lax.[102] Lest it be forgotten, European law was instrumental in promoting cooperation and in enacting concrete standards of behaviour. However, the main, if not dominant, actors of the promotion of European integration through the medium of law have been the judges of the European Court of Justice.[103] Less is known, empirically speaking, of the case of the courts of the Member States. However, the regional level is where the dynamics of constitutional adjustment can best be tracked, particularly given the interventionism which is instrumentalised at the regional level.

The use of economic leverage channeled through the PHARE (Assistance for Economic Restructuring Poland and Hungary) program, for instance,[104] in order to support the institutionalization of regional policies of the CEECs is a useful case in

---

98 Sacha Prechal, 'National Courts in European Constitution', Paper given at a conference at the European University Institute, The Emerging Constitution of the European Union on April 19 and 20, 2002, which deals with the position in The Netherlands.

99 See Robert Inglewood, *Culture Shift* (Princeton: Princeton University Press 1990), at p. 377.

100 James Hughes, Gwendolyn Sasse and Claire Gordon, 'Saying "Maybe" to the "Return to Europe": Elites and the Political Space for Euroscepticism in Central and Eastern Europe', *European Union Politics*, 3 (2002).

101 See Data Set on Preliminary References in EC Law (1961–1998), Robert Schuman Centre, European University Institute, 1999, available http://www.iue.it/RSC/RSC_TOOLS/.

102 See Anthony Arnull, Modernising "Community Courts", *Cambridge Yearbook of European Legal Studies*, 3 (2000), at pp. 37, 62.

103 See Miguel Poiares Maduro, *We, the Court. The European Court of Justice & the European Economic Constitution* (Oxford: Hart Publishing 1998).

104 Council Regulation (EEC) No. 3906/89 of 18 December 1989, O.J. L375/11 as last amended by Regulation (EC) No. 753/96, O.J. 1996 L 103/5.

point. Thus, for example, the Hungarian government's use of PHARE assistance to elaborate and explore a legal-institutional arrangement of EU compatible regional policy making laid the foundations of the 1996 law on Regional Development in Hungary. To this extent, constitutional lawyers should broaden their perspective to include an appraisal of the impact of the implementation of the *acquis* at the regional level and the consequences for the judicature in a decentralized sense. This entails a multi-leveled evaluation of decisions of courts—that is to say, not only the highest courts seized of the matter as well as an assessment of the behavior of the legal elites, in a broad sense. Thus, for example, *La Doctrine*, which has been referred to by some as being composed of professors of public, European and international law including former and future justices[105] should surely also include legal elites from a broader scope, that is to say, the elites who staff the local courts and other administrative bodies in order to address the following: to what extent does the evidence of negative public opinion towards EU membership in the CEECs foretell a story of the period of post-accession?[106] Can such evidence be found amongst the legal elites and if so, what effect will it have on the process of constitutional adjustment? In other words, to what extent, if at all, will it affect the willingness of the legal elites to implement the *acquis*, both in substance and in form? The legal elites will have to be persuaded not only to work within the new system of rules which the *acquis* engenders but also there will have to be an incentive and indeed a motivation for them to do so.

Whether the ultimate arbiter constitutional discourse of dissent will be reproduced in the candidate countries depends on how supranational law is framed in the respective constitutions and how it is viewed from the perspective of lawyers who apply the norms arising therefrom. For example, in the case of Slovakia, the 1999 Slovak Language law which regulates the language use of national minorities in Slovakia in their "official contacts" with local self-governments,[107] is not only full of inconsistencies and contradictions,[108] but provides a high threshold (of 20%) for it to be applied.[109] Whereas it has satisfied the conditionality imposed the EU accession process, internally, the law has divided both Slovak nationalists and

105 See Julianne Kokott, 'Report on Germany' above n. 7 at p. 79.

106 Comments made by the former Polish minister for European affairs, Jacek Saryusz-Wolski reported by EU Observer on April 22, 2002. See http://www.euobserver.com.

107 Such as having all correspondence between the local and state administration in the minority language (article 2(3)) with the exception of public documents, the distribution of official forms of the local administrative bodies in a minority language upon request (see Article 2(6), to conduct meetings of the local administrative bodies in a minority language only with the consent of all present (see Article 3(1)).

108 For example, no definitions of "official contacts" (Article 2(1)) or of "public documents" (Article 2(3)) is given.

109 Thus, minority language use in official contacts is restricted to those municipalities where minorities constitute according to the last census at least 20% of the inhabitants of a municipality (see Article 2(1)).

ethnic-Hungarians alike. Needless to say that the Nationalists are well represented by elites which staff the state and local administrative institutions. The same cannot be said of the case of the ethnic-Hungarians. Both cases illustrate the issue of formal implementation triumphing over substantive implementation. They also show how dependent recognition of rights are on elites, who, as in the case of the CEECs have had to re-learn political support in relation to a new regime in the age of transition post-1989 and currently, as regards the EU in the accession process. Both elites and citizens in these new democracies have spent most of their lives under an undemocratic regime.[110] A corollary to willingness to implement the *acquis* by the legal elites is the reception and recognition of the norms by citizens. In addressing this question, one must bear in mind that legal elites have a low standing in the CEECs due to the fact that law was traditionally politicized and was subject to the administration of political power. Capacity is often seen in terms of physical capacity like resources, personnel and structures. Capacity is also, however, about skill assets, training and trust.

4.1. Allegiance and Trust

If one supports the tendency by scholars to equate political legitimacy with political support, it follows that one must also consider the distinction between two types of support, namely, specific and diffuse support. Briefly stated, the former refers to a set of attitudes towards institutions based on the fulfillment of expectations of politics or actions. The latter is more contentious given that every citizen will disagree with, dislike or distrust the policies of political institutions. However, whilst they may disagree with the actions of these institutions, they may nonetheless concede its authority as a political decision maker. The importance of maintaining the allegiance of the People to the source of political power emphasizes the relational aspect of sovereignty to the extent that it represents the quality of the political relationship that is formed between the state and the people and is thereby tied up with the notion of political power and public law. Trust of the citizens is essential in order to maintain state sovereignty.[111] The very notion of sovereignty as operating at the state level to sustain the affiliation of the citizen is clearly an argument in favor of the Nation State which sees the transfer of sovereignty to supranational instances as weakening the affiliation of the citizen, an issue which is repeatedly discussed in the multiple citizenship discourse, and also the debates, such as those leading up to the reforms of the Citizenship laws in Germany concerning the concept of dual

---

110 See William Mishler and Richard Rose, 'Learning and re-learning regime support: The dynamics of post-communist regimes', *European Journal of Political Research*, 41 (2002), at p. 5.

111 See Martin Loughlin, 'Ten Tenets of Sovereignty', in Walker, above n. 11 at p. 55.

citizenship.[112] My contention is that if one regards sovereignty of the Nation State as being pooled by virtue of European and International obligations that this also gives rise to the following corollary, which goes to the heart of the issue of democratic legitimacy and consent, namely, trust is also "pooled", or "qualified" or "lost"—depending on whichever way one regards the effect of European integration on the sovereignty of the Member States.[113] Whether sovereignty resides at the level of the Nation State or elsewhere is largely irrelevant. What is important is that sovereignty *exists*. It will, by nature, command affiliation and trust. The level at which sovereignty resides is irrelevant to the affiliation of the trust of the citizen because sovereignty is intrinsic to whether citizens feel confident that states perform certain duties and the citizens feel comfortable with the obligations. Drawing on performance theories, the following expectation can be voiced: if the EU performs, it will attract both support and affiliation. Thus, for example, many Catalans feel a stronger affiliation with the EU as compared to the Spanish state as such. The same can be said for the case of Scottish nationalists *vis-à-vis* Westminster. This, however, is more linked to the internal political situation in Spain and in the United Kingdom and the impact which the autonomous community of *Catalunya* has in Spain and the limited impact which the Scottish Executive has in a devolved United Kingdom.[114] Much depends on the sphere of public administration, public policy and law.

The challenge to consumer confidence in the face of food scares, particularly in relation to the BSE crisis and Genetically Modified (GM) food is a useful illustration of the concomitant challenge to the citizen's identification with his or her community.[115] This identification is embedded in culture and identity.[116] Thus, particular foods are associated with festivities, rituals and a sense of belonging to a particular community, be it national or regional. The effects of globalization including the consequences of EU membership has opened up internal food markets and has also disaggregated the tacit trust which has traditionally been active between

112 Jan Halfmann, 'Immigration and Citizenship in Germany: Contemporary Dilemmas', *Political Studies*, 105 (1997), at p. 260.

113 See generally Neil MacCormick, *Questioning Sovereignty: Law, State and Nation in the European Commonwealth* (Oxford: Oxford University Press 1999).

114 See Michael Keating, *Plurinational Democracy: Stateless Nations of the United Kingdom, Spain, Canada and Belgium in a post-Sovereign World* (Oxford: Oxford University Press 2001).

115 See Roberta Sassatelli and Alan Scott, 'Novel Food, New Markets and Trust Regimes: Responses to the erosion of consumers' confidence in Austria, Italy and the UK', *European Societies*, 3 (2001) at p. 213. See also Ellen Vos, 'EU Food Safety Regulation in the aftermath of the BSE crisis', *Journal of Consumer Policy*, 23 (2000) at p. 227.

116 See generally Aleksander Surdej, *Enlarging the EU Food Safety Regime. Adjustments of Polish Food Safety Regulations to the Requirement of EU Membership*, European Forum 2002/03 Discussion Paper EF.RC&RC/02/3/13.

members of particular communities in relation to its particular institutions.[117] This gives rise to a reconfiguration of the notion of boundaries beyond customary conceptualizations predicated on territory. The complexity which attaches to food consumption and the risks posed by the use of pesticides and food additives not to mention the use of new technologies has placed increasing reliance on experts who have increasingly monopolized the debate concerning the perception of risk.[118].

Matters of trust and loyalty also have to be reconfigured in the face of the plurality of public spheres, an issue which has been recognized in the context of Food Safety in the EU and the proposal for the creation of a European Food Authority, the mandate of which would be the responsibility concerning risk assessment and communication on food safety issues.[119] The process of reconfiguration has also been accompanied by a re-entrenchment of national and local identity.

There is need for differentiation in order to come to terms with different regimes of trust which operate at a number of levels. Thus, bearing the CEECs in mind, Polish citizens, for example, would undoubtedly trust their government to defend their agricultural interests more than the European Union negotiators for accession.[120] Agriculture is at the heart of Poland's accession to the EU given that it accounts for 3.3 percent of the Polish GDP (as compared with 2 percent in the EU), but employs 18.8 percent of all working people (as compared with 4.4 percent in the EU).[121]

By contrast, the same might not be true as regards police protection where they might look to the EU as providing a form of supranational "checks and balances" to safeguard their rights. This is also the case of minorities in the CEECs who embrace the EU as a way of escaping the constraints of unwanted sovereignty at the state level, particularly as the states' regional policy tend to discriminate against them such as the cases of Romania and Slovakia where the respective states drew regional boundaries in order to preclude minorities having regional power, authority and competencies.

---

117 See Alan O. Sykes, 'Exploring the need for international harmonization: domestic regulation, sovereignty and scientific evidence requirements. A pessimistic view', *Chicago Journal of International Law*, Fall (2002).

118 See Ulrich Beck, *The Risk Society: Towards a New Modernity* (trans. from the German by Mark Ritter) (London: Sage 1992) who refers this in terms of "primary scientization" at p. 158. See also Cass Sunstein, *Risk and Reason: Safety, Law and the Environment*, (New York: Cambridge University Press 2002).

119 White Paper on Food Safety, COM (99) 719 final at Chapt. 4.

120 Indeed, a climate of "unnecessary mistrust" has been reported to underpin Polish-EU negotiations. See Stephen Holmes, 'Introduction', *East European Constitutional Review*, 9 (2000).

121 See Susan Senior Nello, 'Food and Agriculture in an Enlarged EU', *Robert Schuman Centre Working Paper No. 58/2002* at p. 3.

5. CONCLUSION

What does this teach us? Not only must the approach to affiliation and trust be more nuanced, that is to say that there are degrees of affiliation and trust, but also, there are degrees of sovereignty for which there are likely to be different degrees of multi-level dissent. The case of Germany and the judicial response to the European integration project in particular, illustrates the nature of dissent at the level of constitutional court decisions. The CEECs by contrast indicate the need to widen the analytical framework in order to include a multi-leveled approach in order to monitor and track not only their adaptive capacity, but also the adaptive capacity of the current member states. To this extent, much can be learned by the current member states of the EU and by the EU itself from the experience of legal orders which have had to address these issues within a new supranational architecture. The flexibility with which the CEECs have had to both view and reconfigure their own traditions of state theory and practice in the face of EU membership, particularly as regards rights, may serve as a useful example to the EU and its members, not only in terms of burdens but also in terms of benefits.

11. Europeanization Through Judicial Activism? The Hungarian Constitutional Court's Legitimacy and the "Return to Europe"

Christian Boulanger

1. Introduction

There are various ways to approach the relationship between constitutionalism and the "Europeanization" of post-Communist accession countries to the European Union. First, one could take the lawyer's perspective and analyse the impact of accession and of the *acquis communautaire* on the constitutional systems of these countries. Such an analysis would point out the ways in which EU Integration induced changes in the constitutional structure of accession countries. For example, constitutions have to be changed in order to accommodate the transfer of certain sovereignty rights to the EU, and therefore to allow for the supremacy of EU law over domestic law. Second, if one thinks of a national constitution as incorporating the totality of the legal regulations of its political structure, rather than consisting purely of *constitutional* laws, EU accession obviously has an enormous impact. Laws pertaining to all fields of political life have to be changed in order to comply with the new European law regime—many concerning technical details, others profoundly changing the legal structure of the countries.[1]

Conversely, political scientists tend to study the effects of EU Integration on institution building and governance. They argue that the effects of Europeanization were visible long before the candidate countries began the accession process. They changed institutions and behaviours in anticipation of accession. These changes do not simply mirror the demands of the formal legal rules that candidate countries are supposed to adapt to (the "legal harmonization" process). In some cases, they go beyond what is being asked, and in other cases they fall short of the EU's expectations. The latter comes as no surprise, given the incredibly short time frame

1 See, for example, Andrew Evans, "Voluntary Harmonisation in Integration Between the European Community and Eastern Europe," *European Law Review*, 22 (1997), pp. 201–220, and, for a socio-legal analysis of "legal harmonization," Armin Höland, "EU-Recht auf dem Weg nach Osten: Rechtssoziologische Fragen," in C. Boulanger (ed.), *Recht in der Transformation* (Berlin: Berliner Debatte Wissenschaftsverlag 2002), pp. 79–102. For a "holistic" concept of the constitution, see Alec Stone Sweet, *Governing With Judges. Constitutional Politics in Europe* (Oxford: Oxford University Press 2000).

Wojciech Sadurski et al. (ed.), Spreading Democracy and the Rule of Law?, 263–280.

in which the candidate countries have had to roll back half a century of Leninism and a few years of independent law-making.[2]

Other analyses look at the transfer of law from the opposite direction. They ask whether there is a cultural basis for constitutionalism in individual post-Communist countries in general,[3] and for an "EU-constitutionalism" in particular. They do this by studying public opinion[4] or by speculating on the significance of deep cultural legacies, which affect the (non)functioning of today's legal institutions.[5] Such analyses assume that constitutions and laws do not exist in a socio-cultural vacuum. Rather, they work against the background of discourses and practices inherited from the past in various ways, i.e. in the context of what is often called "culture".

One area that has so far received only limited attention in this context is the role of the newly established constitutional courts in the region. Their remarkable activity has been studied in various contributions,[6] but the relationship between their jurisprudence and EU Integration has not systematically been researched. This research would have to point out the various ways in which the jurisprudence of the constitutional courts has promoted smooth EU Integration or slowed it down.

In this chapter, I am interested in a different, rather more informal way that "Europe" and EU Integration affected constitutional politics in the decade after the regime change and vice versa. I am going to explore an argument formulated by Kim Lane Scheppele, namely that "the success of a constitution depends less on its constitutional pedigree than on the political culture into which the constitution

---

2 See Darina Malová and Tim Haughton, "Making Institutions in Central and Eastern Europe, and the Impact of Europe," *West European Politics*, 25 (2002), pp. 101–120 and Heather Grabbe, "How does Europeanization affect CEE governance? Conditionality, Diffusion and Diversity," *Journal of European Public Policy*, 8 (2001), pp. 1013–1031 for the effects on institution-building.

3 Philip Selznick, "Legal Cultures and the Rule of Law," in M. Krygier and A. Czarnota (eds.), *The Rule of Law After Communism: Problems and Prospects in East-Central Europe* (Aldershot: Ashgate/Dartmouth 1999), pp. 21–38; Rett R. Ludwikowski, "Constitutional Culture of the New East-Central European Democracies," *The Georgia Journal of International and Comparative Law*, 29 (2000), p. 1.

4 Jan Stankovsky, Fritz Plasser and Peter A. Ulram, *On the Eve of EU Enlargement. Economic Developments and Democratic Attitudes in East Central Europe* (Wien: Signum 1998).

5 Georg Brunner, "Rechtskultur in Osteuropa: das Problem der Kulturgrenzen," in *Politische und ökonomische Transformation in Osteuropa* (Berlin: Arno Spitz 1996), pp. 91–112.

6 See for case studies and comparative analyses Herman Schwartz, *The Struggle for Constitutional Justice in Post-Communist Europe* (Chicago: Chicago University Press 2000), Radoslav Procházka, *Mission Accomplished: On Founding Constitutional Adjudication in Central Europe* (Budapest: Central European University Press 2002) and Wojciech Sadurski (ed.), *Constitutional Justice, East and West. Democratic Legitimacy and Constitutional Courts in Post-Communist Europe in a Comparative Perspective* (The Hague: Kluwer Law International 2002).

is inserted. The ideas that judges, lawyers and politicians have about how constitutional cultures work are more important than the actual text, and even more important than the actually existing reality of the constitutional cultures that serve as a model."[7]

In particular, I would like to discuss one of the ideas that she presented in a conference paper: The claim that notions of Hungarian "Europeanness" has influenced the development of the Hungarian constitutional jurisprudence in terms of the receptiveness of Hungarian politicians and publics towards the court's activism. Talking about the so-called "Sólyom court" which worked from 1990 to 1998, she argues that "the Court's power to override the democratically elected Parliament comes from the image it forwards of the Hungarian nation firmly anchored in European culture."[8]

This chapter takes up this argument and tries to draw some theoretical conclusions from it since it touches on several broader socio-legal debates. First, it departs from the dominant theoretical paradigm of the study of constitutional courts, which perceives their power as dependent upon strategic power-plays in the political arena.[9] Second, the argument contributes to a discussion, which has been around since Max Weber first spoke of the relevance of elite "world views"[10] which act as "switchmen" in the institutionalization of new regimes. Third, Scheppele positions herself in the heated debate on the "counter-majoritarian difficulty" (Bickel) of judicial review: contrary to many who think that judicial review is undemocratic, she argues that the Sólyom court in many cases responded to the aspirations of Hungarian society more adequately than the democratically legitimated parliament.

The empirical puzzle I am interested in solving in this context is the following: After the demise of the Hungarian Socialist regime, a powerful Constitutional Court emerged from the round-table-talks between the Socialist Party and the opposition. Equipped with broad jurisdiction and the possibility of easy access by citizens to the court, it began, under the leadership of chief justice László Sólyom, to aggressively challenge the legislature about new legislation. Since access to the court was very easy (everybody could challenge any law without any requirements of "standing"),

7 Kim Lane Scheppele, "The Accidental Constitution," paper presented at the conference *Contextuality and Universality: Constitutional Borrowings on a Global Scale*, March 20–21, 1998, University of Pennsylvania, Philadelphia.

8 Kim Lane Scheppele, "Imagined Europe," paper presented at the conference *Annual Meeting of the Law and Society Association*, July 1996, Strathclyde University, Glasgow, Scotland.

9 Lee Epstein and Jack Knight, *The Choices Justices Make* (Washington, DC: Congressional Quarterly 1998); Tom Ginsburg, *Judicial Review in New Democracies: Constitutional Courts in Asian Cases* (Cambridge, UK: Cambridge University Press 2003); Georg Vanberg, *The Politics of Constitutional Review in Germany* (Cambridge: Cambridge University Press 2005).

10 Max Weber, *Gesammelte Aufsätze zur Religionssoziologie* (Tübingen: J. C. B. Mohr 1988), p. 252.

basically all of the legal and political problems of the transformation ended up at the court and had to be decided. And in spite of severe criticism by parliamentarians and the government, virtually all decisions of the court were complied with and no attempt was made to curtail the court's powers, as has occurred in other countries of the former Soviet bloc,[11] leading Scheppele to characterize the Hungarian political system of the first years after the regime change as a "courtocracy."[12] It is beyond the scope of this paper to provide a detailed account of the court's activities, which are, however, well documented.[13] This sudden rise to power requires explanation. After all, it is received wisdom by now in the social sciences that despite what jurists tell us, courts are not all-powerful and above politics. They depend on the political elite to execute their decisions and therefore have to act strategically and with self-restraint. As Martin Shapiro has pointed out, it took the US Supreme Court more than a century to accumulate enough political capital before it would challenge the political establishment in civil rights cases.[14] My claim here is not that judicial and political strategies are less important than cultural factors. Instead, I take the (hardly) original position that history and culture matters more than is usually admitted by studies that rely on strategic models. In sum, the argument is that cultural dispositions help to bring about political outcomes, they do not *cause* them. Thus, the degree to which the Hungarian elites in the early 1990s were imagining Europe as a cultural space might not differentiate them from Poland or the Czech Republic, it certainly differentiated them from other places such as Slovakia at that time, Belarus, Ukraine, and Russia, of then and today. And this is the reason why I think the cultural analysis presented in this chapter is worthwhile.

---

11 Compare this, for example, to what happened to the Slovak, Russian, or Kazakh court. See Herman Schwartz, "Defending the Defenders of Democracy," *Transition*, 4 (1997), pp. 80–85.

12 Kim Lane Scheppele, "Democracy by Judiciary (Or Why Courts Can Sometimes Be More Democratic than Parliaments)," paper presented at the *Conference on Constitutional Courts*, 1–3 November 2001, Washington University of Saint Louis, p. 16.

13 The only monograph on the court in English so far is Cathrine Dupré, *Importing the Law in Post-Communist Transitions. The Hungarian Constitutional Court and the Right to Human Dignity* (Oxford: Hart Publishing 2003); László Sólyom and Georg Brunner (eds.), *Constitutional Judiciary in a New Democracy: The Hungarian Constitutional Court* (Ann Arbour: University of Michigan Press 2000) provide a collection of cases and commentaries, an extension and English translation of Georg Brunner and László Sólyom, *Verfassungsgerichtsbarkeit in Ungarn* (Baden-Baden: Nomos 1995). A comprehensive legal analysis in German, covering the early years of the court is provided by Gábor Spuller, *Das Verfassungsgericht der Republik Ungarn: Zuständigkeiten, Organisation, Verfahren, Stellung* (Frankfurt a.M.: Peter Lang 1998). For a sympathetic reading of the Solyom court's activity see Schwartz, *The Struggle for Constitutional Justice in Post-Communist Europe* (Chicago: Chicago University Press 2000), Chapt. 4.

14 Martin Shapiro, "Some Conditions for the Success of Constitutional Courts: Lessons from the U.S. Experience," in W. Sadurski (ed.), above n. 6, pp. 37–59.

2. DEMOCRACY, JUDICIAL REVIEW, AND EUROPEANIZATION

I want to start the theoretical discussion by exploring the relationship between democracy, judicial review, and Europeanization, in terms of the concept of legitimacy. As it is well known, there are two ways the concept of legitimacy can be investigated: legitimacy has a normative and an empirical dimension.[15] Normative legitimacy is the subject of political philosophy. The debate focuses on questions of justification of the political order, and the appropriate behaviour of an institution within this order. Since Lambert's famous critique of US American judicial involvement in politics as a "gouvernement des juges," much has been written on the extensive literature on the legitimacy of judicial review.[16] Surprisingly, the external and internal debate on the legitimacy of the activism of Constitutional Courts in CEE countries has been limited.[17] Western scholarship has, thus far, generally been supportive of a strong constitutional court, with a few exceptions.[18] Internally, there was more dissent. In Hungary, for example, Béla Pokol and András Sajó, among others, have accused the Constitutional Court of overstepping its authority.[19]

The social scientific debate on empirical legitimacy tries to distance itself from the normative debate. As Lipset argued, following Weber, in this understanding "legitimacy involves the capacity of a political system to engender and maintain the belief that existing political institutions are the most appropriate or proper ones for the society."[20] It does not matter if we, as observers, share this belief. All that matters is that people subjected to the authority of the institution believe it.

15 Rodney Barker, *Legitimating Identities. The Self-Presentation of Rulers and Subjects* (Cambridge, UK: Cambridge University Press 2001), pp. 7–29.

16 E. Lambert, *Le gouvernement des juges et la lutte contre la legislation sociale aux Etats-Unis. L'experience américaine du contrôle judiciaire des constitutionalité de la loi* (Paris: Giard 1921); for the vast literature on the subject see Mauro Cappelletti, "Repudiating Montesquieu? The Expansion and Legitimacy of "Constitutional Justice," in M. Cappelletti (ed.), *The Judicial Process in Comparative Perspective* (Oxford: Clarendon 1989), pp. 182–211.

17 Wojciech Sadurski, "Constitutional Justice, East and West: Introduction," in W. Sadurski (ed.), above n. 6, pp. 1–18.

18 See for a generally positive assessment Schwartz, *op. cit.* n. 6. One of the very few critical voices was Stephen Holmes, "Back to the Drawing Board," *East European Constitutional Review*, 3 (1993), pp. 21–25.

19 Béla Pokol, "The Constitutionality of Legislation," in V. Gessner, A. Höland and C. Varga (eds.), *European Legal Cultures* (Aldershot: Dartmouth 1996), pp. 451–454; András Sajó, "How the Rule of Law Killed Hungarian Welfare Reform," *East European Constitutional Review*, 5 (1996), pp. 31–41, which is an abbreviated translation of an originally Hungarian, widely circulated manuscript.

20 Seymour Martin Lipset, "Some Social Requisites of Democracy: Economic Development and Political Legitimacy," *American Political Science Review*, 53 (1959), p. 68.

As Max Weber put it, legitimacy is the "prestige of being exemplary or binding" (*das Prestige der Vorbildlichkeit oder Verbindlichkeit*).[21]

Constitutional Courts have, so far, largely been left out of focus of "transitology." But over the past few years, a new field of research is emerging, spilling over from the research on the "Global Expansion of Judicial Power."[22] In this context, different theoretical paradigms are used in the analysis of courts. Many political scientists start with Robert Dahl's assertion that a constitutional court can be analyzed just as any other political institution, "an institution, that is to say, for arriving at decisions on controversial questions of national policy."[23]

One major school of thought used in political science to analyze political actors and institutions is the theory of rational choice.[24] Epstein, Knight and Shvetsova have proposed an approach to study post-Communist constitutional courts using rational choice theory.[25] The authors explain the fate of the first Russian Constitutional Court under Chief Justice Zorkin. The court, acting overtly "political", violated what Epstein et al. have called the "tolerance intervals" of President Yeltsin and the legislators. After it had provoked the power centre, the court was left without allies and was subsequently disbanded. In their model, it is assumed that there are certain strategic imperatives Constitutional Courts have to respect if they want to command obedience from the other branches of government. If they disregard the interests of the major political players, they have no chance of survival.

The rational choice model provides us with some significant theoretical insights. It shows us that although we usually consider a constitutional court to be a "legal" institution only subordinated to the commands of "the law," it is actually an institution that has to take part in power-plays in the political arena. The judges have to consider the political effects of their actions, they have to strategically choose opponents and allies, and this will in turn have an influence on their decisions. Starting from a rational choice approach, we can predict that no court will decide cases with complete disregard for daily politics. Scholars of judicial politics have operationalized the rational-choice paradigm on a macro-institutional level by using the concept of "veto-players."[26] They argue that courts will become more

---

21 Max Weber, *Wirtschaft und Gesellschaft: Grundriß der verstehenden Soziologie* (Tübingen: Mohr 1980), p. 16.

22 C. Neal Tate and Torbjörn Vallinder (eds.), *The Global Expansion of Judicial Power* (New York: New York University Press 1995).

23 Robert A. Dahl, "Decision-Making in a Democracy: The Supreme Court as a National Policy-Maker," *Journal of Politics*, 6 (1957), pp. 279–295, p. 2.

24 Jon Elster (ed.), *Rational Choice* (Oxford: Blackwell 1986).

25 Lee Epstein, Jack Knight and Olga Shvetsova, "The Role of Constitutional Courts in Establishment and Maintenance of Democratic Systems of Governments," *Law and Society Review*, 35 (2001), pp. 117–164.

26 Nicos Alivizatos, "Judges as Veto-Players," in H. Döring (ed.), *Parliaments and Majority Rule in Western Europe* (New York, 1995), pp. 566–592.

powerful if few other institutions exist that can act as veto players, i.e. institutions which can delay, or prevent altogether, a decision already taken by a different institution. Looking at Hungary comparatively, this approach has many merits. Certainly, the fact that in Hungary the court was the only effective remedy against decisions by the parliamentary majority was crucial in putting the court into focus within the political process, given the importance of the questions to be decided. Some observers have spoken about a binary division of power in the 1990s: the opposition of government and Constitutional Court.[27] By way of contrast some have observed that the Polish political system, with an upper chamber and a very politically active Ombudsman, took conflict over many issues into arenas other than the constitutional judiciary.

A different theoretical approach, which stresses structural characteristics of judicial review more than individual choices, has been proposed by Alec Stone Sweet, in his comparative analysis of Western European constitutional courts.[28] Constitutional Courts' main role, in Stone Sweet's interpretation, is one of an arbiter in situations of "triadic dispute resolution": Two parties in the political arena cannot solve their conflict over interpretation of the constitution (understood by Stone Sweet not simply as the written text, but as the sum of all legal norms and political practices of a political community). Without constitutional courts, the "real meaning" of the constitution can only be determined by the majority principle: the political majority in parliament decides what the constitution "means" by adopting laws that shape the constitutional order and practice itself. This is the British practice.[29] But in post-Word War II Europe, constitutional courts have been entrusted with this task, and, as Stone Sweet argues, the institutional arrangement has produced the end of parliamentary supremacy. By way of the mechanism inherent in the institution of judicial review, especially of abstract review, over time, more and more decision-making power shifts from the democratically elected parliament to the constitutional court, or, more precisely, to its jurisdiction. An increasingly dense web of constitutionally mandated norms restricts the scope of the legislative will. Judges start acting like legislators and politicians internalize the constraints of constitutionality.

Stone Sweet's model explains many of the "social mechanisms" in the game of constitutional politics. We can expect that much of what he describes for Western Europe is also applicable in the new democracies of the East. In Stone Sweet's model the legitimacy of judicial review is mainly a function of the constitutional courts arbitration role. As long as the court is able to portray itself as a neutral "third"—for which there are a couple of techniques such as giving partial victories

---

27 Füzér, K., "Wirtschaftlicher Notstand: Konstitutionalismus und Ökonomischer Diskurs im Postkommunistischen Ungarn," in Christian Boulanger (ed.), *Recht in der Transformation* (Berlin: Berliner Debatte Wissenschaftsverlag 2002), p. 188.

28 Stone Sweet, *op. cit.* n. 1.

29 Now undermined by the Human Rights Act (1998) which allows the jurisprudence of the European Court of Human rights to override domestic legislation.

to all sides—the legitimacy of judicial review is preserved. Once this belief breaks down, however, nothing can save the court.

There are two aspects both rational choice and triadic dispute resolution models neglect, and they tie in the subject of this paper: the influence of external normative influences, on one hand, and the political–cultural socialization of the political elite with which Constitutional Courts have to deal, on the other.

The first has been described in a recent contribution by Radoslav Procházka.[30] As a lawyer, Procházka does not frame his argument within the social scientific literature on the topic. But he shows convincingly how the dynamics of international relations, and more specifically, European Integration, has a powerful influence on the nature and development of the constitutional judiciary. He compares the cases of Poland, Hungary, and the Czech and Slovak Republics and argues that there are two major ways in which this influence has been played out.

First, the candidates for integration into the European Union knew that they were being watched, and that any violation of what they perceived to be "European" norms and values could be a potential obstacle in their candidacy. Second, there was even, Procházka argues, an intra-regional competition as to constitutional adjudication. He interprets the acquiescence of the Hungarian elite to their Court's activism as a way of actually using the court as a public relations instrument. In this way, the behaviour of the political elite is also directed towards an audience, i.e. the governments of those EU countries which have to give their permission for them to join. This behaviour, however, can be interpreted as "strategic" or "opportunist" by rational choice analysis.

My claim is, by contrast, that all of these analyses neglect the nature and socialization of the political elite. I therefore propose that in order to understand the development of the constitutional judiciary in a specific country, we should not only have to look at the material interests of the political elite, but also at its cultural aspirations, including the definition of national identity. The behaviour of these elite towards the court, or, more specifically, the kind of claims to legitimacy that these elite is going to accept, strongly depends on the Central European context and also on what they think is appropriate behaviour, both on a national and an international level. In the case of Hungary, as I will demonstrate in the next section, the political elite tolerated much more than a simple model of interest congruence would predict. "Europe," in this perspective, is an imagined cultural space to which elites like to belong, and will, if necessary reorder their preferences accordingly.

3. THE FIRST HUNGARIAN CONSTITUTIONAL COURT

The idea to set up a constitutional court originated in the negotiations between the last socialist government and the democratic opposition at the so-called national round table. There is evidence that both sides—the socialist government and

30 Procházka, *op. cit.* n. 6.

the opposition—viewed the court as one of the institutional guarantees that would protect them in case the other side would win a decisive victory in the first elections, and the court was therefore equipped with a vast number of competencies.[31] The court's design[32] is particular in several regards, but for the purpose of this paper, I only mention the so-called *actio popularis*: the abstract, de-individualized constitutional complaint. This feature means that everybody (even foreigners) can appeal to the court to declare a certain law invalid on the ground that it violates the Hungarian constitution. This eliminates all barriers created by the conditions of *standing* required by other constitutional courts and, of course, it puts the court right in the centre of legislative politics. Almost every major legislative project in connection with the regime change ended up at the Constitutional Court.

The Court began its work on January 1, 1990, even before the first democratic parliament was elected. It was the first new institution of post-Leninist Hungary, and it began its work immediately. The victorious coalition of the conservative Hungarian Democratic Forum (MDF) with the small Christian Democrats and the Smallholders' party were quite surprised to find out what a constitutional court is capable of doing. In fact, the court showed little respect for what they had expected to be a system of parliamentary sovereignty. It has, for example, struck down the death penalty, against the opinion of the overwhelming majority of the population and probably also of legislators.[33] It found fault with the conservative government's restitution plans, which included giving land that had been taken by the Communists, back to the peasants.[34] It also became the centre of attention in a conflict between the prime minister and the president, the so-called "media war." After the constitutional court had ruled against the government, the far-right wing of the MDF mobilized demonstrations against, among other things, this decision in the streets of Budapest. This attempt to put public pressure on the court, however, failed after huge counter-demonstrations showed that the public was not going to tolerate this kind of politics.[35]

Two decisions were especially controversial: when the government introduced a measure to punish those responsible for atrocities during the 1956 revolution by changing the statute of limitations, the court thwarted these plans. In its decision, the court declared that Hungary was a "Rechtsstaat" and that in a Rechtsstaat, it

31 Scheppele, "The Accidental Constitution," above n. 7; John W. Schiemann, "Explaining Hungary's powerful Constitutional Court: A Bargaining Approach," *Archives européennes de sociologie*, 42 (2001), pp. 357–390.

32 For details see Sólyom and Brunner (eds.), above n. 13; Spuller, above n. 13.

33 Tíbor Horváth, "Abolition of Capital Punishment in Hungary," *Journal of Constitutional Law in Eastern and Central Europe*, 3 (1996), pp. 155–160.

34 Péter Paczolay, "Judicial Review of the Compensation Law in Hungary," *Michigan Journal of International Law*, 13 (1992), pp. 806–831.

35 Elemér Hankiss, "Die Zweite Gesellschaft," in S. Kurtán (ed.), *Vor der Wende* (Wien: Böhlau 1993), pp. 83–104.

was not possible, for reasons of legal security, to retroactively expand the statute of limitations.[36] When, in 1994, the conservatives experienced a crushing defeat at the polls and the Ex-Socialists (MSzP) and the Social-Liberals (SzDSz) formed a new governing coalition, the court did not loosen its firm control of the legislative. The socialist-liberal government watched with disbelief how the tables were turned on them. In the so-called "Bokros-package" decision, which annulled austerity measures that had been designed by finance minister Bokros to restore a balanced state budged, the court ruled that parts of the hastily enacted austerity laws violated the principle of legal security. This decision was a shock to the government, since it lost around a third of the savings already earmarked for the next budget. It sharply criticized the court but nevertheless complied. The court allowed for similar measures to take effect some months later, but still insisted that legal security was a constitutional value which could not be abridged by political or economic considerations.[37]

Why was the Hungarian Constitutional Court so strong in the first years of its existence? The government or parliament could have simply ignored the rulings, as it did with some low-visibility orders by the court to create certain laws within a specific time limit.[38] While it was unlikely that politicians would try to reinstate the death penalty—Hungary's membership in the Council of Europe and its prospective membership in the EU effectively prohibited this option—on other issues the compliance of the mostly hostile legislature is quite striking. After all, its suffices to look to its neighbour country Slovakia, where the autocratic prime minister Vladimir Meciar and the parties in his coalition government bullied judges and ignored many important rulings.[39] Not to speak of the already mentioned Russian case or the developments in Kazakhstan, where the President simply deleted the court from the constitution in 1995.[40]

To be sure, there is a way of explaining this phenomenon in the language of interests. The so-called "International Socialization Theory" argues that it is rational for elites to take over normative commitments of the regional environment

36 Gábor Halmai and Kim Lane Scheppele, "Living Well is the Best Revenge: The Hungarian Approach to Judging the Past," in A. J. McAdams (ed.), *Transitional Justice and the Rule of Law in New Democracies* (Notre Dame, IN: University of Notre Dame Press 1997).

37 Füzér, "Wirtschaftlicher Notstand: Konstitutionalismus und Ökonomischer Diskurs im Postkommunistischen Ungarn," in Boulanger (ed.), *Recht in der Transformation* (Berlin: Berliner Debatte Wissenschaftsverlag 2002), pp. 173–195.

38 András Sajó, "Educating the Executive: The Hungarian Constitutional Court's Role in the Transition Process," in J. J. Hesse, G. F. Schuppert and K. Harms (eds.), *Verfassungsrecht und Verfassungspolitik in Umbruchsituation* (Baden-Baden: Nomos 2000), pp. 229–242. Some of this "disobedience" can be explained by the inability of parliament to agree on the required new legislation.

39 Schwartz, above n. 6, Chapt. 5.

40 Schwartz, "Defending the Defenders of Democracy," *Transition*, 4 (1997), pp. 80–85.

in exchange for material benefits.[41] If we apply this theory to our case, it predicts that Central Europe elites, interested in being integrated into Western European economic and political structures, will adapt to what they perceive as the reigning norms of "constitutionalism." Hungarian and Polish elites, who were determined to follow through with European Integration, respected their Constitutional Courts. In Slovakia, Meciar and his cronies, who were running the country using illegal and authoritarian measures, could only lose by the establishment of West European standards, including a strong Constitutional Court. Procházka's argument goes in a similar direction: the Constitutional Court's internal power and the corresponding compliance (i.e. lack of *visible* resistance) were used by Hungarian elites as a showcase towards the West, demonstrating the "democratic" nature of Hungary and its competitive advantage.

But this is only half of the story. Why did the Hungarian elite think that the West cared whether they had a strong constitutional court or not? Procházka points out that neither EU nor Council of Europe required accession countries to have a Constitutional Court, even less a powerful one. Why did they think that a constitutional democracy had to put up with such aggressive activism? András Sajó warns against a perspective which relies too much on "legitimacy" to explain the court's success. He argues that the political elite were too divided to retaliate against the court. The court only ever mobilized a part of the elite, and sometimes a part of the population, against its decisions.[42] But even if we acknowledge that a part of the political elite's compliance can be explained "instrumentally," the compliance still remains striking. Stone Sweet's model helps to explain a further part of the story. Hungarian politics became constitutionalized because the Court became an effective dispute resolution forum, especially in questions of state organization. For example, it had to resolve the ambiguities of the constitution outlining the relationship between the president and the prime minister. The mere existence of the court could avoid constitutional crises which would have arisen from struggles over the "correct" interpretation of the constitution. It was able to preserve its triadic legitimacy by the techniques that Stone Sweet outlines: First of all, it justified its decisions with legal, not political, arguments therefore claiming to be a neutral body above politics. The Hungarian Court solved the "crisis of triadic legitimacy" by offering a jurisprudence based on a on the whole coherent system of principles which made it difficult for political actors to argue that the court was deciding the cases "politically."[43] The message Chief Justice of the Court László Sólyom

---

41 Frank Schimmelfennig, "International Socialization in the New Europe: Rational Action in an Institutional Environment," *European Journal of International Relations*, 6 (2000), pp. 109–139.

42 Sajó, *op. cit.* n. 38, p. 226.

43 Alexander Schmitt, "Die Rolle der Verfassungsgerichte im verfassungspolitischen Transformationsprozess in Polen, Ungarn und Russland," *Jahrbuch für Ostrecht*, 43 (2002), pp. 31–52.

incessantly voiced in the decisions of the court, in interviews, and articles, was that the court's reasoning could not be ad-hoc or arbitrary (and therefore political), but based on a coherent system of principles.

But again, this can only be a partial explanation, because there is no reason to believe that the Slovak Court, for example, could not have functioned the same way. Its decisions were prudent, and based on constitutional principles just as much as other more successful courts in the region.[44] To be sure, as Procházka points out, the legalistic reading of the constitution and the great delays in its decisions did not make the Slovak court an effective check on the Meciar government comparable to the Hungarian court.[45] But I argue that without looking at the elites to which the court's claim to legitimacy is directed, we cannot explain what happened in the post-Communist "judicial review" game. In Hungary, the Kádár-regime had undergone a slow legalization and rationalization of power in the late seventies and eighties.[46] Communist ideology had lost the little legitimation it might have gained after the 1956 uprising. On the other hand, the peculiarity of Hungarian socialism is the extensive exposure of its scientific and economic elite to Western ideas. Its critical intelligentsia was not thrown in jail, but rather sent off to the West to study or do research and upon its return was either co-opted into the system or simply left alone. Chief Justice László Sólyom, for example, spent long periods of time in Germany like many of his colleagues in the first court.[47] The reformers inside the party shared with the opposition the belief that Hungary should become a "Rechtsstaat", a state ruled by law, long before the advent of democracy.[48] To be sure, there was a wide gap in what "Rechtsstaat" meant specifically for the regime and for the opposition. But for both, the "law" became an important legitimating device. Similar developments could be witnessed in Poland,[49] but certainly, such a consensus was missing in the Slovak case.[50]

---

44 See Karel Vodicka, "Das Slowakische Verfassungsgericht im Transformationsprozess," in C. Boulanger (ed.), *Recht in der Transformation* (Berlin: Berliner Debatte Wissenschaftsverlag 2002), pp. 195–216.

45 Procházka, *op. cit.* n. 6, Sections 3.4 and 4.4.

46 Ágnes Zsidai, "Legitimität Kraft Legalität. Funktionswandel des Rechts in Ungarn," *Zeitschrift für Rechtssoziologie*, 17 (1996), pp. 249–258.

47 Georg Brunner and Herbert Küpper, "Der Einfluß des Deutschen Rechts auf die Transformation des Ungarischen Rechts nach der Wende durch Humboldt-Stipendiaten: Das Beispiel Verfassungsgericht," in Holger Fischer (ed.), *Auswirkungen der deutsch-ungarischen Wissenschaftsbeziehungen*, forthcoming.

48 Antal Örkény and Kim Lane Scheppele, "Rules of Law: The Complexity of Legality in Hungary," *International Journal of Sociology*, 26 (1997), pp. 76–94.

49 Klaus Ziemer, *Polens Weg in die Krise: eine politische Soziologie der "Ära Gierek"* (Frankfurt am Main: Athenäum 1987), p. 414.

50 On (missing) elite consensus in post-communist societies, see J. Higley, J. Pakulski, and W. Wesolowski (eds.), *Postcommunist Elites and Democracy in Eastern Europe* (London: MacMillan 1998).

To be sure, this does not mean that a strong constitutional judiciary was the inevitable result. "Rechtsstaat" is not the same as "Constitutionalism", and its relationship with judicial review is, I would argue, one of the historical developments rather than a theoretical logic. Legal positivism is hard to reconcile with judicial review in its modern form—that is, including basic rights. But in an environment of uncertainty and constitutional courts as institutions being largely unknown, this difference was not noticed. The Constitutional Court claimed to interpret "the law", in this case, the constitutional law. And no Hungarian politician from the mainstream of the political elite was prepared to openly advocate "illegal" measures such as defiance of Constitutional Court. The only exception was the extreme right which openly advocated the abolition of the Constitutional Court. But they never gained significant influence.

The final piece of the puzzle could be that of "Europe," and here I come to Kim Scheppele's argument. She has conducted interviews with parliamentarians whose legislative projects had been frustrated by the veto of the constitutional court. Asked why they accepted the sweeping judgements of the court, instead of relying on their own interpretation of the constitution, many of them reacted with surprise—how should they have not accepted given that a strong constitutional court was part and parcel of European constitutionalism. Scheppele argued that the Constitutional Court half relied on, half constructed itself, a "national imagery." This imagery was half "nationalist." It referred to a 19th century myth still alive in Hungarian collective memory, of a 1000-year-old constitutional tradition. According to Scheppele, this myth provided a resource for the legitimacy of post-transition Hungarian judicial constitutionalism. But it was also "European" as it referred to the idea, widespread among Hungarian intellectuals and policy-makers, that Hungary had always belonged to Europe and was currently "returning" to it. According to Scheppele, Europe was seen as the base of liberal Constitutionalism, and having a powerful court was part of being "European."[51] To be sure, rational choice theorists of all flavours will be quick to point out that we should not really believe these parliamentarians. Their answers might be nothing other than rationalizations of the motives that Procházka has pointed out in his comparative study: in the race to be first entrants to the European Union any argument might do. I would not dismiss the sceptics' allergy against cultural explanations since it represents a healthy antidote against Huntingtonian simplifications. But as Max Weber has taught us, arguments based on ideas, culture, or history can be made in a more sophisticated manner.

And in this case, there are a couple of indicators that Scheppele has pointed out as an interesting cultural phenomenon. As put forward by many authors, the idea of the "Europeanness" of Hungary has a long history.[52] The image of Europe

---

51 Scheppele, "Imagined Europe," above n. 8.

52 See, for example György Ránki and Attila Pók (eds.), *Hungary and European Civilization* (Budapest: Akadémiai Kiadó 1989) and György Borsányi et al., "Zwischen Zwei

has not been static, but has changed with the geo-political context. Europe was always a model for Hungarian intellectuals and a source of culture and advancement, favourably compared to their, half-feudal and under-industrialized country. However, after the end of the First World War (WWI), when Hungary lost two-thirds of its territory in the Treaty of Trianon, Europe was, for Hungarians, equated with the victorious *entente* resented as being responsible for its plight. After WWII, however, this image began to shift. During Soviet domination, "Europe", and especially "Central Europe," was a source of identification used to contrast Hungarianness from "Eastern Europe", meaning, the Soviet Union and its culture. This sentiment was shared among Hungarian, Polish, and Czechoslovak dissidents.[53]

Again, some of these developments can be found in other East Central European nations as well. There is nothing inherently "European" in a strong Constitutional Court—they only appear in a few model countries such as Germany. The Scandinavian countries do without such a court, and Britain still maintains parliamentary supremacy.

But what might have differentiated Hungary from Poland or the Czech Republic was the extent to which Hungarians were willing to submit to the imagined European standards. Elémer Hankiss writes about public attitudes at the beginning of the 1990s: "[It] was enough to utter the magic words DEMOCRACY, MARKET ECONOMY, EUROPE—words that resounded all around the country and everybody was happy."[54] While people did not associate the Court with market economy, ironically both "democracy" and "Europe" turned out to be symbolic resources for the court. Thus, damaging this picture in international opinion by attacking the court was out of the question. And even if some MPs within the coalition parties of the first and second parliament harboured thoughts to lash out against the court, the Prime Ministers would stifle any plan in this direction.

4. "DEMOCRATIC COURTOCRACY'?

I have already pointed to the "confusion," in the public sphere (which in Hungary is basically the Budapest public sphere) of positivist legalism and constitutionalism, which helped the court to established its authority. In a later paper, Scheppele points to a different confusion: between democracy and constitutionalism. According to Scheppele:

Ufern: Wandlungen des Ungarischen Europabildes," in Bundeszentrale für politische Bildung (ed.), *Europabilder in Mittel- und Osteuropa* (Bonn: Bundeszentrale für politische Bildung 1996), pp. 139–156.

53 See the well-known essay by Timothy Garton Ash, "Mitteleuropa?," in S. R. Graubard (ed.), *Eastern Europe . . . Central Europe . . . Europe* (Boulder: Westview Press 1991), pp. 1–22.

54 Elemér Hankiss, "Imponderabilia. The Formation of Social Conscience and the Government," in C. Gombár, E. Hankiss, L. Lengyel and G. Várnai (eds.), *Balance. The Hungarian Government 1990–1994* (Budapest: Korridor 1994), p. 35.

one way to see the other meaning of democracy—as a set of substantive commitments directed to policy and not just as a set of procedures for getting there—was in daily conversation (not with lawyers, but with others). It was common in the 1990s for Hungarians to say that something was "undemocratic" when it violated basic rights.[55]

Scheppele's claim that "courts can sometimes be more democratic than legislatures" (thus the subtitle of her paper) is instructive in this respect. She identifies democracy not with a formal distribution of decision-making power to the legislature, but as a "set of substantive commitments" and the possibility of participation in the political process. According to her, the Hungarian constitutional court became a forum for the general population. Whenever the government and the political parties often looked "like the communist-era government in the way they treated the citizenry (claiming laws should be applied retroactively, tampering with the media, picking out favourites for special treatment, picking out enemies for deprivations of rights)", the people could address all their complaints to the court by way of the *actio popularis*, and the "court sprung into action."

However sympathetic one might be towards the jurisprudence of the Hungarian Constitutional Court, it seems to over-stretch the concept of democracy to characterize the "courtocracy" of the early 1990s in Hungary. The *actio popularis* was basically a petition system, which left the judges with broad discretion as to what they wanted to decide. One basic element of a democratic arrangement, it seems to me, is accountability. This was not present in this system—the judges could not be recalled by the electorate for their decisions. Moreover, this is not how the judges themselves viewed their role. They did not think of themselves as serving the majority of the day, or even be the correctors of individual grievances. Their task, as they saw it, was to re-establish the "majesty of the law" in times of turbulence and short-sighted political passions. On the other hand, many people who put their trust into the Constitutional Court[56] did not so because of its democratic pedigree, but—as Holmes had sarcastically noted—probably because they yearned for an all-powerful institution, which would restore order and stability in the midst of chaotic and frightening social change.

For the purpose of my argument, it suffices to note that in Hungarian political discourse, the tension between democratic parliamentarism and constitutional adjudication was not urgently felt. There were few public critics of the court until late

---

55 Scheppele, above n. 12.

56 In public opinion surveys, the Constitutional Court was consistently the institution with the highest levels of trust, see Dóra Husz, "Intézmények presztízse 1989 és 1998 között," in S. Kurtán, P. Sándor and L. Vass (eds.), *Magyarország evtizedkönyve, 1988–1998* (Budapest: Demokrácia Kutatások Magyar Központja Alapítvány 1998), pp. 821–829. But the same is true for the Slovak case, see Martin Bútora and Thomas W. Skladony (eds.), *Slovakia 1996–1997. A Global Report on the State of Society* (Bratislava: Institute for Public Affairs 1998).

into its term, which ended around 1999. Their views were unpopular, especially among the liberal press in Budapest, which cheered the court's censures of the conservative government of the first four years. When the socialist-liberal government's legislative projects were equally censured by the court, the practice was too well established already.

The Hungarian public reacted with deep disillusionment and disappointment to the fact that democracy was not how they had thought it would be. László Sólyom's mission to establish the court as the "guardian of the rule of law revolution" succeeded, because the constitutionalism turned out to have higher legitimacy than parliamentarism. Of course, this is neither a full explanation for what happened in Hungary, nor a normative justification. As to the first, I have already mentioned the enormous importance of institutional rules. Without the *actio popularis*, the Solyom-court certainly could not have played the role it has. Had the roundtable negotiations instead implemented a German-type constitutional complaint procedure, the court might have decided a completely different set of questions, or might have gotten involved in a struggle with the ordinary judiciary, just as it has happened in the Czech Republic and, to a lesser degree, in Poland. Equally clear is the impact of judicial personalities. The first Hungarian court was to a very large degree a product of the ambitions and the vision of its first president. Had Géza Kilényi, the candidate of the reform communists, been given the post, we would have seen a very different court.[57]

5. CONCLUSION

Mauro Cappelletti has argued that for the "mighty problem" of judicial review—namely the implications of its counter-majoritarian character for the theory of democracy—there "can only be a relative solution, determined by contingent variables such as a given society's history and traditions, the particular demands and aspirations of that society, its political structure and processes, and the kind of judges it has produced."[58]

Cappelletti's argument is clearly borne from the case of Hungary. He takes both dimensions of legitimacy into account. While stressing that there is a legitimacy problem with the practice of judicial review, he does not—like many commentators—base this argument on purely abstract considerations. It is, however, important to note that by explaining judicial activism in this way I am not making a general case for "aristocratic" judicial activism in "transitional" times. Jurists are not, as a matter of fact, better suited to decide upon the structural

---

[57] This is disputed by Procházka, *op. cit.* n. 6, p. 263, who, based on a very structural reading of the situation CEE courts were in, claims that the Courts' jurisprudence would have been very similar even with different judges.

[58] Mauro Cappelletti, *op. cit.* n. 16, pp. 149–150.

dilemmas of (post-Communist or similar) regime changes, such as dealing with the past, property redistribution, welfare reform, and so on.

Let us take a step back from the case of Hungary and reconsider the social science perspective. At the beginning of this chapter, I reviewed empirical theories on the real-world limits of judicial activism, which have, so far, largely concentrated on the interests and ambitions of political actors.[59] In the section on Hungary, I have presented Kim Scheppele's argument on the "European" factor explaining part of the compliance of Hungarian elites towards controversial judicial rulings. I argued that the part of the compliance can be attributed to an abstract appeal of the "Rechtsstaat"—concept (a kind of "impersonal charisma"[60]) among Hungarian elites. Both ideas point in the same direction, that is, cultural dispositions which work as the background in front of which real-world politics occur. As Max Weber writes, in a commonly cited paragraph:

> Not ideas, but material and ideal interests, directly govern [human] conduct. Yet very frequently the "world images" that have been created by "ideas" have, like switchmen, determined the tracks along which action has been pushed by the dynamic of interest.[61]

Less often cited is the next sentence in which Weber refers to salvation strategies: "From what and for what one wished to be redeemed and, let us not forget, could be redeemed, depended upon one's image of the world." Hungarians, like Poles and Czechs, wanted to be saved from the communist, lawless, "Eastern European" past. But in Hungary, the Constitutional Court also offered to be a "salvatory" institution, one that promised to make Hungary better and more "European", in short: a "normal" country. This offer had been taken up by less-than-democratic attitudes in the Hungarian population. The yearning for an enlightened institution, which oversees the messy politics of the day—a sort of "philosopher-king."

I do not want to stretch the argument too far, since it would require more comparative analysis and empirical proof than I can offer in this short chapter. I would have to (as Scheppele would) present more evidence how the cultural background of Hungary was different from that of, for example, Poland or the Czech Republic, and how this affected the working of their Constitutional Courts. Procházka,

---

59 Vanberg, *op. cit.* n. 9, refers to public opinion as a factor in strategic power plays, but he does not explore the cultural background of public sentiment.

60 On the concept of "charisma" applied to "law", see C. Boulanger, "The Charisma of Law in Times of Transformation. Max Weber's Relevance for Understanding Institutional Change," paper presented at the conference *Law and Society Association and ISA RCSL Joint Meeting*, July 4–7, Budapest.

61 Hans H. Gerth and C. Wright Mills (eds.), *From Max Weber: Essays in Sociology* (London: Routledge 1948), p. 280. Had social scientists been attentive to this argument, formulated in the early 20th century, many of the fruitless "rational choice vs. cultural explanation" debates could have been avoided.

in his excellent comparative analysis of the Hungarian, Czech, Slovak and Polish court, points out the differences in legal traditions and notions of parliamentary sovereignty that differentiates the legal cultures of these countries.[62] Also, one cannot overlook the fact that the Hungarian court did not continue to be as powerful as it was in the early nineties, no matter how "European" the Hungarian elite or population felt.[63] Parliamentarians resented the court for its activism, and made sure that the next court would be much tamer.

My point is a different one. Maybe the argument could be rephrased in the context of the debate on "Geography and Democratic Destiny."[64] The thesis concerning where a country is located and which other countries it has historically been exposed to (through neighbourhood, occupation, colonization, cultural links, etc.) matters for its contemporary democratic development.[65] Due to reasons of historic tradition and exposure, Hungarians felt closer to Europe than Russians, who have for centuries fought an identity battle over whether they were Europeans, Westerners or something else. There were more Hungarians who could travel to Austria and Germany than citizens of, for example, Kazakhstan.[66] Hungarian thinking has been historically influenced by European developments in a much stronger way than elites in countries further in the East. In the more recent past, Hungarian constitutional lawyers did their research mostly in Germany and studied the *Bundesverfassungsgericht*, rather than the Supreme Court. It is true that "European Culture" is an ideological construction that has more to do with exclusion than inclusion—it is usually used to separate "us" and "them"—to differentiate "European civilization" against the "uncivilized" East or West.[67] But no matter how easily scornful analysts might want to deconstruct "Europe" as a myth, it remains a potent myth, and might be viewed as a self-fulfilling prophesy: those, but only those, who imagine being Europeans strongly enough will become Europeans over time.

---

62 Procházka, *op. cit.* n. 6.

63 See, for unfavourable comparisons of the "Németh"-court with the previous one, K.L. Scheppele, "The New Hungarian Constitutional Court," *East European Constitutional Review*, 8 (1999), pp. 81–87, and Scheppele, above n. 12.

64 Laurence Whitehead, "Geography and Democratic Destiny," *Journal of Democracy*, 10 (1999), pp. 74–79.

65 See also Jeffrey S. Kopstein and David A. Reilly, "Geographic Diffusion and the Transformation of the Post-Communist World," *World Politics*, 53 (2000), pp. 1–37.

66 Regimes matter, of course. There were also more Hungarians studying abroad than Czechs, because the Hungarian regime was much more "liberal" than the Czech.

67 On the latter, see Europe's attempt to distinguish itself from the U.S. regarding capital punishment, international conflict, and welfare state ideas.

Part III: The Rule of Law

12. *Barbarians ante portas* or the Post-Communist Rule of Law in Post-Democratic European Union

Adam Czarnota

1. Introduction

It is quite difficult to write about my topic due to the extensive debate on the Constitutional Treaty, prepared by the European Convention. The work of the European Convention has been closely connected with the first wave of eastern enlargements. This connection was confirmed by Chancellor Gerhard Schroeder who, in the *Palazzo dei Congressi* in Rome on October 4, 2003, the first day of the inter-governmental conference, said that "enlargement and the constitution are two sides of the same coin."

The complexity in writing about the enlargement process is that it is difficult to decide which perspective to adopt—that of the Eastern European, which I am, or that of the Western European. It is also possible to adopt a third perspective, that of a sympathetic external observer. In this chapter I have opted for a different approach: not the position of an impartial judge nor a prosecutor or defence lawyer but that of a sceptical lawyer, similar to what is known in legal procedure as an expert witness. The arguments for such an approach are partly obvious. I am an academic lawyer with interest in the constitutional structure of the European Union. I am also an Eastern European with some insight into the problems faced by the citizens of the new Member States.

The structure of this chapter is simple. I argue that Eastern Europeans wanted, and still want to, join the European Union but a Europe from the past rather than the present. I go on to look at the issues connected with the relationship between enlargement and constitutionalization in the European Union. I finish with some sceptical remarks relating to the prospects for a European rule of law.

2. Two Visions of Europe: Enlargement and Constitutional Treaty

There is a tendency to discuss the enlargement process from a short-term perspective. This is rather normal—it is what politics is about: not too much past unless it is used politically and not too much future since the electorate does not really care too much. What is left is the present. So in the media, as well as in scholarly studies, one can find plenty of articles debating the preparation of different future member states in adopting the *aquis communitaire* and fulfilling the criteria for the adoption

Wojciech Sadurski et al. (ed.), Spreading Democracy and the Rule of Law?, 283–297.

of some policies as per the accession treaty.[1] However, even the latter issue has been overshadowed by a new one—the fiasco of Rome's inter-governmental conference and the refusal to accept the draft Constitutional treaty by Spain and Poland. After the transfer of the Presidency to Ireland discussion on the constitutional treaty continued. In the end the Constitutional Treaty was adopted before the end of the Irish presidency, i.e. signed before the end of June 2004. This was made possible by the change in Spain's position after the last election and consequently the change in Poland's position in relation to the proposed voting system.

The entire presentation of the enlargement process has been overshadowed by the constitutional debate. Is this a correct approach? There is undoubtedly more to enlargement than the new Constitutional Treaty, but it is the treaty itself which is the most important event that will determine the direction of the process of European integration. As a result it is justifiable to look at enlargement from the constitutional point of view.

Another justification is historical. The collapse of communism was a historic moment and it was clear from the very beginning that the aim of Central and Eastern European states was to join NATO and the European Union. Post-communist Central and Eastern European states wanted security and economic prosperity. Security with the enlargement of NATO in March 2004 where Slovenia, Romania, Bulgaria as well as member states from the former Soviet Republic (Lithuania, Latvia and Estonia) were included as members. Still few countries which frequently express their ambitions to join the European Union and NATO, such as Georgia, have been left out. Nevertheless, the main precondition of security is in pretty good shape. That cannot be said about prosperity.

From the very beginning the Central and Eastern European approach to the European Union was partly utilitarian (money from Brussels) and partly status oriented (being reunited with the West). In other words post-communist Central and Eastern European states had their own image of the European Union, which they wanted to join, thus focusing more on the European Economic Community rather than the "European Union" as such. The difference lies in the perception of the constitutional structure of the Union as well as the scope of state sovereignty.

Eastern Europeans looked (and it seems to me they are still looking), at Europe as an infrastructure for economic benefit. That was the case at the time of the European Economic Communities. Even before the Maastricht Treaty which established the European Union with pillars II and III and the Amsterdam Treaty which deepened political Union there was more than just the European Economic Communities. There was a constitutional structure based on supremacy of European law and shared institutions, especially the European Court of Justice. The liberation

---

[1] See for instance B. Kaminski, "The Europe Agreements and Transition: Unique Returns from Integrating into European Union," in S. Antohi and V. Tismaneanu (eds.), *Between Past and Future. The Revolutions of 1989 and Their Aftermath* (Budapest: CEU Press 2000), pp. 306–331.

of Central and Eastern European countries from Moscow's yoke, with the consequent disintegration of the Yalta arrangement after the autumn of nations in 1989, has had a profound influence on the European Communities. It soon became obvious that integration will spill over the Elbe River.[2] Poland and Hungary after obtaining sovereignty expressed the desire to "join Europe." Other countries such as Czechoslovakia, and after the "velvet divorce" the Czech Republic, Baltic states, Slovenia, Bulgaria and Romania followed the same path. Very soon nearly all of the former communist states started to knock at the door of the European Union.

This enlargement not only required institutional change to prepare for a relatively smooth management of a larger number of member states. It became clear that a deeper integration over and above the economic area was necessary if integration was to be kept a live process. The outcome of that was acceleration of integration in the 1990s.[3] The Maastricht Treaty laid the political foundations for a deeper integration with the introduction of the Euro as a common currency. However, the violent lesson of the disintegration of the former Federal Republic of Yugoslavia shows how impotent Europeans were in coordinating foreign policy. This was partly addressed in the Treaty of Amsterdam with the creation of a new position of High Commissioner for Foreign Affairs. This institutional design is the outcome of a temporary political compromise. The acceleration of political integration after Maastricht is more than visible. The creation of a hard core of integration is also visible. Some countries opted out of the Euro zone or from the *Schengen aquis*. The response to that was an institutional acceleration, especially after the Treaty of Nice. The original six founding members played a crucial role in the preparation and work of European Convention.

The Treaty of Nice represented the logic of the old pattern of integration in its focus on enlargement. That is visible in its decision-making procedures and the distribution of votes between existing member states and future member states in the Council. The stress was on empowerment of the small member states at the expense of big member states. Such an institutional arrangement, which will exist until 2009, did not satisfy the powerhouse of the European Union, especially Germany, and prolonged the life of an institutional structure not suited for a Europe Union of 25 or 30 member states. Already at the inter-governmental conference in Nice, work started on future more radical changes in the European Union's institutional structures. As usual a crucial role was played by the original six founding members, especially France and Germany.

As expected, the outcome of the Convention is a compromise, but a few goals have been achieved. First, simplification of institutional structures and, second,

2 See Gary Marks, Fritz W. Scharpf, Phillipe C. Schmitter and Wolfgang Streeck, *Governance in the European Union* (London: Sage Publications, 1996).

3 See John Gillingham, *European Integration, 1950–2003. Superstate or New Market Economy*? (Cambridge: Cambridge University Press 2003), pp. 228–293.

simplification of the decision-making process. All of these changes will make the management of Union affairs a bit simpler. There are also proposed changes in the area of political integration in foreign affairs and defence. The most important meaning of the Constitutional Convention proposal is to shift from an inter-governmental decision-making process to a majority approach. That strengthens big states since votes will be based on population size.

This is not only a symbolic change, as some commentators suggest. Since the draft Constitutional Treaty presented by Valery Giscard d'Estaing in Thessaloniki, then discussed but with no result due to the opposition of Spain and Poland, was accepted at the inter-governmental conference under the Irish presidency, there was a more radical shift in the pattern of European integration. After the introduction of the provisions of the constitutional Treaty there will be an institutional structure to a new type of polity or using Phillippe C. Schmitter's words, a Euro-Polity.[4] A polity which does not have any parallel in history: neither an international organisation nor a federal state but a new polity which in order to be understood requires a new approach to the problem of sovereignty and democracy as well as accountability. The changes in the European Union are side effects of the collapse of communism and a direct effect of enlargement.

Are the countries of Central and Eastern post-communist Europe ready to become full members of such a Euro-Polity? Are they ready to accept limitation of their freshly discovered sovereignty? It seems to me that the answers to these questions do not have to be negative, but there is a chance that the entire project of European integration could be derailed or radically slowed down as a result of eastern enlargement. These countries are ready to become a part of a Euro-Polity in some areas and not in others. It is probably better to discuss the problematic areas involved in enlargement. Nevertheless the Union they apply to is no longer the Union they originally considered. The candidate countries applied to join an economic community and now they find themselves in a new type of polity.

3. EASTERN ENLARGEMENT: PROBLEMS AND PROSPECTS

In order to understand the peculiarities of eastern enlargement we have to take a closer look at the countries which became members of the European Union on 1 May 2004. But first I wish to make one historiosophical remark. Membership of the European Union is an enormously significant event in the history of the region. There is a chance that the eastern periphery of Europe will be reconnected to the main pattern of historical development. The region could be incorporated into Europe, but even with membership of the European Union it does not have to happen mechanically.

4 Phillippe C. Schmitter, "Imagining the Future of the Euro-Polity with the Help of New Concepts," in Marks *et al.*, *op.cit.* n. 2, pp. 121–150.

1. First of all, with the exception of Poland which is a middle weight, they are small countries.
2. Second, eastern enlargement includes countries which do not share long democratic and liberal traditions.[5] One exception is Czech Republic. This was not the case in other waves of enlargement. Even the case of Spain, Portugal and Greece was different to that of post-communist Central and Eastern Europe. They did not suffer from what is called the "simultaneity" problem characteristic of post-communist transformations. Their transformations were primarily centred on the polity. The new members have the task of transforming the polity, the economy and the society at the same time.
3. Third, their economies and infrastructure are far behind the European Union average. In other words there are huge discrepancies between efficiency of the economies in former communist states and in member states of the Union on the other side of the Oder River. Just to give some illustration. According to Eurostat, after enlargement, the population of the European Union grew by 20%—this is not the impact of Malta and Cyprus but of Central-Eastern Europe. At the same time the gross domestic product growth was only 5%. The economic power of all Central and Eastern new member states is roughly the same as the Netherlands. For example, the average cost of labour is 2.42 Euro, in Lithuania it is 2.71 Euro, in Estonia, 3.03 and in Poland an hour of labour costs 4.48 Euro. At the same time there is a huge gap in productivity. In the 15 countries of "old" Europe, a worker earns on an average 57.6 Euro, while in Poland the figure is 16.9 Euro. The lowest productivity is in Lithuania at 10.7 Euro. This data shows huge discrepancies in the economy, technology, know-how skills, organisation of labour, etc; in other words the traditional economical backwardness of Central and Eastern Europe since the XVI century continues. The good news is that Central and Eastern Europeans produce less rubbish. For instance, the average in the old Europe of 15 is 559 kg rubbish produced by person per year while in Poland it is only 272 kg. In this case it is evident that backwardness has its advantages.
4. Last but not the least, not all of these countries have a long history as an independent sovereign nation-state. As a result, they are over-sensitive to any attempt to limit their national sovereignty. We have to remember that apart from Slovenia, the new member states were independent for 20 years in between war periods. Before that, all of them were parts of three European empires: Russian, Austro-Hungarian and German. Independence and sovereignty lay behind the dismantling of Moscow's power or, in case of Slovenia, Belgrade's power. None of the new countries have any experience in being fully independent members of a world state system. Thus prevailing in public opinion and within the political

[5] Some scholars try to identify liberal nationalism, which for me is an oxymoron, especially in Central-Eastern Europe. See for instance Stefan Auer, *Liberal Nationalism in Central Europe* (London and New York: Routledge Curzon 2004).

class is that the notion of sovereignty is understood as total independence and self-government in all areas. This became clear in the debate in Poland on the constitutional treaty. The slogan "Nice or death" illustrates that approach.

It is not difficult to discern that all these areas include different political and social institutions and also collective consciousness. In other words the hardware and the software differs between the Europe of 15 and that of 25. One way of analyzing these differences is to distinguish between three types of constitutional legitimacy: polity legitimacy, regime legitimacy and performance legitimacy.[6]

3.1. Polity Legitimacy

We understand polity legitimacy as the overall support for the polity in question. Two elements are present in that notion:

1. a political element—the degree of autonomous political authority; and
2. a community dimension—a sense of common attachment and identification with the polity.

There is no problem of a shortage but rather of an oversupply of polity legitimacy in all Central and Eastern European post-communist countries. All of those countries are very proud to have recovered or received national independence. The political struggle against communism was mainly fuelled by national ideology. Support for national independence is shared by a broad spectrum of political opinion in these societies. It is visible in the *invention of traditions* of the glorious past of the nation and the belief that the nation can only flourish in the form of an independent nation-state. There are plenty of examples of growing nationalism.[7] The Constitutions of those countries reflect that rather romantic nationalism. A dominant attitude is expressed that the nation is based on primordial bonds of blood, culture and language. That the nation is a pre-political and pre-constitutional entity. The state belongs to the nation and the nation is more than just a political community of citizens. Citizens are bearers of rights but those rights are secondary to the interests of the nation.[8] The constitutions are not simple expressions of constitutional nationalism, but they are closer to constitutional nationalism than liberal constitutionalism.[9]

6 N. Walker, "The Idea of Constitutional Pluralism," *Modern Law Review*, 65 (2002) and attempt of application in "EU Constitutionalism in Transition: The Influence of Eastern Enlargement," *European Law Journal*, n. 9(3) (2003), pp. 365–385.

7 See Vladimir Tismaneanu, *Fantasies of Salvation. Democracy, Nationalism and Myth in Post-Communist Europe* (Princeton: Princeton University Press 1988), pp. 65–87.

8 A. Czarnota, "Constitutionalism, Nationalism, and the Law. Reflections on Law and Collective Identities in Central European Transformation," in *Teoria Prawa, Filozofia Prawa, Współczesne Prawoznawstwo* (Toruń 1998), pp. 29–48.

9 See J. Kis, *Constitutional Democracy* (Budapest: Central European University Press 2003).

Polity legitimacy is expressed in constitutions of member states usually in the form of a grand historical narrative in the preambles to the constitutions. Legitimacy expresses itself in a historical narrative, which plays an important role for the legal system of the state and has a very important role in the functioning (or non-functioning) of the rule of law. The historical narrative provides the legal system with normative coherence. Polity legitimacy is necessary for the existence of any state. Polity legitimacy based on a historical narrative is concentrated on high values and quite often is very difficult if not impossible to operationalize in the form of specific legal institutions. Polity legitimacy provides members of a nation with a historical roadmap giving answers to the questions where we come from and where are we going. That type of legitimacy is usually overlooked by constitutional lawyers and legal theoreticians. But the fact that it is overlooked by lawyers does not mean that it does not exist.

Polity legitimacy is not static but the process of its change is rather slow. It is always in the process of change. One thing is necessary for the very existence of polity legitimacy—namely a *demos*. Neither a *demos* in the form of citizens or nations, political community or romantic notion of a nation, exists at the EU level. Such nations exist in member states or future nation states but this does not mean that the sum of all *demoi* will create a *demos* of the European Union. The European Union, as a new type of a polity, does not possess its own *demos*. That is why there is so far no European discussion on the future of European Union. There is no sense of collective sharing of a foundational myth either.

As I mentioned above only nation-states need and depend on polity legitimacy. The European Union is a new type of polity and does not need that type of legitimacy. This does not exclude the possibility of creation of such legitimacy for the European Union in the distant future. In the discussion on the work of the Constitutional Convention there were some shy voices expressing hopes that Eastern European countries will be able to give a new life to the European integration process, including some input on how to lay the foundations for polity legitimacy. This was a wishful thinking. Eastern Europeans support the European Union but for totally different reasons. Some sociologists in the early 1990s formulated the theses that Central and Eastern European states were not ready to join the European Union since they did not go through the period of enjoyment of sovereignty. Arguably, they will find it difficult to surrender their own sovereignty to the EU, when they are only beginning to enjoy it themselves.

The problem of polity legitimacy is present in social rather than legal institutions, and especially in collective memory. The crux is the remembrance of collective experiences. Eastern enlargement is not only unhelpful in the creation or stimulation of polity legitimacy but it also triggers new problems. The European integration project has been premised on the negative experiences during WW II and the Cold War. The foundational myth for post-communist Central and Eastern European polities is the memory of suffering during the communist period as well as the struggle for independence and freedom. There is no one unified collective memory in the European Union but rather two different collective memories and thus at least two expressions of European identity. Perhaps Jacques Derrida's claim that Europe bears a crisis of memory, that it has forgotten its past was somewhat premature.[10] There is an explosion of memories in Western, Central and Eastern Europe. The problem lies in the fact that such memories are often incompatible and contradictory. Furthermore collective memories are not about the past but about the present. An example of two different memories dividing Europe was given by a recent reaction to the speech by Sandra Kalniete (Latvian Minister for Foreign Affairs and a future commissioner of the European Commission) at the Leipzig Book Fair on the 17 March 2004 in the historical *Gewandhaus* concert hall. In her talk she expressed what all people in post-communist Central and Eastern Europe accept as a given, namely the equality of suffering under two totalitarian regimes: Nazism and Communism. Such a statement, with which the large majority of Central and Eastern Europeans agree, caused enormous critical reaction from the German media. As a consequence the Western European, especially German, media accused Central and Eastern Europeans of moral relativism and . . . anti-semitism. Another example of this division can be found in the variant reactions to the publication "Black Book of Communism."

Due to the fact that historical collective memories diverge from one another the construction of a common European identity becomes a difficult (albeit possible) task.

Over the past two decades the European Commission has sponsored actions to enhance European identity using flags, hymns, TV channels and space programs as the means to create a sense of unity. These efforts have been useful but, as emphasised by Gerard Delanty,[11] what remains lacking is the "emotional value" of European identity. This "emotional value" is usually expressed by a memory of collective suffering. In Europe this idea of suffering has a different meaning for Western and Central and Eastern Europeans. So far, negative identity is enough to start the process of building a positive one. André Malraux observed that "(t)here is no Europe. There never was one." The history of European integration, and especially eastern enlargement, has undermined that statement. Political legitimacy is still a dream to be realised and the European Constitutional Treaty has provided the trigger for old and new member states to embark on this challenging journey.

3.2. Regime Legitimacy

This form of legitimacy relates to the type of organisation of the state, its institutional structure and the basic principles of operation, the constitutional structure of the state, and its socio-political organization. Regime legitimacy is a politically

10 Jacques Derrida, *The Other Heading: Reflections on Today's Europe* (Bloomington: Indiana University Press 1994), pp. 2–5.

11 Gerard Delanty, *Inventing Europe: Idea, Identity, Reality* (London: MacMillan 1995), p. 132.

contested area, and in comparison with polity legitimacy is not only about high values but about the implementation of values in institutional practices. From this perspective, it is interesting to compare the European Union of 15 and Central and Eastern European states.

The European Union has some problems with regime legitimacy but they are not, at present, considered serious problems. It appears that the task of the European Convention was to improve regime legitimacy. But it is possible to say the same about each new inter-governmental conference which initiates a new political push. With eastern enlargement further problems will occur with respect to regime legitimacy, and will be quite distinct from the normal criticism of democracy deficit.

So far the main criticism of the European Union's institutional structure has been focused on this deficit. If we apply the dominant criteria of liberal-democratic constitutionalism, we will easily discover that the European Union institutional structure does not fit in that matrix. The institutional structure does not express the basic principles of a democratic polity, such as one person one vote or majority rule, and also does not express the basic principles of constitutionalism, such as a clear division of powers between the legislative, the executive and the judiciary. Even the independence of the judiciary could be doubted since judges of the European Court of Justice and the Court of First Instance are restricted to teleological interpretations of European law. This is all true, but the criticism is, in my view, based on a misconception. The European Union is not a state in the traditional sense. It is not an authoritative state but rather a "not yet fully conceptualised" *new type of polity*. This new type of polity is similar to network organisations. From the constitutional point of view it is better to apply the so-called new constitutionalism to the analyses of the operation of the institutional regime of the European Union.[12] Such an approach has a better explanatory power than the traditional sovereignty centred understanding of constitutionalism. A distinguished legal theoretician and former MEP, and also member of the European Convention, calls it "*suigenericity.*"[13]

Notwithstanding the fact that the European Union is not organised according to the principles of democratic-liberal constitutionalism, it has presented itself as a guardian of (the implementation of) such principles at the member state level. The incoming eastern enlargement plays an important role in this. The European Union has for a long time already possessed a functional constitution but not a formal one. It is possible to argue that the Constitutional Treaty displays two tendencies with respect to governance of the Union.

1. A populist approach—which focuses on the election of representatives to European offices by the mythical population of Europe. That approach is based on

---

[12] J. H. H. Weiler, *The Constitution of Europe. "Do the new clothes have an emperor?" and other essays on European integration* (Cambridge: Cambridge University Press 1999), pp. 221–286.

[13] Neil MacCormick, *Questioning Sovereignty* (Oxford: Clarendon Press 1999), Chapt. 9.

the presupposition that state sovereignty continues to exist but that each state exchanges its autonomy for some other goods. It assumes that at any moment it is possible to exit the Union and return to the *status quo ante* of full sovereignty. Such an approach underlies the equality of actors in the European Union. The borders of sovereignty are blurred, however. In effect stronger actors can manipulate the weaker members of the Union.

2. The second approach is legal where the sovereign is the law. Politics is not perceived as arena of struggle for power but as the means to achieve the aims. The crucial issue is the autonomy of the Union's institutions that create their own rules of the game. These are created through law. Thus it follows that strong states should control the lawmaking institutions.

In earlier waves of succession, prior to the eastern enlargement, issues relating to political regimes were not articulated. The criteria for accession were codified with the adoption of the *acquis*. The question only arose when the former communist states began to knock on the European Union's door. The political criteria for membership was formally specified at the European Council meeting in Copenhagen in 1993, thereby creating the "Copenhagen criteria." The Council announced what Wojciech Sadurski has called the "canonical yardstick" where the applicant state, in order to be successful in the pursuit of full membership, must enjoy, inter alia, ensure the "stability of institutions guaranteeing democracy, the rule of law, human rights and respect for and protection of minorities." Thus future membership becomes conditional upon the fulfilment of some regime criteria therefore crossing the threshold to liberal constitutional-democracy. It is interesting to note that all candidate states were, at the time, members of the Council of Europe. This meant that they had ratified and complied with the European Convention of Human Rights and were under the monitoring system established by the Council of Europe. Since 1990 the Council of Europe set up the European Commission for Democracy through Law, the so-called Venice Commission, with the aim of helping draft constitutions for Eastern European states. Despite the assurances by Eastern European brothers and sisters to embrace democracy, the rule of law and human rights the EU adopted a suspicious approach. Political criteria conditionality was assessed in yearly reports of each candidate country, but I doubt if these played any significant role in the process of building human rights and constitutional culture in Central and Eastern Europe. It is true that Slovakia was admitted to the process once again after Meciar lost the last election but in all the 8 plus 2 (Bulgaria and Romania), this process was rather insignificant. We now know, after the successful and completed accession negotiations in Copenhagen in December 2002 and after the signing of the accession treaty in Athens this year, which of these criteria did not play an important role in the negotiation process. As a symbolic weapon these criteria help to distinguish between "old" and "new" Europe, to use the expression born of a totally different situation by US Defence Secretary Rumsfeld. It shows the sort of ambivalent approach to poor fellow Europeans from the East tainted by a communist past. The more positive interpretation of this is the EU's point of view that they are trying to encourage Central and Eastern European countries to develop institutions similar to those of Western Europe. A more cynical understanding is that the political criteria were designed to be used as a deterrent should there not be enough political will to include a certain member state.

The political criteria used for Central-Eastern Europeans—let us call them here "B" Europeans, started to be mentioned in relation to old Europe. In article 6(1) of the Treaty of Amsterdam we read "(t)he Union is founded on the principles of liberty, democracy, respect for human rights and fundamental freedoms, and the rule of law, principles which are common to member states." In that way the principles in the Amsterdam Treaty became an explicit precondition for European Union membership.[14]

Austria's boycott in 2001, when the Freedom Party became a member of the ruling coalition, was not a complete but a partial application of these criteria to member states. A higher emphasis on political criteria can be seen in Parts 1 and 2 of the Draft Constitutional Treaty prepared by the European Convention and presented to the Council in Thessaloniki.

Sociological polls conducted in the countries of Central and Eastern Europe show that there are great expectations connected with the membership of the European Union. These not only relate to the love of the Euro as a mighty currency. It is true that in the past 13 years one can observe a shift in the approach of Eastern Europeans, from Eros to Euro, but still the perception that the EU represents a rise in status persists and exists. One important expectation is that of improvement, not only of efficiency in government and administration but also in the basic structural sense of organising the institutions of future member states. People do believe that the Union will fix the constitutional structure of the state. Such an expectation is unrealistic but it could happen as a side effect of membership in the Union. There will be pressure coming from the Union and other countries for adjustment of the institutional structure. For instance, institutions dealing with customs and border control within the *Schengen aquis* or the court system within the new member states. We have to keep in mind that, in the European Union, institutions of member states play a crucial role in the implementation of Community law and policy. The relationship between Union and member states is not based on a classic federal distribution of powers but on dependency and cooperation.

This leads me to one of the crucial issues—namely the rule of law in post-communist countries and its relation to enlargement. One of the crucial problems which undermines the legitimacy of regimes in Central and Eastern Europe is related to issues of law and order as well as the delay in the implementation of justice. The first problem is partly connected with the almost permanent crisis of public

---

14 Manfred Novak, "Human Rights "Conditionality" in Relation to Entry to, and Full EU Membership in the EU," in Philip Alston (ed.), *The EU and Human Rights* (Oxford: Oxford University Press 1999), pp. 689–690.

finances whereas the second is concerned with constitutional and institutional decisions. The majority of Central and Eastern Europe cases before the European Court of Human Rights in Strasbourg are due to the delay of justice. One problem is the inefficiency of the court systems, which in turn impacts upon the operation of the market. The implementation of Community law in member states was mainly through the direct application of that law by state courts of the lowest magistrate level. The two basic principles of the Community law, namely supremacy and direct applicability were realised through active support given by member state courts. This requires judges that are competent in Community as well as their own legal system. The main legal device which worked in the implementation of Community law was the preliminary ruling which enabled local judges to be able to ask questions to the judges in the European Court of Justice and the Court of First Instance. I am not sure that judges in Central and Eastern European countries are ready to use this mechanism. I am not confident that they are sufficiently familiar with Community law. One of the indications in the Polish case could be the direct use of the Polish Constitution by ordinary courts. In recent years judges are able to do so albeit cautiously. Years of training in a positivist perception of law and with "judicial dependence" in thinking has left Central and Eastern European courts ill prepared to become part of the European legal space.

This very centralised system of courts does not support efficient harmonisation of domestic law with the *acquis communataire*. Harmonisation can not solely be left to national legislature but should be pursued by the actions of the courts. However, during the candidacy period this was not the case since the method of harmonisation by courts was controlled by the highest domestic judicial bodies.[15]

3.3. Performance Legitimacy

This type of legitimacy is sometimes referred to as "output legitimacy." This concerns the capacity of the state to produce effective and efficient performance in accordance with chosen criteria that are important from the point of view of the particular political community. It focuses on "delivering the goods" understood over and above the purely economic sense. This type of legitimacy is closely connected with regime legitimacy and sometimes it is difficult to analytically separate the two.

In all eight countries there is a problem with the efficiency of the government, with ineffective administration, with corruption and all the ills connected with "political capitalism" where public position is translated in order to extract economic rents. The blurred boundary between the public and private sphere, connected with

---

15 See Zdenek Kuhn, "Application of European Law in Central European Candidate Countries," *European Law Review*, 18 (2003), pp. 551–560. For an overview of the problem with the system of the administration of justice in post-communist states, see J. Priban, P. Roberts and J. Young (eds.), *System of Justice in Transition. Central European Experiences Since 1989* (Ashgate: Aldershot Burlington 2003).

the extraction of public funds to private pockets, is one of the obstacles, from the citizens point of view, of efficiency of the economy. This phenomenon was described by a sociologist as a "recombined property system" or "hybrid type of property."[16] There also exist organised markets with restricted entry depending on political decisions.

Citizens of Central and Eastern European countries have the expectation that membership to the European Union, and thus the role of the European Commission, will solve the problems of inefficiency and corrupt administration. The surprisingly high turnout in referenda on the association treaty shows that these expectations are pretty high. The choice made by those who voted in favour was a "civilizational" one. They voted for efficiency and economic well-being. They believe that the European Union will provide proper infrastructure for "life with dignity." This of course can not be fully done by the European Union alone. After signing the accession treaty in Copenhagen in December last year, more clouds have appeared over the expected enjoyment of full membership by new member states. It looks as though they will not be able to use all the funds committed in Copenhagen due to inefficiency of domestic administration and lack of matching funds in the state budget.

In the opening discussion about the next European Union budget there are already deliberations on the nationalization of the structural fund, which shows that European solidarity after enlargement is not in good shape. The Lisbon strategy is not in the interest of the new underdeveloped countries but rather of the developed countries of the hard core of the European Union, which wants to stimulate their own stagnant economies. High technical, ecological and social standards are not in the economic interests of new member states. The idea to compete with the USA in the so-called frontier technologies is also not expressing the interests of new member states. Similarly, the financing of the super speed train (TGV–Paris–Berlin) from the Union's budget is also not taking the new member states into account.

In other words the economies of new member states before their full convergence, which will take a generation, require soft standards in the regulation of the market. The example of the former DDR, which is in stagnation since 1996 despite huge amounts of subsidies from the German federal budget, shows how not to integrate Central and Eastern European markets.

Adjusting to this hard economic reality by soft, exceptional regulations could, however, collide with expectations regarding efficiency of the law itself. The rule of law requires clear, stable, predictable legal frameworks. Soft economic regulation is based on discretion which in turn stimulates corruption or other types of abuse of the system.

---

16 J. Staniszkis, *Postkomunizm: Próba Opisu* (Gdańsk 2001), pp. 190–227 and D. Stark and L. Bruszt, *Postsocialist Pathways. Transforming Politics and Property in East Central Europe* (Cambridge: Cambridge University Press 1998).

One of the specialities of Central and Eastern Europe is the pattern of informal operations due to the distrust of authorities.[17] Such a phenomenon was independently discovered in two parts of the region at the beginning of the XX century—Leon Petrażycki called it intuitive law and Eugen Ehrlich gave it the name living law. After accession the informality present in eight new states will undoubtedly become a noticeable phenomenon in the European Union. According to legal sociologists, such informal practices will have a corruptive effect on the rule of law. Would membership in the European Union be a remedy for informal practices? Would it provide another stimulus to strengthen the very fragile rule of law in post-communist Central and Eastern Europe? There is no clear answer to these questions. One way to approach the question is to show tendencies present in the European Union and then speculate upon their impact on the rule of law in Central and Eastern Europe.

Within the European Union there are two different tendencies, described above in the context of constitutional debate, as far as vision of the governance of the Union is concerned. The choice of direction—more rule of law oriented or more populist oriented—will have a profound impact on prospects for the rule of law in new member states. In any case, the contemporary institutional structure of governance of the European Union favours the executive branch of power. Taking into account the weakness of the judiciary it does not promise a bright future for rule of law.

4. Infranationalism and Post-Communist Rule of Law

There is another phenomenon which shows some similarities between the European Union and Central and Eastern European states. Some more intelligent lawyers and political scientists have noticed a new development in the governance of the European Union. Joseph Weiler called it *infranationalism*,

> based on realisation that increasingly large sectors of Community norm creation are done at the meso-level of governance. The actors involved are middle-range officials of the Community and the member States in combination with a variety of private and semi-public body players. Comitology and the remaining netherworld of Community committees is the arena, and the political science of networks is the current analytical tool which tries to explain the functioning of this form of governance. From the constitutional point of view infranationalism is not constitutional or unconstitutional. It is outside the constitution. The constitutional vocabulary is built around "branches" of government, around constitutional functions, and around the concept of delegation, separation, checks and balances among the arms of government, etc. Infranationalism is like the emergence of viruses for which antibiotics, geared towards control of microbes

[17] See for instance D. J. Galligan and M. Kurkchiyan (eds.), *Law and Informal Practices. The Post-Communist Experience* (Oxford: Oxford University Press 2003).

and germs, were simply ill-suited. Infranationalism renders the nation and state hollow and its institutions meaningless as a vehicle for both understanding and controlling government. . . .[18]

If Joseph Weiler is right, and I believe he is, then post-communist Central and Eastern European countries with their own networks and façade-type rule of law are well prepared to become part of an *infranational* European Union.[19] In this sense post-communist rule of law will join a post-democratic European Union. But then such a marriage will be at the expense of the average citizen on both sides of the Elbe River.

---

18 Weiler, *op. cit.* n. 12, pp. 98–99.

19 See M. Łoś and A. Zybertowicz, *Privatizing the Police-State. The Case of Poland* (New York: St. Martin's Press, 2000).

13. Transformation and Integration of Legal Cultures and Discourses—Poland

Marek Zirk-Sadowski

1. Introduction: the Transformation of Law and its Integration—an Attempt to Periodize

The initial period of the transformation of law can be compared to Balcerowicz's reforms in the economy. The transformation was primarily manifest in building the foundations of the rule of law. The beginning of this process was not identical to the beginning of the new state. The turning point was the Act of 1988 on business activity, which proclaimed economic freedom for the citizens and opened a possibility to reconstruct a free market economy. Other civil liberties and rights as well as their content had been discussed as early as in the 1980s in the circles of opposition lawyers, and it was not difficult to accept them. They were primarily derived from international treaties signed by Poland. As the process of building the catalogue of these rights assumed at the same time the continuity of Polish law and taking over of the former commitments of the People's Republic of Poland, it proved relatively simple to formulate them and it took, altogether, about three years, culminating in the promulgation of the so-called Small Constitution. Prime Minister Bielecki's government closed this process, approximately.

It should be noted that the old Constitution of 1952 was not annulled; some fragments of it were merely modified and the Small Constitution was added. This was in the period preceding the integration of Polish law with European Union law. Within the framework of this law, "a social device" was constructed and it was only this that was able to integrate. There was a shift from the Law legalizing a certain political order (where law was subordinated to politics and economy), to a Law that legitimizes a political order and is, therefore, autonomous in relation to politics and the sphere of economics. It can be said that a new constitutional order was created and consisted of the gradual inclusion of unwritten constitutional customs. This was the background for the first divisions within the legal order. They were mainly connected with the conflict of different conceptions of the structure of power in Poland.

The dispute primarily concerned the relationship between the executive and the legislative powers: for instance, deciding upon the President's powers or, more fundamentally, deciding whether the Polish system was to be presidential or cabinet-parliamentary. In attempting to gain an for the advantage the President, a very active interpretation of the Constitution and fundamental laws was applied. It was only then that the general public recognized, for the first time, the role of interpretation

Wojciech Sadurski et al. (ed.), Spreading Democracy and the Rule of Law?, 299–311.

in public law, even though this was perceived of as some form of abuse or avoidance of law. This role was even given a special name: "Falandisation of law" (from the name of Professor Lech Falandysz, President Walesa's legal adviser) which has remained in use until today.

During this period, society did not regard law as a phenomenon requiring a discourse and specification in the communication processes. Lawyers played the role of "guardians of law" whose main task was to recognize law as the content of the Sovereign's will and possibly to explain it.

This period ended around 1993 when new legal acts were being introduced, and partly implemented from the European Community order. Fundamental changes took place between the citizen–state relationship due to the appearance of a new tax system. The universality of income tax and the act on goods and services tax (VAT) significantly complicated economic activity. Notably, VAT was the first to reveal the "strangeness" of the new law. VAT is a mechanism of transferring invoices and it works without being complemented with any moral norms. The question of guilt or causality is of no significance under the conditions of a legal error and is not applicable when determining the sanctions for violating the rules of VAT calculation. Since this tax is based on self-calculation, one cannot safely be its payer without the help of a skilled accountant or tax adviser.

With these foregoing measures, the Law—for the first time—went beyond the framework of everyday moral and conventional duties. And subsequent implementations of European law only intensified this feeling. As a result, a transformation of the law coupled with its integration took place. Society, however, perceived this process as the price of the law's European character and not as the construction of law serving a more complex economic role.

Another feature of the post-1993 period was the discussion on the limits of acquired legal rights. The activity of the Ombudsman (E. Łętowska) led to the preservation of a number of rights acquired in the former state, even if it was against the newly established law and moral assessments. The most important discussions concerned car purchase coupons, combatant's rights and co-operative law. The sphere of the so-called rightfully acquired legal rights became manifest for the first time. This construction was also not very transparent for the general public, which was used to treating law as a kind of instruction. The case law of the Constitutional Tribunal, the Supreme Court and the Supreme Administrative Court proved that it was necessary to shift from the understanding of law as a sort of Leviathan (Hobbes) to law understood as an order anchored in a citizen's sense of freedom and an individual's rights (Locke). However, no appropriate legal discourse appeared at the social level. Individual rights were defined by an elite group of lawyers. This gave the impression that individual rights were independent from the political dimension.

This process, in principle, ended in 1997 with the new Constitution. During its drafting, the catalogue of human rights and civil rights was finally defined. From the point of view of the system, foundations were built in for the Parliament's (the Sejm's) advantage in the structure of the state which at present manifests itself as a kind of parliamentocracy. Courts receded into the background regarding the formulation of the content of law, and their place was taken up by political discourse which is now perceived of as a primary source of legal regulation. Thus the third period of law began. Whereas the first period consisted of building the basic structure of the state and the rule of law, and the second in defining the citizen's freedom in relation to the law made by the state, a distinctive feature of the third period was the fight for the principles of translating political interests into legal categories and legal rules limiting the political game.

In the second and the third periods, society perceived law as a construct made somehow without its participation. Between 1993 and 1997, law was regarded as a product of lawyers' elites, and after 1997—as a product of the political class.

Introducing the principles of the rule of law and building the fundamental law institutions was obvious from the social point of view, and the citizens did not find it difficult to assimilate the mechanisms of the system. To begin a more sophisticated legal–political–economic game and anchor individual rights into culture required argumentative activation on the part of society, as well as its participation in the discursive conception of legal obligations. However, in public consciousness legal obligations continued to be treated as a derivative of coercion, and legal rights were perceived as a kind of good. It was not possible to leave out this stage. A certain analogy with business activities can be noticed here: after a period of simple management in a small enterprise some capital is accumulated and it is necessary to pass to a new, more complex phase of management based on communication in the economic process.

The interests protected by law were still regarded as "received" and not resulting from negotiations or discussions. Those who received them sought to keep them at all costs, not joining the game of arguments revolving around the content of legal duties. This phenomenon can be defined as the "lack of consolidation", i.e. authoritative reforms introducing new rules of the game are effected but in order for these reforms to "work", large groups of society must incorporate the new rules of the game into their activities. However, these new rules have not even been fully understood; nor have interest groups, founded on these new rules, appeared—as a consequence the "entrenching" of known or already articulated interests took place.

The law of the period of the Polish People's Republic was based on orders and so was a sort of instruction. During the transformation, it should have turned into an argumentative game but instead, it became a more complicated hyper-instruction. In this way, the court stopped being regarded as "justice" and is perceived as a place of granting social "bonuses", i.e. it generates a division into bonus-granters and bonus-receivers. The interpretation of law is perceived as "justifying decisions" and not as the argumentative development of the content of the law.

2. DISINTEGRATING FACTORS IN THE LEGISLATURE

An ideal social position in this game is to be a "hyper-instruction" maker. Besides the division into lawyers and citizens, a new division became visible: into "hyper-instruction" makers and those who are subject to it. The legislature is not perceived as a place of the translation of political interests into legal categories but as a place of granting secret privileges.

From the legal point of view, the legislature translates the political, economic, social interests, articulated in democratic discourse, into legal categories. The primary set of legal categories is created by the doctrine of the "rule of law" state. What results from the legislature's activity are general norms (addressed to classes of receivers and regulating classes of behaviours), expressed in natural language and published in the form of legal text. This text must, by the nature of things, be interpreted since natural language is an imperfect tool of communicating norms, of controlling human behaviors.[1] Even in direct communication it is a fallible instrument. The legislature, in turn, is a source of indirect communication in which language itself plays a decisive role. The generality and totality of legal norms (following from the prohibition of building law as a set of privileges) intensifies the problems of communicating legal norms. In principle, there is no possibility of the direct application of legal provisions contained in a legal text. Passing a sentence and a decision and then its enforcement requires prior "adjustment" of the text to a concrete case through a special legal discourse called the adjustment of law.

The application of law is from this point of view a discourse conducted by lawyers and the legal text is its point of departure. Using special types of argumentation and associating legal and actual issues (hearing of evidence or explanatory proceedings) they formulate judgments deciding in individual and concrete legal problems.

In this approach, building a good model of the legislature is highly dependent on the quality of democracy itself. Democratic discourse of bad quality, difficulties with determining political, economic or social interests and a wrong choice of interest diminish (from the point of view of the content) the quality of the legislature itself. This is a principal matter in Poland. However good the legal service of the legislative process is, it cannot repair the deficits of democracy itself. Thus, the legislature cannot be improved without improving the democratic process of articulating social interests; therefore this issue is an object of research in the political dimension. At this point, it is necessary to note the isolation of Polish political, economic and legal thought. The weakness of the Polish reflection on the quality of the legislature comes from the lack of syntheses, which would embrace all these aspects. The legislature is usually investigated in one of the mentioned dimensions without attempting to give holistic diagnoses.

---

1 Jerzy Wróblewski, *The Judicial Application of Law*, trans. Zenon Bankowski and Neil MacCormick (Dordrecht, Boston, London: Kluwer Academic Publishers, 1992), p. 97.

This problem is to a great extent transferred into the public discourse on the legislature. Initially, in the period of introducing the fundamental institutions of the state of rule of law the dimension of legislative technique was mainly discerned in law-making. The quality of the legal text was considered and in its defects the weakness of the legislature was seen. Discussions on the clarity of legal text dominated.

With legal regulations becoming more and more complicated, there appeared considerations on the economic dimension of the legislature. Only recently have the so-called corruption affairs led, paradoxically, to understanding the multi-dimensionality of the legislature. The public discourse, taking place primarily in the mass-media, concerns the problem of the legislature's ties with the quality of democracy as such and its capability of expressing the political interests of particular social groups in terms of the rule of law state.

During the third term of office, as many as 640 Acts were adopted while the previous also full term of office the Sejm, adopted 473 Acts. The current Sejm also works very fast: 394 Acts have already been adopted and it is not even half-way through the fourth term of office. During the previous term of office five Acts on average were adopted at each of the meetings and last year the number of adopted Acts exceeded an average of nine falling on each meeting.

The evaluation of the works of the Polish legislature made in the mentioned institutions is not good: a lot of legislative work is being done but its quality is low. In the first place, the translation of economic and political interests into the categories of the rule of law state is often incomplete in the sense that legal categories are most frequently sacrificed in favor of the economic or political good. Retroaction can be regarded as an obvious error in the art of legislation. However, the most frequent error consists of formulating normative acts in a lengthy and descriptive language, which results in it losing its normative force.

There are legal regulations whose function is not to express and protect the economic interest of a specific social group but only to delay the moment of facing the real solution to the problem. Through apparent legal categories, i.e. those which have weak normative force as a result of using vague formulations in the legal text, the political authority gains time to prepare itself for the next stage of the dispute.

Such measures sometimes serve to transfer political responsibility for the content of a normative act onto the judicial power since the vagueness of the text requires that a court, in the process of the application of law, effects its purposive interpretation. From the argumentative point of view, this kind of interpretation weakly connects a judgment with the legal text. The doubtful rules of reasoning based on purpose relationships result in the fact that the judgment itself loses its normative force. In this way, the political authority which created a vague legal text to simulate a solution of a social conflict shifts the responsibility for this conflict onto the judicial authority.

A similar role is played by the lack of terminological uniformity, using notions from different branches of law, which leads to the incompleteness of patterns of procedures which are subject to regulation. In many cases, even acts do not contain definitions of the notions used in them. This makes it possible to use the legal text to omit law and to apply acts contradictorily to the aim of regulation.

All this results in an increase in the number of amendments and, at the same time, in shortages of consolidated texts of laws. The numerous amendments of law are not formulated in consolidated texts, which make it impossible for an ordinary citizen not only to apply them but even to become acquainted with their content. These phenomena raise particular concerns with regard to tax law since its application by tax-payers is, for this reason, difficult.

Of course, a significant number of these errors are not only technical errors. Many of them result from politics. Political trade-offs become visible in the translation of political and economic interests into legal categories. Very often, for reasons regarding the real condition of the state's finances, legal texts are apparent regulations. The vagueness of legal expressions and the absence of legal definitions are used for manipulation in order to water down the financial effects of the regulation.

The deficits in the activity of the legislature result in a significant degree of haste and poor preparation of legal acts. However, the primary problem lies in disturbances in the process of communicating political interests within legal discourse which is conducted in the institutions of the "rule of law" state. The Polish political class is not prepared to use these categories and regards legal notions as purely conventional which is why there is not only a lack of cohesion in the system of law but also a dysfunction within it. In this way a whole chain of communication barriers is formed, which results in poor legislation. With respect to society, the inability to use arguments and practical discourses can be observed. Thus the processes of articulating group interests are hindered. In turn, the political discourse not being linked to the social (practical) discourse is increasingly incapable of extracting general interest from group interests and to a high degree serves to present private interests as political interests. Since this phenomenon is impossible to hide within legal categories because of the guarantee of procedural protection of fundamental civil rights, the infringement of the structures of legal notions and institutions takes place. At the same time, manipulating the structure of law serves to hide the "privatization" of general interest since the legal text is almost unintelligible for an ordinary citizen. In this way legal measures become the lens through which all the deficits of Polish democracy can be viewed. Thus the legislature in Poland has become primarily a political activity in which the translation of political interests into legal categories is of no significance for the legislators.

3. Disintegrating Factors in Application of Law and its Enforcement

In the wide meaning of this word, the enforcement of law is the application of law, i.e. constructing individual and concrete norms (judgments, administrative decisions) on the basis of abstract and general norms issued by the legislature. In the narrow meaning, the enforcement of law is only the effecting of judicial and administrative decisions. The condition of the Polish judiciary constitutes the primary problem of the widely understood enforcement of law.

The increasing number of cases subject to consideration by courts results from the extending scope of the rule of law state. However, this is being done without a reform in the judicature, within the framework of the conception of a judiciary which decided two million cases at the most by the end of the 1980s. So justice requires very strong financial support. The development of the institutions of the "rule of law" state cannot take place without developing the judicature. The present situation hangs a big question mark over Poland's implementation of a citizen's right to reliable court proceedings.

The above phenomena result in society's growing dissatisfaction with the operation of legal institutions. Of course, there are some factors which arouse in citizens a sense of disappointment with the judicature. Some of them are not connected with irregularities in the work of Polish courts.

However, Polish society is only starting to understand the model of legal culture characteristic of liberal countries. The 1980s crisis of law and the obvious defects of the legal order from those years created a simplified ideal of legal order where the accent was put on consistency of law with morality and fundamental human rights. The complex form of liberal legal culture, based on the conception of attitudinally neutral law, granting access to courts to everybody, granting vast guarantees of formal justice and the right to a reliable trial was not easily accepted by society who desired a quick and explicit reaction to infringements of law. Also the low quality of legal provisions was transferred to the evaluation of the quality of judicial decisions since it yielded a significant lack of uniformity of judicial interpretation. The large scale of implementation of new legal institutions into Polish law results in the fact that law cannot be understood by its addressees, at least in its functional sense.

And lastly, a social belief about the presence of bureaucratic anarchy in the state is spreading widely. The state is perceived by its citizens as a facet of disorder, the removal of bonds and anarchization of social life, and courts are regarded as part of this mechanism.

Besides financial expenditure, an overall reform of the system of justice is necessary: it should be based on the simplification of procedures, particularly in so-called small cases, on raising the judges' ethical level and changing their attitude towards the applied law. Judges are accused of misunderstood professional solidarity. Lawyers' corporations are blamed for excessive defence of their members' interests, even at the cost of the good of the administration of justice. The specific "guildicization" of lawyers is regarded as a manifestation of the ethical crisis of the judicature.[2]

---

2 Marek Zirk-Sadowski, "Uczestniczenie prawników w kulturze" [The participation of lawyers in the culture], *Panstwo i Prawo*, 9 (2002), pp. 3–14.

However, the poor assessment of courts is also caused by phenomena which have appeared inside the machinery of justice and which can be called the crisis of professional ethics and the crisis of the sense of responsibility for the content of the applied law. In the opinion of society, the judicial community does not, in principle, respond to public condemnation of corruption in the courts. The lack of explicit public disapproval of corrupted judges often results in the erroneous impression that the judicial community tries to conceal these phenomena and handle them among themselves. In this situation, appeals from judges for the autonomy of the courts in the system of authorities are often understood as an attempt to "seal" their community. These objections are also raised against the other lawyers' corporations whose reaction to breaches of the rules of professional ethics by their members is, according to public opinion, too weak.

A similar diagnosis of crisis is formulated in relation to the application of law by the state administration. In particular, the organizational and technical dimension of the administration's activity decisively raises objections. The deficits in the administration's IT equipment, the low level of its staff, and its dependence (especially at a local level) on the political sphere are common knowledge. Poland is in the course of building a modern state administration and this task will require significant financial support.

However, the crisis in the system of state administration manifests itself still more seriously when analysing the legality of its decisions. The case law of the Supreme Administrative Court can serve as an indicator of the efficiency of the state administration. For many years in almost one case in three, the Supreme Administrative Court has reversed the decision under appeal and nearly 39% of the acts of supreme authorities, e.g. the ministers, have been reversed or annulled.[3]

4. SOCIETY AND INTEGRATION OF LAW

In the normative dimension over the cultural process of assimilating values and legal principles the process of developing legal institutions dominates. The implementation of Community law was not a process of historical evolution but a purely formal operation of introducing certain legal texts into the system of law. Thus legal institutions have been left suspended in a specific culture vacuum and therefore the actors of the legal institutions assume a purely instrumental attitude towards them; they are not able to fill the legal institutions with rational discourse. This purely external attitude to law, the absence of a social hermeneutics of law, results in the fact that legal institutions do not generate common, socially accepted symbols and meanings.

3 Informacja statystyczna o działalności wymiaru sprawiedliwości [Statistical information on the functioning of the justice system], Part I (Warszawa: Ministerstwo Sprawiedliwości. Dział Organizacyjny, 2002).

Society reads law as a source of rights, which are, however, regarded as specific bonuses in individual strategies. The number of lawsuits in courts increased from two million in 1989 to about eight million in 2002. This is not only a result of the expansion of the range of juridicization. To a significant extent, society perceives law as an important element of social play. The rights derived from law are not, however, regarded as manifestations of individual freedoms in relation to others and to the state. No need to negotiate the limits of this freedom in the process of the application of law is felt. An instrumental attitude prevails, and rights are regarded as goods distributed by law: they can simply be used in individual strategies and therefore it is necessary to win them.

The lack of the rooting of law in culture brings about attitudes of legal nihilism and legal instrumentalism. No connections are discerned between the normativity of law and morality; conventional normativity. The normativity of law is perceived as a sort of convention covering at most a political game, hence, the attitude which that legal regulations entail dishonest intentions. There is an impression that legal normativity does not, in principle, compete with any other normativity and is not supported by any other normativity. Normative disorder is felt in which both, good law and good customs as well as moral norms are absent. At the beginning of the 1990s this state was perceived as temporary disintegration of legal culture coming from the specific "restructuring" of the normative sphere, which, despite raising an impression of chaos, remained, however, under the control of some social elites. Since the end of the 1990s, after testing the variants of governance of all the political elites, the sense of permanent disintegration, the lack of homeostasis manifesting itself in the destruction of normativity, has been dominating.

Thus disintegration in legal consciousness consists of a paradox: there exists a sense of the presence of law, of its validity but it is accompanied by the sense of destruction of normativity. Law is a collection of texts, a source of certain goods but it is not a duty. If it works, it happens so only through the assistance of state coercion. Legal normativity is not of an argumentative nature. Law exists, as do legal institutions, but there is no legal order.

A crisis of legal culture brings the threat of anomy, i.e. lack or atrophy of social recognition for the binding rules of conduct. It may manifest itself as the disorganization of human relationships in large social groups (rural areas, roadblocks, the nihilistic attitudes shown by folk leaders).

Finally, a crisis of legal culture can lead to the destruction of normativity, i.e. the process of destroying the binding force of legal norms. The destruction of normativity is a result of the declining quality of law itself and the effectiveness of its enforcement by the state apparatus. Law loses its basic features: generality, ability to be universally binding, and to obtain rational justifications. Unlike with anomy, citizens become disoriented—they cannot differentiate between a norm and an exception. So violating law becomes thoughtless, a loss of critical assessment of self and others takes place.

5. LAWYERS AND INTEGRATION OF LAW

Lawyers themselves went the same way. The "department of justice" was not successfully transformed into the "administration of justice." Like the whole society, lawyers, subjected to the same factors, regarded law as a specific "bonus" in their individual strategies, i.e. they assumed a typically departmental attitude. Law was only expected to be more "elegantly", accepted in Europe. They did not presume that a new role in the social discourse was required of them, and especially of judges. As yet, lawyers have not accepted the requirement of giving an internal dimension to legal texts. The external attitude towards law dominates, reinforced by positivistic legal education, i.e. law is treated as an instruction, a sort of a stimulus. The argumentative nature of legal obligation, which would require the assumption an internal attitude towards a legal norm, i.e. the assumption of responsibility for the final content of law in the process of judging, is hardly noticed.[4] Such phrases as "judging" and "the administration of justice" almost do not exist in the lawyers' everyday discussion. They use such terms as the application of law, judicial decision, etc. which suggest law's instrumental nature and its stimulus character. Lawyers do not accept their participation in the argumentative cognition of law. Like the whole society, they regard "the play of law" as the distribution of bonuses. This attitude must be accompanied by corruption phenomena. As I have already remarked, this attitude of lawyers is to a great extent affected by their education.

Among lawyers, a conception of the profession prevails referring to legal positivism in which law is regarded as an object entirely external in relation to a lawyer, who is not responsible for its content. In Poland, legal positivism played, from this point of view, the role of a doctrine which protected the Polish lawyers' education after the war against excessive ideologisation since positivism as a method offers a conviction about the autonomy of law in relation to political and economic developments. Positivism showed that the notional apparatus of law and jurisprudence used by the lawyer is universal. Using this method in education greatly protected Polish legal culture from the belief that law was only a derivative of economic and political phenomena. Thus positivism, at least in its methodological sense, formed a pattern of the lawyer which was easily applicable also in the concept of the state of the rule of law. It regards law as the sovereign's order which the lawyer, equipped with the methodology of law, only subjects to formal analysis and arranges notionally. In this way, law as the content of the sovereign's will becomes, the subject of lawyers' cognition.[5]

In primitive positivism, participation in culture, understood as the lawyers' attitude to normative culture patterns, consists solely in the cognitive relation. The

---

4 Neil MacCormick, *Legal Reasoning and Legal Theory* (Oxford: Oxford University Press, 1978), pp. 282–292.

5 Marek Zirk-Sadowski, *Prawo a uczestniczenie w kulturze* [Law and Participation in Culture] (Łódź: University of Łódź Press, 1998), Chapt. 3.

lawyer is defined here as the sovereign's delegate. The sovereign delegates the law-making and the application of law to a number of institutions and primarily to the judiciary. Each legitimated use of this delegation must be based on the assumption that it is only the fulfilment of the sovereign's orders. The formal-dogmatic method coupled with the code excludes the lawyer's influence on culture patterns related to law.

Thus in primitive positivism the lawyer's participation in culture must be reduced only to the cognition of law and the epistemology of law which becomes part of the model of the science of law. So, in the act of cognizing law the lawyer does not constitute the law as a cultural object, assuming a passive, solely cognitive attitude towards it, the same as is assumed towards natural objects.

In the positivistic approach, participation in culture via law is predominantly achieved in the cognition of law. Law presented as an object of cognition separated from the cognizing subject must be sufficiently "objectivised", shown as an object resembling natural objects. For this reason, a basic problem in primitive positivism is the removal of subjective elements from the act of cognition of law. Preserving a borderline between subjectivity and objectivity in the cognition of law is one of the foundations of positivistic epistemology.

This model of lawyers' participation in culture now has a disintegrating effect on the professional roles of lawyers in the integration of Polish law and Community law. Legal positivism is based on the domination of the "hard" law conception, i.e. law built on rules and having strictly determined limits. The demand is that these rules be explicit so that they could effectively perform the function of controlling society. The task of legal institutions is to bring legal rules into effect while functioning under conditions of very limited discretion. We can say that bureaucratic institutions are an ideal of such institutions.

In Community law, the so-called "soft law" model has been predominating as an instrument of the EU Institutions' activity for many years. Most generally speaking, it can be understood as the "principles of conduct" which are not a legal binding but have considerable practical consequences. In this conception of law it is easier to omit the consequences of the lack of political agreements, but at the same time it requires a common understanding of the principles of Community law since in practice the application of soft law consists in "weighing" the principles within the discourse conducted in the Institutions. In EU law this imposes an active, adaptable understanding of law based on referring to principles. The rational discourse taking place in the European Institutions serves to "weigh" principles and not only to apply rules. Thanks to this, there is no clear-cut distinction between legal and social institutions. What finally affects the determination of borderlines between these two types of institutions is the application of the subsidiarity principle.

Assessing the cultural "distance" between the professional roles of lawyers in Poland and in the European Union, we can say that our conception of lawyer is based on the conception of autonomous law (cf. our last year's report) in which an important role is played by the application of rules, interpreted, however, on the basis of the adopted conception of the "bill of rights" which guarantees law its autonomy in culture, while the European institutions are already developing the concept of reflective law which is created on the basis of discussing principles, which is significantly negotiable in character and refers to social self-control mechanisms.

In Poland, legal positivism entirely leaves out this cultural and communicative character of law by assuming that the content of law becomes known due to the linguistic correctness of the text which guarantees, to a significant degree, its reading in accordance with the legislator's intention. The opposite of this approach is the concept of the content of law as an effect of the argumentation conducted within a culturally determined discourse.

The absence of discursive legal culture (created by lawyers) capable of negotiating the content of law is a source of interpretative disintegration and an ordinary lawyer's inability to engage in the culture of soft, responsive "subsidiary" law. Such a role can be played only by the highest judicial institutions which establish specific, small communication communities, capable of generating new meanings against the background of a legal text created by the legislature. In this situation it is justified to suppose that we are approaching a model of the judicature with the strong domination of the hierarchically highest level courts, which will in fact perform the function of a specific controller of the limits of interpretative swings and which will be incapable of the discursiveness of the lower level judiciary.

The public law of the Polish People's Republic period was based on orders; it was a kind of instruction. During the transformation new texts were included in it, containing provisions guaranteeing human and civil rights as well as the institutions of a free-market economy, pluralistic society and a liberal-democratic state. The autonomy of such law in culture, i.e. its resistance to economic and political instrumentalization, is possible when a change of the text of law is accompanied by a new legal discourse in which the scope of legal obligation and its authority result from argumentation and not from the direct imposition of duties by the legislature.

A legal text is always written in natural language and is a collection of general provisions. So it cannot be directly applied to the settlement of a specific case which is always individual and concrete. The substance of the third power in this new model does not consist in creating new legal texts but in establishing the meaning of legal texts via argumentation. Power over the meaning of law is the essence of administration of justice in which the judge is a kind of negotiator of the content of law and, as a result, of morality and politics.[6] Within this meaning, the power of interpretation is the essence of the law.

Meanwhile, the mechanism for creating a new legal discourse was lacking in the transformation process. The organisation of legal education was, to a large extent, to blame. The absence of argumentative attitude to law and the appearance of very complicated legal regulations finally resulted in the "hyperinstruction" effect. As

[6] Ronald Dworkin, *Law's Empire* (London: Fontana Press, 1986), pp. 166–167.

a result, justice became a chaotic distribution of bonuses, dependent on the quality of judges—on their qualifications, their sense of morality and law—where the majority of judges played the role of little gods.

6. CONCLUSION: INTEGRATION VS. DISINTEGRATION OF POLISH LEGAL CULTURE

This problem became manifest in the integration processes. So, paradoxically, the implementation of EU law led to the strengthening of the tendency to instrumentalize law. The disintegration of the legal order is a result of the narrow understanding of the harmonization of law in the implementation of new legal texts. They were introduced to the Polish legal order without a reference to the achievements of the European legal discourse. The consequences of this primitive implementation of law have led today to alarming phenomena, e.g. in the area of fiscal law. As it turns out, a number of institutions, e.g. goods and services tax and excise (VAT) are understood in entirely different ways by Polish courts and European courts.

Although the way in which Polish legal culture determines the role and principles of the legal discourse resembles that of European culture, this resemblance, however, concerns only the legal culture of professionals—the lawyers engaged in legal practice and doctrine—and at the same time its nature is formal. The disintegrating elements manifest themselves early, such as in the field of attitudes assumed by lawyers towards law, the willingness to actively develop legal normativity, the perception of law, its creation and application as a kind of social negotiation in which lawyers play the role of social arbiters.

The problems concerning citizens' legal awareness are unknown. The poor development of civil society in Poland is of particular importance. The autonomous sense of civil freedom, which constitutes a criterion of assessment of positive law, is probably weakly developed in Poland. Again, we do not mean here the tendency to "copy" the social institutions of the West which began after 1989, but civil society understood as a capacity to articulate needs autonomously via social discourse and the appointment of political representations for interests established in this way. The appearance of such a society is a fundamental condition for successful legal integration with an active, adaptable and argumentative European legal culture. The direct effectiveness of Community law presupposes the possibility of exercising individual rights and their semantic development by society. This requires the existence of social institutions such as voluntary civil associations and, as a result, the emergence of a public sphere remaining beyond the reach of the state's direct control. Of course, the appearance of such society must naturally be a slow process whose course will also be influenced by economic as well as educational conditions. Only then will the current disintegration of legal culture have a chance to become positive integration, i.e. creating a new kind of legal culture in Poland.

14. EU Enlargement and the Constitutional Principle of Judicial Independence

Daniel Smilov

1. Introduction

At the end of 2002, the Bulgarian Constitutional Court (BCC) took a key decision invalidating the plan of the government to reform the judicial system. The judges argued that many provisions in the amendments to the Law on the Judicial System, sponsored by the cabinet of PM Simeon Sax-Cobburg-Gotha,[1] violated the principle of judicial independence in the Bulgarian Constitution.

The BCC has a history (although not a fully consistent one) of defending judicial independence against interference by the political branches of power—the legislature and the executive. Especially prominent in this regard was the resistance of the Court against the plans of the 1994–1996 Videnov[2] government to introduce substantial judicial reforms, which were in many respects similar to the more recent plans for reforms.

In 1994–1995 the stance of the Constitutional Court was widely hailed by commentators of Bulgarian politics, and by representatives of the EU and the Council of Europe. In fact, the Videnov government was much criticized by European analysts and politicians for its controversial policies.

Somewhat paradoxically, the 2002 decision of the BCC, which was similar to its predecessors in many ways, was interpreted in negative terms by the EU Commission, and became the major reason for a temporal "freezing" of the negotiations between Bulgaria and the EU on issues concerning the judiciary. After the decision, further reform of the judicial system could proceed only by means of a constitutional amendment. The Commission insisted on the introduction of such amendments as a condition for the closing of the negotiation "chapters" concerning the judicial system. In order to comply with these requirements the Bulgarian government drafted the amendments which were adopted by parliament, rather hastily, in September 2003. These amendments limited significantly the immunities previously enjoyed by Bulgarian magistrates, and made it possible for the government to introduce limited terms of office (mandates) for senior judges and prosecutors. What would have been seen in 1991–1996 as a significant attempt to limit judicial independence, in 2003 was deemed constitutionally compatible and necessary for

1 Leader of the ruling party—Movement Simeon II.
2 Bulgarian Socialist Party.

Wojciech Sadurski et al. (ed.), Spreading Democracy and the Rule of Law?, 313–334.

a successful judicial reform. For a Martian anthropologist on a field trip to Earth, it might have appeared that the principle of judicial independence is a convenient rhetorical instrument for justifying positions which do not fit well together.

This chapter takes its cue from the insights of Martian scholarship, and attempts to analyze the politics behind the constitutional principle of judicial independence in the EU enlargement process. This process is commonly described in normative terms as *harmonization* of the legal systems of the accession countries with the rules and principles of the EU. There are strong assumptions behind this misleadingly simplistic picture however. One of these assumptions is that the EU normative order is itself internally coherent and complete: what is necessary is just its "transplantation" to the legal systems of the accession states. The paper will question this assumption, as far as the issue of judicial independence is concerned. The starting point will be to demonstrate that Western European legal systems provide *a plurality of models* of judicial independence, and that there is no prospect of convergence among them on key issues. Therefore, there is no sufficiently specific common European theory of judicial independence. Of course, at a very abstract level it could be claimed that similar principles are being followed. But when it comes to their application, interpretation, and implementation through different institutional arrangements, it becomes clear that the balancing of different competing values has produced a variety of different models. The European normative space, therefore, is characterized by competing conceptions and theoretical dilemmas, as much as by agreement on common general principles. These problems are discussed in section one.

Section two analyses the language of the Commission Regular Reports. These Reports are the major EU instruments of monitoring the progress of the accession countries in their preparation for Union membership, and therefore, reveal the standards used in this process. Two interpretations of these reports as related to the issue of judicial independence are possible. One is that the Commission has made particularistic and contextual judgments in assessing the legal systems of the accession countries regarding the issue of judicial independence. On this interpretation, the reports synthesize the conclusions of careful contextual analyses, which focus on country-specific problems without the ambition to construct a coherent pan-European theory of judicial independence.

A second, more ambitious reading, which is probably more consistent with the aspirations of the Commission, is that the reports rely on some consistent set of common standards concerning judicial independence. Yet, the irony is that, as was claimed above, there are arguably no such common standards easily derivable from the legal traditions of member states. Therefore, on the second interpretation, the Commission reports develop and rely on a certain myth: the *myth of a common European theory of judicial independence*. This interpretation, as it will be argued, does have evidential support. Thus, for instance, the reports often criticize the structure of the judicial systems of different countries, as well as specific institutional arrangements, as violating putatively common constitutional principles of judicial independence while, at the same time, similar arrangements could be found in European Member States, or other applicant countries, which are not criticized. Of course, the same institutional model could perform differently depending on the context: criticisms of the Commission are often well founded and justified. The question which is raised is rather about the advantages and costs of the perpetuation of the *myth* of a common European theory of judicial independence? In other words, why do the Commission and the participants in the EU enlargement process prefer to use a *constitutional* language implying the existence of some common theory of judicial independence, in the actual absence of such a theory?

Section three of the chapter attempts to show that the preservation of the myth is instrumentally convenient for certain actors. A number of hypotheses are explored, which purport to explain the eventual perpetuation of the myth through its uses in enlargement politics. First, it is argued, constitutional language and constitutional arguments do save time. For instance, it is not necessary to develop complex contextual cost–benefit analyses of the performance of different institutional models if there is an "argument of principle" ruling them out as unconstitutional. Although rather simplistic, this hypothesis has explanatory power because of the bureaucratic character of the enlargement process, with its emphasis on timeliness and efficiency. The bureaucratic character of the process places also an emphasis on common "standards", "benchmarks" and "performance criteria", the availability of which is dependent on the existence of a common detailed theory of judicial independence.

Second, the myth of judicial independence is instrumental in the creation of a certain picture of the European Union as a polity based on common principles and standards. The discussions of the future Constitution for Europe have spurred the debates about the character of the European polity. A community of integrity of principles is seen by many as an important ideal, which could mobilize the support of the people of Europe for the new constitution.

Third, the myth of a consistent theory of judicial independence has instrumental uses in the process of negotiations as well. At the start, it strengthens significantly the bargaining position of the Commission *vis-à-vis* the governments of accession countries: the existence of common European norms and standards is a "self-explanatory" argument in favour of certain recommendations. Further, however, the myth has empowered national governments, pursuing reform of the judicial system, against the opposition of domestic judiciaries and other actors. This use of the myth is gaining some prominence at the moment: national governments and the Commission form coalitions against "recalcitrant" judiciaries in the promotion of "European standards and values".

This curious patchwork of bureaucratic, normative, and pragmatic uses of the described myth of the constitutional principle of judicial independence comes at a certain price, however. Section four of the chapter attempts to give an account of the various problems to which its perpetuation is likely to lead. Two of these are singled out for special analysis. First, the myth conceals a common, pan-European problem:

the growing political power of judges and courts. It perpetuates the Weberian image of the judge-administrator, who just applies previously existing rules without much innovation and law-making. Contemporary judges and magistrates, as it will be argued, increasingly serve important political functions. So the real question is not how to devise institutional solutions withholding the political powers of the judiciary, but how to "structure" their discretion so that they produce socially beneficial policies. A franker approach to this problem in the accession process could have been more useful not only to the accession states, but the Union at large.

Second, the myth of a common theory of judicial independence reinforces a grander myth—the myth of the EU as a community based on common normative principles and values. Although probably instrumental for the construction of a European identity, an inflation of the grander myth of EU as a community of principles threatens to "bureaucratize" and "judicialize" the integration process, and thus to deprive it of its most important dimension—the *political* dimension. After all, European integration, as many hope, is a political project in which people with similar, but still distinct, cultural histories and values come together to build a common future on the basis of mutual trust and understanding. It is not just a project of *following* common principles and *endorsing* common values, but primarily of *creating* new normative solutions which will give a chance to every member to present themselves in their best light.

2. JUDICIAL INDEPENDENCE AS A MYTH

Giacomo Oberto, Deputy Secretary General of the International Association of Judges,[3] has attempted to extract from a number of international agreements a set of common standards and rules concerning the independence of the judiciary.[4] The following principles will be elaborated, and used as a starting point for our discussion:

> The Judiciary is an autonomous body. It is not subject to any of the other two powers of the State. Public prosecutors should enjoy the same guarantees provided for by the law concerning the judicial status. More specifically:

---

3 http://space.tin.it/edicola/goberto/.

4 The main agreements he focuses on are the following: the United Nations "Basic Principles on the Independence of the Judiciary", approved in 1985; the "Judges' Charter in Europe", adopted on March 20, 1993, in Wiesbaden (Germany) by the European Association of Judges, regional group of the International Association of Judges; Recommendation No. R (94) 12 of the Committee of Ministers of the Council of Europe to Member States on the Independence, Efficiency and Role of Judges, adopted on October 13, 1994; the European Charter on the Statute for Judges of the Council of Europe, approved in Strasbourg on July 8–10, 1998; the "Universal Charter of the Judge", unanimously adopted in November 1999 in Taipei (Republic of China, Taiwan) by the International Association of Judges.

1. Judges and public prosecutors are only subject to the law.
2. Judges and public prosecutors should be appointed for life or for such other period and conditions, that judicial independence is not endangered. Any change to the judicial obligatory retirement age must not have retroactive effect.
3. Judges and public prosecutors should be selected through competitive examinations. The selection and appointment of a judge or of a public prosecutor must be carried out according to objective and transparent criteria based on proper professional qualification. Where this is not ensured in other ways that are rooted in established and proven tradition, selection should be carried out by an independent body that includes substantial judicial representation.
4. The Executive or to the Legislative power should have no influence in the process of selection of judges and public prosecutors.
5. A High Council for the Judiciary should be established. This Council should be entrusted with the appointment, assignment, transfer, promotion, and disciplinary measures concerning judges and public prosecutors. This body should be composed of judges and public prosecutors, or at least have a majority representation of judges and public prosecutors.
6. Judges and public prosecutors cannot be transferred, suspended or removed from office unless it is provided for by law and then only by decision in the proper disciplinary procedure.
7. Disciplinary action should be carried out by independent bodies that include substantial judicial representation. Disciplinary action against judges and public prosecutors can only be taken when provided for by pre-existing law and in compliance with predetermined rules of procedure.
8. Each judge and each public prosecutor has the right to be provided with an efficient system of initial and further judicial training; attendance to these two forms of training should be, for a certain period, compulsory for each judge or public prosecutor, or at least it should represent an essential condition for moving to a higher post. Judicial training should be provided by an independent institution, such as the French *Ecole Nationale de la Magistrature*, or by the independent body, that includes substantial judicial representation.
9. Judges and public prosecutors must be granted proper working conditions.
10. Salaries of judges and of public prosecutors be fixed by statute (and not by an act of the executive power) and linked to the salaries of parliamentarians or of ministers. They should not be reduced for any reason.
11. Judges and public prosecutors must be granted full freedom of association, both on national and international level. Activity in such association must be officially recognized as judicial work.

These principles, or a similar set, form the normative framework for the doctrine of judicial independence in modern liberal democracies. At this level of abstraction, most liberal democracies would arguably espouse these principles.

Yet, when it comes to concrete interpretations and the institutional implementation of these principles, consensus no longer exists, even among established western democracies.

One focus of substantial disagreement in the interpretation of judicial independence concerns the checks and balances between the major branches of power (principles four and five from the list above). In some western legal systems, the Minister of Justice, or its functional equivalent, is authorized to make judicial appointments upon the advice or nomination from senior members of the judiciary. Also, the Minister of Justice may have certain powers related to the promotion and demotion of already appointed magistrates, as well as to the imposition of disciplinary sanctions.[5]

Other systems prefer to deprive the Minister of Justice of the power of appointment, promotion and demotion of magistrates. In these systems, this function is entrusted to an independent body, governing the judicial branch.[6] The composition of these bodies, however, also reflects different levels of involvement of the legislative and the executive branches in the personnel and management affairs of the judiciary. It could be argued, that the very fact that the executive and the legislative branch are entitled to appoint members of the body governing the judicial system is already a compromise of principle four as formulated above. This compromise is, however, deemed necessary in order to preserve a degree of *accountability* of the judiciary *vis-à-vis* the political branches of power, and ultimately, the citizens as electors. Having this in mind, it could be said that the principle of judicial independence should always be balanced against the principle of accountability of the judicial branch. The judiciary should not be out of tune with the preferences of the citizens, and should be representative of these preferences to a degree.

However, different legal systems of established democracies balance these competing values—accountability and independence—in different ways. Some systems rely on highly unrepresentative judiciaries as a social group. Other systems attempt to achieve a greater degree of representation including through popular elections of magistrates. Further, different ideas of accountability of the judiciary are also in operation. Some systems rely on political accountability, and in them political bodies (like the Minister of Justice) have greater powers in determining the personnel policies of the judicial branch. Other systems rely more on the professional ethics of the community of lawyers as a self-regulating body: in these systems, accountability is treated as accountability to peers on the basis of professional standards, rather than as accountability to other branches of power.[7]

---

5 Typical of the Anglo-Saxon model, the UK and US in particular.

6 This is the Mediterranean model, exemplified most clearly by Italy.

7 For a recent, very illuminating discussion of the institutionalization of the principle of judicial independence in the major established western democracies, see Carlo Guarnieri and Patrizia Pederzoli, *The Power of Judges: A Comparative Study of Courts and Democracy*, (Oxford: Oxford University Press 2002). See also S. Shetreet and J. Deschenes (eds.),

Another point of divergence among the legal systems of established democracies is the character of internal accountability within the judiciary. The legal systems of continental countries (especially these of Latin Europe) rely on strong internal accountability, which means that senior magistrates exercise significant control in terms of career promotion and demotion over junior magistrates. In contrast, in common law countries, there is greater internal independence of the magistrates.

A further difference in the interpretation of the principles of judicial independence involves the position of public prosecutors in the constitutional model. In some systems, the prosecutors are part of the executive, and thus fully accountable to politically elected bodies. In other systems they are part of the judiciary and enjoy different degrees of autonomy both *vis-à-vis* the other branches, but also *vis-à-vis* the other parts of the judiciary as well.

Finally, a controversial issue worth mentioning is the elaboration and the adoption of the budget of the judiciary. Again, different systems allow for various degrees of judicial "independence" in this sense. In some systems, the government and parliament have greater leeway in the appropriation of funds for the judicial branch, while in other systems the draft budget is closely coordinated with the independent body governing the judicial system. The formulation of principle 10 from the list above could hardly address the complexity of the problem with the funding of the judicial system. Since financial independence is one of the key components of judicial independence, the vagueness of principle 10 illustrates a general point: convergence on normative principles exists only at a very high level of abstraction, a level which is not very helpful when it comes to the assessment of different institutional solutions.

The existence of a plurality of different institutional models of judicial independence could be interpreted in at least two different ways. The first one, and probably the more plausible, is that, from a constitutional point of view, there is a plurality of legitimate competing solutions to the question of judicial independence. Democracies resolve this question in different ways depending on their constitutional traditions, the character of their political process, etc. There is no overall best solution: all of them have advantages and disadvantages. On this view, there is a minimal set of requirements which all democracies must meet: after these requirements are met, however, a wide variety of institutional models, reflecting different conceptions of underlying principles and values, are acceptable.

A second interpretation of the existing variety could be called *contextualist*. The contextualist argues that all legal systems (of established democracies) follow the same (or very similar) sets of normative principles. However, differences in the context entail that these principles should lead to different institutional solutions. The contextualist would argue that if we have taken into account all the relevant social, political, and economic differences among the given countries, we would be

---

Judicial Independence: The Contemporary Debate (Dordrecht: Martinus Nijhoff Publishers 1985).

able to explain how the following of the same normative principles lead to different institutional solutions. A difficulty of the contextualist position is that the normative theory of judicial independence that it advances must be incredibly detailed and complex, so as to explain all institutional differences by simultaneously preserving normative unity and coherence. Such a theory would contain propositions such as the following:

> In countries with majoritarian politics, executive domination over the parliament, and a low level of separation of powers, it is necessary to have as little interference of the political branches as possible, while in countries with weaker executives, stronger parliaments, and extensive separation of powers (for instance, through federalism), a greater degree of political involvement in the governing of the judiciary could be tolerated.

Through the construction of such complex normative principles of judicial independence, a contextualist could claim that there is a single normative theory on this issue (at least in Europe or concerning the established western democracies). The empirical institutional divergence would be explained away by differences in the context in which this theory is applied.

The contextualist view is arguably theoretically possible. The problem with it is that a super complex theory of judicial independence has not been yet elaborated either for Europe or for the western democracies in general. Of course, academics and constitutionalists do their best, but there is no candidate theory on the horizon which would command universal acceptance. Reasonable, deep disagreement persists at the theoretical level as well, as is evident at the level of substantive constitutional principles, institutional arrangements, etc. Thus, the fact that a super-contextualist theory is in principle possible should not be confused with the question about its existence. The confusion of these two issues creates constitutional myths—in the present case, the myth of a single coherent theory of judicial independence in Europe or in the established democracies in general. One of the consequences of the myth, as will be shown below, is that under the guise and authority of mythological common normative principles, usually purely contextual, sometimes controversial or simply unfounded assessments could be made.

3. THE MYTH IN THE REGULAR REPORTS OF THE EUROPEAN COMMISSION

The Copenhagen criteria do not explicitly mention the issue of judicial independence as a condition for the accession of the candidate countries to the European Union. The language of the criteria rather focuses on the stability and efficiency of judicial institutions: "stability of institutions guaranteeing . . . the rule of law". This extremely vague language has posed serious problems for the Commission in developing a suitable strategy for monitoring and evaluating the progress of the candidate countries. Throughout the monitoring process, the Commission has placed an emphasis on different aspects of judicial reform. An influential study of the monitoring process conducted by the Open Society Institute in Budapest, the findings of which are used below, summarizes the areas of interest for the Commission in the following way:

> The Commission has placed great emphasis on the ability of judiciaries to safeguard citizens' rights, contribute to a favourable business environment, and implement EU legislation, as well as more recently (2001), on the judiciary's adjudicative and administrative independence.[8]

The Regular Reports of the Commission from 2001 onwards consistently mention judicial independence as an area of judicial reform which deserves closer monitoring. Thus, in the overview of the developments in the candidate states, in the 2001 Regular Reports the Commission argues that:

> Further progress was made in reforming and strengthening the judicial system, as a vital element in ensuring respect for the rule of law and in the effective enforcement of the *acquis*. Several countries advanced in adopting basic legislation, strengthening human resources and improving working conditions. Efforts in this area need to be further stepped up, with particular attention to ensuring the *independence of the judiciary* [emphasis added].[9]

After the peak of interest in judicial independence between 2001 and 2002, the Commission shifted its attention to differently formulated problems—such as judicial capacity—which are broader (and even vaguer) than judicial independence.

One of the most critical 2002 reports of the Commission concerning Latvia asserts that:

> The issue of the independence and efficiency of the judicial system, including the establishment of an independent court administration, still needs to be addressed. Furthermore, other issues such as the absence of well-defined criteria and transparent methods for selecting judicial apprentices and appointees, and the Ministry of Justice's influence over career paths, also need to be tackled. . . . (The Ministry of Justice determines the number of Judges and administers the budgetary resources of the judiciary. It supervises the organisation of activities at regional and district courts.)[10]

A positive report—the one on the Czech Republic—contains almost identical language concerning the powers of the Czech Ministry of Justice, and yet, there is no criticism that the principle of judicial independence has been endangered. Nor is there an explanation why the model works in the Czech Republic but obviously fails to work in Latvia:

---

8 EUMAP, "Overview: Judicial Capacity," (Budapest: Open Society Institute 2002), p. 19.

9 http://europa.eu.int/comm/enlargement/report2001/ (Section 1 a, Overall Development).

10 http://europa.eu.int/comm/enlargement/report2002/lv_en.pdf, p. 22.

> [In the Czech Republic], judges are nominated by the Ministry of Justice and appointed for life by the President of the Republic . . . The Ministry of Justice determines the number of judges and state prosecutors and their promotion, and administers the budgetary resources of the judiciary . . . The Constitution enshrines the independence of the judges, although the Minister of Justice is responsible for appointing, transferring and terminating the appointment of the President and Vice Presidents of courts.[11]

As could be anticipated, the Eastern European models of judicial independence differ from one another as much as the western European models discussed in the previous section. There are similar puzzles and similar dilemmas, such as the legitimate powers of the Minister of Justice in the appointment and promotion policies of the judiciary, the existence and composition of supreme judicial councils, etc. The variety is indeed significant. Some countries have followed the Latin European model of self-governing judiciaries, through the establishment of independent bodies—Judicial Councils. Yet, the composition of these bodies varies—in Bulgaria, for instance, only half of the members are appointed by Parliament, while the other half are appointed by the different branches of the judiciary—the judges, the prosecutors, and the investigators. In Romania, all of the members of the Council are elected by parliament through a majority vote, although they are nominated by the judiciary.

Other countries, the Czech Republic for instance, have opted for judicial administration through the Ministry of Justice, which is responsible, in fact, for the governance of the judicial system, and is empowered to determine key questions of personnel policy through the appointment of Court presidents. A reform in 2002 introduced Judicial Councils in the Czech judicial system, but these are just consultative bodies with no formal powers regarding the appointment, promotion, or disciplining of judges. A similar model has been in operation in Latvia, as already mentioned, and has been the focus for criticism from the Commission. In Slovakia such a model existed until 2001, when it was replaced with a model with a Judicial Council, partly under pressure by the Commission.

Given this variety in institutional implementation of the principle of judicial independence in the region, the Commission has apparently faced a very difficult task in trying to introduce any consistent scheme of evaluation of the performance of the different models. Ultimately, it seems, the Commission has failed to do so, and its Regular Reports should be read mainly as contextual assessments, which are based, not on any uniform model of evaluation, but rather on the particular agreements reached between governments and the Commission, as well as on the opinions of local and EU experts (peer review).

This conclusion is supported by the findings of the EUMAP project as well, whose authors argue that:

---

11 http://europa.eu.int/comm/enlargement/report2002/cz_en.pdf, p. 22.

> To date, however, the accession process has shown that the Union itself needs a more comprehensive approach to the [judicial] reform question. There are few standards on how the judiciary should be organised and how it should function, and the existing expert support system is often uncoordinated and ineffective... Determining the acceptability of different arrangements requires clear articulation and understanding of the standards the EU wishes to apply to itself and its candidates. The candidate States are under an effective obligation to fulfil the Copenhagen criteria, but the EU has yet to elaborate any standards by which the candidate States' efforts—or member states continuous performance—can be measured. More precise standards are necessary to encourage a uniformly high level of respect for judicial independence across Europe.[12]

The lack of a coherent theory of judicial independence, and the corresponding lack of a consistent scheme of evaluation of the performance of different models, has led to occasional problems:

> There have been... instances where the Commission has sent mixed signals to the candidate states. On occasion, the direction of the judicial reforms in different countries has been dependent on expert advice from EU member states; in the absence of EU-wide standards, pre-accession advisors and representatives of twinning institutions have often simply encouraged the adoption of specific solutions imported from their own states... Candidate states cannot be reasonably expected to bring their judiciaries in line with standards that are themselves not defined.[13]

It has to be kept in mind that the Regular Reports of the Commission have been tremendously important in determining the course of judicial reform in the accession states. Only in the period 2001–2003, under pressure from the Commission have there been constitutional amendments concerning the status of the judicial system in Slovakia and Bulgaria (and a proposal for constitutional amendment in Romania), as well as adoption of major legislation in Poland, Bulgaria, Slovakia, the Czech Republic, Estonia, and Slovenia. Many of these pieces of legislation have tried to change the institutional balance of power within the judiciary and among the major branches of power as well, with the goal of strengthening the performance of the judicial system. The lack of a coherent theory of judicial independence, and its link to the performance of the judicial system as a whole, has led the Commission to endorse some projects of reform and reject others in a somewhat opportunistic way.

Thus, in Slovakia the Commission repeatedly advocated the abolition of the probationary period for judges (obviously with the view to strengthen judicial

---

[12] EUMAP, "Judicial Independence," in *Judicial Independence in the EU Accession Process* (Budapest: Open Society Institute 2001), p. 26.

[13] Ibid., pp. 20–21.

independence) while in Bulgaria it supported a constitutional amendment in 2003 which extended the probationary period from three to five years. Curiously, the government in Slovenia has argued that a similar extension of the probationary period for judges for up to five years is *necessary* for EU accession. As another controversial example from the evaluation practice of the Commission, the Latvian case could be cited, where EU experts suggested the appointment of judges in the Ministry of Justice in order to improve its efficiency in administering the judicial system: this has been seen by independent analysts as a violation of the principle of the separation of powers itself.[14]

All in all, it is difficult to argue that a coherent scheme of principles could be derived from the overall record of the Commission as an evaluator and inspiration behind the reforms of the judiciaries in the accession countries. In some of them, the Commission has accepted that models with extensive powers accorded to the Minister of Justice are legitimate and perform well (the Czech Republic). In others, the Commission has suggested and supported the introduction of independent Judicial Councils (Slovakia). In others still, as in Latvia, the Commission had been ready to experiment with institutional innovations (as the appointment of judges in the Ministry of Justice). Also, the balance between independence and accountability has been struck differently in separate countries, depending mostly on the context and the past performance of different institutional models. Probably a super-theory could fit all differences into a coherent whole by taking into account all contextual differences between the countries. The problem, however, is that the Commission has not tried to elaborate even the rough outlines of such a theory, and has left this task to inventive academics and analysts.

In this chapter, unfortunately, such a Herculean task cannot be pursued. Furthermore, there are some suspicions that such a super-complex theory does not exist at all. This is so, not only because cross-country analysis would be unable to establish a single pattern, but also because some of the positions taken by the Commission regarding *single* accession countries do not fit well together. Take as an example Bulgaria, and the Regular Reports of the Commission for this country for 2002 and 2003. There are some important differences in these two reports, concerning key areas of reform of the judiciary in the country. Thus, in 2002, the Commission argues that:

> The Supreme Judicial Council represents judges, prosecutors, and investigators, and its members comprise representatives of all three groups, as well as a number of members elected by Parliament. The three groups have different roles in the judicial system, and hence different interests and management structures. This makes it difficult for the SJC to play a fully effective role in the professional management of judges and the court system.[15]

---

14 The last two examples are taken from the cited above *EUMAP* study.

15 http://europa.eu.int/comm/enlargement/report2002/bu_en.pdf, p. 24.

This analysis should be read to support the exclusion of prosecutors and especially investigators (a long standing concern of the Commission) from the Supreme Judicial Council. In the context of the Bulgarian debates on the reform of the judicial system, the Report could be read also to support even the exclusion of the Prosecution from the judicial system: an option which was openly advocated in 2002 by the Minister of Justice and some of the leading political forces.

The 2003 Report contains no criticism on the composition of the SJC. In terms of institutional reform, the Report argues again for the exclusion of the investigators from the judicial system, but there is no suggestion for a change in the role of the prosecution either in the SJC or more generally as a part of the judiciary. (Although there is subdued criticism that reforms towards greater accountability of prosecutors are needed, without specifying in what direction.) It is true that by 2003 the government had abandoned its plans to significantly change the position of the prosecution in the overall governmental structure due to a series of decisions of the Constitutional Court, which postulated that such reforms would require constitutional revisions through a Grand National Assembly—a specially elected parliament authorized to amend the Constitution on issues affecting *inter alia*, the separation of powers. But this procedural difficulty cannot be a conclusive reason for a change of the view of the Commission, if its previous criticism was based on a *normative* principle.

A second example of a change of position of the Commission in the period 2002–2003 concerns the issue of the so-called fixed mandates for senior magistrates in Bulgaria. In 2002, the Commission acknowledges as legitimate the *concerns* of the SJC regarding the introduction of such fixed mandates:

> During the work on reform, co-operation between the Ministry of Justice and the Supreme Judicial Council has developed considerably . . . The SJC has raised concerns where it considered reforms did not fully respect judicial independence (e.g. introduction of time-limited mandates for some appointments . . .)

In 2003 the Report hailed a constitutional amendment which actually authorized, among other things, the introduction of such limited mandates. In fact, the Report even fails to mention this aspect of the constitutional amendment, which the Commission required in a very straightforward way. If there were a set of coherent, even though not explicit, principles behind the position of the Commission, there would have been a need to explain in more detail how such significant changes of position could be justified.

Of course, a convinced contextualist could hardly be dissuaded by the present attempts to show that there is no coherent *normative* theory of judicial independence illuminating all the Regular Reports of the Commission, and possibly even the reports on specific countries. For present purposes, suffice it to say that the extraction of such a theory would be a very difficult task indeed, and that neither the Commission, nor independent analysts, such as the EUMAP project, has been able to articulate such a theory.

Yet, the paradox is that the *de facto* absence of such a theory has not deterred the Commission from endorsing the view that the evaluation contained in the Regular Reports follows a rigorous standardized methodology. In the 2003 *Strategy Paper: Towards the Enlarged Union*,[16] it is argued that:

> Under this methodology, the Regular Reports assess progress in terms of legislation and measures actually adopted or implemented. This approach ensures equal treatment for all candidates, and permits an objective evaluation of the situation in each country. Progress towards meeting each criterion is assessed on the basis of *detailed standard checklist*, which allows account to be taken of the same aspects for each country and which ensures the transparency of the exercise [emphasis added].[17]

Although the Commission has been careful to directly state that there are common principles in the interpretation of the different Copenhagen criteria, the understanding that such principles do exist is evident from scattered remarks in the text of the Regular Reports themselves. Typically, there are references to "benchmarks" and "standards" as in the following example from 2001: "Benchmarking and peer pressure is increasingly used inside the Union in order to develop interoperable and compatible administrative structures."[18]

Thus, through the ambiguity of diplomatic language, the Commission has smuggled a myth of a standardized normative theory of assessment of the progress of the accession countries towards meeting the Copenhagen criteria. At least in the area of judicial independence, such a standardized normative theory is most likely missing.

Some would be willing to dismiss this fact as being of minor importance. After all, diplomatic language is necessarily vague, and one should not try to look for profound conceptual and normative coherence in it. In the next section, it is argued that the existence of certain myths in the Regular Reports is hardly just a side effect of diplomatic linguistic subtlety.

4. USES OF THE MYTH

The myth of a standard, coherent theory of judicial independence has not found its way into the Regular Reports by chance. The explanation for its existence is rather that it is convenient for the major stakeholders in the accession process—the Commission and the national governments of the accession countries. The myth, as argued below, could be put to at least three different types of use: a bureaucratic, a normative, and a diplomatic one. Each of these is examined in turn.

---

16 http://europa.eu.int/comm/enlargement/report2002/strategy_en.pdf.

17 Ibid., p. 9.

18 http://europa.eu.int/comm/enlargement/report2001/(c) (Administrative capacity beyond accession).

4.1. The Myth as a Bureaucratic Instrument

The existence of coherent constitutional theories of judicial independence, which would have given a basis for comparative analysis of the different institutional models, would have undoubtedly provided a very transparent and efficient tool for the assessment of the progress of different countries in meeting the political Copenhagen criteria. Yet, in the absence of such a theory, a myth about it may serve the same function—cutting the costs of lengthy contextual explanations based on time-consuming empirical surveys. It is not that the Commission, its experts, and the national governments have spent insufficient time on the analysis of the legal systems in the accession states. But the reform of an entire judicial system is not a simple matter, which could be successfully accomplished within a couple of years. Institutional reforms show all their effects only after some time has elapsed and the true effects of the reforms inspired by the Commission are to be seen only in the future. There is bound to be unintended consequences, failures, or less-than-optimal arrangements.

In such circumstances, the myth of a coherent normative theory of judicial independence could be used to cut a few corners in the justification of particular institutional choices and options. As observed by the EUMAP project, in many countries the course of the reforms has been determined by EU experts. In Eastern Europe, common "European models" and "European experience" are often overriding or knock-down arguments in domestic politics, especially if they come from the mouths of EU experts or administrators. Indeed, again as noted by EUMAP, what happens is that at least some of those experts simply advocate solutions with which they are most familiar from their own countries: nevertheless, this local knowledge often passes for a universal truth in the Eastern part of the continent.

It should be noted that *not* using the myth of a coherent theory of judicial independence would have imposed significant costs on the Commission in the assessment of the legal systems of the candidate countries. There would have been two options. First, very detailed contextual analyses of the legal systems of the countries done through the commissioning of empirical research concerning the performance of different models. Again, due to the complexity of the issue, and the time constraints, the results of such an effort would not have been perfect, but arguably they would have been more frank and helpful than the "mythological" approach.

A second option would have been to attempt to design a complex, pan-European normative theory of judicial independence, which would have introduced common standards both for the eastern and the western parts of the continent. Assuming that such a theory is in principle possible (which is doubtful), its creation would have presented the Commission with a really Herculean task.[19] After all, judicial

---

[19] For an attempt to construct such a theory see the EUMAP project and its methodology, which is indeed rather sophisticated. Yet, the result of this project could hardly be described as a common European theory of judicial independence, which illustrates the point that even

independence is only one aspect of one of the Copenhagen criteria. In its Regular Reports, the Commission has provided roughly two pages of analysis of the judiciary in general for each of the countries. Within such a space, a truly helpful, coherent normative theory is difficult to construct. Assuming that these two pages reflect the resources at the disposal of the Commission for the assessment of judicial capacity, it is clear that the very rules of efficient bureaucracy would dictate the endorsement of time-saving constitutional myths against other, much more costly options.

4.2. The Myth as a Normative Argument in European Constitutionalism

The myth of a coherent normative theory of judicial independence is instrumental in the reinforcement of a particular view of the European Union as a community based on common values—a community of principle. This view is dominant in the theoretical discussions about the nature and character of the EU, and understandably illuminates the conceptions with which EU politicians and administrators approach practical problems, such as the evaluation of the progress of the accession countries.

The view of the European Union as a community of common values has direct implications for the European legal order. As Bengoetxea, MacCormick, and Moral Soriano have convincingly argued, this view would entail that EU law and EU constitutionalism should be based on comprehensive legal coherence, which would allow for the common set of values to permeate all spheres of communal life, by the creation of specific, common constitutional doctrines.[20] Indeed, they have claimed that the creation of such specific doctrines is at the heart of European integration:

> It seems no mere pun to link [integrity] with the idea of integration . . . The guiding value is integration of the states and their peoples into a community or union that succeeds in being more than an international association of treaty-observing states, while not yet leaping to the other pole of becoming a sovereign union state (like the UK or Spain) or a sovereign federal union (like the USA or Australia or India).[21]

The idea of the EU as a community of principle is capable of inspiring EU officials and illuminating their understanding of the character of the Union. There is a tiny step from the argument that the Union is based on common principles, to the idea that there are detailed common constitutional principles in the EU. If this is so, one should admit that there is, or at least that there should be a common theory of judicial independence, applicable to all member states.

---

a more focused review of the candidate countries would have not necessarily produced a single, coherent theory of judicial independence.

20 "Integration and Integrity in the Legal Reasoning of the European Court of Justice," in Grainne de Burca and J. H. H. Weiler (eds.), *The European Court of Justice* (Oxford: Oxford University Press 2001), p. 82.

21 Ibid., p. 85.

Taking this tiny step is the cognitive mechanism through which the ideal of a community based on common principles ends up re-enforcing the creation and perpetuation of specific constitutional myths, as the myth of a coherent theory of judicial independence.

4.3. The Myth as a Pragmatic Argument in Accession Negotiations

Probably the most important use of the myth of common constitutional principles and standards in the area of judicial independence has been registered in the negotiations between the Commission and national governments in the elaboration and the implementation of the so-called Action Plans—the strategies of the accession countries in meeting the Copenhagen criteria.

First of all, the myth of the existence of common principles of judicial independence could be used as a powerful argument to put pressure on particular governments to pass specific reforms. This has, however, not been the most important use of the myth, since the Commission has hardly had a specific agenda for reforms in each and every country. Therefore, it is most likely that domestic governments would form a coalition with the Commission in order to pass a particular reform of the judicial system, which in most cases would meet the resistance of the domestic judiciary. Reforming the judicial system always involves interpretation of domestic constitutional principles: it is no coincidence that domestic constitutional courts have been heavily involved in adjudication concerning reforms of the judiciary.

In these circumstances, the myth of a common European theory of judicial independence is particularly handy for a coalition between a domestic government and the EU Commission. If a domestic court (or some part of the judiciary) raises an objection against a specific reform proposal on the grounds of a contradiction with domestic (constitutional) rules, the government sponsoring the reform could argue that it is required by the common European constitutional principles. Such was the case, for instance, in the already mentioned episode from the Slovenian accession efforts, in which the government argued that an extension of the probation period for judges was required for EU membership against objections that it was unconstitutional on domestic constitutional grounds.

Probably the most spectacular instance of such a use of the myth of a common theory of judicial independence was the saga of the introduction of constitutional amendments in Bulgaria which allowed for the prolongation of the probationary period for judges, the introduction of time-limited mandates for senior magistrates, and the reduction of the immunities enjoyed by the magistrates. The whole problem started with the fact that some of the measures from the Action Plan agreed by the government and the Commission had been found unconstitutional by the Bulgarian Constitutional Court. Therefore, upon the explicit insistence by the Commission, an urgent amendment of the Constitution was arranged, which was defended at least partly on the grounds that, in this way, Bulgaria would adopt a model reflecting common European values and principles. On the basis of the previous discussion, it is not difficult to discern that this was largely a mythological justification. More importantly, however, the normative priority of the Action Plans over domestic constitutions is quite problematic, and hardly serves the purpose of creating a culture friendly to the rule of law.

Finally, it should be said that the discussed myth could have other strategic uses in the interaction between domestic and EU politics: it is by no means impossible for domestic judiciaries and especially domestic constitutional courts to use this myth as an argument against the government and the legislature. If the view of the domestic court is close to the views of the Commission, the domestic government would find itself in a difficult position. The general point is that the myth is instrumental in bridging domestic and EU politics, and this accounts for much of its popularity.

5. THE COSTS OF THE MYTH

Despite being instrumental for a variety of purposes, the use of a myth is accompanied by certain costs. In this section, I explore two types of costs, which seem to be especially high. Taking them into account might counsel against the use of the myth of a coherent theory of judicial independence in accession politics.

5.1. The Irreducible Political Role of Judges: A Challenge to Traditional Views of Independence

First, despite various short-term benefits, the use of the myth of a common European theory of judicial independence conceals a long-term common European problem, and delays its adequate treatment. This is the problem of the growing and irreducibly political power of the judiciary in contemporary constitutionalism. There is a rich literature on the political power of constitutional and high appellate courts, in the activities of which the processes of the "judicialization of politics" and "politicization of jurisprudence" are most visible. Yet, these processes could also be seen in the activities of other parts of the judiciary, such as the prosecutors, for instance. At the bottom of this problem is, on the one hand, the irreducible vagueness and indeterminacy of law, and especially constitutional law. With the expansion of the regulatory state, the need for interpretation of legal norms permeating more and more areas of social life has become particularly acute. In such a context, the powers of the judiciary, as the traditional ultimate interpreter of legal norms, have dramatically increased.

A second source of the expansion of the political powers of the judiciary has been the growing need for a specific type of policy decision—adjudicative decisions between competing comprehensive ideological views and doctrines. In contemporary pluralistic societies, reasonable disagreement reaches deep into what Rawls has called the "basic structure of society". Sometimes disagreement concerns not only issues relating to the *common good* of the given community, but also to the *principles of justice* according to which disputes should be resolved.

In the "circumstances of politics" marked by profound disagreement, as argued by Waldron, there is a need for an adjudicative procedure, which is not based on some specific contested substantive view of justice. Waldron himself believes that procedural views of democracy provide the answer to the predicament of profound disagreement. Waldron's views presuppose the restriction of the powers of courts, and greater reliance on democratically elected assemblies.[22]

A different answer to the same problem—the problem of pluralism and disagreement—draws on the insight of Martin Shapiro that the central rationale for the operation of courts is that of *neutral arbiters* in disputes between two parties.[23] In the circumstances of profound disagreement between competing conceptions of justice, it is no surprise that there is a growing need for neutral arbiters. Courts, especially constitutional and high appellate courts, are rather well suited to act as such arbiters in modern constitutional democracies. Therefore, their very constitutional position accounts for their growing powers.

The problem with this solution, however, is that because of the typical vagueness and indeterminacy of law, and constitutional law in particular, the neutrality of courts as arbiters cannot be anchored in constitutional rules and even principles—the discussion of the principle of judicial independence above has demonstrated this claim.[24] Another traditional way of ensuring their (political neutrality) is through institutional isolation from the other branches both in terms of appointment and promotion, but also in budgeting terms. Indeed, modern judiciaries are self-regulating and self-evaluating to a great degree, which is clearly demonstrated in Eastern Europe in the almost universal process of setting up of Judicial Councils. This second traditional way of ensuring the "neutrality" of courts as arbiters admits that the distinction between "principle" and "policy" in judicial work is significantly blurred. Courts *are* policy makers on this view, but their institutional isolation from other branches is sufficient to guarantee that their policies of adjudication between the claims of individuals and groups disagreeing on issues of justice and the common good are fair and impartial.

In order to strengthen the legitimacy of courts as specific policy makers a number of scholars argue in favour of increasing the accountability and political responsibility of judges and magistrates through the mechanisms of popular elections. Inspired by American models (at the state level), these proposals aim to make the judiciary more responsive to and more representative of the preferences of the citizens.

---

22 Jeremy Waldron, *Law and Disagreement* (Oxford: Clarendon Press 1999).

23 Martin Shapiro, *Courts: A Comparative and Political Analysis* (Chicago: University of Chicago Press 1981).

24 See Wojciech Sadurski, "Legitimacy and Reasons of Constitutional Review after Communism," in Wojciech Sadurski (ed.), *Constitutional Justice, East and West* (The Hague, London, New York: Kluwer Law International 2002).

There are at least three different, traditional ways of interpreting and responding to the problem of the growing political powers of the judiciary, which I sum up in Table 1.

As shown in Table 1, all three models have their own advantages and disadvantages. While the first two attempt to address the problem of the growing power of the judiciary through an increase of its political accountability, the third model attempts to ground the legitimacy of the judiciary in its role as a neutral arbiter between competing political views. In terms of weaknesses, the first two models may lead to the weakening of the traditional democratic institutions, or to the emergence of rampant political majoritarianism: in many countries of Eastern Europe, aggressive majoritarianism is a problem which needs to be taken seriously. The third model risks the capturing of the judiciary by special interests not controllable by the democratic process. This is also a real danger for many of the countries in the region.

Not surprisingly, therefore, the Commission has oscillated between the different models (especially the second and the third one) in its Regular Reports assessing the progress with judicial reforms in the accession countries. Even within single countries, the Commission has hesitated between the second and the third view over the years. Yet, despite the lack of a single best answer to the problem of the expansion of judicial power, for a variety of reasons (already discussed) the Commission and national governments have preferred to work on the assumption that they are implementing common European norms and solutions, which actually has resulted in the concealment of a common problem.

One of the most negative results of this concealment has been the neglect of actual *policy-making* decisions by the judiciaries in the accession countries, and an exclusive focus on the *institutional model* of independence. The Commission preferred to trigger institutional reforms rather than to look into the specific policy-making processes in the judiciary in a given country. In other words, the accession negotiations were carried out on the assumption that the choice of institutions can guarantee the adequacy of policies. As shown in Table 1 above, however, this is hardly the case—all institutional models may sometimes lead to wrong and dangerous policies adopted by the judiciary.

5.2. A Grand Myth of the EU as a Community of Principle?

The second cost associated with the endorsement of myths of common constitutional principle is that it in fact takes for granted the ideal of Europe as a community of principle as the best or even as the only political ideal about the EU. The defenders of the ideal of the EU as a community of principles usually portray the existing alternatives to their view as mere *modus vivendi* justifications of the Union as an instrument for the advancement of narrowly understood economic interests of the Member States. Indeed, if the choice were simply between a community of principles and such a *modus vivendi* society, few would argue that the former is not a more valuable form of human cooperation.

Table 1 The growing political power of the judiciary—institutional answers

	Third legislative chamber model	*Politically accountable judiciary*	*Strongly independent judiciary*
Rationale of the operation of constitutional and high appellate courts	Judges are policy-makers, similar to the legislative branch, but having a political programme structured in a different way	Judges administer and implement decisions and programmes of the politically elected branches	The judiciary lacks a specific political programme and acts in an opportunistic way as a policy-maker
Body administering and supervising the judicial system	An independent body, composed of appointees of the political branches of power	Minister of Justice or an equivalent political figure	An independent Council composed of appointees of the judiciary
Appointments	Senior judges appointed by the political branches or directly by the electorate	Senior judges appointed by the political branches of power, and especially the Minister of Justice	Appointments by independent judicial councils
Guarantees of independence	Different composition than the other political branches; different political agenda	Professional ethics	Institutional separation from the other branches
Representative character of the judiciary	Essential	Not essential	Not essential
Advantages	Ensures a degree of political responsibility for policy decisions	Ties responsibility for policy-making to traditional channels of democratic representation	Preserves better the character of the judiciary as a "neutral arbiter"
Disadvantages	Competing with democratically elected branches and weakening of traditional democratic institutions; danger of aggressive majoritarianism	The judiciary cannot be an effective check against aggressive political majoritarianism	The judiciary may start defending only their own corporate interest, and become captured by strong special interests, because of the low level of accountability

However, this dichotomy is misleading, because there are numerous possible intermediate positions, in which although the members of a given community are not fully committed to the same basic normative framework, they might consider staying together valuable not only from a narrow self-interested point of view. They all might actually be motivated by *different ideals of the common good*, and believe that cooperation with the other members of the society is their best chance to realize their own ideals.

All societies may rely on myths for the purposes of social mobilization and integration. One should not expect Europe to be the great exception from this rule. Yet, an account of the costs of the myths should be kept as well. This is not the place to explore all the costs of the grand myth of Europe as a community of principle. One of them should be at least indicated, however. This myth seems to lead to an excessive emphasis in the integration process on *normative harmonization* rather than on *political invention* of new normative solutions. The former requires the following of existing common normative frameworks, while the latter is centred on the notion of trust in the capacity of members having different normative agendas to understand each other, and resolve their disputes in a just, equitable and creative manner. Probably the *normative harmonization* view was sufficient for the accession process; it would hardly be sufficient for the further consolidation of European constitutionalism, however, in the circumstances of growing disagreement about the ultimate goals of the Union.

6. CONCLUSION

In this chapter, the issue of judicial independence in the accession process was examined, and it was argued that any claim that the Commission assessment of the legal systems of the accession countries has been based on a coherent theory of judicial independence is deeply problematic. Despite the lack of such a theory, factors diverse as the dominant intellectual understanding of the nature of the Union and pragmatic considerations in the negotiations process, have presupposed the construction of a certain myth of such a coherent theory. The chapter examined some of the uses of this myth and the costs related to these uses.

The issue of judicial independence was a tiny aspect of the accession process. Therefore, one should be careful in generalizing on the basis of the finding of this study. Yet, it seems what has been said for the issue of judicial independence might have some relevance for the assessment of the accession process in general.

15. Post-Communist Legal Orders and the Roma: Some Implications for EU Enlargement

*István Pogány**

1. Introduction

The ousting of communist regimes across Central and Eastern Europe (CEE), in 1989–1990, is frequently portrayed as the triumph of popular democracy, human rights and market economics.[1] However, for the bulk of an estimated six million Roma, or Gypsies, constituting by far the largest ethnic minority in the region, the post-communist era has brought neither improved living standards nor the genuine enjoyment of democracy or basic freedoms. On the contrary, Roma poverty has worsened dramatically during the transition from communism. As a recent World Bank report notes: "[w]hile Roma have historically been among the poorest people in Europe, the extent of the collapse of their living conditions in the former socialist countries is unprecedented."[2] At the same time, the incidence of anti-Roma assaults (and of Roma stereotyping by opportunistic politicians and by elements in the media) has risen sharply, particularly in the early to mid 1990s.[3] According to a

* I should like to acknowledge the generous financial support of the Nuffield Foundation. This enabled me to interview officials, NGO spokesmen and scholars concerned with minority affairs in Hungary and Romania, to work in specialist libraries and to carry out fieldwork in several Romanian towns and villages with significant Roma communities. The Office for National and Ethnic Minorities, in Budapest, Hungary, supplied me with numerous materials and were very helpful in responding to my queries. Finally, I should like to thank my colleague at the University of Warwick, Dr. Andy Williams, for his perceptive and helpful comments on an earlier draft of this paper.

1 See, e.g. Timothy Garton Ash, *We the People* (London: Granta Books 1990).

2 Dena Ringold, Mitchell A. Orenstein and Erika Wilkens, *Roma in an Expanding Europe: Breaking the Poverty Cycle* (Washington, DC: International Bank for Reconstruction and Development 2003), p. 1. See, generally, *ibid*, at pp. 1–2, 13, Chapt. 2.

3 For details of the pattern of violence directed against Roma in the CEE states and of anti-Roma stereotyping see, e.g. OSCE High Commissioner on National Minorities, *Report on the Situation of Roma and Sinti in the OSCE Area* (The Hague: OSCE 2000), Chapt. 2. The Report is available at http://www.osce.org/hcnm/documents/reports/ (accessed September 3, 2003). See, also, the Country Reports series issued by the Budapest-based European Roma Rights Center. See, in addition, the entries on various post-communist states in the annual World Report published by Human Rights Watch. The World Reports are available at: http://www.hrw.org/reports/world/reports/ (accessed March 28, 2003).

Wojciech Sadurski et al. (ed.), Spreading Democracy and the Rule of Law?, 335–356.

broad range of inter-governmental organisations and human rights NGOs, the new era of democracy and of supposed economic opportunity in the CEE states has been characterised by the partial exclusion—economic, social and political—of the mass of the region's Roma.[4]

The European Union has an obvious interest in the predicament of the Roma people of Central and Eastern Europe. The process of eastward enlargement of the EU means that the Roma 'problem' has ceased to be a largely external affair.[5] If transitional arrangements had not been introduced by existing EU members, severely limiting the potential flow of job seekers from the accession states for an interim period, the chronic economic and social marginalization of the Roma in the CEE region might have triggered waves of Roma migration, particularly from the Czech Republic, Slovakia and Hungary, to more prosperous and apparently liberal countries in Western Europe.[6] The eventual admission of a further tier of CEE states to the EU, Romania and Bulgaria—each of which has a substantial and mostly impoverished Roma minority—will result in an enormous additional pool of potential Romani migrants to the West.[7] At the very least, as emphasised in a recent World Bank report, the failure to address the economic, social and political exclusion of the Roma in the CEE countries will pose a serious challenge to sustained economic growth and to the consolidation of democracy and respect for human rights in the region.[8] Put simply, a large and expanding 'underclass' of semi-destitute, poorly educated and alienated Roma is likely to prove a massive

---

4 In addition to the sources cited above, n. 2–3, see, e.g. the relevant sections of the European Commission's 2002 Regular Reports on Progress Towards Accession of the then candidate states from the CEE region. These are available at: http://europa.eu.int/comm/enlargement/report2002/ (accessed January 12, 2004).

5 Even before the accession of a sizeable group of post-communist states to the European Union, on May 1, 2004, EU member states were confronted with the problem of Roma asylum seekers fleeing Central and Eastern Europe. See, e.g. Mít'a Castle-Canerová, "Romani Refugees: The EU Dimension," in Will Guy (ed.), *Between Past and Future* (Hertfordshire: Hertfordshire University Press 2001), Chapt. 6. See also Dallal Stevens, "The Migration of the Romanian Roma to the UK: A Contextual Study," *European Journal of Migration and Law*, 5 (2004), pp. 439–461.

6 At the time of writing, severe restrictions have been introduced by most EU members on the numbers of job seekers from accession states who will be admitted during a transitional period. In some cases, EU members have chosen to restrict access to welfare benefits by job seekers from accession states, rather than actual entry. The size of Roma populations in the CEE states cannot be given with any degree of precision for a variety of reasons. For an estimate see, e.g. Ringold, Orenstein, Wilkens, above n. 2, p. 12. In Bulgaria, FYR Macedonia, Romania and Slovakia, Roma are thought to comprise between 6 and 11% of the population of the respective countries.

7 It is currently envisaged that Bulgaria and Romania will accede to the European Union in 2007.

8 Ringold, Orenstein, Wilkens, above n. 2, p. 1.

economic burden on the CEE states, while also straining inter-communal tensions in these societies. These are important and obvious concerns for the EU, whether in terms of its economic objectives or its more recent commitment to the recognition and protection of human rights.[9]

Beginning with a case-study of a Transylvanian village which has a mixed population of ethnic Romanians, ethnic Hungarians and Roma, this chapter goes on to examine the nature and extent of the problems confronting the Roma of the CEE region in the transition from communism. The chapter further considers some of the causes of the chronic difficulties experienced by the Roma since the collapse of state socialism. It should not be assumed that the plight of this minority can be ascribed solely to racism and to anti-Roma discrimination in the countries concerned, even though the continuing importance of these factors should not be discounted. In Part IV of this chapter, I review the efforts of the EU to monitor the situation of the Roma in post-communist states and to address some of the underlying problems.

2. VOICES FROM A TRANSYLVANIAN VILLAGE: THE ROMA OF *SOMEŞ* IN THE TRANSITION FROM COMMUNISM[10]

Someş (not its real name) is a fairly typical village in north western Transylvania, in Romania. Like many of the villages in this region it has a mixed population. The residents of *Someş* comprise over 800 ethnic Romanians, more than 300 ethnic Hungarians and approximately 265 Roma, or Gypsies. In terms of religious affiliation, the ethnic Romanians are Orthodox, the Hungarians belong to the Reformed, or Presbyterian, Church, while the Roma adhere to one or the other of these religious denominations.

The Roma of *Someş*, as elsewhere in Romania and in the CEE region as a whole, insist that they were comparatively well off during the communist era. In particular, they were freed from material insecurity as the state provided them with jobs that assured them a regular income. Many of the Roma in the village, who had had little

---

[9] Article 6(2) of the consolidated text of the Treaty of European Union, dated December 24, 2002, declares that: '[t]he Union shall respect fundamental rights, as guaranteed by the European Convention for the Protection of Human Rights and Fundamental Freedoms . . . and as they result from the constitutional traditions common to the Member States'. For the text of the treaty see, e.g. http://europa.eu.int/eurlex/en/treaties/dat/EU_consol.pdf (accessed January 12, 2004). Note, also, the Charter of Fundamental Rights of the European Union, dated December 18, 2000. For the text of the Charter see, e.g. http://europa.eu.int/eurlex/pri/en/oj/dat/2000/c_364/c_36420001218en00010022.pdf (accessed January 12, 2004).

[10] This case study of the Roma living in the Transylvanian village of *Someş* is based on semi-structured interviews that I conducted with Roma families and community leaders in the village, in April 2003.

schooling, moved to towns and cities with their families where they were given work, frequently in newly constructed factories. Rapid and often ill-considered industrialisation was a key feature of the post-war sovietization of the region.[11] Other Roma from *Someş* found work locally, whether as labourers on recently established cooperative farms or at a nearby quarry. Traditionally, a large number of Roma in the village, as many as 47 at one time, had been popular and successful semi-professional musicians. At weekends, in groups of three to six, they played at wedding feasts and at other celebrations in the surrounding villages. In such a multicultural environment, Gypsy musicians learnt to be flexible and to maintain an extensive repertoire. Each of the principal ethnic communities in this part of Transylvania—Romanians, Hungarians and Roma—had their favourite songs and dances that they expected the Gypsy musicians to perform.

Miklós, a Romani resident of *Someş*, has spent his whole life in the village. Now in his late sixties he is retired and living on a small pension. For 30 years he worked as a stonemason at the local quarry, supplementing his wages with his earnings as a musician. In the single downstairs room of his tiny but immaculate wooden house he keeps the accordion that is his pride and joy, although now he is too frail to play the cumbersome instrument. Like most of the Roma in the village, Miklós recalls the communist years with undisguised nostalgia:

> When the communists were around, life was good! Back then, poor people, peasants, everyone had something. Whether you wanted to or not, you had to go [to work]. You got what you got, but it was enough to live on! It wasn't a lot of money, maybe fifteen hundred or two thousand Lei. I earned two thousand Lei. I never managed to earn more than that.

For most of his adult life, Miklós was in great demand as a musician. At weekends, along with his father, well known locally for his skills as a violinist, and his wife, who accompanied them on the drums, they performed at weddings and other festivities. Frequently, other instruments were added to the line-up: a second accordion, a double bass and a *kontra*.[12]

Since the end of communist rule and the gradual introduction of a market economy under successive governments, most of the Roma of *Someş*, as in other parts of Romania and within the CEE region as a whole, have experienced economic dislocation and plummeting living standards. As factories closed down or shed

---

11 See, e.g. Ivan Berend, *Central and Eastern Europe 1944–1993* (Cambridge: Cambridge University Press 1996), pp. 190–192.

12 The *kontra*, a stringed instrument, was developed in Transylvania, quite possibly by Gypsies. It can be adapted from either a violin or a viola, and has a flat bridge instead of the rounded bridge that is characteristic of string instruments that are bowed rather than plucked. Consequently, a bow can be drawn across three strings of the *kontra* at once, producing a complete chord. I am grateful to the Cluj-based folk musician and musicologist, Kálmán Urszui, for this information.

much of their surplus workforce—measures that impacted disproportionately on the Roma—many newly redundant Gypsies opted to return with their families to villages, such as *Someş*, in which they had spent their childhood. They imagined that it would be easier to survive in a rural environment. Other Roma, who had remained in the countryside during the socialist era and who had worked as labourers on collective farms, lost their jobs as the land was returned to the peasants from whom it had been taken in accordance with communist policies of collectivisation. As in other countries in the region, very few Roma had owned agricultural land in the inter-war period. Therefore, they were excluded from the process of land reprivatization that was implemented in Romania, in the 1990s, in an effort to correct some of the worst 'injustices' perpetrated by the communists. New employment opportunities in or around villages such as *Someş* remain scarce, particularly for Roma. In addition to the general shortage of regular work, Roma job applicants have to contend with pervasive anti-Roma prejudice. The Roma are also disadvantaged by their generally low level of formal education. The fate of the two adult sons of Miklós, the retired stonemason and former accordionist, is instructive. Referring to his elder son, Miklós told me indignantly:

> He worked, he worked on the roads for twenty years! Now he doesn't work anywhere, because where could he [find a job]? He and his family are here with me. Then there's my younger son. He worked for ten years. He learnt to be a stonemason [like me]. He has three children. Now he can't earn anything, anywhere. He went to the authorities and asked them for money. Once they gave him some after three months. After three months they gave him something.

Even music has ceased to be a source of ready income for the Roma in the village. Musical tastes have changed and the availability of cassette and CD players offers a much cheaper means of entertainment than hiring a Gypsy band. Many younger Roma, including Miklós' sons and grandchildren, have even lost the desire to learn to play a musical instrument. Miklós told me, with evident sadness, about one of his grandsons:

> Here's my younger son's son. I thought to myself, he'll be like my father, he'll be a good musician! He made a good start [on the violin]. Then he got bored of it. There are no longer Gypsies coming into the world who'll grow into musicians.

A Romani community leader in *Someş* explained to me how most of the Roma in the village earn a living since the end of communism. Some hire themselves out as labourers to *gadje* (i.e. non-Roma) smallholders, although such work is seasonal, at best, and very poorly remunerated. Sometimes, the Roma are paid in kind, i.e. with flour, *szalona* (a fatty bacon), or other foodstuffs. Many Roma, like Miklós' younger son, rely on occasional handouts from the local administration. Gathering mushrooms and medicinal plants that grow in hedgerows near the village constitutes another, albeit irregular, source of income. Virtually identical modes of subsistence have been identified by a Hungarian ethnographer, Péter Szuhay, amongst a community of *Vlach* Roma in a village in south eastern Hungary.[13]

Paradoxically, the end of communism has partially reversed the slow process of social and economic integration on which many Roma had embarked under state socialism, or sometimes significantly earlier. For many Roma in the CEE states, the post-communist transition has become synonymous with abject poverty, insecurity and heightened social marginalisation.

Ironically, two or three *Kalderara* Romani families in *Someş*, who resisted the communist authorities' efforts to integrate them within Romanian society, have experienced far fewer problems of adjustment since 1990 than the numerous Roma in the village who readily accepted jobs. Preferring the freedom of self-employment to a more regulated life as factory workers, or as laborers on agricultural cooperatives, the *Kalderara* worked as rag and bone men during much of the socialist era. Over time, they found a new niche for themselves, trading in 'antiques' such as XIX century jugs and vases, for which there was a growing market. Although entrepreneurial activity was generally frowned upon by communist ideologues, a minority of Romania's Gypsies, often belonging to Roma subgroups such as the *Kalderara* or the *Gabori*, were permitted to work as self-employed traders or as craftsmen during much of the socialist era.

The commercial flair and spirit of self-reliance of the *Kalderara* Romani families of *Someş* has proved a major asset in the new market oriented, post-communist environment. The former rag and bone men of the village—who at one time were looked down upon by the other Roma in *Someş* as backward, semi-nomadic and unwilling to integrate—have transformed themselves into successful businessmen. Acquiring nineteenth century hand-painted wooden chests and other family heirlooms from a younger generation of peasants, who frequently prefer modern, factory-made furniture, they sell the assorted antiques to dealers from abroad who find a ready market for them in Western Europe. The Romani traders of *Someş* have become adept at identifying the provenance of these sturdy, hand-painted chests, each of which was built to accommodate a bride's trousseau.

However, for the vast majority of Roma in *Someş*, life has become increasingly bleak. Like Miklós' adult sons, most of the Roma in the village lack marketable skills or land on which to produce food for themselves and their families. And, as a result of their experiences under communism, they have become dangerously dependent on the state, whether as a source of employment or of social assistance. One of the village's handful of *Kalderara* Romani entrepreneurs told me that as many as 80% of the men in the village are currently unemployed, Roma and non-Roma alike. However, he insisted that, apart from the *Kalderara* Roma who have their own businesses, the local Gypsies are in a much worse position than either

[13] Péter Szuhay, "Foglalkozási és megélhetési stratégiák a magyarországi cigányok körében," in Ferenc Glatz (ed.), *A Cigányok Magyarországon* (Budapest: Magyar Tudományos Akadémia 1999), p. 139.

the Romanians or the Hungarians: "[t]hey [Romanians and Hungarians] can still get by, because they have land, everything. But round here the Roma don't own any land, horses, cows, pigs, or sheep. They have nothing."

3. THE PLIGHT OF THE ROMA OF CENTRAL AND EASTERN EUROPE IN THE TRANSITION FROM COMMUNISM

The plight of most of the Roma in the Transylvanian village of *Somes* offers a stark insight into the difficulties experienced by the bulk of the Roma of Central and Eastern Europe in the transition from Communism. These problems are different in character, scope and in sheer intractability from those encountered by most other national or ethnic minorities, of any size, in the region. Thus, there are few, if any, analogies that can be drawn between the predicament of the Roma in the CEE states and problems faced by national minorities such as ethnic Serbs in Croatia or ethnic Hungarians in Slovakia, the Ukraine, Serbia or Romania. National and ethnic minorities in the post-Communist states, other than the Roma, frequently complain about the lack of educational provision in minority languages or the need for greater cultural and political recognition by the authorities. By contrast, the Roma have experienced an acute economic crisis, since 1990, as well as heightened social marginalisation. In many areas, increased antipathy towards the Roma has resulted in vicious, racially motivated physical assaults.

3.1. The Economic Crisis Affecting the Roma in the Transition from Communism

In the shift from command to market economies, the Roma have suffered disproportionately, experiencing mass unemployment and growing poverty throughout the CEE region.[14] In Hungary it has been estimated that 70% of Romani men of working age are currently unemployed as against less than 10% of the non-Romani population.[15] The extent of Romani unemployment in other CEE states with significant Romani minorities,[16] including the Czech Republic, Slovakia, Bulgaria

---

[14] On the worsening poverty experienced by the bulk of the Roma since the end of communism see, e.g. Ringold, Orenstein, Wilkens, above n. 2, Chapt. 2. See, also, Zoltan Barany, The *East European Gypsies* (Cambridge: Cambridge University Press 2002), pp. 157–183; István Pogány, *The Roma Café* (London: Pluto 2004), especially Chapts. 1, 6, 9. On the economic gains experienced by many Roma during the socialist era see, e.g. Barany, above n. 14, pp. 125–143; Pogány, above n. 14, Chapt. 4.

[15] European Union's 2002 Regular Report on Hungary, p. 31. This is available at http://europa.eu.int/comm/enlargement/report2002/ (accessed March 28, 2003).

[16] For the reasons given above, the size of Romani minorities in the CEE states cannot be given with any degree of precision. However, according to figures cited by the European Commission, there are up to 800,000 Roma in Bulgaria, 300,000 in the Czech Republic, 600,000 in Hungary, 2,500,000 in Romania, and 520,000 in Slovakia. In Poland, where the bulk of the Roma were killed during World War II, it is estimated that there are up to

and Romania, is comparable.[17] Soaring levels of Romani unemployment in the post-communist states, together with the rising cost of rents, utilities and basic foodstuffs, have contributed to worsening poverty and deprivation amongst a significant proportion of the Roma people. As noted in a recent World Bank Report:[18]

> Roma are the most prominent poverty risk group in many of the countries of Central and Eastern Europe. They are poorer than other groups, more likely to fall into poverty, and more likely to remain poor. In some cases poverty rates for Roma are more than 10 times that of non-Roma. A recent survey found that nearly 80 percent of Roma in Romania and Bulgaria were living on less than $4.30 per day . . . Even in Hungary, one of the most prosperous accession countries, 40 percent of Roma live below the poverty line.

The root causes of the current high levels of Romani unemployment in the CEE states, a prime cause of Romani poverty, cannot be reduced to a single factor. In some instances, Roma may have a culturally informed preference for informal entrepreneurial activity of various kinds, or even subsistence occupations, over wage labour with its inevitable and far-reaching restrictions on individual freedom and autonomy.[19] However, Roma frequently have little or no choice in such matters due to the scarcity of secure, full-time employment of the kind that was readily available under communism.

In part, the scale of Romani unemployment can be explained by the fact that, during the communist era, the authorities encouraged (sometimes even coerced) the Roma to take semi-skilled or unskilled jobs in sectors of the economy, such as heavy industry, that were to prove uncompetitive. Many of these former state-owned enterprises, employing large numbers of Roma, were closed down during the hasty transition to a market economy, or shed much of their workforce.

Thus, it can be argued that the communist policy of integrating the Roma in the general economy, while providing them with limited training or opportunities for professional advancement, amounted to little more than proletarianization. Such policies conspicuously failed to equip the bulk of the Roma with the skills or outlook needed to obtain regular employment in increasingly modern, competitive societies. Michael Stewart has referred dismissively to the "creation of phantasmagorical "socialist" jobs for the Gypsies which disappeared as soon as consumers had any choice over what they purchased."[20] In fact, there is a case for saying that, by

---

60,000 Gypsies. See European Union Support for Roma Communities in Central and Eastern Europe, p. 4. The text is available at http://europa.eu.int/comm/enlargement/docs/pdf/brochure_roma_oct2003_en.pdf (accessed February 23, 2004).

17 See, e.g. Ringold, Orenstein, Wilkens, above n. 2, pp. 35–37.

18 *Ibid*, at 1–2.

19 *Ibid*, at 36.

20 Michael Stewart, "Communist Roma Policy 1945–89 as Seen Through the Hungarian Case," in Will Guy (ed.), above n. 5, p. 87.

generally discouraging the Roma from pursuing traditional trades or crafts, or from engaging in commerce, the communists in Central and Eastern Europe may have unwittingly rendered the Roma *less capable* of adjusting to modern economic conditions than they would have been if the authorities had been less dogmatic in their approach to the Gypsy "question."

However, blatantly discriminatory practices by employers are also to blame for the current unacceptably high levels of Romani unemployment in the region. There is a widespread disinclination on the part of employers in the CEE countries to hire Gypsies, other than as casual labourers. The virulence of anti-Roma prejudice has led some lighter skinned Roma to try to pass themselves off as *gadje*, or non-Roma, in an effort to gain social and professional acceptance.[21]

As emphasized above, in the case study of the Roma living in the village of *Someş* in Transylvania, a comparative lack of marketable skills and of educational qualifications also helps to account for the difficulties experienced by Roma in finding regular employment. The statistics of Romani educational under-performance are alarming. According to research done in Hungary, in the mid 1990s, only 2% of Roma aged 25–29 had completed secondary school.[22] Levels of educational achievement amongst Roma in other Central and Eastern Europe states are broadly comparable. A Romanian study, carried out in 1998, found that 18.3% of Romani children aged 7–16 had not even attended elementary school.[23] In the mid 1990s, 2.5% of Czech Roma and 2.8% of Slovak Roma attended (but did not necessarily complete) secondary school.[24] Only 0.2% of Hungarian Roma, 0.7% of Romanian Roma and 0.9% of Bulgarian Roma undertook tertiary education of any kind.[25]

The chronic educational underperformance of the Roma in the CEE countries is a product, to some degree, of cultural insensitivity. Not infrequently teachers have low expectations of their Romani pupils as they simply do not understand the cultural context that may shape some Romani childrens' behaviour in class.[26] In other instances, there is compelling evidence of institutionalised discrimination. For example, human rights experts assert that Romani children in the Czech Republic have been systematically allocated to 'special' schools intended for the educationally subnormal without regard to their individual abilities.[27] A detailed

21 For a discussion of this phenomenon see Pogány, above n. 14, Chapt. 5.

22 István Kemény, "Tennivalók a cigányok/romák ügyében," in Glatz, above n. 13, p. 230.

23 Barany, above n. 14, pp. 169–170. See, generally, *ibid*, at 164–172.

24 *Ibid*, p. 170.

25 *Ibid*, p. 171.

26 The educational 'ghettoization' of Romani pupils in parts of Central and Eastern Europe and related problems are discussed in Pogány, above n. 14, Chapt. 1.

27 See, generally, European Roma Rights Center, *A Special Remedy: Roma and Schools for the Mentally Handicapped in the Czech Republic* (Budapest: ERRC Country Report Series No. 8, June 1999).

report issued by an influential NGO, the Budapest-based European Roma Rights Center, notes that:[28]

> According to reasonable estimates, Roma are at least fifteen times more likely to be placed in remedial special schools than non-Roma. A student who has completed remedial special school has greatly restricted choices in secondary education compared to a student who has completed mainstream primary school. Romani children are thereby effectively condemned from an early age to a lifetime of diminished opportunity and self-respect. In addition, the segregation of Roma in inferior schools is used as constant legitimation for discriminatory attitudes and actions by members of the majority society.

These alleged practices in the Czech Republic are currently the subject of a complaint to the European Court of Human Rights. In Hungary, a recent study of elementary schools found that pressure from non-Romani parents had resulted in the allocation of large numbers of Gypsy pupils to "special classes."[29] Researchers, who examined 192 Hungarian elementary schools, concluded that almost 85% of the children in "special classes" are of Roma extraction.[30] The standard of instruction provided to the mostly Romani pupils in the "special classes" is often unsatisfactory, while the teachers assigned to these classes are frequently poorly qualified.

However, the educational under-performance of significant numbers of Roma pupils can also be ascribed to the residual effects of deep-seated Romani cultural norms. Traditionally, the Roma generally viewed 'education' as the intergenerational transfer of skills, usually within families or communities, rather than as passing exams or attendance at schools. A failure to appreciate the growing importance of formal qualifications as the most reliable route to secure and well paid work remains a widespread problem, particularly in poorer or more traditional Romani communities. In the view of social workers and numerous Romani community leaders, many Romani parents continue to attach insufficient importance to their childrens' schooling.

Not infrequently, Romani children are expected to play a part in generating income for the family from an early age, whether by hawking goods, begging or, in rural areas, helping to collect medicinal plants, nuts and other commodities that can be sold to wholesalers. For example, children from the Romani settlement of *Pata Rât*, on the outskirts of the city of *Cluj* in Romania, worked alongside their parents at the municipal rubbish dump until a few years ago, combing through the

---

28 *Ibid*, p. 11.

29 Gábor Havas, "A cigány tanulók elkülönitése az általános iskolában," in Terézia Reisz and Mihály Andor (eds.), *A Cigányság Társadalomismerete* (Pécs: Iskolakultúra 2002), p. 152, at pp. 166–172.

30 *Ibid*, p. 170.

rubbish for items of value. A local Romani NGO, *Wassdas*, finally persuaded the parents to let their children attend school.[31]

In some instances, traditional notions of "shame" continue to play a decisive role in shaping the attitudes and way of life of Romani sub-groups, with important implications for the education and general status of women in these communities. Amongst the *Gabori* Roma of north western Romania, for example, girls are only permitted to receive 2–3 years of schooling out of concern that an adolescent girl, attending school, might become the subject of gossip, thereby bringing shame on her family.[32] The strict division of the sexes and the right of parents to select marriage partners for their children, while the latter are in their early teens, remain widely observed customs amongst this community.

Although the entrepreneurial culture of Romani subgroups, such the *Gabori*, has enabled them to adapt comparatively well to the demands of a market economy, the vast majority of Roma in Central and Eastern Europe have been far less successful. Spiralling unemployment amongst the Roma—particularly at a time of economic transition when former communist states have been shedding many of the subsidies and welfare structures built up during the socialist period—have impacted massively and disproportionately on Roma living conditions throughout the region.[33] Unable to keep up the rent on apartments in towns and cities, or to meet the rising cost of utilities, hundreds of thousands of Roma have vacated their homes, moving to cheaper accommodation in the countryside, or to flimsy shacks in overcrowded settlements such as the one at *Pata Rât*. Still others have become squatters, occupying buildings that frequently lack proper sanitation, water or electricity.[34]

At both the national and international levels there has been increasing, if belated, recognition of the fact that the impoverishment and marginalisation of the bulk of the substantial Romani population in the CEE region threatens the long-term prosperity of several CEE states, as well as endangering their internal cohesion and democratic institutions. Since the mid to late 1990s, governments throughout the region have introduced programs aimed at alleviating the acute socio-economic problems experienced by their Roma minorities.

Beginning in 1995, Hungarian governments have adopted a series of legal measures to address some of the worst problems experienced by the Roma.[35] These

---

31 For details of conditions at the *Pata Rât* settlement and of the work of *Wassdas* see Pogány, above n. 14, Chapt. 1.

32 For a discussion of *Gabori* notions of shame see *ibid*, Chapt. 7.

33 See, generally, Ringold, Orenstein, Wilkens, above n. 2, Chapt. 2. On the dismantling of social and economic rights in the CEE states and the effects of this process on the region's Roma see Pogány, above n. 14, Chapt. 6.

34 Ina Zoon provides many examples of this phenomenon. See, e.g. Ina Zoon, *On the Margins: Roma and Public Services in Romania, Bulgaria and Macedonia* (New York: Open Society Institute 2001), pp. 184–185, 188.

35 The first of these measures was Government Resolution 1121 of 1995. This authorised the establishment of a Public Foundation for the Roma to 'decrease the imbalance'

instruments include, for example, Government Resolution No. 1047/1999 (V.5), concerning 'Medium-Term Measures to Improve the Living Standards and Social Position of the Roma Population'.[36] Laying down a series of objectives for government departments concerned, variously, with education, employment, housing, health and social affairs, the Resolution tried to tackle the multiple roots of Roma disadvantage and under-achievement, with the ultimate aim of promoting "the integration of the Roma population in society" and improving "their living standards and social position."[37] However, it would be naive to imagine that these ambitious policy objectives have been realized.[38]

According to official documents, the goal of integrating the Roma within Hungarian society is not to be pursued at the expense of the preservation of Roma identity. Thus, a discussion paper issued by Hungary's former Minister of Justice, in July 2001, emphasised that, "[t]he aim of the long-term [Roma] strategy . . . is to promote the social and economic integration of the Roma population living in Hungary and to ensure simultaneously the appropriate conditions for the preservation of their minority identity."[39] Though exemplary as a matter of principle this strategy fails to take account of the fact that, partially as a result of successive programs of state-sponsored assimilation, most Hungarian Roma have already lost any real sense of "minority identity", apart from the consciousness of their social and economic marginality.[40]

Since 1990, Hungary has created a liberal and innovative minority rights regime, allowing the country's minorities, including the Roma, to form national and local self-governing councils. The creation of these self-governing bodies constituted a radical initiative in constitutional terms, allowing national and ethnic minorities a degree of autonomy in cultural and educational affairs and embodying the still controversial principle of collective rights. As of October 2002, there are

---

experienced by this minority. See, also, Government Resolutions Nos. 1120/1995 (XII.7); 1125/1995 (XII.12) For an English-language translation of Government Resolution 1121 see http://archiv.meh.hu/nekh/Angol/6-1-23.htm (accessed February 24, 2004).

36 For an English-language translation of the 1999 Resolution see http://archiv.meh.hu/nekh/Angol/6-1999-1047.htm (accessed February 24, 2004). See, also, Government Resolution No. 1093/1997 (VII.29) on the medium-term package of measures to improve the living standards of the Roma population, and Government Resolution No. 1107/1997 (X.11) on the measures aimed at improving the situation of the Roma ethnic minority. These earlier Resolutions expired with the entry into force of Government Resolution No. 1047/1999 (V.5).

37 Para. 4, Government Resolution No. 1047/1999 (V.5).

38 For a discussion of Roma poverty and marginalisation in Hungary see, e.g. Pogány, above n. 14, Chapts. 4, 7.

39 For an English-language translation of the discussion paper on 'Guiding principles of the long-term Roma social and minority policy strategy' see http://archiv.meh.hu/nekh/Angol/guiding.htm (accessed February 24, 2004).

40 On successive efforts to assimilate Hungary's Roma see, e.g. Pogány, above n. 14, Chapts. 2, 4.

1004 Romani, or Gypsy, councils of this type in Hungary.[41] However, it is doubtful whether Hungary's minority rights regime has done much to address the fundamental problems experienced by the country's Roma—unemployment, inadequate living standards and widespread discrimination.[42]

In 2001, Romania unveiled an ambitious "Roma Strategy" designed to increase Roma employment opportunities while at the same time significantly improving Roma access to public services, including education and healthcare. In accordance with the Strategy, experts on Roma affairs have been appointed to advise county prefects, while a total of 42 local Roma offices have been established across the country.[43] At the national level, fifteen commissions have been created to develop sectoral strategies for tackling a wide range of problems affecting the Roma, including unemployment. However, a report issued in 2003, by the European Commission, noted that[44]:

> Discrimination against the Roma minority continues to be widespread in practice and the social inequalities to which the Roma community is exposed remain considerable. Living conditions are poor and access to social services is limited . . . the Government has continued with implementation of the Roma Strategy (adopted in 2001), although the results have been uneven . . . Progress in . . . [several] areas covered by the Roma Strategy has been limited due to a lack of clear policies and limited funding.

In June 2000, the Czech Government issued a resolution on the "Concept of the Government policy towards the members of the Roma community, supporting their integration into society."[45] Czech authorities subsequently launched a strategic action plan, for the period 2001–2020, with the aim of implementing the resolution. However, in a Report issued in 2002, the European Commission concluded that, "[i]n spite of these efforts, widespread discrimination continues to exist and the

41 See *National and Ethnic Minorities in Hungary* (Budapest: Office for National and Ethnic Minorities, 13 May 2003), p. 5.

42 On the limitations of minority rights regimes as a means of advancing the basic interests of the Roma in the CEE region see, e.g. Pogány, above n. 14, Chapt. 5.

43 For details see, e.g. *2002 Regular Report on Romania's Progress Towards Accession* (Brussels: Commission of the European Communities 2002), pp. 35–36. See, also, *2003 Regular Report on Romania's Progress Towards Accession* (Brussels: Commission of the European Communities 2003), p. 30. These Reports are available at: http://europa.eu.int/comm/enlargement/report2002/#report2002 (accessed February 25, 2004).

44 *2003 Regular Report on Romania's Progress Towards Accession*, above n. 43, p. 30.

45 For details of the Czech Roma strategy and of steps taken to implement it see, e.g. Barany, above n. 14, pp. 332–334. See, also, 2002 Regular Report on the Czech Republic's Progress Towards Accession (Brussels: Commission of the European Communities 2002), pp. 30–33. The 2002 Report is available at: http://europa.eu.int/comm/enlargement/report2002/#report2002 (accessed February 25, 2004).

Government's efforts to date have not yet reached a threshold capable of bringing about structural change."[46]

Thus, notwithstanding a series of welcome initiatives by the CEE states, intergovernmental organisations, NGOs and independent experts remain deeply concerned at the scale of the problems that the region's Roma are still experiencing. In a recent report, cited above, senior economists at the World Bank felt it necessary to issue a stark warning as to the likely consequences for the CEE region of a continued failure to tackle the multiple difficulties confronting the Roma people[47]:

> National governments have a large stake in the welfare of Roma, for human rights and social justice concerns, but also for reasons of growth and competitiveness. In countries where Roma constitute a large and growing share of the working-age population, increasing marginalization of Roma in poverty and long-term unemployment threatens economic stability and social cohesion.

3.2. The Escalation of Physical Assaults against the Roma in the Transition from Communism

The worsening economic and social marginalisation of the Roma in the CEE region, in the transition from communism, has been accompanied by an escalation of physical assaults against Roma in several states, notably Slovakia, Romania and the Czech Republic. For example, in its 2002 World Report, Human Rights Watch, a highly respected NGO, drew attention to several incidents of anti-Roma violence in both the Czech Republic and Slovakia. With respect to Slovakia, the Report noted "a continuing pattern of police failure to prevent racist violence against Slovak Roma", offering the following damning picture of the Slovak criminal justice system[48]:

> In a week of incidents, racist gang members beat and harassed Roma in the town of Holic, culminating in an August 13 assault on Milan Daniel that left him needing brain surgery. Roma residents asserted that the police had failed to protect them despite repeated complaints. On August 20, police finally charged two youths with the attack on Daniel. On August 30, Peter Bandur was sentenced to seven years' imprisonment for his part in the beating to death of a Roma woman, Anastazia Balasova, a year earlier... While Bandur was convicted of the more serious crime of racially motivated assault, his two accomplices received three and five years respectively for simple assault (without racist intent).

As suggested by these grim developments in Slovakia (similar examples could be provided with respect to the treatment of Roma in the Czech Republic, Romania,

---

46 *2002 Regular Report on the Czech Republic's Progress Towards Accession*, above n. 45, p. 32.

47 See Ringold, Orenstein, Wilkens, above n. 2, p. 1.

48 See entry for 'Slovakia' in Human Rights Watch, *World Report 2002*, at http://hrw.org/wr2k2/europe.html (accessed September 3, 2003).

Bulgaria and elsewhere), the Roma have had to contend with discriminatory and unsympathetic treatment by criminal justice systems in the post-communist transition, in addition to a surge of racially motivated violence. The Roma have also faced routine denigration by sections of the media and by opportunistic politicians, eager to exploit popular prejudices. This contrasts with the broadly paternalistic, if authoritarian, treatment that the Roma generally experienced during the years of state socialism, when racial stereotyping by the press or electronic media would not have been tolerated.[49] Unsurprisingly, thousands of Roma have sought asylum in North America and Western Europe.[50]

4. THE EUROPEAN UNION'S POLICIES CONCERNING THE ROMA OF CENTRAL AND EASTERN EUROPE

The European Union's policies concerning the Roma of Central and Eastern Europe have to be understood in the context of the Union's general approach to enlargement. These policies can be analysed in terms of three separate but closely linked functions: (a) laying down standards for the applicant states with respect to the observance of human rights and the treatment of national and ethnic minorities including the Roma; (b) monitoring states' compliance with these norms; (c) funding projects in the CEE region that are intended to aid Roma communities, as well as providing material incentives to the applicant states to fulfil their responsibilities towards the Roma. For reasons of convenience, the standard settling and monitoring functions of the EU will be examined together.

4.1. Standard Setting and Monitoring

In 1993, the European Council adopted the "Copenhagen criteria." This sets out, in broad terms, the political and economic conditions that candidate states must satisfy in order to qualify for membership of the EU.[51] According to the Copenhagen formula applicants must demonstrate, *inter alia*, that they have achieved "stability of institutions guaranteeing democracy, the rule of law, human rights and *respect for and protection of minorities*."[52] Thus, with the adoption of the Copenhagen test, the

---

49 On the treatment of the Roma by the former communist regimes see, e.g. Barany, above n. 14, Chapt. 4.

50 See above, n. 5.

51 In addition to the political and economic conditions, specified in the Copenhagen criteria, candidate states must also demonstrate that they have the ability to assume the obligations of EU membership, i.e. the *acquis*.

52 My emphasis. The Copenhagen criteria are reproduced, for example, in European Union Support for Roma communities in Central and Eastern Europe (undated), p. 4, at http://europa.eu.int/comm/enlargement/docs/pdf/brochure_roma_oct2003_en.pdf (accessed March 1, 2004. Subsequently, the political criteria recognized at Copenhagen were included,

situation of the Roma (and of other national and ethnic minorities in the candidate states) came under formal EU scrutiny. From that date, candidate countries have understood that their efforts to join the EU hinge, at least in part, on their treatment of various national and ethnic minorities, including the Roma.

As indicated above, the problems facing the Roma of the CEE states, particularly since 1990, are different in character, scope and in sheer intractability from those encountered by most other national or ethnic minorities, of any size, in the region. Consequently, in applying the Copenhagen formula, the EU Commission has been particularly concerned at the desperate situation of the Roma in several candidate states in Central and Eastern Europe. As already indicated, in Parts II–III of this chapter, the Roma in the CEE countries have experienced sharply increased levels of economic and social marginalisation, since the collapse of state socialism, resulting in a state of affairs that economists and human rights experts regard as catastrophic. According to conservative estimates, there are almost six million Roma currently living in the CEE region, representing by far the largest ethnic minority in the area.[53]

The European Commission first drew attention to the problems experienced by Central and Eastern Europe's Roma in July 1997. In Agenda 2000, a document that dealt with a range of issues including EU enlargement, the Commission noted that the integration of national and ethnic minorities in the candidate countries

---

albeit in modified form, in both the consolidated Treaty on European Union, as amended by the Treaty of Amsterdam, and in the Charter of Fundamental Rights of the European Union proclaimed at the Nice European Council. Thus, Article 6(1) of the Treaty of European Union emphasizes that, '[t]he Union is founded on the principles of liberty, democracy, respect for human rights and fundamental freedoms, and the rule of law'. For the text of the Treaty of European Union see above, n. 9. However, there is no express reference in the Treaty to the rights of national or ethnic minorities. The Charter of Fundamental Rights, of December 18, 2000, while articulating the rights recognized by the EU, is notably cautious in its treatment of minority issues. Article 21 prohibits discrimination on the grounds of "membership of a national minority", while Article 22 stipulates that "[t]he Union shall respect cultural, religious and linguistic diversity". For the text of the Charter of Fundamental Rights of the European Union see above, n. 9. However, the Charter falls some way short of the commitment, enshrined in the Copenhagen formula, of "respect for and protection of minorities". In particular, the terms "minority" and "protection" have been omitted from Article 22 of the Charter, resulting in a considerably weaker and less clearly defined obligation. However, the Charter of Fundamental Rights and Article 6(1) of the Treaty of European Union must be understood, first and foremost, as setting out the duties of EU institutions and bodies with respect to the recognition and protection of basic freedoms. See, e.g. Article 51, Charter of Fundamental Rights of the European Union. By contrast, the Copenhagen criteria embody the standards, political and economic, that applicant states must satisfy in order to qualify for membership of the EU.

53 *European Union Support for Roma communities in Central and Eastern Europe*, above n. 52, p. 4.

was, in broad terms, satisfactory "except for the situation of the Roma minority in a number of applicant [countries], which gives cause for concern."[54] The Commission emphasized the extent of the difficulties, including discrimination and social hardship, facing Roma minorities in Bulgaria, the Czech Republic, Hungary, Poland, Romania and Slovakia.[55]

Since 1998, at the invitation of the European Council, the Commission has produced "Regular Reports" on the progress made by the candidate states towards compliance with the Copenhagen criteria.[56] These Reports, some of which were cited in Part III of this chapter, provide detailed information about the continuing difficulties experienced by the Roma in the CEE region, including poverty, inadequate housing, as well as discrimination in employment and in the provision of public services. The Reports also present the Commission's assessment of efforts by the candidate countries to tackle these problems through wide-ranging programs, such as the Roma Strategy adopted by the Romanian authorities in 2001.[57] As a result of the admission of the Czech Republic, Hungary, Poland, Slovenia and Slovakia to the EU, in May 2004, along with five other candidate countries, the Commission's most recent Regular Reports no longer deal with these countries. However, the Commission has continued to publish Reports on Bulgaria, Romania and Turkey.[58]

The broad requirement contained in the Copenhagen formula, to ensure 'respect for and protection of minorities', has been translated by the European Commission into more specific obligations for the various CEE states with respect to the situation of the Roma in each of these countries. Accession Partnerships drafted in March 1998 for CEE states with substantial Roma minorities—Bulgaria, the Czech Republic, Hungary and Romania—referred expressly to the plight of the Roma. The Partnerships stipulated that continued improvement in the situation of the Roma in these countries constituted "a medium-term political priority."[59] The obligations contained in the original Accession Partnership for Slovakia differed only insofar as further measures were considered necessary by the Commission to strengthen the protection available to *all* national and ethnic minorities in the

---

54 The Commission's observations concerning the Roma in the applicant states, in Agenda 2000, are summarised at *id*.

55 For the full text of Agenda 2000 and the European Commission's 1997 opinions on the various candidate states see: http://www.europa.eu.int/comm/enlargement/intro/ag2000_opinions.htm (accessed February 28, 2004).

56 The Reports are available at: http://europa.eu.int/comm/enlargement/report2002/ (accessed February 28, 2004).

57 The Hungarian, Romanian and Czech programs, which are aimed at improving the overall situation of the Roma minorities in these countries, are discussed above, Part III.

58 The most recent regular reports, for 2003, are available at: http://europa.eu.int/comm/enlargement/report_2003/index.htm (accessed February 28 2004).

59 *European Union Support for Roma communities in Central and Eastern Europe*, above n. 52, p. 5.

country. Revised Accession Partnerships, adopted in 2001, emphasised the urgent need for continued progress in improving the overall situation of the Roma in Bulgaria, the Czech Republic, Hungary, Romania and Slovakia. For example, the Accession Partnership for Slovakia called on the Slovak authorities to[60]:

> Continue improving the situation of the Roma through strengthened implementation of the relevant strategy, including the provision of the necessary financial support at national and local levels; measures aimed at fighting against discrimination (including within the public administration), fostering employment opportunities, increasing access to education, improving housing conditions; provide adequate financial support.

Reference should also be made to the EU's Equal Treatment Directive, adopted on June 29, 2000.[61] This provides for equal treatment of all persons, without regard to their racial or ethnic origins. The Directive, which applies to both the public and private sectors, covers the fields of employment, education, social protection (including both health care and social security) and access to goods and services, including housing. In addition, Member States are required under the Directive to "designate a body or bodies for the promotion of equal treatment of all persons without discrimination on the grounds of racial or ethnic origin" (Art. 13(1)). This body shall provide, *inter alia*, "independent assistance to victims of discrimination in pursuing their complaints about discrimination." As the Directive forms part of the Community *acquis*, candidate countries are bound to give effect to it by the date of their accession to the EU.

Although the Directive was not adopted solely, or even primarily, with the candidate states in mind, it has obvious and important implications for the Roma in these countries. As indicated in Parts II–III of this chapter, the Roma have experienced widespread and severe discrimination, particularly since 1990, whether in access to public services such as education, housing and health care, or in terms of employment. However, the scale of Roma disadvantage in the CEE states, including discrimination by public services and employers, cannot be explained solely by reference to the problems confronting the Roma since the collapse of state socialism.

Undoubtedly, the monitoring and standard setting functions of the EU have had a significant, albeit variable, impact on candidate states' efforts to improve the situation of their Roma minorities. Countries in Central and Eastern Europe have been acutely conscious of the need to satisfy the European Commission's expectations in terms of establishing a satisfactory legislative and administrative framework, together with programs aimed at boosting Roma educational performance and Roma access to employment.

---

60 For the text of the 2001 Accession Partnership with Slovakia see, e.g. http://www.europa.eu.int/comm/enlargement/report2001/apsk_en.pdf (accessed March 1, 2004).

61 See Council Directive 2000/43/EC of June 29, 2000, *Official Journal of the European Communities* (19.7.2000), L.180/22.

However, it would be wrong to exaggerate the extent to which the EU has been the catalyst for the development of concerted policies to tackle Roma disadvantage in at least some of the CEE states. For example, Hungary's efforts to address the causes of Roma poverty and social exclusion began in 1995, at least two years before the EU Commission first drew attention to the socio-economic problems experienced by the Roma. As noted in Part III of this chapter, the Hungarian authorities adopted three separate government resolutions, in 1995, on the alleviation of Roma disadvantage and on the promotion of the minority's social integration.[62] Thus, the influence of the EU on Hungary's policies concerned with the Roma, though useful and constructive, has been limited. At most it has served to highlight various deficiencies in government programs aimed at eradicating Roma poverty and disadvantage and in the legislative framework—notably the lack of a comprehensive anti-discrimination law. Under persistent pressure from the EU, a draft anti-discrimination law, prepared by Hungary's Ministry of Justice, was finally approved by the government in September 2003.

If the EU's monitoring function has had a beneficial impact on the development of Roma policies in the CEE region, there remains a widespread perception amongst Roma activists and community leaders that this function has not been exercised with sufficient rigor. For example, a well-placed Romani official in Budapest, whom I interviewed in September 2003, told me that 'experts' had been dispatched from Brussels whose knowledge is superficial, at best: "[t]hey know little of Hungary and are easily persuaded that things are OK."[63] In Romania, in March 2003, an experienced Romani community leader assured me that, despite the adoption of a wide-ranging Roma Strategy by the government, in 2001, little had changed. He described the efforts of the Romanian authorities to improve the situation of the country's Roma as largely a "*teatru spectacol*", or 'theatre performance', intended to convince Western audiences that something constructive was being done.[64]

While the observations of Roma commentators (as of any interested parties) should be treated with a degree of caution, there is considerable evidence to support the view that the European Commission's Regular Reports, on candidate countries, could have been more searching with respect to the situation of the Roma. For example, the 2002 Regular Report on Romania stated[65]:

> The Government has made steady progress in implementing last year's Roma Strategy, which is explicitly aimed at addressing discrimination. During the reporting period, the structures for the implementation of the Roma Strategy were progressively established. At the county level, the Roma offices provided for

---

[62] See Government Resolutions Nos. 1120/1995 (XII.7); 1121/1995 (XII.7); 1125/1995 (XII.12).

[63] Interview recorded September 2003 (on file with the author).

[64] Interview recorded April 2003 (on file with the author).

[65] *2002 Regular Report on Romania's Progress Towards Accession*, above n. 43, at 36.

> in the strategy have become operational. Over 400 Roma have been hired as experts, the responsibilities of these experts have been clarified, and all 42 local Roma offices have elaborated Action Plans for the 2001–2004 period.

I know of at least one Roma 'expert', appointed to a senior post under the terms of Romania's Roma Strategy, who had no previous work experience of any kind. In another case, I was told of a Roma adviser to a County Prefect who had been told not to try to see his boss unless the Prefect specifically summoned him. The adviser's numerous and elaborate proposals, for tackling the problems of the local Roma went unheeded. A meaningful evaluation of the implementation of the Roma Strategy in Romania would have had to consider not simply whether Roma experts had been appointed across the country, as provided for by the Strategy, but the background and qualifications of those appointed, as well as the extent to which the advisers have been permitted to initiate or influence the formation of policy. These issues are not even touched upon in the Commission's subsequent Regular Report on Romania, for 2003.

4.2. Financial Incentives and Funding for Roma-Related Projects in the CEE Region

In addition to standard setting and monitoring the performance of candidate countries, the EU has used financial incentives to encourage these states to comply with EU objectives, including the adoption of appropriate measures to improve the situation of Roma minorities in the CEE region. Thus, financial assistance to a candidate country, in accordance with the PHARE Programme or other schemes of EU-funded assistance, can be suspended if a state is in breach of its obligations under EU instruments.[66] As noted above, for several CEE states—Bulgaria, the Czech Republic, Hungary, Romania and Slovakia—such obligations included the adoption of far-reaching measures to improve the situation of their Roma minorities.[67]

The scale of financial assistance from the EU to candidate countries, in order to prepare them for EU membership, has been impressive. For example, for the period 1995–1999, grants under the PHARE Programme amounted to almost 6.7 billion Euros.[68] For the period 2000–2006, the total value of grants available under the PHARE Programme, for infrastructure and other projects, represents 1.5 billion Euros annually.[69] Potentially, at least, this has served as a strong incentive

---

66 This is spelt out in the 1998 Accession Partnerships drawn up by the European Commission for the then candidate countries. The revised Accession Partnerships, of 2001, reaffirm this principle of conditionality.

67 These obligations are specified, for example, in the various Accession Partnerships.

68 *European Union Support for Roma Communities in Central and Eastern Europe*, above n. 52, p. 6.

69 *Id.*

to candidate countries to discharge their obligations under EU instruments, including the requirement to improve the situation of the Roma in various ways.

Funds from the PHARE Programme have also been allocated to projects that are directly concerned with improving the situation of the Roma in the CEE states. Funding for Roma-related projects rose from 11.7 million Euros in 1999 to 31.35 Euros in 2001.[70] For example, in 2001, a grant of 1,700,000 Euros was awarded for a project concerned with improving educational provision to the Roma in Slovakia, while a further grant of 8,300,000 Euros was made to secure improvements in the infrastructure in Roma settlements in Slovakia.[71] In the same year, a grant of 7,000,000 Euros was awarded to promote access to education for disadvantaged groups, particularly the Roma, in Romania.[72]

Significant, though smaller, sums have also been allocated by the EU to NGO-focused projects, in accordance with the LIEN and ACCESS Programmes that have benefited the Roma.[73] The European Initiative for Democracy and Human Rights has also funded various projects for the Roma in the CEE states. Finally, mention should be made of the EU's SOCRATES and Youth for Europe Programmes. Each of these has given extensive support to Roma projects.[74]

Yet, despite the variety and evident usefulness of these EU programmes, they have broadly failed to tackle the multiple and deep-seated problems confronting the mass of the Roma of the CEE region. The scale of financial support for Roma-related projects under the single largest EU scheme, the PHARE Programme—11.7 million Euro in 1999, rising to 31.35 million Euros in 2001—has not been sufficient to meet the massive educational, housing, health care and other needs of up to six million Roma in the CEE region. A far more ambitious level of funding and of assistance is necessary to address the wide-ranging concerns of the Roma people.

5. CONCLUSIONS

The eastward enlargement of the EU, in May 2004, has represented a decisive moment in European history, bringing to an end the division of the continent that was formalized in the aftermath of World War II. However, from the perspective of the Roma of Central and Eastern Europe, it may seem as if the *territorial division* of the continent has been replaced by the erection of new 'borders' that are essentially social, cultural and economic in character, rather than geographical.[75] As described

---

70 *Ibid*, at 7.

71 *Ibid*, at 22.

72 *Ibid*, at 20.

73 For details see, e.g. *ibid*, at 9.

74 *Ibid*, at 10–11.

75 As yet, the old territorial borders remain largely in place, in addition to the new ones. As indicated above, n. 6, most EU member states have introduced transitional arrangements restricting the entry of persons from accession states.

in Parts II–III of this chapter, the collapse of communist administrations in the CEE countries has led to the partial exclusion—social, economic and political—of an estimated six million Roma. Despite commendable efforts, whether in terms of standard setting, monitoring or the provision of financial incentives and assistance, the EU has not succeeded in reversing the severe marginalization of Roma in the CEE region. In particular, the scale of material support provided by the EU, to improve Roma social integration, education levels, housing and infrastructure, has been completely inadequate. As emphasized by World Bank economists, in a report published in June 2003, the Roma of Central and Eastern Europe remain in a state of crisis.[76]

Paradoxically, the accession of several post-communist states to the European Union, in May 2004, may actually have made matters worse. In particular, these states are no longer subject to the stringent monitoring of their minorities policies that they experienced as candidate countries. In addition, having achieved their goal of EU membership, accession countries may prove less susceptible to political or other pressures with respect to their treatment of Roma minorities. The rhetorical and overblown claims of Article 2 of the Treaty of European Union, in which member states pledge "to maintain and develop the Union as an area of freedom, security and justice", are likely to prove hollow and illusory for the mass of the Roma in accession states.

---

[76] See Ringold, Orenstein, Wilkens, above n. 2.

16. A Europe of Variable Geometry: Still a Winning Model?

*Lauso Zagato**

1. Introduction

The tragic scenes of exodus from Africa, which perturb the current debate on the future of Europe, strongly recall the dominant (but perhaps too hastily forgotten) apocalyptic predictions of a decade ago with regard to the anticipated waves of mass migration from Eastern and South-East Europe, from the Central Asian republics of the former Soviet Union and furthermore, from the endless hinterland of Southern Asia. Such predictions did not come true. It is unanimously agreed that the situation evolved differently, thanks to the decisive role played by the EU. It is, therefore, useful to analyse in detail the complex process of subdivision and re-composition in a hierarchy of State and sub-State entities on a primarily (but not exclusively) territorial basis and to examine the sophisticated system of legal instruments utilized by the EU institutions to win a difficult match. The most tangible trophy of this victory is the recent enlargement.

This research, however, is not inspired by futile optimism. Indeed it will become clear through analysis that it is not possible to confront other "geographical fronts" of the global movement of populations with similar panoply of instruments. A more complex task will be to offer some introductory reflections on the relationship between a Europe of variable geometry and a Europe of rights in the context of the new EU, as well as to indicate the contradictions on the horizon marked out by the Constitutional Treaty.

2. The Legal Instruments of Enlargement

It is imperative to start by taking time to survey, in brief, the panoply of legal instruments which the Europe of variable geometry makes use of. The reason for this is not to list a pointless catalogue of sources and acts, but to enable us to understand better how it has been possible for such a Europe to take shape and know what its working mechanisms are.

In the first place, the development of a relationship between the EU and the Central and Eastern European Countries (CEEC) throughout the 1990s materialized specifically by recourse to a wide range of Treaty provisions. On the one hand, it stands out that even the Treaty of Nice did not bring together external

---

* Language assistance and consultancy by Alison Riley, LL.B.

Wojciech Sadurski et al. (ed.), Spreading Democracy and the Rule of Law?, 357–378.

competences[1] under a single Title.[2] On the other hand, provisions relevant for the purposes of enlargement do not only concern external relations, but, on the contrary, also substantially pertain to other fields, including in particular Economic and Social Cohesion (Title XVII, Articles 158–162) and the Area of Freedom, Security and Justice (AFSJ).[3] This has given rise to uncertainties and confusion, thus contributing to the strong discretionary element that, as we shall see, has characterised the policy of the EU-apparatus towards the candidate countries right up to the eve of enlargement.

Only the Europe Agreements (EA), stipulated in the 1990s between the EU and its Member States on one hand, and the single CEEC on the other,[4] are international agreements concluded in solemn form. However, we should also add the Stabilization and Association Agreements (SAA) concluded or currently being concluded with the West Balkan States (WB).[5] As is well known, the single EA initially envisaged the establishment of a common market between the EU and the individual candidate countries for 2004, not the entry of those States into the EU.

---

1 Among recent contributions on this issue: Enzo Cannizzaro (ed.), *The European Union as an Actor in International Relations* (The Hague: Kluwer Law International 2002), pp. 1–345; Enzo Cannizzaro, "Le relazioni esterne della Comunità dopo il Trattato di Nizza," *Diritto dell'Unione Europea*, VII (2002), pp. 182–191; Luigi Daniele (ed.), *Le relazioni esterne dell'Unione europea nel nuovo millennio* (Milano: Giuffré 2001), pp. 1–359; Alan Dashwood, "External Relations Provisions of the Amsterdam Treaty," *Common Market Law Review*, 35 (1998), pp. 1019–1045; Ian McLoad, I.A. Hendry and Stephen Hyett, *The External Relations of the European Communities* (Oxford: Oxford University Press 1998), pp. 1–432; Antonio Tizzano, "Note in tema di relazioni esterne dell'Unione europea," *Diritto dell'Unione Europea*, III (1998), pp. 464–491; Ramses A. Wessel, "The Inside Looking Out: Consistency and Delimitation in EU External Relations," *Common Market Law Review*, 37 (2000), pp. 1135–1171.

2 On one hand, external competences are divided between the EC Treaty and the TEU (Title V: Foreign and Security Policy). On the other hand, the EC Treaty provisions relating to external competences are scattered in different Titles of the Treaty. Only the Treaty Establishing a Constitution for Europe—if and when it comes into force—provides for a unified structural settlement of the matter (Part III Title V, Articles III-193 to III-231, of the Draft Treaty).

3 The provisions relating to the AFSJ are divided between the EC Treaty (Title IV: Visas, asylum and immigration) and the TEU (Title VI: Justice and Home Affairs).

4 On mixed agreements as the normal practice in the EU external relations system and for an extensive bibliography, see Stefano Nicolin, "Modalità di funzionamento ed attuazione degli accordi misti," in Luigi Daniele (ed.), *Le relazioni esterne dell'Unione europea*, *op. cit.* n. 1, pp. 177–213.

5 Only the SAA with Macedonia and Croatia have been concluded, for the moment. See Stabilisation and Association Agreement between the European Communities and their Member States, on one side, and the former Yugoslav Republic of Macedonia (the Republic of Croatia), on the other, done in Brussels, 26 March 2001 (9 September 2001). See also the Communication from the Commission to the Council and the European Parliament, 21/05/2003, *The Western Balkans European Integration*.

It was only later, at the Copenhagen Summit of 1993, that the EU set in motion the enlargement process, thus accepting the request to do so from the countries of Central and Eastern Europe.[6] No new International Agreement was concluded, however. In other words, the EU did not undertake formal commitments: even the Copenhagen Declaration, with its pronouncement of the famous three criteria for enlargement, is a purely *unilateral* act, issued by the Union through the Council, which does not commit the Union itself to accepting the membership request of the associated countries, even where the latter effectively comply with the said criteria.

What took place, rather, in the years that followed, was a series of converging acts effectuated internally by each legal system, especially in relation to the third Copenhagen criterion (implementation of the Community *acquis*).[7] On one hand, we find the EU making use of a wide range of non-binding instruments (White Paper, Agenda 2000) and binding instruments. A particularly important instance of these is Regulation 622/98[8] establishing the Accession Partnerships and the ensuing Partnerships decided in relation to the relevant CEEC (thus, despite the name, these are unilateral instruments of the Union!); these instruments envisage an elaborate system of punishments and rewards that the EU Council may apply at its discretion depending on the progress or lack of it made by each CEEC along the way. On the other hand, we find the relevant CEEC beginning to issue a stream of acts within its national legal system that are mainly binding in character, so as to ensure the implementation of the Community *acquis* envisaged by the Community instruments as an indispensable precondition for membership. This is done over a certain period of years following the stages set by the *Accession Partnerships*. This

---

6 On the first phase of the EA: Elisa Baroncini, "Gli accordi europei di associazione con i paesi dell'Europa centrale ed orientale," *Nuove Leggi Civili Commentate*, XIX (1996), pp. 130–151; Marc Maresceau, "Les Accords Europeens: Analyse générale," *Revue du Marché Commun et de l'Union Européenne*, 369 (1993), pp. 507–515; Marc Maresceau and Elisabetta Montaguti, "The Europe Agreements Compared in the Light of Their Pre-Accession Reorientation," *Common Market Law Review*, 32 (1995), pp. 1327–1367; Lynn Ramsey, "The Implications of the European Agreements for an Expanded European Union," *International and Comparative Law Quarterly*, 44 (1995), pp. 161–171; Antonio Toledano Laredo, "L'Union européenne, l'ex-Union soviétique et les Pays de l'Europe centrale et orientale: un aperçu de leurs accords," *Cahiers de droit européen*, XXX (1994), pp. 543–562.

7 See Graham Avery and Fraser Cameron, *The Enlargement of the European Union* (Sheffield: Sheffield Academic Press 1998), pp. 19–48; David Katz, "Les 'critères de Copenhague," *Revue du Marché Commun et de l'Union Européenne*, 440 (2000), pp. 483–486; Richard Poláček, "Le débat élargissement-approfondissement dans la perspective de l'élargissement de l'Union européenne aux Peco," *Revue du Marché Commun et de l'Unione Européenne*, 425 (1999), pp. 112–120; Milada A. Vachudovà, "EU Enlargement: An Overview," *East European Constitutional Review*, 9(4) (Fall 2000), pp. 64–69.

8 Council Regulation No. 622/98 of 16 March 1998, on assistance to the applicant States in the framework of the pre-accession strategy, and in particular on the establishment of Accession Partnerships, Official Journal L 85, 20/03/1998.

practice evolves "freely", in order to earn the reward (passage to the next phase of the accession process) and avoid the punishment set by Article 4 of Reg. 622/98: formally, then, each of these States acts freely and has given no undertaking regarding the complete implementation of the *acquis communautaire* in its own legal order.[9]

On the international plane, it is obviously a case of an *agreement by conclusive conduct* between the two parties, a perfectly legitimate and operative accord thanks to the principle of freedom of form of international agreements. In fact, this is a type of accord that has met with a recent revival on the international scene; this revival may be linked in theory to the spread of *positive sanctions* as an instrument in relations between international subjects.[10]

We still need to inquire what the relationship is between this second agreement and the earlier accord (the Europe Agreement), incorporated within the legal orders of all the international subjects involved, according to the specific procedures of each. Each individual Europe Agreement not only remained in force, but further, became subsumed within the new pre-accession strategy, as is shown by the Partnership Agreements (PA), each of which peremptorily states in the introduction that the Europe Agreement in question continues to form the basis of the relationship between the EU and the candidate country. This amounts to saying, then, that the text of each Europe Agreement was tacitly amended by agreement between the Parties, according to a practice recognized by the international legal order.[11] The diversity of structure among the various generations of Europe Agreements carries weight in confirming the position stated above. Particularly in the most recent Europe Agreements (those with the Baltic States and Slovenia), there are

---

9 Michael Blecher, "Aspetti istituzionali dell'allargamento EU verso est e principali strumenti di assistenza e sostegno dei Paesi candidati," in Marco Polo System (a cura di), *Il GEIE nella prospettiva di Agenda 2000* (Proceedings of the Seminar Held in Venice at the Fondazione Querini Stampalia, 28 September 2001), pp. 8–15; Kristyn Inglis, "The Europe Agreements Compared in the Light of the Pre-Accession Reorientation," *Common Market Law Review*, 37 (2000), pp. 1173–1210; Gilles Joly, "Le processus d'élargissement de l'Union européenne," *Revue du Marché Commun et de l'Union Européenne*, 457 (2002), pp. 239–246; Marc Maresceau, "From Europe Agreements to Accession Negotiations," in Mario Ganino and Gabriella Venturini (eds.), *L'Europa di domani: verso l'allargamento dell'Unione* (Milano: Giuffré 2002), pp. 15–37; Phedon Nicolaides et al., *Guide to the Enlargement of the European Union. A Review of the Process Negotiations, Policy Reforms and Enforcement Capacity* (Maastricht: European Institute of Public Administration 1999), pp. 1–103; Karen E. Smith, "The Conditional Offer of Membership as an Instrument of EU Foreign Policy: Reshaping Europe in the EU's Image," *Marmara Journal of European Studies*, 8 (2000), pp. 2–15.

10 Lauso Zagato, "Qualche riflessione (e alcuni cattivi pensieri) sul processo di allargamento," in Marco Polo System (ed.), *Il GEIE nella Prospettiva di Agenda 2000*, pp. 16–29. On positive sanctions, see Bernardo Cortese, "International Economic Sanctions as a Component of Public Policy for Conflict-of-Laws Purposes," in Picchio Forlati and Sicilianos (eds.), *Economic Sanctions in International Law* (Leiden/Boston: Martinus Nijhoff 2004).

11 Zagato, *op. cit.* n. 10, p. 17.

innovative elements that can only be explained in the framework of the prospect of *accession*, and not mere *association*.

A further development has taken place with the Stabilisation and Association Agreements (SAA): in this case, the enhanced approach typical of the final phase of the relationship with the CEEC has become the basis of the relationship with the five new countries. These States are asked to proceed immediately, *inter alia*, to a far more radical legislative alignment than the one on which the Europe Agreements are based, and with no prospect of entry into the EU in the medium term (except perhaps for Croatia).

We still have to focus on the instruments enacted by the EU to ensure implementation of the *acquis communautaire* on the part of the candidate countries. In the first place, the PHARE programme is prominent[12]: At the outset, this was used by the Commission for funding reform projects in a vast range of sectors, from restoration of sewerage systems to law reform. In other words, it was meant to ensure technical assistance for the transformation process, with no prior indication whatever that in future the countries in question would be admitted to full membership of the European Union. To give an example, legislative reform in the CEEC was carried forward in that period under the auspices of PHARE, but initially such reform did not coincide at all with straightforward implementation of the Community *acquis*. PHARE responded, rather, to the demands of the governments of the countries in transition without being tied to the framework of an association agreement and without a compulsory scheme of priorities. Strong criticism was rightly provoked by the dissipating effect of this type of assistance, unfortunately leading in the first place to a bureaucratisation of the programme.[13]

Starting with the Accession Partnerships, the entire range of Community assistance has been coordinated by the Commission: the reorientation of PHARE thus took place, accompanied by the launch of the ISPA and SAPARD programmes.[14] Since then, PHARE has been remodelled on the basis of the third Copenhagen criterion, that is to say, implementation of the Community *acquis* by the candidate countries. The programme has become the fulcrum of assistance for developing institutional capability to give effect to the principles of the European legal order,

---

12 Council Regulation (EEC) No. 3906/89 of 18 December 1989 on economic aid to the Republic of Hungary and the Polish People's Republic, Official Journal L 375, 23/12/1989.

13 Blecher, *op. cit.* n. 9, p. 10.

14 See Council Regulation No. 1266/1999 of 21 June 1999 on coordinating aid to the applicant countries in the framework of the pre-accession strategy and amending Regulation No. 3906/89, Official Journal L 161, 26/06/1999; Council Regulation No. 1267/1999 of 21 June 1999 establishing an Instrument for Structural Policies for Pre-accession (ISPA), Official Journal L 161, 26/06/1999; Council Regulation No. 1268/1999 of 21 June 1999 on Community support for pre-accession measures for agriculture and rural development (SAPARD) in the applicant countries of central and eastern Europe in the pre-accession period, Official Journal L 161, 26/06/1999.

since it is in this domain that the greatest problems of all the candidate countries lie. After the SAA, implementation of the *acquis communautaire*, meant as full legislative alignment with Community law is also the object of the Community Assistance for Reconstruction, Democratization and Stabilization programme (CARDS) addressed to the West Balkan States (WB).[15]

Also among the array of instruments to which the European Union has had recourse are instruments implementing the EU policy for *economic and social cohesion*,[16] and in particular, the INTERREG III programme, aimed at ensuring a "cross-border, transnational and interregional cooperation intended to encourage the harmonious, balanced and sustainable development of the whole of the Community". To complete the picture, another Community policy should be mentioned, one characterized both by the wide involvement of public and private subjects and by its growing concern with the States of Eastern and South-East Europe, candidate countries in the near or more distant future: reference here is to the policy for research and technological development, in particular in the light of the Fourth Framework Programme.[17] This Programme gives unusual scope for the participation of public and private bodies of the States affected by the programmes indicated above, especially as far as universities are concerned.

As regards in particular the area of freedom, security and justice (AFSJ),[18] it must be underlined at once that the commitments undertaken by candidate countries in relation to external border controls, asylum and immigration "go far beyond the

15 Council Regulation No. 2666/2000 of 5 December 2000 on assistance for Albania, Bosnia and Herzegovina, Croatia, the Federal Republic of Yugoslavia and the Former Yugoslav Republic of Macedonia, Official Journal L 306, 07/12/2000.

16 Council Regulation 1260/1999 of 21 June 1999 laying down general provisions on the Structural Funds, Official Journal 161, 26/06/1999. Article 20 paragraph 2 specifies that under the INTERREG Initiative "due attention should be given to cross-border activities, in particular in the perspective of enlargement, and for Member States which have extensive frontiers with the applicant countries, as well as to improved coordination with the PHARE, TACIS and MEDA programmes. Due attention shall also be given to cooperation with the outermost regions". See: Council Regulation (EC, Euratom) No. 99/2000 of 29 December 1999 concerning the provision of assistance to the partner States in eastern Europe and Central Asia (TACIS), Official Journal L 12, 18/01/2000 and Council Regulation No. 2698/2000 of 27 November 1999 amending Reg. 1488/96 on financial and technical measures to accompany the reform of economic and social structures in the framework of the Euro-Mediterranean partnership (MEDA), Official Journal L 311, 12/12/2000.

17 Decision No. 1513/2002/EC of the European Parliament and of the Council of 27 June 2002 concerning the sixth framework programme of the European Community for research, technological development and demonstration activities, contributing to the creation of the European Research Area and to innovation (2002–2006), Official Journal L 232, 29/08/2002.

18 See: Joanna Apap, "Questioni pratiche e probabili conseguenze derivanti dall'ingresso nell'area Schengen: allargamento e area di libertà, sicurezza e giustizia, alla ricerca di un miglior equilibrio," *Diritto, Immigrazione e Cittadinanza*, V (2003), pp. 3–26; Christina

mere adoption of the EU *acquis*", with consequent, grave concerns relative to observance of those standards of human rights protection, which the EU declared in the Copenhagen Criteria to be a basic condition for enlargement.

3. A CITIZENSHIP OF VARIABLE GEOMETRY AND THE ROLE OF THE COURT OF JUSTICE

The concept of Community citizenship, as we all know, is evolving fast. This is particularly due to the activism of the Court of Justice, which has repeatedly intervened in recent years[19] to expand the content of the right of citizenship. Thus, albeit with innumerable precautions, the Court is leaning towards removing certain rights from the ties dictated by "economism" still present in the Treaty text at Articles 39, 43 and 46,[20] specifically the rights of Member States' citizens to freedom of movement, residence and establishment in other Member States.

Rather than getting to the heart of the concept of European citizenship, our concern here is to observe how the rights granted to non-EU citizens within the European Union act in relation to that concept. These are rights deriving from the various agreements concluded by the EU with the respective home States. The inner circle is made up of citizens of EEA countries[21]: both natural and legal persons

---

Boswell, "The 'external Dimension' of EU Immigration and Asylum Policy," *International Affairs*, 79 (2003), pp. 619–638; Charles Elsen, "Le Conseil européen de Thessalonique," *Revue du Marché Commun et de l'Union Européenne*, 471 (2003), pp. 516–518; Paolo Mengozzi, *Istituzioni di Diritto Comunitario e dell'Unione Europea* (Padova: Cedam 2003), p. 298 *et seq.*; Bruno Nascimbene, "Il 'Libro Verde' della Commissione su una politica comunitaria di rimpatrio degli stranieri irregolari: brevi rilievi," *Rivista italiana di diritto pubblico comunitario*, XIII (2003), pp. 445–449; Bruno Nascimbene (ed.), *Expulsion and Detention of Aliens in the European Union Countries* (Milano: Giuffré 2001); Massimo Condinanzi, Alessandra Lang e Bruno Nascimbene, *Cittadinanza dell'Unione e libera circolazione delle persone* (Milano: Giuffrè 2003), pp. 219–277; Catherine Phuong, "Enlarging 'Fortress Europe': EU Accession, Asylum, and Immigration in Candidate Countries," *International and Comparative Law Quarterly*, 52 (2003), pp. 641–663.

19 See: Case C-85/96, *María Martínez Sala* v. *Freistaat Bayern*, [1998] ECR. I-2691; Case C-274/96, *Criminal proceedings against Horst Otto Bickel and Ulrich Franz*, [1998] ECR I-7637; Case C-184/99, *Rudy Grzelczyk* v. *Centre public d'aide sociale d'Ottignies-Louvain-la-Neuve*, [2001] ECR I-6193; Case C-224/98, *Marie-Nathalie D'Hoop* v. *Office national de l'emploi*, [2002] ECR I-6191; Case C-413/99, *Baumbast*, [2002] ECR I-7091.

20 With reference to the three Directives of 28 June 1990 (in Official Journal L 180, 13/07/1990): 90/364/EEC on the right of residence, 90/365/EEC on the right of residence for employees and self-employed persons who have ceased their occupational activity and 90/366/EEC on the right of residence for students. On the role played by the ECJ in the evolution of the concept of European Citizenship, Mengozzi, *op. cit.* n. 18. See also Condinanzi, Lang and Nascimbene, *op. cit.* n. 18, p. 26 *et seq.*

21 Agreement on the European economic Area, done at Oporto on the second day of May in the year 1992 (Official Journal L 1, 3 January 1994).

coming from Iceland, Liechtenstein and Norway and are fully entitled to the rights of freedom of movement and establishment in a Member State in relation to the performance of economic activities (whether for wages or not), which until recently constituted the limits of the right of freedom of movement enjoyed reciprocally by citizens of Member States. A corresponding situation exists in relations between the EU and Swiss citizens.[22]

Apart from nationals of the States just mentioned, only citizens of Turkish nationality—and to a very small extent those of the Maghreb countries—enjoy directly applicable rights on which an action can therefore be founded directly before a national Court in the Union, following the Association Agreement of 1963 as integrated by certain decisions of the Association Council, in particular Decision 1/80.[23] Such rights mainly concern the prohibition of discrimination[24] and the right for families to be reunited (though there are some very serious restrictions, especially concerning the wife's status). Alone among migrant workers, the Turkish citizen also has the right to remain in the Member State where he has performed regular work for four years, and to have unimpeded access to the labour market of that same country.

For immigrants coming from any other country, it is true that a noteworthy variety of rights exists based on the different agreements stipulated by the EU with the home countries. Nevertheless, the fact remains that such agreements do not confer directly effective rights, even where they include a certain number of provisions that are favourable to immigrants, as in the case of the cooperation agreements with the ex-Soviet Union countries. It was thought that the same applied to the provisions contained in the Europe Agreements.

Instead, the CJEC has taken a stand on the direct effect of the EA, with a substantial set of judgments handed down between late 2001 and January 2002,[25]

---

22 See Bilateral Agreements between Switzerland and the EU, done in Luxembourg, 26 June 1999. The Agreements became effective on 1 June 2002 (in Official Journal L 114, 30 April 2002).

23 Agreement Establishing an Association between the European Economic Community ant Turkey, done at Ankara 12 September 1963 (Council Decision 64/732 Of 23 December 1963 in Official Journal 217 of 29 December 1964); see also Decision No. 1/80 of the Association Council of 19 September 1980 on the Development of the Association.

24 In the Association Agreements with Tunisia (done in Tunis, 25 April 1976, in Official Journal 265 of 27 September 1978), with Algeria (done in Algiers, 27 April 1976, in Official Journal 264 of 27 September 1978) and with Morocco (done in Rabat, 27 September 1976, in Official Journal 263 of 27 September 1978) only Article 40 (abolition of any discrimination based on nationality between workers of the Member States and workers of Algeria, Morocco and Tunisia as regards employment, remuneration and other conditions of work and employment) is subject to direct application. See Judgment of the Court of 31 January 1991, C-18/90, *Kziber*, [1991] *ECR* I-199.

25 Judgments of the Court of 27 September 2001: Case C-63/99, *Gloszczuk*, [2001] *ECR* I-6369; Case C-257/99 *Barkoci and Malik*, [2001] *ECR* I-6557; Case C-235/99, *Kondova*,

pronouncing in particular on the provisions contained in the Agreements with Poland, the Czech Republic and Bulgaria concerning freedom of establishment. The Court lay down that the provisions of the EA concerning the free movement of workers, the right to be reunited with one's family and the right to national treatment in the matter of the right of establishment, all have direct effect. This position was adopted despite the fact that the Member States had taken steps to protect themselves in advance by inserting in each EA a safeguard clause (Article 58 or 59) asserting that "nothing in the Agreement shall prevent the Parties from applying their laws and regulations regarding entry and stay, work, labour conditions and establishment of natural persons and supply of services . . . ".

The Court went further: it is true that the right of establishment granted by the EA does not exclude preventive control by the Member State of entry over the conditions for issue of a visa (necessary in the case of stays that are by definition longer than three months), such control to be carried out in the country of departure; however, the Court declared that such controls cannot be performed in such a way as to deprive of its sense the right granted to the non-Community national by the Europe Agreement with the EU.

It is not within the scope of this article to examine the matter in depth. It is sufficient to establish that the Court has shown favour towards citizens coming from the countries that have concluded the Europe Agreements with the EU, in such a way as to distinguish their situation from that of any other class of migrant. Since the category in question also includes immigrants from Romania and Bulgaria, countries which have concluded Europe Agreements with the EU but are expected to enter the Union only years from now, it will be possible to verify whether the Court has established a way to achieve *de facto* regularisation for migrants coming from those countries, or whether it means to stop short of that.

In not dissimilar terms, the Court's most recent case law concerning the application of the Association Agreement with Turkey shows further receptiveness compared with the previous cautious approach that had still inspired the set of judgments pronounced in 2000.[26] The judgment in the *Bülent Kurz* case of 19 November 2002[27] sheds light on this development.

[2001] *ECR* I-6427; Judgment of the Court of 20 November 2001, Case C-268/99, *Jany and Others*, [2001] *ECR* I-8615; Judgment of the Court of 29 January 2002: Case C-162/00, *Pokrzeptowicz-Meyer*, [2002] *ECR* I-1049. See: Martin Hedemann-Robinson, "An Overview of Recent Legal Developments at Community Level in Relation to Third Country Nationals Resident within the European Union, with Particular Reference to the Case Law of the European Court of Justice," *Common Market Law Review*, 38 (2001), pp. 525–586; Christophe Hillion, "Case Law," *Common Market Law Review*, 40 (2003), pp. 465–491.

26 Judgments of the Court: 10 February 2000, Case C-340/97, *Nazli*, [2000] *ECR* I-957; 16 May 2000, Case C-329/97, *Egart*, [2000] ECR I-1487; 11 May 2000, Case C-378/98, *Savas*, [2000] *ECR* I-2927; 22 June 2000, C-65/98 Safet *Eyüp*, [2000] *ECR I-4747.*

27 Judgment of the Court of 19 November 2002, C-188/00, *Kurz*, [2002] *ECR* I-10191.

Something remains to be said about the SAA; in effect, these Agreements are extremely careful to exclude provisions liable to be applied directly. Thus, the provisions on freedom of establishment at the moment apply exclusively to freedom of establishment of undertakings; Article 48(4) of the SAA with Macedonia[28] provides, for example, that the SAA Council (the supervisory body for the application of the Agreement) will only take into consideration the possibility of extending the provisions on freedom of establishment to nationals of both sides who intend to perform work as "self-employed persons" in the territory of the other side, once five years have elapsed from the date the Agreement entered into force and on the basis of the situation in the labour market *and the development of the case law of the CJEC.* The rules governing freedom of movement of employees are also extremely cautious. However, we should not be too worried by the defence screen: even the EA of the early 1990s seemed to leave no room for possibilities of direct applicability.

In conclusion, a picture emerges, based to a large extent on the case law, of a citizenship of the Union of variable geometry. Possible outcomes and consequences of that picture can only emerge at the end of this article, once we have completed our scrutiny of how the EU-apparatus has used the wide range of legal instruments that we have seen were available to it, in the process of enlargement.

4. EXPORTING THE COMMUNITY *ACQUIS* BY MEANS OF THE LEGAL INSTRUMENTS DESCRIBED ABOVE: BETWEEN A GUIDING FUNCTION AND A TAKEOVER

4.1. Foreword

During the process of German reunification a controversy arose over whether, with respect to the way it was handled, it was correct to talk about the "accession" of East Germany based on freedom of contract, or whether it was correct to speak of a basic acquisition or "takeover" by the Federal Republic.[29] This allusion brings up some necessary considerations about the way the countries of Central and Eastern Europe have implemented the Community *acquis*, not only after 1989, but especially since Copenhagen and by the standard of the third criterion set there.

It might appear to some that the problem is on the way to being solved: on 1 May 2004, these countries entered the EU, and the singular forced implementation of the Community *acquis* (to speak plainly, the legislative takeover) imposed on these States has become history. This is not quite right: in the first place, Bulgaria and Romania did not join the EU immediately; in the second place, the process is being repeated with greater force in relation to the West Balkan States. In fact, the latter are required to ensure prompt, immediate and full incorporation of the Community *acquis a priori*, with no assurance as to the future and Turkey is also in the background. In the third place, and chiefly, the scope and effects of the policy of

[28] See *op. cit.*, n. 5.

[29] Blecher, *op. cit*, n. 9, p. 8.

Accession Partnerships developed over the last decade need to be precisely assessed with respect to the current situation.

4.2. *Vertical Instruments, or the Tough Side of Asymmetry in the EU–CEEC Relationship (and Beyond)*

We need to observe, in general terms, how exporting the *acquis* has often consisted in a blind, bureaucratic operation, carried out in some countries without any criterion. There are some salient examples. One instance is the implementation by one candidate country's legal system of Community law on consumer contracts, which took place, at the very beginning, without the participation of consumer associations, with hostile indifference on the part of the judiciary and with notable legislative confusion; all this occurring in a situation complicated by a political crisis, with total silence from the press.

An equally salient example is that of Albania. This country found itself having to put into effect a law reform which, after having been designed on the basis of a plan to enact two separate codes (civil and commercial), then made an about turn (1994–1995) seeing the enactment of a single code. The change was fortunate, but none the less abrupt, and perhaps not everything in the new code had been adequately thought through.[30] In both these cases the decision was taken by experts from the Member States and by a succession of team leaders, in a situation that increased the bewilderment and difficulties of the (few) local experts. It was also severely testing for the very institutional structures of the new State, faced with new problems and not helped to take on the role of protagonists in the process of legislative reform.

It is useful at this point to mention the way the accession policy introduced by the *White Paper* and launched with *Agenda 2000* (with its resulting tacit amendment to the content of the EA) has influenced trade in goods between the Parties. In fact, creating an area of free trade in goods is quite different from creating an internal market, which involves not only a customs union, but also complete freedom of movement of goods, persons, services and capital, as well as setting common policies in the sectors concerned. We must consider in the first place that the results of the asymmetrical bargaining power between the EU and the CEEC were discernible right from the start of negotiations on trade liberalization, i.e. before the opening up of the accession policy. True, with the Europe Agreements, the EU offered the CEEC rapid and asymmetrical liberalization of trade in industrial products; but in the same Agreements the EU reserved wide anti-dumping and safeguard measures for itself and, moreover, imposed a series of exceptions precisely in those sectors in which the CEEC's economies, or at least some of them, were competitive:

30 Lauso Zagato, "I contratti di distribuzione nel recente codice civile albanese: suggestioni comunitarie," *Rivista di Diritto Civile*, XLII (1996), pp. 537–558.

agriculture, coal, iron, steel and textiles. As a result, these countries worked up a permanent trade deficit with the Community, particularly in the case of the more advanced CEEC economies.[31]

Second, and in broader terms, it should be stated that the paradigmatic shift from the prospective creation of a free trade area and the approximation of laws to the prospect of accession has had a mixed, if not mainly negative, influence overall on the relative competitiveness of the CEEC in relation to the Member States of the European Union. It should be noted that the prospect of accession referred to involved no commitment at the time on the part of the EU, but immediate, complete and actual acceptance of the Community *acquis* on the part of each CEEC; and in some respects, the negative consequences converged on the CEEC best prepared for accession. This is particularly evident in the areas of *competition* and protection of *intellectual property*.

To take *competition* policy first: as far as the rules aimed at undertakings are concerned (Articles 81 and 82 CE), it can be said that the CEEC have largely completed implementation of the *acquis* by now. Paradoxically, however, this has ended up weighing especially heavily on the legal systems of the more advanced CEEC, the first States which managed to enact legislation on competition (Poland, the Czech Republic and Hungary). In these countries the provisions were modelled *roughly* on Community law, but had their basis in the local system. This is particularly true of the Polish legislation on concentrations. Local experiences of this sort (involving the creation of expertise on the part of administrative and judicial organs, and of the operators themselves) have been wrecked by the activity conducted by the Association Councils of issuing Implementing Rules (IR). The latter have naturally imposed immediate implementation, pure and simple, of primary and secondary EU law, in the manner of pre-accession strategy. The question is different again on the subject of *State aids* and above all as regards the competition rules applicable to public undertakings or undertakings entrusted with the operation of services of general economic interest (Article 86 EC, formerly Article 90).

Indeed, there is cause to reflect on the difficulties encountered at EU level *in subiecta materia*, despite the fact that an organised Community structure independent of the Member States exists, and further, that individual organs of the States may find themselves in a subordinate position to the Community apparatus. For this reason, and also because of their past experience in terms of political and economic organisation, it is impossible to see how the States of Central and Eastern Europe can go ahead with the reorganisation of their systems required by the EU legal order, beneath the goad of decisions taken unanimously by structures such as the Association Councils. It is no coincidence that there is a lack of such

31 See Frank Schimmelfenning, "The Community Trap: Liberal Norms, Rhetorical Action, and the Eastern Enlargement of the European Union," *International Organization*, 55 (2001), pp. 55–56.

decisions *in subiecta materia*.[32] The telecommunications sector is an exception and in fact this is the sector most clearly regulated at Community level.

There are equally remarkable things to be said about *intellectual property*.[33] From the first angle, given that the CEEC had in any case to adjust to international law in this area, they would clearly encounter greater difficulty and burdens (such as costs, but also for productive renewal needed by undertakings) as a result of renouncing the standard of protection laid down by the TRIPS Agreement, which is lower than that required by EU law. Further, the TRIPS standard is to be reached by each State within five years of the WTO Agreement entering into force (or of WTO accession for States that were not founder Members). States would renounce all this in the name of immediately having to adjust to the far more penetrating parameters for protection in force in the EU.[34] It is equally clear that the price paid by some countries to do this is all the more dramatic in proportion to how distant the prospect of actual accession to the EU is.

From the second angle, we must focus our attention on an issue pertaining directly to the free movement of goods: the *exhaustion* of intellectual property rights. The principle of *exhaustion* is only applicable within the Union, i.e. it is valid as *Community exhaustion*: consequently, the holder of the right cannot oppose the importation and circulation within a Member State of products that have been marketed in the exporting State by the holder itself or with its consent, or by a person bound to the holder by legal or economic ties. However, the principle is not applicable to *association* agreements or *free trade* agreements, as the Court of Justice held in the well-known *Polydor* case in 1982.[35] This is so much the case that when, in an Association Agreement—specifically the European Economic Area (EEA)—the extension of the application of the principle of *exhaustion* later to the ex-EFTA States was desired, provision was explicitly made for this so as to avoid future disputes.

---

[32] See Lora Borissova, "Promoting Competition, Liberalisation and Regulation of the TeleCommunications Sector in the Central and Eastern European Countries," *European Competition Law Review*, 22 (2001), pp. 59–73; Christopher Harding and Marian Kepinski, "The Polish Law against Monopolistic Practices," *European Competition Law Review*, 22 (2001), pp. 181–188; Inglis, above n. 9, pp. 1203–1205.

[33] For an overall view, see "The Enforcement of Industrial Property Rights in Eastern Europe," *International Review of Industrial and Copyright Law*, 32 (2001), pp. 875–1002, with an Introduction by Adolf Dietz.

[34] There is one exception, though it concerns the field of telecommunications, not intellectual property: Slovakia claimed reliance on its status as a less developed country under the GATS Agreement on Telecommunications so as to delay privatisation in the field of voice telephony for 5 years. It accordingly implemented the rules concerned in 2003, instead of 1998, as the EU had asserted.

[35] Judgment of the Court of 9 February 1982, Case 270/80, *Polydor*, [1982] *ECR* 329 *et seq.* (points 15–16). See also Opinion 1/91 of 14 December 1991, [1991] ECR 6079 *et seq.* (point 22).

This amounts to saying that the *free trade area* created between the EU and CEEC States before accession was decidedly weakened by its being confined exclusively to products not incorporating rights (in practice, to goods low in technological or commercial content). The holders of rights were easily able to partition the market corresponding to the *free trade area* between the internal market on one side and the single national markets of the CEEC on the other.

Certainly, the possibility of segmenting the market for the most innovative products (marked by the absolute prohibition of *parallel imports*) may also possess features of interest for the firms holding the rights, making localisation in certain CEEC markets attractive, while the same markets would present very few benefits if they were not partitioned. It goes without saying that only those CEEC currently furthest from accession will be able to benefit from this advantage if they are able, since these countries would offer a stable, partitioned market for a period of 10 years or so for products incorporating protected technology (industrial or commercial). The countries that have not acceded can certainly not benefit and over the last few years they have suffered only harmful consequences to their productive renovation as a result of this situation.[36]

The Polish Industrial Property Act (IPA) of 30 June 2000[37] deserves a more careful analysis. Indeed, the Act purposely regulated Geographical Designations in a way not coinciding in important respects with the provisions of Regulation 2081/92.[38] Geographical Designations are a new type of subject matter for the Polish system of industrial property rights protection.[39] This is to some extent surprising in the light of the long established tradition of Polish folklore, nevertheless it must be admitted that the choice made by the Polish legislator not to comply with the European law was not due to the strength of local legal traditions, nor can it have been a mistake. It was rather an attempt by the Polish legislature to develop adequate legal and administrative expertise in an increasingly important field in which Poland lacked previous experience. To achieve that, even "short term" legal provisions intentionally not complying with the *acquis communautaire*—the deadline being in any case 1 May 2004—became admissible. Further investigation is

---

36 See Lauso Zagato, "Il rapporto tra Romania e UE in materia di proprietà intellettuale nel periodo che precede l'accesso," in Luigi Carlo Ubertazzi (ed.), *TV, Internet e new trends di diritti d'autore e connessi* (Milano: Giuffré 2003), pp. 82–91.

37 In Official Journal, 21 May 2001, n. 49, item 508. See Marian Kępinski, "Geographical Designations under Polish Industrial Property law," *International Review of Industrial and Copyright Law*, 34 (2003), pp. 751–771.

38 Council Regulation (EEC) No. 2081/92 of 14 July 1992 on the protection of geographical indications and designations of origin for agricultural products and foodstuffs of 14 July 1992 Official Journal L 208, 24/07/1992.

39 On the historical reasons leading to this situation, and in particular the "partitioning powers" policy of not allowing the development of an organized Polish "folklore", Kępinski, above, n. 37, p. 751.

needed, therefore, into legislation enacted in CEECs in the years preceding accession not fully complying with the *acquis communautaire*, with a view to establishing, case by case, the significance of the (transient) choice not to comply with the *acquis*.

A problem still to be mentioned is the uniformity of application of Community law as between the EU and associated candidate countries, and as among the latter group of countries themselves. Each *Europe Agreement* provides for an *Association Council* (AC), composed of members of the EU Council and Commission, on one hand, and government members of the single CEEC on the other. The Association Council's tasks are to deal with both the implementation of the Agreement—through the issue of decisions (*Implementing Rules*) binding on the Parties to the specific EA—and the resolution of disputes relating to it. If the parties fail to agree, certain procedures provide for a hazy solution using arbitrators, which would be very difficult to put into practice.

The obligation to comply not only with the *acquis communautaire* subsisting at the time of the signature of the EA, but also with the *acquis* subsequent to signature, had constitutional implications in the domestic systems of the candidate countries; all the more so when, as often happened, the IR were drawn up in vague terms. It is hardly surprising, therefore, that the constitutionality of some provisions of the EA and of the IR has been challenged before the Constitutional Courts of various CEEC. In particular, the Hungarian Constitutional Court[40] found Articles 1 and 6 of the Association Council IR, relating to the application of Article 62(2) of the EC-Hungary EA, unconstitutional.[41] According to that provision, "any practice contrary to this Article shall be assessed on the basis of criteria arising from the application of the rules" of Articles 81 and 82 (*inter alia*) of the EC Treaty, dealing with competition law. As for Articles 1 and 6 of the IR, the former provided that the cases referred to in Article 62 EA were to be dealt with, on the Hungarian side, by the Office of Economic Competition (OEC), while the latter provided that, in applying Article 62, it was the OEC's task to ensure that the block exemption Regulations in force in the EU were applied in full; and this was so even though up to that moment no provision of Hungarian competition law contemplated any block exemption Regulation.

The Hungarian Supreme Court found Articles 1 and 6 IR unconstitutional on two grounds. First, according to Article 62 EA, the relevant criteria that the OEC had to take into account in the proceedings contemplated under the IR, were to be inferred only "by way of reference [. . .] to internal legal rules and to the legal practice of internal fora (European Commission, ECJ, CFI) of another subject of

[40] Hungarian Constitutional Court, Decision 30/1998 (VI.25) AB, in Hungarian Official Gazette, 1998/55, p. 4565. See Allan Tatham, "Constitutional Judiciary in Central Europe and the Europe Agreement: Decision 30/1998 (VI.25) AB of the Hungarian Constitutional Court," *International and Comparative Law Quarterly*, 48 (1999), pp. 913–920.

[41] Decision 2/1996, in Hungarian Official Gazette, 1996/120.

international law".[42] Secondly, the OEC was required to take into account criteria emerging in EC law and practice even after the signing of the EA. In other words, a Hungarian organ was required to apply directly criteria to be generated in the future by a legal order other than the Hungarian legal order. It must be underlined that the Hungarian Court, in this part of its decision, gets to the root of the asymmetry in the EC–CEEC relationship which characterizes the third Copenhagen criterion.

Still, the Court managed to avoid taking the consequences of its reasoning to the extreme. True, the OEC must apply exclusively the rules of Hungarian competition law; but the content of these rules must be determined in a manner allowing "the proper assertion in the domestic legal order of the relevant EC criteria". The "persuasivity" of the EC criteria for the OEC when interpreting substantive domestic competition law is strengthened in light of the fact that the aim of the Hungarian substantive competition law is proper harmonisation with EC substantive competition law. In the end, the Hungarian Supreme Court's decision appears to be consistent with the decisions of other CEEC high courts, in particular the Administrative Supreme Court in Warsaw and the Polish Constitutional Tribunal.[43] According to the latter Tribunal, although EC law had no binding force in Poland, by virtue of the provisions of Articles 68–69 of the EC-Poland EA, Poland was obliged to use "its best endeavours to ensure that future legislation is compatible" with Community legislation. The Constitutional Tribunal held that the duty to ensure compatibility also included "the obligation to interpret the existing legislation in such a way as to ensure the greatest possible degree of such compatibility".

It would be senseless to underline that the original EA provisions discussed here were supposed to refer only to a gradual approximation of laws between the EC and the candidate countries to be pursued over a period of years; the conclusive fact is that the constitutional courts of different CEEC have agreed upon the necessity for a "Euro-friendly interpretation of domestic legislation".[44] It is important to note how both the burden of controlling the degree of harmonisation of national legislation and the coherence of interpretative criteria used in applying national law fall in the last analysis on national judges deciding cases in candidate countries.

Have such judges been equipped to face this difficult task? In the case of the European Economic Area, this problem is solved by a clever system which guarantees that both the judicial decision in the Community and in the EEA *effectively*

---

42 Tatham, above n. 40, p. 917.

43 See Decision of the Czech High Court, Decision of 14 November 1996 (Re Skoda Auto, Collection of Decisions of the Constitutional Court, vol. 8, p. 149); Decision of Supreme Administrative Court in Warsaw, 13 March 2000 (English transl. in 1999–2000 *Polish Yearbook of International Law*, pp. 217 *et seq.*); Decision of the Constitutional Tribunal k. 15/97 (English transl. *East European Case Reporter of Constitutional Law*, pp. 271 *et seq.*). See Zdenek Kühn, "Application of European Law in Central European Candidate Countries," *European Law Review*, 28 (2003), pp. 551–560.

44 Kühn, above n. 43, p. 553.

develops in parallel, and that the rules applied in the EEA are given uniform interpretation. The latter is ensured by special consultation procedures between the Court of Justice and the EFTA Court, and by the chance for an ex-EFTA State to allow its judges to refer to the ECJ where they consider it necessary, for a decision on the interpretation of the EEA rules. Nothing of the sort has happened in the case of the Europe Agreements. The national judges of each candidate country have been left completely alone to interpret a system of law and case law that is, on the whole, alien to them, with all the resulting lack of certainty.

In this connection it is useful to recall an event that took place during negotiations for the EA with Poland. Poland had proposed that a provision should be inserted in the Agreement which would allow the Polish national court to make a reference to the Court of Justice under former Article 177 (234 EC) when the domestic court was called upon to apply a provision that had become part of the national legal system in order to implement the Community legal system. The Commission refused, on the grounds that access to the European Court of Justice is reserved to judges of the Member States alone.[45] The fact remains that the Polish proposal had picked out right from the start a weak point in the framework about to be built with the passing of the Europe Agreements. At the present time, as the legal systems of the new Member States implement the Community *acquis* in the various fields more extensively and in greater depth, the problem of identifying instruments capable of ensuring *uniformity* of application of Community law as between the EU and associated candidate countries, and as among the candidate countries themselves, has become more and more urgent.

4.3. A Europe of Variable Geometry: Midway between Centralisation/Re-centralisation and Flexibility

It is time to draw our conclusions about what has been stated so far. EU external relations with the CEEC developed in the 1990s on the basis of a complex network of legal instruments (almost always including also Article 308). The aim of arranging the process in this way was to ensure implementation of the Community *acquis* by the CEEC countries, meaning the body of primary and secondary legislation (as well as the case law of the CJEC) developed by the EU over 50 years. This process has displayed good and bad aspects.

It would be unjust, certainly, to burden the Community-apparatus with what lies outside its province; indeed, the asymmetry in relations between the Union and the candidate countries was already written into the Copenhagen criteria (especially the third), and into the practice decided at European Council level; the Accession Partnerships were the instrument for that practice.

It follows that the preferred use of vertical instruments to guide the incorporation of the *Community acquis* in these countries was inevitable. The Community

[45] As provided in Opinion 1/91: above n. 35.

authorities, as we have seen, reacted with force to the risk of the PHARE project becoming bureaucratized and centralised, for instance by favouring decentralisation in the performance of assistance projects to the advantage of the EU Delegations in the field. This means that the Delegation task managers can take an increasingly active part in performing the activities requested. In many cases, though, this has led to a bureaucratic re-centralisation of projects under the local Delegation (an effect still being felt in the Western Balkan States, following a chain reaction).

While wishing to avoid second-rate anecdotes, another point to make is that the choice of favouring, as far as possible, the admission of qualified local personnel to the Delegations, though positive in itself, has not always produced the effects hoped for. This strengthening of the local delegations also has repercussions on the consultancy firms that manage the projects. If they want to keep their reputations they must show that they have managed to trigger the change set out in their job descriptions. It becomes more difficult to form tacit agreements of non-interference with stubborn partners (in particular the bureaucratic structures of government organizations, which are particularly inflexible by tradition). On the contrary, the partners begin to recognise the pressure of project management, to become aware and within certain limits accept the pressure bearing on them. They also know that the Delegation will intervene at government level should reform projects under the accession partnership be put at risk.[46] The impression is that the Delegations have often ended up taking on characteristics comparable to the role of the East India Company before the English assumed direct responsibility.

It is a situation not devoid of dangers for the future, as we can see if we examine the CARDS Programme, the instrument of legislative assistance provided for in the SAA. We have already mentioned how, by the standard of the CARDS Programme,[47] the consolidated approach of the first 10 candidates in the final phase becomes the basis for relations with the new countries. Just to be able to begin negotiations on the SAA, the WB States are being asked to ensure a level of legislative alignment far higher than the level on which the EA were based. In this connection, signs of friction with Serbia, which cannot be further investigated here, must not be underestimated. The risk here entails a shift in legislative choices by the Serb Government apparatus towards US models (confirming the dissonant choice of Serbia compared with the other WB countries).

We have also seen, on the other hand, how the range of instruments governing the making of a Europe of variable geometry does not allow itself to be trapped in a pattern of exclusive recourse to vertical instruments on the part of the Community apparatus, which would be almost like a 'soft' version of the attempted takeover of Iraq by the world superpower and a group of allied States that is still ongoing.

From the outset, the use of instruments of *centralisation/re-centralisation* have been accompanied by the use of instruments giving transversal flexibility: the most

---

46 Blecher, above n. 9, p. 14.

47 See above n. 15.

recent example of the former being through the new Title XXI, the realignment of the PHARE Programme and its offshoots; of the latter, through the new wave of projects within INTERREG. The instruments giving transversal flexibility have somehow managed to act together in preparing the technical legal instruments needed for enlargement of the Union.

Bearing in mind especially the countries not due to enter the EU immediately and the new candidates, we should hope to see a more marked corrective contribution of the transversal type, in the nature of a plan that arises from the confluence of competent elements in the territory, and bringing in the bodies representing the different parts of European civil society that are affected; elements of a bottom-up approach should also be brought into play in the process of harmonising the whole of European society.[48] The Court of Justice has, moreover, made a contribution to the process just described. Following a technique already used on other occasions, the Court has intervened at the decisive moment, establishing that a significant part of the immigration law in force in the single Member State is essentially inapplicable to citizens of the EA countries.[49] One of the main obstacles to enlargement was thus cleverly circumvented (in part, at least) even before the final phase of negotiations with those States began. What is more, Romania and Bulgaria will remain outside the EU for many years yet.

As a result, following the case law of the Court, a category of non-Community immigrants has been created possessing rights that are not commensurable with those of any other group; it is a fixed term category, so to speak, since Romania and Bulgaria are due to enter the EU in time, but nevertheless it is a category that is destined to last for years. Further, a similar profile is beginning to take shape in favour of Turkish citizens.

Then, as far as the rights of citizens emigrating from the WB States are concerned, as these countries gradually conclude SAAs with the EU, the Member States cannot rely too securely on the clauses excluding direct applicability that exist in those agreements and are repeated at every turn. The developing sequence of the Community cycle is punctuated by the Court overcoming similar obstacles. All the elements therefore point to the formation of a legal hierarchy over the long term of the rights of citizens from non-Community countries within the EC.

In conclusion, we find confirmation of the tendency during the course of enlargement to mix international law contours belonging to EU external relations, with transnational contours acting as a model and reference point for the activities of both local and foreign private parties. Indeed, the latter often tend to weigh

---

48 Laura Picchio Forlati, "Il diritto dell'Unone europea tra dimensione internazionale e transnazionalità," *Jus*, XLVI (1999), pp. 461–473. Interesting points for reflection also in Marco Frigessi di Rattalma, "Il ruolo del contratto nei rapporti tra Enti pubblici territoriali appartenenti a Stati diversi," in *Regioni, Costituzione e rapporti internazionali* (Milano: Franco Angeli 1995), pp. 93–115.

49 Sec. II, above.

themselves down with ambiguous supranational contours not justified by any basis in treaty law. This is due both to the attitude of the executive staff of the EU structure (and of the national experts) sent to the single candidate States, and to the acceptance of such a role by those at the receiving end of their activity, with the consequent withdrawal of the administrative apparatus of those States.

From the viewpoint of the international law scholar, what is remarkable is the extreme functionality revealed by the instrument of positive sanctions in the process outlined; in short, the positive sanction has proved to be decisive in achieving what seemed at first sight to be an extremely hard objective to attain.[50]

5. CONCLUSIONS

It is not the task of this chapter to examine in depth the prices paid and the risks that lay ahead, at the end of this first phase of the enlargement process, both for the former Eastern Bloc States and for the States historically belonging to the EU. From the viewpoint of the present paper, we must restrict ourselves to posing only certain problems.

In the first place, the way the instruments for a Europe of variable geometry are structured must be set in relation to the tumults going on in the south of the world, in particular in Africa. It is then easy to see how that panoply of instruments directed at creating reorganization and hierarchical system going from the centre to the periphery cannot be re-proposed in relation to the States on the southern side of the Mediterranean. The cardinal element of a Europe of variable geometry is in fact the positive sanction. This is an instrument that for obvious reasons can be used in an incomparably less effective way in relation to any countries other than the States of Central Eastern, South Eastern and Eastern Europe. Indeed the policy of granting economic aid as a means to a certain end is one thing (in this case, preventive control of migrations towards Europe, readmission agreements centralised at EU level for illegal immigrants who are nationals of that State or a third State, but are assumed to have crossed the frontiers of that State, etc.) while the outlook of co-opting the State apparatus over the medium or long term in the Union venture is quite another thing. Anyone who, like the present writer, has had the opportunity to witness at first hand the break-up of a Country's State apparatus (in this case, Albania) and then to see its unexpected return to life when confronted with an explicit takeover on the part of the Community apparatus, can easily appreciate how decisive such an element is.

The present author does not wish to escape the onerous consequences of this reasoning. The opposition between a short-sighted EU policy of externalising

---

50 See Laura Picchio Forlati, "La partecipazione al dialogo del diritto internazionale," in *Giornale di Diritto del Lavoro e delle Relazioni Industriali*, XIV (1992), pp. 799–781. Also Cortese, above n. 10, *passim*.

repressive control of the migration phenomenon, as against a virtuous policy based on prevention, cherished in some scholarly writings[51] and relying on the successes achieved in South-East Europe, does not exactly hit the point. Since one of the two horns of the dilemma is unworkable, I fear that such a dichotomy would end up leaving room for the other—the repressive method—which really is workable in the short term. A watery Auschwitz would thus be round the corner.

Other solutions are to be thought of, then. They must be capable of claiming for themselves those aspects from the experience of a Europe of variable geometry, of interweaving between the transnational and international dimensions (enhancing the transnational) that have been developed in the last decade in relations with the CEEC and WB States.

From other standpoints, too, moreover, a Europe of variable geometry does not seem destined to end. This is not so much because of the geographical fact that there are still European countries waiting behind the acceding or candidate countries. What should be borne in mind, instead, is the formidable development that has taken place over the last decade of the issue of the protection of minorities, and above all, the transformation of that issue from a claim to prohibit forms of discrimination, to the active pursuit of a policy protecting individuals' right to their identities and cultural differences.

On the one hand, events in ex-Yugoslavia have influenced this development as well as the reflections on it sparked off both within the Council of Europe and at the EU. On the other hand, also as a consequence of global phenomena that there would be no point dwelling on here, we have witnessed a process of revival of local cultural entities in the Member States themselves; one scholar refers to this as an opportunity for a new, third way between Westphalia and Cosmopolis.[52] Again, we must not forget an important institutional aspect: in the tough political and administrative clash with the biggest Member States and their government apparatuses, and at the expense of a certain lack of coherence with the past (although one might speak of making an important evolutionary leap), the Commission has become the champion of the plurality of cultural identities within the EU in the hard-fought battle over the constitutional Treaty, both at State level and more especially at sub-State level.

So, the imminent enlargement creates a series of new contradictions and the task of this paper will be brought to a close by indicating what they are. On the one hand, minorities are pushing at the other side of the borders of States that are more or less close to joining the EU, and they can only be coped with in a trans-Union dimension (we refer firstly to the question between the Turks and the Kurds, but it is not necessary to look so far afield). Even involuntarily, this alone brings the

---

51 Boswell, above n. 18, *passim*.

52 Peter A. Kraus, "Cultural Pluralism and European Polity-Building: Neither Westphalia nor Cosmopolis," *Journal of Common Market Studies*, 41 (2003), pp. 665–686.

instruments of variable geometry into play.[53] On the other hand, the problem of protection of minorities affects the legislative choices of a nationalistic character of certain new Member States: see, for example, the recent Hungarian legislation on citizenship. To be sure, the Commission is watching over the problems stemming from that tendency.[54]

Nonetheless, it is the Commission itself that seems willing to take upon itself a policy of dramatic closure towards the planetary migrations of desperate hordes, in pressing for the creation of a European immigration agency, requiring new Member States meanwhile to incorporate in their laws the full weaponry with which the historical Member States are endowed: readmission agreements, etc.[55] There is a strong impression that the "archangel" approach within the Union and at its immediate borders counterbalances an extreme carelessness verging on cynicism on the part of the Unionist institutions in handling relations of a global character. Nor would this be for the first time.[56]

---

53 Christin Henrard, "The Impact of the Enlargement Process on the Development of a Minority Protection Policy within the EU: Another Aspect of Responsibility/Burden-sharing?", *Maastricht Journal of European and Comparative Law*, 9 (2002), pp. 357–391.

54 See Barbara Brandtner and Allan Rosas, "Human Rights and External Relations of the European Community: An Analysis of Doctrine and Practice," *European Journal of International Law*, 9 (1998), pp. 468–490; Henrard, above n. 53; Gaetano Pentassuglia, "The EU and the Protection of Minorities: The Case of Eastern Europe," *European Journal of International Law*, 12 (2001), pp. 3–38.

55 See Caroline Forder, "Common Minimum European Standards in Immigration Matters," *Maastricht Journal of European and Comparative Law*, 9 (2002), pp. 221–229; Catherine Phuong, above n. 18, *passim*.

56 See Laura Picchio Forlati, "Contratto (diritto internazionale privato)," *Digesto delle discipline privatistiche, sezione civile*, IV (1989), p. 235.

Concluding Remarks

Conclusions: The Adhesion of New Member States to the European Union and the European Constitution

Sergio Bartole

1. Introduction

In dealing with the problem of the adhesion of new member States to the European Union and with the question of the Constitution of the Union at the same time, we have to adopt two different points of view, looking, on one side, at the legal order, and, on the other side, taking into account the internal system of law of the interested States. Moreover, all three major items have to be considered which are respectively studied in the three parts of this book: democratic institutions, constitutionalism and rule of law. The topic of the European Constitution and that of the accession of new Member States to the Union, as far as they are connected, are at the center of a knot of different strands of research relating to some of the main questions of the constitutional studies: for instance, sovereignty, alternative models of direct or deliberative and parliamentary democracy, coexistence of parliamentary and judicial making of law, national and supra-national protection of human rights and fundamental freedoms, judicial review of legislation and its justification in the frame of a democratic order, and so on.

Therefore the task of drawing the conclusions of the debate raised by the papers collected in the book is extremely complex and engaging. Complying with it in a satisfactory way would require more space and more time than the editors are ready to allow the author of these notes. I shall limit my attention to a few key issues and I hope that such a summary presentation will offer an idea of the conclusions reached during the workshop while promoting new research which could be started on the basis of these conclusions. As a matter of fact, some of the hypotheses concerning the mutual interference between the adhesion of the new member States to the European Union and the adoption of the Treaty establishing the Constitution of the Union have to be tested in the framework of the future developments which we might be able to envisage, but certainly not in the position of describing with exactitude.

2. Direct Effect and Democratic Deficit

The first judicial elaboration of the concept of the European Constitution by the European Court of Justice highlighted two key elements, which interest not the substantial normative content of European law but rather its legal effects. In emphasizing the direct effects of European law in the internal legal order of the

Wojciech Sadurski et al. (ed.), Spreading Democracy and the Rule of Law?, 381–390.

Member States and its supremacy over the national law of those States the Court has taken a formal approach to the problem in a very Kelsenian way. The main principles of the European Constitution, that is, the principle of supremacy of the European law and the principle of direct effect are the *Grundnorm* of a legal system which is made up by European and national law. If European and the national law of the Member States concur in shaping a unitary legal order according to a peculiar hierarchy of the relevant sources of law, the result is made up by the specific legal force of the different legislations and by their mutual relations. But these technical aspects, which deserve to be appreciated specially, if not exclusively by the legal scholars and by the professional interpreters of European law, have a political relevance if we look at the impact of European law on the people of the Member States.

The content of the European Constitution is more and more frequently developing a substantial nature. Therefore, the direct effects of European law on the status of the citizens of the Member States should require—according to the political theory of democracy—the direct participation of the people concerned in the making of both the European Constitution and the law of the European Institutions. On the one hand, the people should not be excluded from the choices concerning the organization and the formation of the law-making bodies of the Union and, on the other, the citizens and their representatives ought to be given a say in the decision-making processes aiming at the adoption of the European law.

The implementation of these theoretical consequences apparently conflicts with the generally accepted idea that the European Union is characterized by the so-called democratic deficit, the presence of which is emphasized by comparing the constitutional organization of the European Union with the form of the governments of the member States.

Many are of the opinion that the new European Constitution ought to be approved by referenda in all member States: only this method of direct democracy would guarantee an immediate participation of the people concerned in a decision affecting the shape and the role of the European Union and its relations with the citizenry. It is true that the procedure for the revision of the European Treaties was already modified when the newly established European Convention was entrusted with the task of drafting the text of the Constitution. But the Convention only played a preparatory function, and the relevant formal deliberation was adopted by the intergovernamental conference. Moreover the members of the Convention were not directly elected by the citizens, but were nominated by various European and national bodies whose authority is in different ways, directly or indirectly, based on the vote of the people.

As a matter of fact, the adoption of the European Constitution (or of the Treaty establishing it) by referendum would be a partial novelty in Western European countries. Only in Denmark, France and Ireland was the innovative Treaty of Maastricht approved by referendum, while in all the other countries the relevant decisions were adopted by the Parliaments. On the contrary, in all the Central European countries which became member States on May 1st 2004, a referendum was called to ask the people about adhesion to the Union. This choice was not formally required by the governing bodies of the Union—sometimes there are constitutional provisions on the matter (e.g. Art. 7 of the Slovakian Constitution). But it is well known that a popular vote on the matter was considered essential to establish the legitimacy of accession by those bodies. Therefore, should all the Member States choose to adopt the Constitution by way of referendum, this could be construed as an interesting development of the accession of the new Member States: the Western European States would follow *ex post* the soft suggestion which was given *ex ante* to the Central European new democratic States, and it is interesting to note that, according to the established principle, referenda might be called again to approve the Constitution also in the ex-communist new Member States.

It is ironic, but well known, that the European Union which itself is supposed to suffer from a democratic deficit, not only cautiously and indirectly suggested the approval of the accession by referendum, but also strongly influenced the constitutional reforms of the Central European countries before and after the take-off of the process of adhesion. At the beginning, after the fall of the Wall, it was the Council of Europe that offered its help at the moment of the adoption of the new constitutions of the ex-communist States. Help and support meant not only guidance and advice but also a soft revision of the early drafts adopted by the competent national bodies. The membership of the ex-communist States to the Council was dependent on the implementation of its models of democracy, rule of law and protection of human rights and fundamental freedoms. As a matter of fact, separation of powers and indirect parliamentary democracy with anti-majoritarian guarantees were central to the dialogue between the Council of Europe and the Central Eastern European countries. Referenda did not have a central position in the new constitutions because they were supposed to be decision-making devices whose majoritarian nature does not allow a fair, participative and inclusive deliberation of the State's decisions. Nevertheless some of those countries had already shown a preference for the adoption of the institutions of direct democracy in the presence of fundamental decisions when at the moment of the proclamation of their independence Estonia, Latvia, Lithuania and Slovenia (but not Slovakia and the Czech Republic) decided to leave to the people the relevant decisions. Therefore, notwithstanding that the process of accession has been seen by the European Union as a follow-up of this very dialogue between the Council of Europe and the interested States, it is evident that the choice of referendum for the approval of the adhesion to European Union is strongly connected with the history of these States, even if its adoption is evidently an exception to the models of the deliberative and parliamentary democracy which were and are prevailing in Western European democracies. It is the price which has to be paid when the sovereignty of the concerned States and the revision of their national constitutions are at stake. Therefore I think that the approval of the European Constitution by referenda may be justified in the same way.

3. THE ROLE OF THE JUDICIARY AND THE LEGISLATURE

The principle of direct effect and the doctrine of supremacy of the European law impinge at the same time both upon the power of the national Parliaments and the national sovereignty of the concerned States. The importance of the decisions aimed at insuring the compliance of the internal orders implies the adoption of a special decision-making processes. But in the framework of an approach which emphasizes the moment of the deliberation of normative acts or by representative bodies or by referenda, the problem of the coexistence of these traditional ways of making law with the judicial law-making by the precedents of the case remains-law which is characteristic of European constitutional law. According to the construction of Joseph Weiler,[1] the judicial formation of the main principles of the European Constitution on the superiority of European law supported its expansion as far as (and because) the relevant developments were controlled by the Council of Ministers of the European Communities where the Member States were bound by the Luxembourg compromise and by the connected agreement of complying with the principle of the unanimity for the adoption of the decisions of the Council. The States accepted that European law has internal effects in their legal order and they profit from these effects in introducing with a unanimous vote, new common rules in many matters according to their common political conveniences. If this hypothesis is correct, there has been a mutual underpinning between the judicial making and the deliberative formation of European law.

But what is the position of judicial law-making in the development of the European Constitutional heritage? Is the common law tradition a part of this heritage? Or is the principle of the separation of powers prevailing over the partial confusion of judicial power and law-making which the common law system implies? Is judicial law-making compatible with the lesson of Montesquieu that the judiciary is the mouth of the law, and with Rousseau's theory who taught that the law is the expression of the people and of its representatives?

We cannot deny that in principle the traditional doctrine of the separation of powers of continental Europe did not allow much room for the judicial formation of the law, but it is also true that, after the Second World War, Western Europe has known a large diffusion of constitutional jurisdiction and the contemporary development of judicial law-making in the field of constitutional law by Constitutional Courts. The phenomenon recently interested also the Central Eastern European countries where, at the moment of their take-off, the Constitutional Courts, e.g.

---

1 J.H.H. Weiler, *The Constitution of Europe* (Cambridge: Cambridge University Press 1999), pp. 20–22.

Poland and Hungary, were faced with the problem of the coexistence of the old revised constitutions and the principles of Western constitutionalism. Furthermore, after the adoption of new democratic constitutions, they had to settle the conflicts between the recently approved constitutional legislation, sometimes incomplete or ambiguous, and the previous communist law, which was still in force and could not be easily deprived of its effects without creating dangerous lacunae. If we keep in mind the role that Western European Constitutional Courts had in shaping relations between European and national law in the absence of the necessary constitutional provisions, we can envisage that the Central European Courts will display a similar role at least in those States which, at the moment of adhesion to the European Union, did not adopt specific constitutional rules providing for the direct internal effect and supremacy of European law.

In effect, only three States have specific provisions on the matter. The Constitution of Slovenia states that the European acts shall be applied in accordance with the legal regulations of the Union[2]; in Slovakia, the possibility of direct application of European rules conferring rights and duties is explicitly provided for in the Constitution,[3] however only in Poland does the Constitution state that European law shall be directly applied in the Polish legal order and have a legal force superior to national law.[4] Where similar rules are missing or the constitutional provisions are unclear or ambiguous, the judicial bodies of the new Member States, and especially the Constitutional Courts, shall perform the task of drawing the consequences of adhesion to the Union in the field of relations between European and the national law according to the dicta of the Luxembourg Court.

The enlargement of the scope of judicial law-making will probably be an additional effect of adhesion in connection with the multilevel structuring of the relations between the European Constitution and the national Constitutions. The Constitutional Courts shall take into account the implicit reshaping of the powers of the constitutional bodies of the States induced by the approval of the European Treaties and of the European Constitution. They will have to balance European commitments with internal constitutional principles, but it is evident that the powers of national Parliaments will be curtailed. Moreover, ordinary and administrative courts shall have to take care of the internal effects of European law and with regard to national law, as far as their coexistence is compatible with the principles of the jurisprudence of the Luxembourg Court.

Within this framework, the principle of the rule of law in the European legal system will be construed as a middle way between its old traditional Anglo-Saxon content and the more recent continental principle of legality. The law will be expressed by written documents adopted at the end of deliberative decision-making

---

2 Art. 1 of the Constitutional Act amending Chapter I and Articles 47 and 68 of the Constitution of the Republic of Slovenia, 27 February 2003.

3 Art. 86 of the Constitution of the Slovak Republic.

4 Art. 91 of the Constitution of the Polish Republic.

processes, but the living law, that is the law which has to be applied day by day in the social relations of life, will be made up by the judicial construction and integration of those documents.

Professor Sajo posed the question: is it possible to compare the European Union with the model of the administrative State? The limited expansion of the powers of the European Parliament certainly displays negative effects on the functionality of the democratic principles in the frame of the European institutions. Conversely it emphasizes the role of cabinets in the internal framework of the Member States, where the curtailment of the powers of national Parliaments is balanced by the expansion of the normative functions of the Executives which are jointly exercised in the European Councils of Ministers. But an inversion of this tendency does not depend only on the enlargement of the powers of the European Parliament. It is evident that the democratic legitimacy of the Union is strictly connected with the approval of the European Treaties by national Parliaments (or by the citizens of the Member States). But we can say that compliance of the functioning of the Union with democratic principles depends also on the actual links binding national Parliaments and the members of the Cabinets who sit in the Council of Ministers. The accountability of the Ministers (who are members of the Council) before the national legislative Assemblies can partially compensate the internal democratic deficit of the Union. Therefore it is extremely important that the constitutional amendments adopted by some of the new Member States provide for the active participation of national Parliaments in the formation of European policies. This is the case of the Czech and Slovenian Constitutions which require the establishment of an active cooperation between the Cabinets and the Parliaments in the implementation of the State's obligations flowing from the Treaty on European Union. The governments shall inform the chambers which have to be given the possibility of expressing their views on the decisions which the European institutions are preparing. Somebody could say that these amendments offer a very weak solution to the problem of the democratic deficit if it looks preferable founding the democratic legitimacy of the functioning of the Union only upon a direct link between European institutions and European citizens. But when we look at them taking into account the special nature of the Union and the role that the Member States display in the frame of the Union, it is understandable that national Parliaments shall have a say in the formation of European policies.

If it is true that the new Member States are very sensitive to the limitations of their sovereignty and the following limitations of the powers of their Parliaments, these constitutional arrangements should be specially fitted to their political exigencies and conveniences.

4. THE FUTURE OF NATIONAL SOVEREIGNTY

It is generally accepted that the problem of limitation of national sovereignty can, for the ex-communist States, be a difficult problem to deal with at the moment of the accession. They obtained their independence only recently and it is possible that adhesion to the European Union could be perceived by their citizens as subordination to a new "Breznev doctrine"[5] The hope is largely shared that accession to the European Union will start a process of further internal democratization, of enlargement of the internal spaces of political freedom, but also of expansion of the economic market and of great social and economic developments. These are purposes which certainly deserve to be pursued, and the European institutions have taken care of them. But it is also well known that the citizens of the new member States understood the proclamation of their newly acquired independence as a recognition and a strengthening of their national identity.

Therefore, in many States of Central Eastern Europe the proclamation of the State's sovereignty is strictly connected with the vindication of national identity. After the fall of the Wall, the return of the nation State was the result of the replacement of the communist economic and social theory with nationalistic ideology. In certain Constitutions[6] the defense of national identity apparently takes precedence over other principles and values. It follows that its coexistence with the safeguard of human rights and fundamental freedoms looks sometimes very difficult, especially when the protection of the national minorities is at stake, even if explicit provisions on the matter were included in the Constitution.

Will these constitutional choices have any impact on the jurisprudence of the Constitutional Courts when these judges deal with the problems of the limitation of sovereignty flowing from adhesion of the new Member States to the European Union? In Western Europe, Constitutional Courts covered the defense of state sovereignty under the guise of the vindication of their task of safeguarding national constitutional principles and rights.[7] Only the Maastricht *Urteil*[8] explicitly responded to the question of the coexistence of and the relations between people's sovereignty and European commitments by giving precedence to the exercise of sovereign rights of the people over the decisions of the European institutions. It is perfectly possible that in the new Member States the vindication of national sovereignty is placed at the center of the debate of constitutional jurisprudence and its limitations are accepted only as far as they don't imply its surrender in favor of the European Union. Constitutional Courts could refuse the substitution of the supranational approach to the European unity for the intergovernmental one. If this were the case, conflicts could arise not only between the interested Constitutional Courts and the Luxembourg Court, but also between the Member States. However, it is evident that the preexisting *acquis communitaire* should prevent

5 It was incorporated in Art. 30 of the 1977 Soviet Constitution.

6 It is worth bearing Art. 6 of the Romanian Constitution in mind, but also Art. 1 of the Estonian Constitution is interesting.

7 M. Zuleeg, "The European Constitution under Constitutional Constraints: The German Scenario", 22 E.L. Rev. (1977), 19–34.

8 Bundesverfassungsgericht 89 (155).

the authorities of the new member States from adopting guidelines which could conflict with the principles of supremacy of European law and of its direct effects in the internal legal orders. If at the moment of take-off of the European Community in the fifties not all the authorities of the founding States were conscious of all the legal consequences implied by adhesion to the Community, the experience of the past years does not allow the interested States to adduce doubts and pretexts in the matter. In any case, while some Constitutions (e.g. in Latvia, Slovenia and Poland) explicitly state that a delegation or a transfer of powers to the European Union has to take place,[9] and in Hungary the exercise of constitutional powers jointly with other States is clearly provided for[10] other constitutional provisions are more ambiguous, such as in Estonia where the amended Constitution declares, on the one hand, that "Estonia may belong to the European Union on the basis of the fundamental principles" of its Constitution and, on the other, that, "when Estonia belongs to the European Union", its Constitution "shall be applied with due regard to the rights and duties arising from the Accession Treaty".[11]

5. CONCLUSION

The present discussion on the problem of sovereignty opens the debate up to the issue of the protection of human rights and fundamental freedoms. Is this protection a task which can be satisfactorily dealt with by European law, or do we have in any case to reserve the last word to authorities of the Member States? The frequently reaffirmed tendency of Western Constitutional Courts could suggest a preference for the second option. However the elaboration of the so called European constitutional heritage by the Luxembourg Court and the provisions of the European Treaties concerning human rights and fundamental freedoms offer a different perspective of a European law which provides directly and in an exhaustive way for the protection of European citizens as well as of third country nationals.

During the workshop it was correctly underlined that both the concept of European heritage and the standards adopted at Copenhagen in view of the monitoring of the constitutional and legislative reforms in the new member States[12] do not always have a clear content. They are used by the interpreters with great freedom and fantasy. For instance, it is difficult to accept the opinion supported by some authors that regional autonomy forms part of the European constitutional heritage when many European States still use a centralistic form government. The organization of the judiciary follows at least two different models in Europe: the Southern

9 Art. 68 of the Constitution of the Latvian Republic and Art. 90 of the Polish Constitution.

10 Art. 2 of the Hungarian Constitution.

11 The Constitution of the Republic of Estonia Amendment Act adopted by way of referendum on 14 September 2003.

12 As put forth during the 1993 Copenhagen European Council.

European model premised on the institution of the Councils of the judiciary and their entrustment with governing functions, and the Central European model which places at the center of government of the judiciary, the executive organs or bodies and limits their discretionality by specific procedural rules. Even European authorities experienced difficulties in using a European constitutional heritage to monitor the constitutional and legislative experiences of the new Member States. For instance, with respect to Estonia, they clearly adopted guidelines for the protection of the Russian minority which gave priority to knowledge of the Estonian language above the safeguard of Russian identity. Also Bulgaria adopted criteria in the evaluation of judicial reforms which are distinct from those they preferred when dealing with other countries.

But the understanding of a European constitutional heritage is not only complicated by the ambiguities of its content as it is construed by European authorities. There are difficulties also on the side of the Member States. The obsession with the value of the national identity which is present in their societies restrains State authorities from correctly complying with some of the main principles of democracy and protection of human rights. Again the experience of the Baltic States in the field of citizenship admonishes us that the myth of national identity can endanger the application of the principles of equality and non-discrimination to the relations among the persons living "within the jurisdiction" (Art. 1 of the European Convention on human rights and fundamental freedoms) of the member States.

The institutions of the Council of Europe and, more recently, those of the European Union have been very attentive to the protection of the ethnic identity of the Roma. These policies are justified not only by the number of interested people, but also by their special nomadic conditions. This is a people of travelers frequently moving around European countries, especially in Central and Eastern Europe. Only if the principle of tolerance is incorporated in the Constitutions of the interested States, can they hope to be welcome and treated according to the needs of the policies of the protection of human rights and fundamental freedoms. But the example of the treatment reserved to the Roma can be a useful precedent for the implementation of the policies regarding the four well known freedoms which support the creation of the European (market and) space. It is worth mentioning that Joseph Weiler strongly and correctly emphasized the basic importance of tolerance in shaping the European Constitution.[13]

Tolerance cannot be established *uno actu* and simultaneously in all European member States. As antisemitism is still present in many countries of Western Europe, notwithstanding the long history of commitment of the European institutions to the protection of human rights and the statements which are present in the European Treaties, it is understandable that in the new Member States the establishment

---

[13] Most recently in *Un'Europa Cristiana: un saggio esplorativo* (Milano: BUR 2003).

of a frame of tolerance, democracy and freedom will take some time. These are problems which can be solved not only by constitutional declarations, in line with Sieyès but also—and, in a better way—according to a Burkeian approach. The long and difficult future developments of the accession process will undoubtedly enrich our research by new materials if we have the patience and the courage to wait and study them.